# THE
# BOOK OF ACTS

the **Smart Guide** to the **Bible**™ series

BE SMART · BE INSPIRED ·™

## Robert C. Girard
## Larry Richards, General Editor

*Published by*
THOMAS NELSON™
*Since 1798*

www.thomasnelson.com

General Editor: Larry Richards
Managing Editor: Lila Empson
Associate Editor: W. Mark Whitlock
Scripture Editor: Deborah Wiseman
Assistant Editor: Amy Clark
Design: Diane Whisner

ISBN 10: 1-4185-0997-3
ISBN 13: 978-1-4185-0997-2

Printed in the United States of America
06 07 08 09   9 8 7 6 5 4 3 2 1

# Introduction

Welcome to *The Book of Acts—The Smart Guide to the Bible*™. This series makes the Bible fun and easy to understand. This is not a traditional Bible study or commentary. It is a new commentary that can change your outlook on the Bible.

## To Gain Your Confidence

The New Testament book of Acts is the history of what the first Christians did with the experiences and teachings of Jesus Christ after their face-to-face experience with him ended. I hope *The Book of Acts—The Smart Guide to the Bible*™ will create in you a thirst to learn even more from the Bible.

## Acts: A Sequel to the Life of Christ

The book of Acts was written to complete the story the author, Doctor Luke, began in the Gospel of Luke. Originally Acts was the second volume of a two-volume history of the beginnings of Christianity, which was circulated together in the early churches. Not long after AD 100 the two volumes were separated, and the Gospel of Luke was circulated as part of a fourfold Gospel along with books by Matthew, Mark, and John—books that record the basic facts about Jesus Christ. The first volume of the history came to be known as the Gospel According to Luke. The second volume came to be called the Acts of the Apostles. The two books are two parts of the same story—the story of Jesus. The first tells about "all that Jesus began both to do and teach" until his ascension (Acts 1:1 NKJV). The second picks up the Jesus story after his resurrection and carries it forward about thirty years, tracing the spread of the gospel from Jerusalem to Rome through the small contingent of true believers he left behind.

## Author! Author!

The author of the Gospel of Luke and the book of Acts writes anonymously. In fact, none of the writers of the four Gospels identify themselves by name. But church tradition as far back as the early part of the second century has always agreed that Luke was writer of both the Gospel of Luke and Acts.

Luke is mentioned by name only three times in the New Testament (Colossians 4:14;

2 Timothy 4:11; Philemon 24). From these passages and Luke's books we discover several things. Luke was a well-educated Greek living in Asia Minor, a Gentile (Colossians 4:12–14)—the only Gentile writer of the New Testament. Luke's use of the Greek language was superior. His lively, entertaining style resembles the writing style of Greek novelists of his time. He was also a careful historian, often tying his story to specific dates and historical incidents and figures. Luke was a physician (Colossians 4:14). His medical training shows in his use of technical medical terms. After he met Paul, Luke was the apostle's constant companion, even in jail. In ninety-seven verses in Acts (the so-called "we passages"), beginning with Acts 16:10, Luke uses the first person ("I," "we," and "us" rather than "they" and "them"), indicating he was there and part of the action.

## Where and How Luke Got His Information

Luke was not an eyewitness to anything he describes in his Gospel nor to most of what he wrote about in the first fifteen chapters of Acts. He never saw Jesus. The opening paragraph in his Gospel of Luke tells where and how he got his information (Luke 1:1–5). He heard about Jesus from the apostles and others who told him what they had seen and heard. Luke's two books were probably written about thirty years after Jesus rose from the dead—between AD 58 and 63.

## The Cure for Writer's Block

Luke tells us that by the time he authored his books, many early Christian writers had begun to feel the urgency to get the facts about Jesus down on papyrus (Luke 1:1). Among them may have been John Mark (Mark's Gospel was written about AD 55) and Matthew (who wrote between AD 50 and AD 70). Several incidents and trends may have triggered this epidemic of writer's itch:

- In many places Christians were under attack (Acts 8:1, 3; 12:1; Hebrews 10:32–34).
- Stephen and James had been martyred (Acts 7:57–60; 12:2).
- Paul was in a Roman prison awaiting trial (Acts 21:33; 24:27).
- The apostles faced intensifying persecution and death threats.
- Many of the original eyewitnesses—people who had known Jesus in the flesh—were getting older and would soon be gone; some had already died (1 Corinthians 15:6).

If the next generation was to have the facts on which the Christian faith was founded, these things had to be written down. Luke was one who felt the urgency to write what he had discovered.

# Pass It On!

How did the early Christians keep alive the facts concerning Jesus and the beginnings of the church before the New Testament was written? Luke says, "Eyewitnesses and ministers of the word delivered them [the facts] to us" (Luke 1:2 NKJV). First-century Christians told and retold the stories. People who had seen Jesus told what they had seen, heard, and felt. Jesus had given his disciples specific responsibility to pass the story on to others accurately and with authority.

God himself oversaw the process from beginning to end (John 16:13–15), so when the writers finally began to write, there was a reliable collection of facts from which to assemble the story. Two men who were involved in this process commented on it:

Peter: "We did not follow cunningly devised fables when we made known to you the power and coming of our Lord Jesus Christ, but were eyewitnesses of His majesty" (2 Peter 1:16 NKJV).

John: "That which was from the beginning, which we have heard, which we have seen with our eyes, which we have looked upon, and our hands have handled, concerning the Word of life" (1 John 1:1 NKJV).

# Investigative Reporter

To ensure accuracy, Luke "had perfect understanding of all things" before reporting them (Luke 1:3 NKJV). Much of Luke's investigative work may have been done during the two years while Paul was in jail in Caesarea. Luke was there too, serving as Paul's physician. Luke had time to interview eyewitnesses and assemble facts from Christians who had fled to Caesarea to escape persecution in Jerusalem.

# A Word About Words

There are several interchangeable terms: *Scripture, Scriptures, the Word, Word of God, God's Word*, etc. All these mean the same thing and come under the broad heading called the Bible. I may use each of these terms at various times.

The word *Lord* in the Old Testament refers to Yahweh, God. In the New Testament *Lord* is a term of respect, like "sir," a reference to God, or a title of Jesus.

# Why Study Acts?

After the four Gospels, where the personal story of Jesus's life, teachings, death, and resurrection are told, Acts may be the most important book in the New Testament. Here are some things you can learn from Acts that you can't get anywhere else:

- Acts is the story of how Jesus continues his work since his death and resurrection.
- Acts shows Jesus in action as head of the church.
- Acts shows how people can know Jesus through the Holy Spirit.
- Acts demonstrates practical application of Jesus's message that God loves the whole world and wants everyone to be rescued from sin.
- Acts records the origins of the church.
- Acts describes what true Christian fellowship is like and how important it is.

Jesus said his Holy Spirit will guide us in discovery of "all truth" (John 16:13 NKJV). It helps to read and study the Bible with an open heart, expecting God to light up your life in some surprising and enriching ways.

## About the Author

Bob Girard spent many years in the pastorate, during which he wrote several influential books and had a popular radio ministry, *Letters to the Church at Phoenix*. For many years Bob wrote adult Sunday school lessons for Scripture Press. He is the author of other books in the Smart Guide to the Bible™ series, including *The Life of Christ* and *The Book of Hebrews*. Bob is retired and living in a house he built in Rimrock, Arizona.

## About the General Editor

Dr. Larry Richards is a native of Michigan who now lives in Raleigh, North Carolina. He was converted while in the Navy in the 1950s. Larry has taught and written Sunday school curriculum for every age group, from nursery through adult. He has published more than two hundred books that have been translated into twenty-six languages. His wife, Sue, is also an author. They both enjoy teaching Bible studies as well as fishing and playing golf.

# Understanding the Bible Is Easy with These Tools

To understand God's Word you need easy-to-use study tools right where you need them—at your fingertips. The *Smart Guide to the Bible*™ series puts valuable resources adjacent to the text to save you both time and effort.

Every page features handy sidebars filled with icons and helpful information: cross references for additional insights, definitions of key words and concepts, brief commentaries from experts on the topic, points to ponder, evidence of God at work, the big picture of how passages fit into the context of the entire Bible, practical tips for applying biblical truths to every area of your life, and plenty of maps, charts, and illustrations. A wrap-up of each passage, combined with study questions, concludes each chapter.

These helpful tools show you what to watch for. Look them over to become familiar with them, and then turn to Chapter 1 with complete confidence: You are about to increase your knowledge of God's Word!

# Study Helps

The thought-bubble icon alerts you to commentary you might find particularly thought-provoking, challenging, or encouraging. You'll want to take a moment to reflect on it and consider the implications for your life.

key point

Don't miss this point! The exclamation-point icon draws your attention to a key point in the text and emphasizes important biblical truths and facts.

go to

**death on the cross**
Colossians 1:21, 22

Many see Boaz as a type of Jesus Christ. To win back what we human beings lost through sin and spiritual death, Jesus had to become human (i.e., he had to become a true kinsman), and he had to be willing to pay the penalty for our sins. With his <u>death on the cross</u>, Jesus paid the penalty and won freedom and eternal life for us.

The additional Bible verses add scriptural support for the passage you just read and help you better understand the <u>underlined text</u>. (Think of it as an instant reference resource!)

How does what you just read apply to your life? The heart icon indicates that you're about to find out! These practical tips speak to your mind, heart, body, and soul, and offer clear guidelines for living a righteous and joy-filled life, establishing priorities, maintaining healthy relationships, persevering through challenges, and more.

This icon reveals how God is truly all-knowing and all-powerful. The hourglass icon points to a specific example of the prediction of an event or the fulfillment of a prediction. See how some of what God has said would come to pass already has!

What are some of the great things God has done? The traffic-sign icon shows you how God has used miracles, special acts, promises, and covenants throughout history to draw people to him.

Does the story or event you just read about appear elsewhere in the Gospels? The cross icon points you to those instances where the same story appears in other Gospel locations—further proof of the accuracy and truth of Jesus' life, death, and resurrection.

Since God created marriage, there's no better person to turn to for advice. The double-ring icon points out biblical insights and tips for strengthening your marriage.

The Bible is filled with wisdom about raising a godly family and enjoying your spiritual family in Christ. The family icon gives you ideas for building up your home and helping your family grow close and strong.

Introduction

something significant had occurred, he wrote down the substance of what he saw. This is the practice John followed when he recorded Revelation on the **Isle of Patmos.**

What does that word really mean, especially as it relates to this passage? Important, misunderstood, or infrequently used words are set in **bold type** in your text so you can immediately glance at the margin for definition. This valuable feature lets you better understand the meaning of the entire passage without having to stop to check other references.

### the big picture

**Joshua**
Led by Joshua, the Israelites crossed the Jordan River and invaded Canaan (see Illustration #8). In a series of military campaigns the Israelites defeated several coalition armies raised by the inhabitants of Canaan. With organized resistance put down, Joshua divided the land among the twelve Israelite

How does what you read fit in with the greater biblical story? The highlighted big picture summarizes the passage under discussion.

### what others say

**David Breese**
Nothing is clearer in the Word of God than the fact that God wants us to understand himself and his working in the lives of men.[5]

It can be helpful to know what others say on the topic, and the highlighted quotation introduces another voice in the discussion. This resource enables you to read other opinions and perspectives.

Maps, charts, and illustrations pictorially represent ancient artifacts and show where and how stories and events took place. They enable you to better understand important empires, learn your way around villages and temples, see where major battles occurred, and follow the journeys of God's people. You'll find these graphics let you do more than study God's Word—they let you *experience* it.

# Chapters at a Glance

# Part Three—FILLED WITH GOD'S SPIRIT

# Part Four—CHAINED WITNESS

# Part One
# FIRE IN THE HOLY CITY

# Acts 1 Lighting the Fuse

## Let's Get Started

The world in which Christianity got its start was ruled by the iron fist of the Roman Empire, which had invaded Europe, North Africa, Egypt, and the Middle East, including Israel, homeland of the Jews. The imperial capital was Rome. In AD 30 the emperor was **Caesar** Tiberius. Nowhere was hatred of the Roman conquerors hotter nor revolutionary skirmishes more likely than Israel. Jewish historian Josephus reports that during the first century there were ten thousand incidents of insurrection in Israel alone![1]

The most radical revolution—the one the official scorekeepers forgot to count—was a nonviolent uprising that began with a handful of mostly fishermen and women in Jerusalem. In less than three hundred years, this uprising brought the mighty Roman Empire officially to its knees before the crucified Galilean, Jesus of Nazareth. This revolution was not driven by hate or political ambition but by love and belief that its hero and commanding officer had given his life for their freedom, risen from the dead, and now directed the revolution from the heavenly throne room of God!

Acts shows the **church** in its finest hour—under fierce attack but unstoppable, spiritually aflame, morally pure, impelled by love, and bound together by the living presence of Christ. It details a movement of pioneers and risk-takers breaking new ground, taking on new challenges, highly energized for assault on spiritual ignorance and wickedness.

**Caesar**
official title of Roman emperors; family name of Julius Caesar

**church**
community of Christian believers, not a building

### what others say

**Maude De Joseph West**

[Acts] is a book about people who thrust their feet into sweat-stained sandals and marched out to conquer the world. They had no visible swords, they had no visible shields, they had no visible commander; nonetheless, they marched with matchless unconcern into the gates of prison, through the valley of persecution, and even into the jaws of death.[2]

**physician**
Colossians 4:14

**Theophilus**
Luke 1:3;
Acts 1:1

**Theophilus**
Greek name meaning "God-Lover"

**Greek**
universal language of Roman Empire in which the New Testament was written

# This Could Be the Start of Something Big

**ACTS 1:1–2** *The former account I made, O Theophilus, of all that Jesus began both to do and teach, until the day in which He was taken up, after He through the Holy Spirit had given commandments to the apostles whom He had chosen,* (NKJV)

The author of Acts is a Greek <u>physician</u> named Luke. Acts is a sequel. The author's former book is the third New Testament version of the Jesus story, the Gospel of Luke.

Both of Luke's books are addressed to an official in the Roman government that Luke calls "<u>**Theophilus**</u>." Theophilus was either a committed follower of Jesus Christ or a serious seeker on his way to becoming one. Luke's Gospel and Acts are written in the purest **Greek** in the New Testament—the language that would best communicate to an educated member of the aristocracy.

Some people think Luke may have been a slave, the personal physician of Theophilus, who was seriously ill. Through Luke's medical skills and care Theophilus was restored to health. In gratitude Theophilus gave Luke his freedom. Luke, in turn, to show his gratitude gave Theophilus the most precious gift he could think of—the message concerning Jesus.[3]

# What Jesus Started

If Luke had given his second book a title, it might have been something like, "The Continuing Work of Jesus" or "More Proof Jesus Is Alive" or "You Read My First Book but Fasten Your Seat Belt, Pilgrim, You Ain't Seen Nothing Yet!" The Gospel of Luke "began" Jesus's story (Acts 1:1). Acts tells the rest of the story. That story is still being written in the lives of Christ's followers today.

The superstar is Jesus Christ. He is the main actor in every scene. In the Gospels he moved about in a single human body and spoke with a Jewish accent. In Acts he speaks in many different voices and languages. His message and goals remain the same.

# Forty Incredible Days

**ACTS 1:3** *to whom He also presented Himself alive after His suffering by many infallible proofs, being seen by them during* *forty days and speaking of the things pertaining to the kingdom of God. (NKJV)*

On April 9, AD 30,[4] demoralized followers of the dead Nazarene, Jesus, huddled in a second-story room in Jerusalem. It was their third day of secret mourning (it was against the law to grieve openly for a condemned criminal). Their teacher, whom they had believed was the long-expected **Messiah** sent to rescue Israel from bondage, was dead. They'd <u>watched him die</u>. The depression in the room was so thick you could slice it with a knife!

Suddenly the door flew open. Breathless women who had gone to embalm the body burst in, babbling confusing things about a rolling stone (Matthew 28:2), a missing corpse (John 20:2–13), angels (Luke 24:4–5), and a risen Christ (Matthew 28:8–10)!

It was the start of the most amazing forty days of their lives.

**go to**

**watched him die**
Matthew 27;
Mark 15;
Luke 23;
John 19

**appeared**
Matthew 28;
Mark 16;
Luke 24;
John 20–21;
1 Corinthians 15:3–8

**Lord's Prayer**
Matthew 6:9–13

**God's will**
Matthew 7:21;
Luke 1:38; 22:42;
Romans 12:1–2

# The King and the Kingdom

ACTS 1:3 *[Jesus spoke of] things pertaining to the kingdom of God. (NKJV)*

Alive and kicking, Jesus <u>appeared</u> to his people in all sorts of places and situations. He spoke their names, touched them, invited them to touch him, ate with them, hiked and fished with them. The scars of the crucifixion were visible in his hands, feet, and side (Luke 24:39–40; John 20:27).

Eager partisans clustered around their **Master** in those post-resurrection meetings. They sat on the edge of their seats, unable to take their eyes off the back-from-the-dead Jesus. "The kingdom of God" had always been on his mind. He spoke of it more than eighty times in the **four Gospels**. Alive from the dead, he talked about it more than ever.

## The Kingdom in a Capsule

The kingdom centers in one major issue. In the <u>Lord's Prayer</u> Jesus taught us to pray: "Our Father in heaven, hallowed be Your name. Your kingdom come. Your will be done on earth as it is in heaven" (Matthew 6:9–10 NKJV). The kingdom is the reign or rule of God. Everything in the kingdom focuses on doing <u>God's will</u>.

**Messiah**
Christ, the king from God

**Master**
teacher, rabbi, Lord

**four Gospels**
New Testament books by Matthew, Mark, Luke, and John

**future world**
Revelation 11:15

**character and values**
Matthew 5–7

**is here**
Matthew 4:17

**taken the punishment**
1 Peter 2:24–25;
Isaiah 53:4–6

**Jesus rules**
Matthew 28:18;
Romans 1:4

**sovereign**
absolute, excellent,
supreme

**agent**
means by which
God accomplishes
his desired results

Kingdom citizens are people who acknowledge God's **sovereign** authority over their lives, their world, and the universe. Their rallying cry is "God is in control!" They are linked with each other in the kingdom community, the church, the kingdom's advance contingent. Together they give the present world a taste of the <u>future world</u> where everything and everybody will bow to God's will. They work to carry out God's grand scheme to bring every person everywhere under his benevolent reign.

**what others say**

**Howard Snyder**

The church is seen as the community of God's people—a people called to serve him and called to live together in true Christian community as a witness to the <u>character and values</u> of the kingdom. The church is the **agent** of God's mission on earth. But what is that mission? It is nothing other than bringing all things and, supremely, all people of the earth under the dominion and headship of Jesus Christ.[5]

## The Reign of God—An Inside Job

ACTS 1:4–5 *And being assembled together with them, He commanded them not to depart from Jerusalem, but to wait for the Promise of the Father, "which," He said, "you have heard from Me; for John truly baptized with water, but you shall be baptized with the Holy Spirit not many days from now." (NKJV)*

As he meets with his followers after his resurrection, Jesus whistles his favorite tune: "The kingdom of God <u>is here</u>!" At last they can see what they could not see before. Having <u>taken the punishment</u> for human sin and beaten death's rap, <u>Jesus rules</u>! Even if they tried they couldn't doubt it. He's won the right to reign. He can expect his instructions to be obeyed. And he has big plans—he intends to conquer the world!

How was this fishy-smelling collection of back-country synagogue dropouts going to conquer the world? Yielding to the reign of God in the practical stuff of life goes against lifelong habits. Sin is like falling off a log! Surrender to the will of God is like climbing Mount Everest every day! Conquer the world? Out of the question!

There is only one way: The King's regime must become an inside job! So King Jesus commands his troops: "Wait for the Spirit!" (see Acts 1:5).

## If You Ain't Been Dipped, You've Been Gypped!

Jesus's strategy for giving people the opportunity to live under the reign of God began with connecting his followers to the source and secret of his own power. "John truly baptized with water," Jesus said, "but you shall be baptized with the Holy Spirit not many days from now" (Acts 1:5 NKJV). In the original language of the New Testament "baptize" means the following:

**John the Baptist**
Matthew 3:1–12;
Mark 1:2–9;
Luke 3:1–20;
John 1:6–8

- To place or dip something in water to wash it clean (like dirty laundry)

- To change the color of fabric by dipping it repeatedly in dye

- To steep, saturate, overwhelm, or fill something or someone

When early Christians spoke of being "baptized with the Holy Spirit," they had these meanings in mind:

- The Holy Spirit cleanses believers' sins away (Acts 15:8–9).

- The Holy Spirit gradually changes believers to be like Jesus (2 Corinthians 3:18).

- The Holy Spirit fills believers with his presence, giving them power to do God's will, immersing them in the thinking, values, and character of Jesus (Acts 2:4).

## Splashing Down Memory Lane

"John truly baptized with water," Jesus said. Three years earlier on the banks of the Jordan River, the desert prophet John the Baptist declared: "I indeed baptize you with water; but One mightier than I is coming, whose sandal strap I am not worthy to loose. He will baptize you with the Holy Spirit and fire" (Luke 3:16 NKJV). With these words of Luke 3:16, John summed up everything Jesus Christ would do—from teaching to dying on the cross to rising from the dead (things he was able to do in the energy of the Holy Spirit); from spiritual rebirth to forgiveness of sins to coming to live in his people's hearts (things he does in believers by giving them the Holy Spirit). Everything Jesus does is the Holy Spirit's work and part of his "baptism."

## Don't Leave Home Without It!

Jesus gives three clues to shape his friends' expectations about the coming of the Holy Spirit into their lives (Acts 1:4–5):

1. "Don't leave Jerusalem without it!" (Acts 1:4). Don't attempt anything for God until you have the Holy Spirit.

2. "Wait for the Father's Promise!" (Acts 1:4; 2:38; 10:45). The Spirit is the fulfillment of God's assurance.

3. "Remember what I said!" (Acts 1:4). Baptism with the Spirit includes everything Christ does in and for people. To understand spiritual baptism, check Jesus's teachings (see the following chart).

key point

It is clear from the beginning of Acts that oversight of the expansion of God's kingdom is directed by Jesus Christ himself, living in his followers in the person of the Holy Spirit.

## What Jesus Said About the Holy Spirit

| Scripture Reference | Jesus's Message |
|---|---|
| Luke 11:13 | The Holy Spirit is given by God to people who ask. |
| John 3:5 | The Holy Spirit is able to give a person "new birth" (a new start with God). |
| John 7:37–38 | The Holy Spirit satisfies spiritual thirst. The Holy Spirit is given to everyone who believes in Jesus. |
| John 14:16 | The Holy Spirit is the Christian's helper, comforter, and guide. |
| John 14:18–23 | The Holy Spirit is Jesus—living in believers, giving life, revealing himself. |
| John 14:26 | The Holy Spirit reminds us of Jesus's teachings. |
| John 15:26–27 | The Holy Spirit is sent by Jesus and tells people about him. |
| John 16:8–11 | The Holy Spirit enlightens the world about sin, righteousness, and judgment. |
| John 16:12–13 | The Holy Spirit guides people to the truth. The Holy Spirit always agrees with Jesus. The Holy Spirit sometimes reveals things before they happen. |
| John 16:14–17 | The Holy Spirit's primary job is to glorify Jesus and make him known. |

## What the Bible Says About the Holy Spirit

| Scripture Reference | What the Bible Says |
|---|---|
| Hebrews 9:14 | The Holy Spirit is eternal (no beginning, no end, not limited to time). |
| Luke 1:35 | The Holy Spirit's works are acts of God. |
| Psalm 139:7 | The Holy Spirit is present everywhere. |
| 1 Corinthians 2:10–11 | The Holy Spirit knows God's thoughts. |
| 2 Corinthians 3:18 | The Holy Spirit is Lord. |
| Acts 5:3–4 | To lie to the Holy Spirit is to lie to God. |

go to

**restored**
Ezekiel 36–37

**only the Father**
Mark 13:32

**worldly power**
Luke 9:46–50;
22:25–27;
Mark 10:35–45

what others say

**Billy Graham**

There is nothing God is that the Holy Spirit is not. All the essential aspects of deity belong to the Holy Spirit. We can say of him exactly what was said of Jesus Christ in the ancient **Nicene Creed**: He is very God of very God! so we bow before him, we worship him, we accord him every response Scripture requires of our relationship to Almighty God. Who is the Holy Spirit? He is God![6]

## Strategy for World Conquest

ACTS 1:6–7 *Therefore, when they had come together, they asked Him, saying, "Lord, will You at this time restore the kingdom to Israel?" And He said to them, "It is not for you to know times or seasons which the Father has put in His own authority.* (NKJV)

Jesus's teaching about the kingdom of God was often misunderstood. Oppressed Jews looked for a military governor to throw off the yoke of **pagan conquerors** and restore national independence. These nationalistic ideas were still a sticking point in his disciples' thinking. Patriotic Jews to the core, they dreamed of reviving the old Jewish monarchy. "Lord, will You at this time restore the kingdom to Israel?" (Acts 1:6 NKJV).

Jesus didn't exactly say "No." Believing Jews would soon put their faith in him, surrender to God's rule, and experience the kingdom. Someday, as the prophets predicted, the kingdom of Israel would be <u>restored</u>. But not yet. Jesus's response was a gentle rebuke, like saying, "The timing of national and international events is none of your business. <u>Only the Father</u> has authority over **times** and **dates**. Give up your dreams of <u>worldly power</u>. More important issues are at stake!" (Acts 1:7).

## The TNT of Christ's Presence

ACTS 1:8 *But you shall receive power when the Holy Spirit has come upon you; and you shall be witnesses to Me in Jerusalem, and in all Judea and Samaria, and to the end of the earth."* (NKJV)

A more important war must be fought before the war for Israel's independence. The original word translated "but" (Acts 1:8) is the

**Nicene Creed**
official statement of Christian beliefs adopted in AD 325

**pagan conquerors**
Assyrians, Babylonians, Persians, Greeks, Romans

**times**
interval till Christ returns to establish political as well as spiritual rule

**dates**
"seasons," events in establishing the kingdom

go to

**witnesses**
Luke 24:48;
Acts 10:41; 22:20;
Revelation 2:13

**apocalyptic**
forecasting the ulti-
mate destiny of the
world

**witnesses**
literally, "martyrs"—
people willing to
give their lives

**gospel**
good news about
Jesus

**apostles**
Christ's specially
chosen ambassadors

**Christendom**
Christianity

strongest word in Greek to indicate contrast. It's like saying, "Hold your horses! Instead of indulging in wishful thinking or **apocalyptic** speculation, hang on to your hats, brothers. You are about to grab a hot wire of power, the likes of which you have not dreamed!"

The original word for "power" in verse 8 sounds like "dynamite." It means authority and energy. To follow their Commander into bat-tle for the kingdom, followers of Jesus need the spiritual TNT of his presence. In a few days, Jesus would supernaturally enter them in the form of the Holy Spirit. This would empower them to be what Christians must be—**witnesses**.

## War Map for Revolution

Three major offensives form Jesus's plan for world conquest. The locations of pins on his war map form a table of contents for Acts[7] (see Illustration #1).

1. Jerusalem (Acts 1–7)
2. Judea and Samaria (Acts 8–12)
3. The ends of the earth (Acts 13–28)

Acts traces the **gospel**'s outreach as far as Rome. Before they died the **apostles** actually took the message of Jesus to Spain, Britain, Africa, and India. Before the revolution is over every people group on earth will hear it (Matthew 28:19). Strategies are in place to take the good news to the last unreached people early this century.

But don't get ahead of the Leader. Wait for the Spirit! (Acts 1:4)!

what others say

**Billy Graham**

If you believe in Jesus Christ, a power is available to you that can change your life, even in such intimate areas as your mar-riage, your family relationships, and every other relationship. Also God offers power that can change a tired church into a vital, growing body, power that can revitalize **Christendom**.[8]

**William Barclay**

The apostles were enjoined to wait on the coming of the Spirit. We would gain more power and courage and peace if we learned to wait. In the business of life we need to learn to be still. . . . Amidst life's surging activity there must be time to receive.[9]

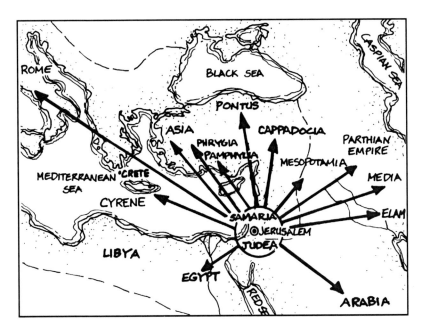

**Illustration #1**
Map of the Gospel's Spread—The circles on this map show where the gospel began in Jerusalem and spread to nearby areas of Judea and Samaria. The arrows show how the message spread to the rest of the known world at the time Acts was written. The dashed lines indicate the boundaries of the Roman Empire about AD 57.

## 5-4-3-2-1 Liftoff!

ACTS 1:9–11 *Now when He had spoken these things, while they watched, He was taken up, and a cloud received Him out of their sight. And while they looked steadfastly toward heaven as He went up, behold, two men stood by them in white apparel, who also said, "Men of Galilee, why do you stand gazing up into heaven? This same Jesus, who was taken up from you into heaven, will so come in like manner as you saw Him go into heaven."* (NKJV)

The strategy sessions with the risen Jesus ended abruptly forty days after his resurrection. He led his friends into the country (Luke 24:50), raised his hands to bless them and, as they watched, he lifted off and disappeared in a strange cloud.

As the group on the hilltop strained for a last glimpse of the ascending Lord, two white-clad figures (**angels**) suddenly "beamed down" beside them. "Why are you gawking into the empty sky?" they asked. "Jesus will come back just as you have seen him go—<u>in a cloud</u>."

**in a cloud**
Mark 13:26

**angels**
spirit beings created to serve God and help people

**descended**
John 1:10–18;
Philippians 2:5–11

**human baby**
Luke 1:31–38

**right hand of God**
Mark 16:19;
Romans 8:34

**Head**
leader, director,
CEO

**intercedes**
prays for

**what others say**

**Howard Snyder**

The Kingdom is both present and future, both earthly and heavenly, both hidden and becoming manifest. It is as concrete and this-worldly as the dust on Jesus' feet or the Galilean wind in his hair; it is as costly as the crucifixion; it is as heavenly as the risen Christ sitting at the right hand of the Father. . . . Its truths and values are those taught and lived by Jesus Christ and delivered to the body of his followers. But this Kingdom can become fully manifest only when Jesus Christ returns to earth.[10]

The Ascension is the game-winning final play of an amazing life. Where did Jesus go? Thirty-three years earlier he <u>descended</u> from the heavenly dimension as a <u>human baby</u> so that he could die as a man for human sins. Mission accomplished, he returned to the heavenly dimension and reassumed his place at the <u>right hand of God</u>. See the following chart.

### Seven Wonderful Things About the Ascension of Jesus Christ

| Wonderful Thing | Scripture |
| --- | --- |
| The ascension fulfilled Old Testament prophecy. | Psalms 24:7–10; 68:18–19; Ephesians 4:7–11 |
| The ascension fulfilled Jesus's prophecy. | John 6:62; 7:33–34; 10:17; 14:28–29; 16:5–7 |
| With the Crucifixion and Resurrection, the Ascension certifies Jesus is Lord, Christ, King, and **Head**. | Acts 2:32–36; Ephesians 1:18–23; 1 Timothy 3:16; Revelation 19:16 |
| The Ascension puts Christ permanently in God's presence where he **intercedes** for us. | Romans 8:34; Hebrews 7:25; 9:24 |
| The Ascension opens the way for Jesus to send the Holy Spirit to us. | John 16:7; Acts 2:33 |
| The Ascension makes it possible for Jesus to be with us at all times. | Matthew 18:20; 28:20; Ephesians 4:10 |
| The Ascension enables Jesus to prepare a place for us to be with him in heaven. | John 14:2–3 |

Jesus directs the affairs and movements of his followers and his church from the place of highest authority in the universe—the right hand of God.

## Anticipation in the Attic

ACTS 1:12–13a *Then they returned to Jerusalem from the mount called Olivet, which is near Jerusalem, a **Sabbath <u>day's journey</u>**. And when they had entered, they went up into the upper room where they were staying:* (NKJV)

The setting for the spiritual explosion that would rock the world was simple. Witnesses of the Ascension returned to Jerusalem and climbed to the upper chamber, an upstairs room large enough to hold 120 people. Ahead lay a heart-pounding adventure. "You shall be baptized with the Holy Spirit not many days from now" (Acts 1:5 NKJV). Precisely what that was going to mean they did not know. They only knew he'd told them they were about to connect with power to be his witnesses "to the end of the earth" (Acts 1:8 NKJV).

All they had to do was . . . wait.

## Upper Room Roll Call: The Eleven

ACTS 1:13b *Peter, James, John, and Andrew; Philip and Thomas; Bartholomew and Matthew; James the son of Alphaeus and Simon the Zealot; and Judas the son of James.* (NKJV)

The upper room aggregation included "the Eleven" (the Twelve minus Judas). The Eleven were men <u>chosen by Jesus</u> as his special ambassadors and church leaders. Before being called to join Jesus's party, most had been blue-collar tradesmen (fishermen, farmers, government workers). Most were synagogue dropouts, "<u>sinners</u>" by reputation. They'd spent three years following Jesus around as his disciples (trainees). They were the original apostles whose acts are being told in Acts.

Those present were as follows:

*Peter*—Called the "Rock." Quick-tongued (Matthew 16:15–16). Denied Jesus three times (Matthew 26:75). Reinstated after Jesus rose from the dead (John 21:15–17).

*James*—The other "Son of Thunder." First apostle **martyred** (Acts 12:1–2).

*John*—Brother James and he were nicknamed "Sons of Thunder" for volatile personalities (Luke 9:51–55). He is the disciple "<u>Jesus loved</u>" of the Gospel of John.

go to

**day's journey**
Numbers 311:31
Luke 2:44

**chosen by Jesus**
Luke 6:14–16;
Mark 3:16–19;
Matthew 10:2–4

**sinners**
Luke 5:8, 30; 15:1–2

**Jesus loved**
John 13:23; 19:26;
20:2; 21:7, 20–24

**Sabbath day's journey**
three-fourth mile, maximum distance allowed on Sabbath

**martyred**
killed for following Christ

**named**
Mark 16:1;
Luke 8:2–3;
John 19:25

*Andrew*—Peter's brother. Brought strangers to Jesus (John 1:35–42; 12:22).

*Philip*—Among first five to connect with Jesus (John 1:43–45).

*Thomas*—Called Doubting Thomas for refusing to believe the Resurrection until he saw Jesus alive (John 20:25–29).

*Bartholomew*—Also called Nathanael. Skeptical at first, then recognized Jesus as "King of Israel" (John 1:46, 49).

*Matthew*—Called Levi. Customs officer. Held banquet to introduce Jesus to friends (Luke 5:29). Student of Bible prophecy.

*James*—"Younger" or "Junior." Matthew's brother (compare Matthew 10:3 with Mark 2:14). Christian legend says he'd been a right-wing revolutionary.

*Simon*—The Canaanite, nicknamed "Zealot" (Acts 1:13; Mark 3:18). From militant wing of Jewish independence movement.

*Judas*—Alias: Jude, Judah, or Thaddeus, to distinguish him from the betrayer Judas Iscariot. May have been the apostle James's son.

## Upper Room Roll Call: The Women

ACTS 1:14 *These all continued with one accord in prayer and supplication, with the women and Mary the mother of Jesus, and with His brothers. (NKJV)*

Some of these women had been part of Jesus's Galilean traveling team along with male disciples (Luke 23:55). Some were wealthy and provided financial support (Luke 8:1–3). <u>Named</u> in other places are Joanna, Susanna, Salome, and a quartet of Marys—Mary Magdalene, Mary the mother of James, Jesus's aunt Mary, and Mary his mother.

*key point*

Luke, more than any other New Testament writer, notes the role of women in the ministry of Jesus and the church. Specially noted is the presence of "Mary the mother of Jesus" (Acts 1:14 NKJV). She once called herself "the maidservant of the Lord" (Luke 1:38 NKJV). Miraculously, she was a virgin until after the birth of Jesus. (Read all about it in Luke 1:27, 34.) The early church held Mary in high esteem. She was a major source of information about Jesus's early years. Mary not only gave Jesus birth, but also she was there to help give birth to his church!

**Craig S. Keener**

Given the culture's usual downplaying of women's public roles, the equal participation of women is noteworthy, especially their apparent mixing with the men.[11]

**leader**
Acts 12:17;
15:13–19; 21:18

**one mind**
Matthew 18:19–20

**Epistle**
letter

## Upper Room Roll Call: Jesus's Relatives

The roster of upper room participants contains a happy surprise: "His [Jesus's] brothers" were there (Acts 1:14 NKJV): James, Joseph, Simon, and Judas (Matthew 13:55). Throughout most of his ministry they'd been quite unwilling to believe in Jesus (John 7:5). In fact, they thought he was mentally ill (Mark 3:21). But they've changed! Here they are among Jesus's closest disciples, waiting for the Holy Spirit. Jesus's brother James became a church <u>leader</u> and authored the **Epistle** of James.

"With one accord" (Acts 1:14 NKJV) means more than occupying the same room. It means with <u>one mind</u> and passion. This was hardly the kind of group that could be expected to launch a worldwide revolution. Most were nobodies in polite society. However, they shared one thing in common—close relationship with Jesus. He was the superglue that held them together.

## How Do You Start a Fire?

Strike a match. Spark flint on steel. Rub two sticks together.

Or . . . jam 120 spiritually passionate people who've met the risen Jesus in a room like sardines, and get them praying. The early church is big on prayer—it's mentioned thirty-one times in Acts. Jesus told the early believers that their Father in heaven would give them the Holy Spirit if they prayed (Luke 24:49).

**Sue Monk Kidd**

When Jesus asked the disciples to wait, he knew that times of prayerful waiting allow something profound and necessary to take place. They create a receptiveness to God's power that enables it to sink down and revitalize our lives. . . . In every transformation there is a time to wait . . . and pray.[12]

**Psalms**
Psalms 69:25; 109:8

**turned traitor**
Luke 22:3–6;
John 12:4–6; 13:27

**guide**
John 18:1–3

**cursed**
Genesis 4:10–12

**cursed**
haunted by his
blood, as a place to
bury paupers and
**aliens**

**aliens**
foreigners, not
native to Israel

## Tragedy at Murder Meadow

ACTS 1:15–20 *And in those days Peter stood up in the midst of the disciples (altogether the number of names was about a hundred and twenty), and said, "Men and brethren, this Scripture had to be fulfilled, which the Holy Spirit spoke before by the mouth of David concerning Judas, who became a guide to those who arrested Jesus; for he was numbered with us and obtained a part in this ministry." (Now this man purchased a field with the wages of iniquity; and falling headlong, he burst open in the middle and all his entrails gushed out. And it became known to all those dwelling in Jerusalem; so that field is called in their own language, Akel Dama, that is, Field of Blood.) "For it is written in the Book of Psalms:*
*    'Let his dwelling place be desolate,*
*    And let no one live in it';*
*and,*
*    'Let another take his office.' (NKJV)*

One familiar face was missing at this upper room caucus: Judas Iscariot, Jesus' friend (see Matthew 26:50). Judas was one of Jesus's original twelve ambassadors (Luke 6:16). He <u>turned traitor</u> and "became a <u>guide</u> to those who arrested Jesus" (Acts 1:16 NKJV). The price of his treachery was a miserable "thirty pieces of silver" (Matthew 26:15 NKJV).

### How Judas "Bought the Farm"

The Bible gives two accounts of Judas's tragic end—here in Acts 1:18–19 and in Matthew 27:3–10. Overcome with guilt, Judas went to the Temple to return the bribe. The priests refused the money. He threw the silver into the Temple, went out, and hanged himself. His body fell, bursting open. Peter's description is graphic enough to make the strongest stomach turn.

The bribe money was used to buy the piece of land where Judas died, now considered **cursed**. Six weeks later, the locals were already calling it "Field of Blood" or "Murder Meadow."[13]

## The Election of AD 30

ACTS 1:21–26 *Therefore, of these men who have accompanied us all the time that the Lord Jesus went in and out among us, beginning from the baptism of John to that day when He was taken up from us, one of these must become a witness with us of His resurrection." And they proposed two: Joseph called Barsabas, who was surnamed Justus, and Matthias. And they prayed and said, "You, O Lord, who know the hearts of all, show which of these two You have chosen to take part in this ministry and apostleship from which Judas by transgression fell, that he might go to his own place." And they cast their lots, and the lot fell on Matthias. And he was numbered with the eleven apostles.* (NKJV)

The yawn factor of 240 hours of waiting becomes apparent when we realize the most exciting thing that happened during those ten days was a church election! Actually it was quite important. The first congregational election involved four steps:

*Step 1—Instruction* (Acts 1:20–21). Qualifications for office: Judas's pinch-hitter must (1) believe in the Resurrection, (2) know Jesus as a result of living with him, (3) know and work well with the rest of the team.

*Step 2—Nomination* (Acts 1:21–23). By **consensus** two candidates were nominated: Joseph, nicknamed Barsabas ("son of the Sabbath") or Justus (Latin for "righteous"), and Matthias. **Eusebius** reports that Matthias was one of the seventy Jesus sent out to prepare the cities of Judea and Perea for his arrival (Luke 10:1)

*Step 3—Prayer* (Acts 1:24). Ask God to <u>reveal his choice</u>.

*Step 4—<u>Casting lots</u>* (Acts 1:26). Today we'd draw straws or flip a coin. In Acts 1 they wrote candidates' names on small stones, put them in a bowl, and shook the bowl till one of the stones rolled out (see Illustration #2 on the next page). The rolling stone announced the winner—Matthias (Acts 1:26).

The story of the first church election shows how Jesus leads his movement through (1) his people's concerns, (2) their willingness to listen to each other, (3) their attitude of dependence on his leadership expressed in prayer, and (4) their consensus—agreement, harmony—about a course of action.

**go to**

**reveal his choice**
Proverbs 16:33

**casting lots**
Leviticus 16:8–10;
Numbers 26:55;
1 Chronicles
26:12–16

**consensus**
agreement of the
entire group

**Eusebius**
early church
historian

**what others say**

**Lawrence O. Richards**

This is the last time we read [in the Bible] any decision being made by casting lots or any similar way. . . . From that moment on the Spirit became our guide. Now we look to him, and in faith commit ourselves to obey when he shows us the way.[14]

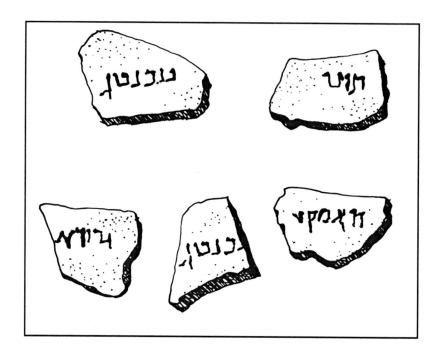

**Illustration #2**
Casting Lots—Small stones or pottery pieces such as these with names or symbols written on them were used to make decisions. Biblical use of lots was not superstitious but based on a belief that God controls everything.

## Chapter Wrap-Up

- Acts is a sequel to the Gospel of Luke, telling how Jesus continued his work through his followers. (Acts 1:1–2)

- For forty days following Easter, Jesus appeared to people, proving he was alive. He talked about God's reign and the baptism of the Holy Spirit. He outlined his strategy for taking his message to the world. The Holy Spirit would come to his people. Then they would take his message in widening circles to the ends of the earth. (Acts 1:3–8)

- Jesus ascended to heaven, assuring vital benefits for believers. Angels promised he would return. (Acts 1:9–11)

- The disciples spent the next ten days waiting for the Spirit. They prayed and experienced oneness based on love for Jesus. (Acts 1:12–14)

- The gathering agreed Judas's vacancy on the apostolic team should be filled. Matthias was chosen by lot. (Acts 1:15–26)

## Study Questions

1. Where did Jesus get his power to teach and do miracles?

2. Identify two things baptism with the Holy Spirit may be expected to accomplish in a person's life.

3. Jesus's strategy for world conquest involves three phases or major offensives. List them.

4. How did the people waiting in the upper room for the Holy Spirit spend their time?

5. What qualifications did Peter say should be looked for in Judas's replacement? Who were the two men who fulfilled the qualifications to be candidates for apostleship?

6. How did the group go about deciding which one should replace Judas?

# Acts 2 God's Promise to the Jewish Believers

**Chapter Highlights:**
- The Annual Jewish Barley Harvest Festival
- God's Spirit Introduces a New Covenant
- The Miracle of the Church

## Let's Get Started

Jesus told his friends they would become world travelers taking the news about him to faraway places (Matthew 28:19–20; Acts 1:8). He promised they would be "endued with power from on high" (Luke 24:49 NKJV). Wherever the adventure took them, he would go with them (Matthew 28:20).

Depending on your perspective, what happened next may seem strange, sensational, or spooky. In all its colorful religious history, Jerusalem had never seen anything like it. The **promise** came to the first trembling collection of 120 Jewish believers on their tenth day of waiting. Jesus suddenly stormed back into their lives like gangbusters! They found themselves with unusual opportunities to tell his story and unusual abilities for getting people to listen. They found courage to confront the people responsible for Jesus's death and to publicly appeal to their listeners to link up with the dynamic personal presence of God.

go to

**harvest festival**
Exodus 23:16;
34:22;
Deuteronomy 16:10;
Numbers 28:26

**Passover**
Exodus 12;
Leviticus 23:5

**promise**
God's unchangeable commitment

**Pentecost**
called Feast of "Weeks" (seven weeks after Passover), "Firstfruits," or "Harvest"

**Passover**
celebration of Israel's freedom from Egyptian slavery

> what others say
>
> **Michael Card**
>
> Our God is the great maker of promises. His word, the Bible, is quite simply a collection of the promises he has made to us.[1]

## The Annual Jewish Barley Harvest Festival

**ACTS 2:1** *When the Day of Pentecost had fully come, they were all with one accord in one place. (NKJV)*

**Pentecost** Day was the annual Jewish barley <u>harvest festival</u> held in late May or early June, fifty days after **Passover**. It was Israel's Thanksgiving Day. In AD 30 Pentecost was the day the Holy Spirit came upon the followers of Jesus (Acts 1:4). What the Jews celebrated on that day helps us understand the Spirit's coming.

**go to**

**guarantees**
2 Corinthians 1:22;
5:5;
Ephesians 1:13–14

**Hebrew**
Israelite, belonging
to the nation of
Israel, Jewish

**Mount Sinai**
mountain on Sinai
Peninsula, between
Gulfs of Suez and
Aqaba

**covenants**
binding agreements
or contracts
between parties

**poured out**
given freely and
abundantly

# God's Spirit Introduces a New Covenant

**Hebrew** scholars calculate that on the fiftieth day after ol' Pharaoh let God's people go (Exodus 12, 19), God gave Israel the Ten Commandments (Exodus 20:1–17) and the Law, at **Mount Sinai**. The Law is also called "the Mosaic Covenant" because God communicated it through Israel's great liberator, Moses.

**Covenants** play a big part in the history of God's relationship with people. God's covenants are formal statements describing his commitments. God made covenants with Noah (see Genesis 9:8–17); Abraham (see Genesis 12:1–3; 15:18–20); David (1 Chronicles 17:7–15); and Moses (introduced in Exodus 19:3–6 and spelled out in Exodus, Leviticus, Numbers, and Deuteronomy). The Mosaic Covenant is also called the "First" or "Old" Covenant (Hebrews 8:6–7, 13).

At Pentecost, the anniversary of the Old Covenant, the Holy Spirit introduced a New Covenant (new terms for relating to God). The Old Testament arrangement based on religious rule keeping and animal sacrifices was canceled (Hebrews 8:13). Since Jesus came and the Spirit was **poured out**, knowing God is a whole new ball game! Today we relate to God through his Spirit who lives in everyone who trusts Jesus. God's Spirit living in us writes God's law on our minds and hearts (Hebrews 8:10; 10:16–17) and guarantees God's commitments will be carried out.

You see, Pentecost was not just a temporary spiritual high. It was the start of a new way to know and live with God.

**what others say**

**Billy Graham**

The Day of Pentecost in the New Testament on which the Holy Spirit came was "a day of first fruits"—the beginning of God's harvest in this world, to be completed when Christ comes again. Pentecost in the New Testament marked the commencement of the present age of the Holy Spirit.[2]

## Lessons from Jewish Pentecost About the Holy Spirit

go to

| What Pentecost Celebrates | How Celebrated | What It Pictures About the Spirit |
|---|---|---|
| Harvest—God's goodness in providing food | The first sheaf of barley is presented to the Lord in thanksgiving and anticipation of a full harvest ahead. | The 120 are the first "sheaves" of a spiritual harvest, which will gather people all over the world to Christ through their witness. |
| Community—Equality of God's people | Most inclusive festival. Everyone invited (Deuteronomy 16:11). All social classes participate as equals. | The Spirit is for the whole church; all who believe in Jesus are equipped by the Spirit to do God's work together (John 7:37–39). |
| Acceptance—God's acceptance of imperfect people | Festival bread is common bread of Israelite homes, made with yeast—symbol of sin (Leviticus 23:17). | God accepts and empowers ordinary people still struggling with spiritual imperfections and uses them as workers in his harvest. |
| Commitment—God's commitments to his people | Remembering God's gift of the Mosaic Covenant, the Law, at Mount Sinai, fifty days after first Passover (Exodus 20:1–17). | Spirit's coming inaugurated the New Covenant in Christ; the Spirit writes God's laws on believers' hearts (Hebrews 8:10). |

**disturbances**
Genesis 9:8–17;
15:6–21; 32:24–31;
Exodus 19

**breath**
Genesis 2:7;
Job 37:10;
Ezekiel 13:13;
John 3:8

**thousands**
100,000 to 150,000
or more[3]

## Prayers Interrupted with a Deafening Roar

ACTS 2:2–3 *And suddenly there came a sound from heaven, as of a rushing mighty wind, and it filled the whole house where they were sitting. Then there appeared to them divided tongues, as of fire, and one sat upon each of them. (NKJV)*

Morning, the tenth day after Jesus was lifted to heaven, **thousands** of pilgrims moved through the streets of Old Jerusalem to the temple area for worship, unaware that in a nearby loft something was about to happen that would change the course of history.

In Bible history new beginnings—especially God's covenants—are often introduced with nerve-racking <u>disturbances</u>.

The prayers of the 120 were interrupted by a deafening roar—as if a tornado had been unleashed inside the house. Today you might have described it as the roar of a super jet taking off! Wind is a symbol of the Spirit (<u>breath</u>) of God, the source of life, and cleansing judgment. The roar of this glorious gale announced that what they had been waiting for—their moment of spiritual rebirth, the beginning of a new life in the Spirit—had arrived.

**go to**

**fire**
Exodus 3:2–5;
13:21–22; 19:18;
Leviticus 6:13

**chaff**
Psalm 1:4

**engulfment**
baptism with the
Holy Spirit

**chaff**
seed coverings,
straw, and other
debris

what others say

**Dallas Willard**

The **engulfment** came upon them—with quite a racket, right out of the sky into which only ten days earlier they had seen Jesus disappear (Acts 2:2).[4]

## A Sudden Ball of Fire

As if the hurricane-sound tearing through the house was not enough to scare the daylights out of them, a ball of fire suddenly appeared, exploded, separated into individual flames, and danced around the room, igniting 120 secondary fires. Each person in the room seemed to be on fire.

In the Bible, <u>fire</u> represents the presence of God. The Holy Spirit is God present.

John the Baptist predicted Jesus would "baptize you with the Holy Spirit and fire" (Luke 3:16 NKJV). Jesus as harvester threshes out the good grain and incinerates the <u>**chaff**</u> (Luke 3:16–17). His incoming Spirit purifies a person's conscience from past guilt (Acts 15:8–9) and starts a process of cleansing away everything destructive and useless.

The Holy Spirit's work meets both group and individual needs. He invades each person, but the impact of his cleansing, empowering work is most fully realized when believers are together, interacting, bumping up against each other, adjusting, dealing with irritation and frustration with each other, reconciling.

what others say

**Paul Tournier**

Human effort is like an endless labor in which, generation by generation, bit by bit, a monument is built, always precarious and never finished. The solution of each problem raises a thousand new problems. But when the spark of the Spirit lights up the darkness that has gathered around a person's life, it is as if there has come down from heaven, perfect and complete, a quite simple truth that sets at rest all the disquiet of the soul.[5]

**Cyril of Jerusalem**

Whatever the Spirit touches becomes holy and transformed.[6]

## Engulfed in the Spirit

**ACTS 2:4a** *And they were all filled with the Holy Spirit* (NKJV)

"Filled with the Holy Spirit"—what does it mean?

1. The Spirit of Christ fills the void created by separation from God because of sin.

2. Paul compares Spirit-filling to being intoxicated! "Do not be drunk with wine, in which is dissipation; but be filled with the Spirit" (Ephesians 5:18 NKJV). To be filled with the Holy Spirit is to be under the Spirit's <u>influence</u>. Getting tanked on wine leads to loss of control and destructive behavior. Spirit-filling produces joy, spiritual singing, and worship.

In order to assure that direction of his movement is dynamic and personal, Jesus comes to live in believers, in the person of the Holy Spirit. He manages the kingdom from the throne of his people's yielded desires and wills.

**influence**
Romans 8:5–9

**tongues**
languages

---

### what others say

**Kilian McDonnell**

The Spirit is the turning-around point by which the way back to God is opened. . . . The Spirit is the sole source of our relationship with God.[7]

**Billy Graham**

All Christians are committed to be filled with the Spirit. Anything short of a Spirit-filled life is less than God's plan for each believer. . . . To be Spirit-filled is to be controlled or dominated by the Spirit's presence and power. . . . We are under the "influence" of the Spirit. Instead of doing things only with our own strength or ability, He empowers us. Instead of doing only what we want to do, we now are guided by Him.[8]

---

## Languages of Wonder and Witness

**ACTS 2:4b–11** *and began to speak with other **tongues**, as the Spirit gave them utterance. And there were dwelling in Jerusalem Jews, devout men, from every nation under heaven. And when this sound occurred, the multitude came together, and were confused,*

**languages**
Isaiah 28:11–12;
1 Corinthians 12–14

**Babel**
Genesis 11:1–9

**Corinth**
1 Corinthians 12–14

**wonderful works**
acts and characteristics of God that reveal his splendor and inspire worship

**cacophony**
discordant sound

*because everyone heard them speak in his own language. Then they were all amazed and marveled, saying to one another, "Look, are not all these who speak Galileans? And how is it that we hear, each in our own language in which we were born? Parthians and Medes and Elamites, those dwelling in Mesopotamia, Judea and Cappadocia, Pontus and Asia, Phrygia and Pamphylia, Egypt and the parts of Libya adjoining Cyrene, visitors from Rome, both Jews and proselytes, Cretans and Arabs—we hear them speaking in our own tongues the wonderful works of God." (NKJV)*

Jews converged on Jerusalem for Pentecost. Thousands of travelers speaking foreign languages filled the streets. A little before nine in the morning, passersby were startled by what sounded like a violent windstorm bearing down on one particular house. They rushed toward the sound.

In the loft above, with a hurricane howl inundating their ears and a vision of flame dazzling their eyes, the roomful of Galileans began to speak in <u>languages</u> other than the Galilean-accented Aramaic they'd spoken all their lives. Men and women poured out of the upper room doors and down to the street below, loudly praising God in the new languages. It was <u>Babel</u> unraveled! What sounded to some like mindless babble, to others was clear declaration of the **"wonderful works** of God." At least fifteen different languages were spoken in this **cacophony** of praise—Even "Cretans and Arabs"! cried one incredulous listener.

Acts 2 gives these facts concerning the "languages" phenomenon:

- Ability to speak was given by the Holy Spirit (verse 4).
- Everyone in the original group was able to speak a new language (verse 4).
- Speakers used their new languages to declare the wonderful works of God (verse 11).
- Some listeners concluded it was the babbling of a bunch of drunks (verse 13).

On two other occasions in Acts, people spoke in strange languages when first introduced to Jesus and the Holy Spirit (Acts 10:44–46; 19:5–6). Other times when people received the Spirit, the language gift is not mentioned (Acts 8:17; 9:17–18). The gift of languages (tongues) also appeared in the church at <u>Corinth</u>. There the languages were not understood and required interpretation.

# Why Would God Give Such a Goofy Gift?

ACTS 2:12 *So they were all amazed and perplexed, saying to one another, "Whatever could this mean?"* (NKJV)

The serious-minded folks were scratching their heads, wanting to know more. At Pentecost, with all those foreign visitors, the Holy Spirit's language gift shifted the worldwide witness to Jesus Christ into gear (Acts 1:8; Matthew 28:19). The pilgrims of Pentecost returned home (see Illustration #1), taking with them news of the new thing God was doing.

**go to**

**diaspora**
2 Kings 17:5; 25:21

**explanation**
1 Corinthians 14:23

**Jewish diaspora**
Jews scattered in foreign countries

**Gentile**
anyone who's not Jewish

**what others say**

### Krister Stendahl

Now the Spirit is the energy and the guide engineering the life and expansion of the church in the world of the **Jewish diaspora** and through it to the **Gentile** world. The ecstatic speech, the speaking in tongues . . . is seen by Luke as a symbol of the global outreach across all barriers of language and culture.[9]

Jesus does not merely tell the church what it should be doing; he gives the spiritual equipment and abilities needed to do it—in this case, the ability to speak the language of the people.

# The "New Wine" of the New Order

ACTS 2:13 *Others mocking said, "They are full of new wine."* (NKJV)

Some people in every crowd try to hide their perplexity with cynical jokes. Or perhaps deciding the disciples were all crocked was the best explanation bewildered detractors could come up with for the puzzling occurrence of a roomful of Galilean yokels making strange noises with their mouths. Ironically, in the spiritual sense, the detractors were right. This was the "new wine" of the new order Jesus said couldn't be contained in old bottles (Mark 2:22). In any case, the snide remark gave the full-of-Jesus believers their first real chance to be witnesses.

# Peter Shouts for Attention

ACTS 2:14–15 *But Peter, standing up with the eleven, raised his voice and said to them, "Men of Judea and all who dwell in*

**go to**

**denied**
Luke 22:54–62

**ran**
Mark 14:50–52

**Rock**
Matthew 16:18

**last days**
2 Timothy 3:1;
Hebrews 1:2;
2 Peter 3:3;
1 John 2:18

*Jerusalem, let this be known to you, and heed my words. For these are not drunk, as you suppose, since it is only the third hour of the day. (NKJV)*

Before their very eyes they saw proof Jesus Christ rose from the dead and lives in his followers! Here's Peter the coward, who, three times, before some of these same people, <u>denied</u> knowing Jesus. Flanking him are eleven other guys, who, when the chips were down seven weeks earlier, <u>ran</u> like rabbits to save their own miserable skins, leaving Jesus to face death alone. But what a difference!

The "<u>Rock</u>" Peter, finally living up to his name, shouts for the crowd's attention. With good humor he pitches the cynics' joke back at them: "Drunk? It's only nine o'clock in the morning, for heaven's sake! Nobody gets drunk before breakfast." (*Laughter.*)

## The Outpouring of the Spirit Will Impact Everyone

ACTS 2:16–21 *But this is what was spoken by the prophet Joel:*
    *'And it shall come to pass in the last days, says God,*
    *That I will pour out of My Spirit on all flesh;*
    *Your sons and your daughters shall prophesy,*
    *Your young men shall see visions,*
    *Your old men shall dream dreams.*
    *And on My menservants and on My maidservants*
    *I will pour out My Spirit in those days;*
    *And they shall prophesy.*
    *I will show wonders in heaven above*
    *And signs in the earth beneath:*
    *Blood and fire and vapor of smoke.*
    *The sun shall be turned into darkness,*
    *And the moon into blood,*
    *Before the coming of the great and awesome day of the* LORD.
    *And it shall come to pass*
    *That whoever calls on the name of the* LORD
    *Shall be saved.' (NKJV)*

"Whatever could this mean?" (Acts 2:12 NKJV). Peter remembered the ancient prophecy of Joel (Joel 2:28–32) and quoted it to explain. The ruckus in the upper room, the happy hubbub in the streets, announced a new age. The "<u>Last Days</u> are here," Peter said. "This is the Age of the Holy Spirit." Expect miracles!

1. Expect the outpouring of the Spirit to impact everyone.

2. Expect ordinary people—men and women—to **prophesy**, see **visions**, dream <u>dreams</u>.

3. Expect awesome occurrences in the sky and on the earth. Cosmic signs were already happening! The <u>day Jesus died</u> the sky had blackened and a rock-splitting, grave-opening earthquake occurred. And now the wind roared, fire appeared, and strange languages were spoken. There would be more.

4. Expect **salvation** to be offered to <u>everyone</u>.

**go to**

**dreams**
Matthew 1:20; 2:13, 19, 22

**day Jesus died**
Luke 22:44–45;
Mark 15:33, 38;
Matthew 27:45, 51–52

**everyone**
John 3:16;
Romans 1:14–16

**destiny**
Matthew 1:21;
Mark 8:31;
Luke 2:34–35;
John 10:14–18

**exalted**
Acts 1:9;
Philippians 2:11

---

**what others say**

**Watchman Nee**

Because the Holy Spirit has been poured out upon all mankind, the merest cry from the sinner to God is enough.[10]

---

## The Big Idea

**ACTS 2:22–24** *"Men of Israel, hear these words: Jesus of Nazareth, a Man attested by God to you by miracles, wonders, and signs which God did through Him in your midst, as you yourselves also know—Him, being delivered by the determined purpose and **foreknowledge** of God, you have taken by lawless hands, have crucified, and put to death; whom God raised up, having loosed the pains of death, because it was not possible that He should be held by it.* (NKJV)

Peter states the central theme of the Christian message. Some form of this message is preached over and over in Acts:

1. Jesus was approved by God (Acts 2:22).

2. His <u>destiny</u> was to die on the cross (Acts 2:23).

3. God raised him from the dead (Acts 2:24–32).

4. Jesus now occupies the <u>exalted</u> position at "the **right hand** of God" (Acts 2:33–35).

**prophesy**
speak God's messages, preach

**visions**
insights, dreamlike revelations from God

**dreams**
images with spiritual significance while asleep

**salvation**
rescue from sin's slavery; restoration of spiritual health

**foreknowledge**
ability to know in advance what will happen

**right hand**
highest place of honor and power in the universe

**go to**

**be like**
Psalm 16:8–11

**descendants**
1 Chronicles
17:11–14

**predicted**
Psalm 16:10

**return**
Psalm 110:1

**what others say**

**William Barclay**

The thought of Acts safeguards us from two serious errors in our thinking about the death of Jesus. (a) The cross is not a kind of emergency measure flung out by God when everything else failed. It is part of God's very life. (b) We must never think that anything Jesus did changed the attitude of God to men. It was by God Jesus was sent. We may put it this way—the cross was a window in time allowing us to see the suffering love which is eternally in the heart of God.[11]

## King David Sings the Wondrous Story

**the big picture**

**Acts 2:25–35**

Peter explained that God showed King David what Messiah would <u>be like</u>. Messiah would be one of David's <u>descendants</u>. The king <u>predicted</u> Christ's resurrection and return to God's right hand.

Speaking to this audience of zealous Jews, Peter used the prophetic poetry of Israel's most popular king to explain Jesus's significance. God showed King David what Messiah would be like (Acts 2:25–28; Psalm 16:8–11). Messiah would be one of David's descendants (Acts 2:29–30; 1 Chronicles 17:11–14). The singing king predicted Christ's resurrection (Acts 2:31; Psalm 16:10) and <u>return</u> to God's right hand (Acts 2:25; Psalm 110:1).

Peter's message is clear: The Christian gospel offers a reality no other system of morality, religion, or philosophy offers. Genuine Christianity is packaged in the person of its founder and present leader—who died on the cross, rose from the dead, holds the most highly exalted position in the universe, and by his Spirit literally lives in his followers!

**what others say**

**George MacDonald**

Jesus departed from our sight that he might return to our hearts; he departed and, behold, he is here![12]

# The Zinger: The True Identity of the Man You Killed

ACTS 2:36 *Therefore let all the house of Israel know assuredly that God has made this Jesus, whom you crucified, both Lord and Christ." (NKJV)*

Peter wraps up his speech with a whack across the head with a spiritual two-by-four. All of this—the prophecies, Jesus's crucifixion, resurrection, and ascension, the Holy Spirit's coming to the disciples, the disturbances of Pentecost—proves one great fact: Jesus (the man you crucified) is **Lord** (Yahweh-God) and Christ (*Messiah King*).

The foremost fact of Christian faith is this: Jesus, who died for our sins, rose from the dead, is alive today, and may be known personally as Lord and Savior.

**his job**
Matthew 16:17;
Luke 10:21–22;
John 6:44–45;
16:7–15

**Lord**
Master; also a title for God

**Messiah**
God's Chosen One, Savior, King

# No Time to Sing "Just As I Am"

ACTS 2:37 *Now when they heard this, they were cut to the heart, and said to Peter and the rest of the apostles, "Men and brethren, what shall we do?" (NKJV)*

Call 911! This is an emergency! The sense of urgency that gripped people as Peter nailed home point after point was a result of the Spirit quietly doing 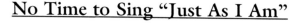his job. Peter's logic was flawless. The Spirit's power energized him as he spoke. They knew about the Crucifixion. They knew who was responsible. They knew Jesus's tomb was empty. They saw what they hadn't seen before: Jesus's death and resurrection fulfilled prophecies they'd read Sabbath after Sabbath in their synagogues. The light dawned. Jesus of Nazareth was the Messiah!

"What shall we do?" they cried.

Were you ever "cut to the heart" by something you heard about Christ? What did you do? Have you made an initial commitment to follow Christ? What convinced you that you needed him?

what others say

### J. Gresham Machen

There must be the mysterious work of the Spirit of God in the new birth. Without that, all our arguments are quite useless. . . . What the Holy Spirit does in the new birth is not to make a man a Christian regardless of the evidence, but on the contrary to clear away the mists from his eyes and enable him to attend to the evidence.[13]

## Quick! Walk This Way!

ACTS **2:38–39** *Then Peter said to them, "Repent, and let every one of you be baptized in the name of Jesus Christ for the remission of sins; and you shall receive the gift of the Holy Spirit. For the promise is to you and to your children, and to all who are afar off, as many as the Lord our God will call." (NKJV)*

Peter was ready with a road map:

**1.** *"Repent"*—Admit you're going the wrong way. Turn to God.

**2.** *"Be baptized"* **in the name of** Jesus Christ for forgiveness of your sins—Let God wash away your sins, forgiving you because of what Christ did on the cross.

**3.** *"Receive the gift of the Holy Spirit"*—To welcome Christ is to welcome the Spirit.

This is a promise for (1) you, (2) your children, and (3) **afar off** people who don't know anything about God.

what others say

### F. F. Bruce

Peter's preaching proved effective, not only persuading his hearers' minds but convicting their consciences. . . . Incredible as it must appear, Peter told them that there was hope even now. Let them repent of their sin and turn to God; let them submit to baptism in the name of Jesus, confessed as Messiah. Then not only would they receive forgiveness of sins, but they would receive also the gift of the Holy Spirit—the gift which had been bestowed on the apostles themselves only a few hours before.[14]

# "Get Out While You Can!"

**go to**

**system was out**
John 12:31–33;
Romans 7:4–6;
8:1–4;
1 John 2:15–17

**obsolete**
Hebrews 8:13

**surprises**
Acts 2:2–12, 17–20

**church**
Matthew 16:18;
18:17;
Acts 5:11; 8:1, 3;
14:23

ACTS 2:40 *And with many other words he testified and exhorted them, saying, "Be saved from this perverse generation." (NKJV)*

The "perverse generation" Peter urged his listeners to get out of was the spiritually dead, morally rotten culture of the world, including a dead religious system riddled with hypocrisy and resistance to God's will thinly masked by a facade of lifeless ritual and crotchety rule keeping. With the arrival of Jesus Christ that old <u>system was out</u> the window! Down for the last time! Kaput! <u>Obsolete</u>! A new generation is born—the generation of the Spirit. A new community, a culture responsive to Jesus as Lord, has hung up its shingle and gone into business.

## Spiritual Dynamite: Terms for the Holy Spirit's Work in Acts 1–2

| Term | Reference | Meaning |
|------|-----------|---------|
| Filled | Acts 2:4 | Under the Spirit's influence |
| Baptized | Acts 1:5 | Initiated into the Spirit's life, washed clean from sin |
| Promise/gift | Acts 1:4; 2:38 | The Spirit is a free gift based on God's promise |
| Come upon | Acts 1:8 | Occupied, taken over, energized by the Holy Spirit |
| Pour out | Acts 2:17 | God's generosity in giving the Spirit, fullness |
| Receive | Acts 2:38 | Open the door to the Holy Spirit by welcoming Jesus |

# The Miracle of the Church

ACTS 2:41 *Then those who gladly received his [Peter's] word were baptized; and that day about three thousand souls were added to them. (NKJV)*

Three thousand people responded to Peter's message and were baptized that very day to seal their deal to follow Christ and to welcome his Spirit into their lives. It was a day of <u>surprises</u>. The most delightful surprise was the emergence of the intense, spiritually lively community that immediately came together around the risen Jesus.

Like a magnet the Spirit drew the people who trusted Jesus to each other. They became part of a new association of people in the process of "being saved" (Acts 2:47 NKJV). Elsewhere this believing community is called the <u>church</u>. The original word for "church"

**go to**

**added**
Acts 2:47; 5:14;
1 Corinthians 12:13

means "called out ones"—identifying people "called out" by the Holy Spirit to live a radically new and different lifestyle.

When a person declared his or her faith in Jesus, he or she was immediately "<u>added</u> to them" (Acts 2:41 NKJV). In New Testament jargon "added" means "fitted and adjoined"[15] (Acts 2:5–11). Fitting believers together as indispensable pieces in God's puzzle is one of the most wonderful wonders the Holy Spirit does!

---

**what others say**

**Tertullian**

How much more justly are those called and considered brothers, who acknowledge the one God as their Father; who have received the one Spirit of holiness; who have awakened from the same darkness of uncertainty to the light of the same truth? . . . We, who are united in spirit and in soul, do not hesitate to have all things in common, except wives.[16]

---

## On Your Mark. Get Set. Grow!

**ACTS 2:42** *And they continued steadfastly in the apostles' doctrine and fellowship, in the breaking of bread, and in prayers.* (NKJV)

As three thousand living pieces were fitted into the early church puzzle, a unique new society developed, driven by four priorities and activities:

1. *The apostles' doctrine.* Jesus had commissioned them to tell his story and teach people to obey his principles (Matthew 28:20; Luke 24:46–48). This involved three kinds of communication:

   - *Preaching*—plain statement of the facts: Who Jesus is, and what Jesus did, including an invitation to make a decision to follow him (Acts 2:16–40)

   - *Teaching*—explanation of the meaning of the facts aimed at helping Christians grow up in their faith (Ephesians 4:13)

   - *Exhortation*—motivational communication urging believers to align their lives with Christ's teaching; counseling, correcting, advising one another (Acts 2:40; Romans 12:1)

go to

**special significance**
Luke 9:16; 22:19;
24:30, 35, 41–43;
John 21:12–13

**Lord's Supper**
Matthew 26:26–29;
Mark 14:22–25;
Luke 22:17–20

what others say

**Larry Richards**

Much of education is concerned with helping people know what their teachers know. Christian education is concerned with helping people become what their teachers are.[17]

2. *Fellowship*. The original word for "fellowship" (*koinonia*) means more than a handshake at the church door! New Testament–style fellowship means partnership, interaction, helping one another, sharing, sympathy, mutual communication. The first faith-based community got the crazy-loving notion that fellowship meant giving their own stuff away to meet the needs of others! (Acts 2:44–45).

3. *Breaking of bread*. Jesus gave eating together <u>special significance</u>. Sharing meals was a regular part of early Christian meetings (Acts 2:42) and day-to-day fellowship (2:46). **Potluck** meals called "love feasts" (Jude 12) served three purposes:

**potluck**
people bring food
and share it
together

**Lord's Supper**
Holy Communion,
Eucharist

- The hungry got a square meal.

- Sharing with each other strengthened fellowship.

- The **Lord's Supper** was celebrated, remembering Jesus and his death (1 Corinthians 11:23–26).

There is something about eating together that makes people more open to each other. A shared meal is a context where conversation happens naturally, needs become known, and friends discover how they can serve each other.

what others say

**Sherwood Wirt**

I have learned there is no point in talking about strong churches and weak churches, big churches and little churches, warm churches and cold churches. Such categories are unrealistic and beside the point. There is only a loving church or an unloving church.[18]

**go to**

**destitute widows**
Acts 6:1

**voluntarily**
Acts 5:4

**law of love**
Luke 6:27;
John 13:34–35;
Romans 13:8–10;
1 John 3:16–18

4. *Prayers.* Fourteen of the first fifteen chapters of Acts and many later chapters tell how they prayed . . . "together" (Acts 4:24–31) . . . "alone" (Acts 10:9) . . . "continuously" (1 Thessalonians 5:17; Romans 8:26–27).

what others say

### Tertullian

We come together for a meeting in order to besiege God with prayers, like an army in battle formation. Such violence is pleasing to God.[19]

## The Jerusalem Philharmonic

ACTS 2:43–46 *Then fear came upon every soul, and many wonders and signs were done through the apostles. Now all who believed were together, and had all things in common, and sold their possessions and goods, and divided them among all, as anyone had need. So continuing daily with one accord in the temple, and breaking bread from house to house, they ate their food with gladness and simplicity of heart, (NKJV)*

It was hard to sleep in that church! Disturbing things kept happening. Apostles touched sick people, and they got well. Miraculous changes took place in people's attitudes toward others and material things. Love developed between people who shouldn't have been able to be in the same room without fighting. Sometimes the only response that made sense was worship.

They were "together"—really together. Jerusalem had many beggars and poor people. Jobs were scarce. Foreign travelers heard Peter's message, believed on Jesus, and stayed to learn more. Travel funds became depleted. Destitute widows joined the church. People spent enough time together to discover where the needs were. What's a Christian to do when a brother or sister in Christ is hungry or homeless? The original Jesus people responded by voluntarily sharing everything (2:44; 4:32). No law demanded it but the law of love. Private ownership was not discouraged nor ended. But surplus property was sold to get money to help the needy.

go to

made it grow
1 Corinthians 3:6–8

The original Christians did not invent this way of living together. They simply followed Jesus's instructions, recorded in the four "Life of Christ" books—Matthew, Mark, Luke, and John. When his energy came to them through the Holy Spirit, they had no other strategy in mind but the one Jesus had given them. In the following chart, compare Acts 2:42–47 with Jesus's instructions to discover the source of the original Christians' ideas about how to do church.

### Jesus's Strategy for the Church

| The Early Church in Action | The Strategy Laid Out by Jesus |
| --- | --- |
| Acts 2:42—The priority of teaching | Matthew 28:20; Luke 6:40 |
| Acts 2:42—The importance of prayer | Matthew 6:5–15; Luke 11:9–13; 18:1 |
| Acts 2:43—Evidence/signs of spiritual reality | Matthew 10:8; John 13:34–35; 15:5 |
| Acts 2:43, 46–47—Awe at God's work | Luke 4:36–37; 8:25; John 7:31, 45–46 |
| Acts 2:44–45—Together, things in common | Luke 12:15, 22–34 |
| Acts 2:42, 46—Shared meals, communion | Luke 10:7; 22:19; John 6:5–14 |
| Acts 2:47—Adding to the fellowship | Luke 9:47–50; John 10:16; Matthew 28:19 |

## Divine Arithmetic

ACTS 2:47 *praising God and having favor with all the people. And the Lord added to the church daily those who were being saved.* (NKJV)

Every day they were together somewhere, meeting, sharing, eating, celebrating, praising. Nothing was "put on" or just for show. Acts 2:46 says they did what they did with "gladness and simplicity of heart" (NKJV). Nonbelievers watched and saw what was happening as real and good. And God made it grow!

When the church is marked by eagerness for Christ's teaching, supportive relationships, wonder at God's working, sharing, prayer, liberality, genuineness, and joy, God adds people to their number.

## Chapter Wrap-Up

- The Jewish Feast of Pentecost was the setting for the initial outpouring of the Holy Spirit. The coming of the Spirit signaled the end of the Old Covenant and beginning of the New Covenant. (Hebrews 8:13)

- The Holy Spirit came with wind and fire. The disciples praised God in new languages. A crowd gathered, amazed at hearing Galileans speak their homeland (foreign) languages. The apostles told the people about the Holy Spirit. (Acts 2:2–16)

- Peter explained that these happenings fulfilled prophecy. He showed from the facts, Scripture, and eyewitness accounts that God had raised Jesus from the dead and that his resurrection proved he was Lord and Messiah. (Acts 2:16–36)

- Some were convinced. Peter explained that if they would turn to God and declare faith in Jesus, the gift of the Holy Spirit would be given to them. (Acts 2:37–40)

- Three thousand people responded and were added to their band. The new body concentrated on four activities to bring converts to spiritual maturity—teaching, fellowship, shared meals, and prayer. (Acts 2:41–42)

- Wonderful things happened. All they owned was available to meet each other's needs. They welcomed one another into their homes. Their sincerity impressed everyone who watched. Their numbers grew. (Acts 2:43–47)

## Study Questions

1. What did the disciples hear, see, and experience when the Holy Spirit was first given?

2. According to Acts 2:4–13, what is the gift of tongues? What purpose did it fulfill? What was communicated? Identify three reactions of the crowd? Where in the New Testament can more information be found on the gift of tongues?

3. According to Peter, what does the Resurrection prove about Jesus?

4. What did Peter say a person must do to receive the gift of the Holy Spirit?

5. To what four activities did the early believers devote themselves?

6. How far did the early Christians go in expressing their oneness and love for each other (Acts 2:44–45)? If they lacked something to give, what did some of them do?

7. Who did Luke say was responsible for the growth in numbers?

# Acts 3-4 Fresh Enthusiasm for the Ancient Faith

**Chapter Highlights:**
- Better Than Money
- Jesus Is Back in Town!
- Sit Down! You're Rocking the Boat!
- Taking Trouble Home

## Let's Get Started

Jews did not stop being Jewish when they believed in Jesus and joined his band. They pursued the ancient faith with fresh enthusiasm because they understood its significance more clearly. They saw Jesus as the fulfillment of the Law of Moses.

For the committed Jew there were three special times of prayer each day—the **third hour** (about 9 a.m.), the sixth hour (noon), and the ninth hour (about 3 p.m.). Most important were the times of the <u>morning and evening</u> sacrifices. Something happened at the evening sacrifice that caused the fire of the new Jesus movement to leap the fireline and spread into the camp of its enemies.

Luke, the author of Acts, does not say God created this breakout of Spirit fire, but it is not hard for believing eyes to see a divine hand arranging its escape from the comfortable parameters of the believers' community.

**go to**

**morning and evening**
Exodus 29:39–42

**third hour**
days were divided into twelve hours based on the position of the sun

## A Gift Better Than Money

> **the big picture**
>
> **Acts 3:1-10**
>
> One day Peter and John went to the Temple. A man who was born with a handicap was begging there. He asked for money from Peter and John. They said they didn't have money to give him, but would give him something better. In the name of Jesus they healed him. The healed man walked and jumped and praised God so much that he attracted lots of attention.

Giving to the poor while entering the Temple was considered especially pleasing to God. So beggars clustered at the temple gates. This beggar chose to lie beside the "gate . . . called Beautiful," an exquisitely crafted bronze gate between the Court of the Gentiles and the Court of Women (see Illustration #3).

**leaping**
Isaiah 35:6;
Luke 1:44

**disease or disability**
Mark 10:46–52;
Luke 16:19–21

"Silver and gold I do not have," Peter said. He and John looked the lame man in the eye. "But what I do have I give you: In the name of Jesus Christ of Nazareth, rise up and walk" (Acts 3:6 NKJV). Peter grabbed the man's hand and pulled him up. The man had never stood on his own two feet before. But now he found his legs and feet supporting his weight. He jumped to his feet. Took his first step at age forty (Acts 4:22)! He was walking! He took a couple of practice leaps and then followed Peter and John through the Beautiful Gate into the Temple, walking and <u>leaping</u> and yelling praise to God! (Wouldn't you?)

**Illustration #3**
Temple Diagram—
This diagram shows
the Court of the
Gentiles where non-
Jews could pray.
The Court of the
Women was in a
more interior place
where both men and
women could wor-
ship. Women were
not allowed farther
into the Temple,
except to sacrifice.

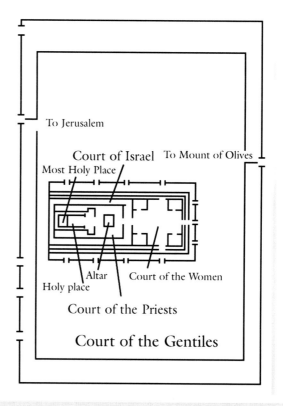

To Jerusalem

Court of Israel   To Mount of Olives

Most Holy Place

Altar   Court of the Women

Holy place

Court of the Priests

Court of the Gentiles

## what others say

**The Revell Bible Dictionary**

In Middle Eastern lands begging has long been recognized as a profession. Yet the Bible has surprisingly few references to beggars. Typical beggars were crippled by some obvious <u>disease or disability</u>. . . . The beggar healed by Peter was lame from birth (Acts 3:1–10). In view of the Old Testament's often-expressed concern for the poor and oppressed, giving money

42 ———— **The Smart Guide to the Bible**

to beggars was considered an important act of piety by the Jews of Jesus' time. But Christ and his disciples went to the root of the problem. They healed the beggars who appealed to them, combating diseases which kept them from earning their own living.[1]

### Richard C. Halverson

"What I have I give you," Peter said. You cannot give what you do not have, but you must have to give. The impotence of many Christians in this exciting, thrilling hour of history is due to the fact that they simply have nothing to offer but a few coins, and alms will not save a sick society. Healing, reconciliation, salvation can be shared only when we have it. We can give only what we have, and some of us are not giving because we do not have.[2]

**go to**

nine times
Acts 3:6, 16; 4:7, 10, 12, 17, 18, 30

authority
John 14:12–14, 26; 15:16; 16:23–24

**power of attorney**
legal authority to act in behalf of another

Jesus does his work through his people as they go about their ordinary daily routines if they simply share what they have with people they are with.

## "In Jesus's Name"—What Does This Mean?

"In the name of Jesus Christ of Nazareth, rise up and walk," Peter said (Acts 3:6 NKJV). <u>Nine times</u> in eight verses in Acts 3–4 the word "name" or the phrase "in the name of" is used to refer to the authority by which a thing is done. To act in Jesus's name is to act with a kind of **power of attorney** granted by him. He gave his followers <u>authority</u> to act in his name—to represent him, speak and pray consistent with his person, character, purposes, and instructions.

key point

## <u>Jesus Is Back in Town!</u>

ACTS 3:11–13a *Now as the lame man who was healed held on to Peter and John, all the people ran together to them in the porch which is called Solomon's, greatly amazed. So when Peter saw it, he responded to the people: "Men of Israel, why do you marvel at this? Or why look so intently at us, as though by our own power or godliness we had made this man walk? The God of Abraham, Isaac, and Jacob, the God of our fathers, glorified His Servant Jesus,* (NKJV)

It was as though Jesus had returned and was at his old game again! Even his enemies were forced to admit that what Peter and John did and said had a hauntingly familiar ring—"These men have been with Jesus!" they bellyached (see Acts 4:13).

"Don't look at us!" Peter began, as the crowd rushed to see the healed cripple at the corner of the Temple where Solomon's Colonnade and the Royal Colonnade met. The crowd authenticated the miracle, recognizing the former lame man (Acts 3:10). "It isn't our power or godliness that makes this man able to walk," Peter said. "The <u>God of Abraham</u>, Isaac, and Jacob, the God of our fathers, glorified His Servant Jesus" (Acts 3:13 NKJV).

## The Master Key to Power

*ACTS 3:13b–16 whom you delivered up and denied in the presence of Pilate, when he was determined to let Him go. But you denied the Holy One and the Just, and asked for a murderer to be granted to you, and killed the Prince of life, whom God raised from the dead, of which we are witnesses. And His name, through faith in His name, has made this man strong, whom you see and know. Yes, the faith which comes through Him has given him this perfect soundness in the presence of you all. (NKJV)*

Peter continued, "You remember Jesus." (I'm paraphrasing.) "He's the one you insisted Pilate execute even though he found him <u>not guilty</u> and wanted to let him go. Jesus is the good guy—"the <u>author of life</u>"—who went around <u>giving people life</u> . . . the one you rejected and killed, voting instead for Barabbas, the <u>hit man</u>.

"I've got news for you. God overturned your verdict! He raised Jesus from the dead. We've seen him! This healing was by faith in Jesus's name."

Surprise! Surprise! Surprise! The secret is out: Acts is the story of what Jesus continues to do since his resurrection (Acts 1:1). Jesus in Acts has the same purposes, mission, and **modus operandi** as Jesus in the Gospels. The difference? He's no longer limited to a single human body, one location at a time, one voice, one set of actions. Since ascending and sending his Spirit, Jesus <u>heads</u> a <u>corporate body</u> composed of all who receive him.

**go to**

**God of Abraham**
Exodus 3:6

**not guilty**
John 18:38

**author of life**
John 5:26; 11:25;
14:6

**giving people life**
John 10:10; 11:25

**hit man**
Luke 23:25;
John 18:40

**heads**
Ephesians 1:22;
4:15;
Colossians 1:18;
2:19

**corporate body**
Romans 12:4–5;
1 Corinthians
12:12–27;
Ephesians 4:4–16

**modus operandi**
method of operation

### F. F. Bruce

There is no merely magical **efficacy** in the words which Peter pronounced when, in Jesus' name, he commanded the cripple to walk; the cripple would have known no benefit had he not responded in faith to what Peter said. But once this response of faith was made, the power of the risen Christ filled his body with health and strength.[3]

## A Call to Turn Toward God

### Acts 3:17-26

After acknowledging that Israel and its leaders had acted in ignorance in their rejection of Jesus, Peter showed how Jesus fulfilled what the prophets wrote about Messiah. He called for people to turn toward God, stop sinning, and listen to Jesus. If they'd do this, certain spiritual benefits are promised.

As the crowd rushed to check out the beggar's miracle, Peter got on his soapbox. He preached the indispensable fundamentals of the Christian faith: Who Jesus is. What Jesus did (Acts 3:13–16). It's the same format as his Pentecost Day sermon (Acts 2:14–40). Because the audience was Jewish, Peter quoted from the Old Testament to show how Jesus fulfilled what the prophets wrote about Messiah (Acts 3:18–25). He called for people to turn toward God, change their lives, quit their wicked ways, and listen to Jesus. If they'd do this, Peter promised these things:

- Their sins would be blotted out (Acts 3:19; see Isaiah 44:22; Colossians 2:13–14).

- Spiritual renewal would come to them (Acts 3:19; see John 7:37–39; Matthew 11:28–30).

- Christ himself would come to them (Acts 3:20; see Acts 2:38; John 14:18–21).

- Everything broken in them would be restored (Acts 3:21; see Joel 2:12–27).

- They'd get the blessings promised to Abraham's offspring (Acts 3:25–26; see Genesis 22:18; 26:4).

But . . . if they refused, there literally would be hell to pay! (Acts

3:23). The early church had no message but Jesus crucified, risen from the dead, and offering a fresh start to people who trust him.

## Sit Down! You're Rocking the Boat!

ACTS 4:1–3 *Now as they spoke to the people, the priests, the captain of the temple, and the Sadducees came upon them, being greatly disturbed that they taught the people and preached in Jesus the resurrection from the dead. And they laid hands on them, and put them in custody until the next day, for it was already evening. (NKJV)*

The official attack against the church started here in Acts 4. Religious leaders who'd tried to terminate Jesus now arrested the first of his followers. Peter and John were hauled off to jail in mid-sermon by the captain of the **temple guard**, acting on orders from the **priests** and **Sadducees**, who controlled temple affairs. The Sadducees did not believe in life after death, the possibility of resurrection, or in the existence of angels or spirits.

## Why Did Peter's Preaching Give the Chiefs the Jitters?

Acts 4:2 gives two "official" reasons Peter and John were booked:

1. *They were teaching the people.* And Peter and John lacked the proper credentials.

2. *They were proclaiming the resurrection of Jesus from the dead.* This was a specific no-no to the Sadducean temple leadership who didn't believe in resurrection.

Peter and John were put in jail under the pretext of protecting **orthodoxy**. Unofficially, temple leaders took a dim view of the apostles' repeated allegations that they were guilty of the Messiah's crucifixion and hoped to shut them up (Acts 2:23; 3:13).

Arrest of Christians by religious authorities for unapproved teaching is a practice that is still alive and well! In a raid on a church in Turkey in 1999, police arrested twenty-five adults and charged them with "terrorism" for "criticizing Islam" and "forcing" people to take Bibles. According to the personal account of one of those involved, after thirty-six hours in jail, repeated interrogations, and negative newspaper publicity, a Muslim judge threw their case out of court. The incident has sparked renewal among Turkish Christians.

**Hall of Hewn Stone**
official meeting place of the Sanhedrin

**Sanhedrin**
Jewish supreme court and high council

## While the Old Guard Fussed, the Church Grew

ACTS 4:4 *However, many of those who heard the word believed; and the number of the men came to be about five thousand.* (NKJV)

As dungeon doors clanged shut, many believed the apostles' message. The Jerusalem fellowship hit a new statistical high—five thousand men (Acts 4:4). Add women and children, and the total number was probably ten thousand or more!

The church grows by ministering to people's real needs and daring in the face of opposition to tell the truth about sin, Jesus, faith, and salvation.

what others say

**Walter Wangerin**

The council and the leaders in Jerusalem . . . were as threatened by the disciples as they had been by Jesus because the assembly growing around them was large and well-knit and committed to this Jesus as to one alive and mighty. It was an assembly distinct from the Synagogue—an Ecclesia, a Church.[4]

## Official Inquest at the Hall of Hewn Stone

ACTS 4:5–7 *And it came to pass, on the next day, that their rulers, elders, and scribes, as well as Annas the high priest, Caiaphas, John, and Alexander, and as many as were of the family of the high priest, were gathered together at Jerusalem. And when they had set them in the midst, they asked, "By what power or by what name have you done this?"* (NKJV)

According to Jewish Law no trial could be held at night, so the next day in the **Hall of Hewn Stone**, the **Sanhedrin** met to consider the case of the unparalyzed unpanhandler. Everybody who was anybody was there:[5]

*Rulers*—Temple priests and officials whose goal was preservation of the status quo.

*Elders*—Community leaders; heads of aristocratic families.

*Scribes*—Experts in Jewish Law, fanatical adherents of religious rules.

**Spirit would teach**
Luke 12:11–12;
21:14–15

**done that**
Luke 22:54–62

deposed
removed from office

full
energized, under
the influence

*Annas, high priest*—**Deposed** by Romans, Jews considered him the rightful high priest.

*Caiaphas*—Annas's son-in-law, official high priest from AD 18 to AD 36.

*John*—Also called Jonathan. Annas's son, replaced Caiaphas as high priest in AD 36.

*Alexander*—Just another pretty face, nothing is known about him.

## Disorder in the Court

ACTS 4:8–12 *Then Peter, filled with the Holy Spirit, said to them, "Rulers of the people and elders of Israel: If we this day are judged for a good deed done to a helpless man, by what means he has been made well, let it be known to you all, and to all the people of Israel, that by the name of Jesus Christ of Nazareth, whom you crucified, whom God raised from the dead, by Him this man stands here before you whole. This is the 'stone which was rejected by you builders, which has become the chief cornerstone.' Nor is there salvation in any other, for there is no other name under heaven given among men by which we must be saved." (NKJV)*

Peter was **full** of the Spirit (Acts 4:8) and champing at the bit. This was precisely the kind of situation Jesus told his disciples they would face. He'd said not to worry because the Holy Spirit would teach them what to say. "By what power or by what name have you done this?" (Acts 4:7 NKJV) the inquisitors asked.

Peter and John stood before the very court that condemned Jesus. They knew the potential consequences of confronting these hostile men with the claims of Christ. But to tell them anything but the truth would be an act of cowardice and denial. (Peter had been there, done that! But no more!)

> **what others say**
>
> **Watchman Nee**
>
> The name of Jesus . . . represents the power and dominion before which every knee in heaven and earth must bow. . . . Today the name tells us that God has committed all authority to his Son, so that in the very name itself there is power. But further, not only is it his, but it is "given to men." He has placed that authority in our hands for us to use.[6]

The members of the high court found themselves being accused by the men they'd met to accuse (Acts 4:10–11). But Peter didn't just accuse. His charges were part of an ardent appeal in which he became a compassionate first-century Billy Graham offering <u>salvation</u> to Israel's powerful if they would put their **faith** in the name (person, character, and work) of Jesus. No "decisions for Christ" are recorded. Acts 6:7 indicates there may have been some.

Christ is "the cornerstone" (Acts 4:11 NKJV), capstone, or keystone. He holds God's salvation plan together.

## Who Killed Christ Jesus?

| Responsible Party | Scripture Passages |
|---|---|
| Sanhedrin/priests and elders (Jews) | Acts 4:5–11; 5:27–30; 7:52; Matthew 27:1, 20–23; John 19:6–7 |
| Roman governor Pilate (a Gentile) | Acts 4:27–28; Matthew 27:24–26; John 19:16–18 |
| Herod (a Gentile) | Acts 4:27–28; Luke 23:6–11 |
| Men of Israel (Jews) | Acts 2:22–23, 36: 4:27 |
| Godless men/Romans (Gentiles) | Acts 2:23; 4:27–28; Matthew 27:27–36 |
| People of Jerusalem (Jews) | Acts 3:13–15; 4:27–28 |
| Judas, the betrayer (a Jew) | Acts 1:16; Matthew 27:3–4 |
| God, to rescue us | Acts 2:23; Romans 3:25–26; 2 Corinthians 5:18–21; Isaiah 53:10 |
| People who reject Christ (Jew/Gentile) | Hebrews 6:6; Isaiah 53:3 |
| Human sin (Jew and Gentile) | 1 Peter 2:24–25; Isaiah 53:4–6 |
| Jesus, to be the sacrifice for our sin | John 10:14–18; Philippians 2:5–8; Hebrews 9:14; 10:5–14 |

go to

**salvation**
Matthew 9:22;
John 3:16;
Romans 5:9;
Ephesians 2:5;
Hebrews 5:7; 7:25

**salvation**
rescue and forgiveness from sin's eternal consequences

**faith**
to respond with love, trust, and obedience

> ### what others say
>
> ### John R. W. Stott
>
> We ourselves are also guilty. If we were in their place, we would have done what they did. Indeed, we have done it. . . . We too sacrifice Jesus to our greed like Judas, to our envy like the priests, to our ambition like Pilate. . . . We may try to wash our hands of responsibility like Pilate. But our attempt will be as futile as his. For there is blood on our hands. Before we can begin to see the cross as something done for us (leading us to faith and worship), we have to see it as something done by us (leading us to repentance).[7]

Peter said, "Nor is there salvation in any other, for there is no other name under heaven given among men by which we must be saved" (Acts 4:12 NKJV). On a scale of 1 to 10, how sure are you that Peter's statement is true (1 = not at all sure; 10 = absolutely sure)?

Who killed Jesus—the Jews? the Romans? Satan? Check the passages in the chart on the previous page to see where the Bible puts the responsibility.

Jesus never allows his people to get into a situation for which he has not made adequate provision through his indwelling Spirit for power to meet the challenge and words to say.

## Poor, Uneducated Fishermen

> ACTS 4:13–14 *Now when they saw the boldness of Peter and John, and perceived that they were uneducated and untrained men, they marveled. And they realized that they had been with Jesus. And seeing the man who had been healed standing with them, they could say nothing against it. (NKJV)*

In spite of their animosity toward the apostles, the council members found themselves admiring their courage. Jerusalem's intellectual elite had not expected such grit and eloquence from uneducated fishermen (Acts 4:13). What was it about Peter and John that showed they'd been "with [schooled by] Jesus"? Perhaps it was the Jesus-like way they rocked the establishment's boat, healed the lame, told the truth, confronted sin, and took command. Whatever it was, it was like Rabbi Jesus was back in town!

## The Smart Guys Paint Themselves into a Corner

> ACTS 4:15–22 *But when they had commanded them to go aside out of the council, they conferred among themselves, saying, "What shall we do to these men? For, indeed, that a notable miracle has been done through them is evident to all who dwell in Jerusalem, and we cannot deny it. But so that it spreads no further among the people, let us severely threaten them, that from now on they speak to no man in this name." So they called them and commanded them not to speak at all nor teach in the name of Jesus. But Peter and John answered and said to them, "Whether it is right in the sight of God to listen to you more than to God, you judge. For we cannot but speak the things which we have seen and heard." So when they had further threatened them, they let them go, finding no way of punishing them,*

*because of the people, since they all glorified God for what had been done. For the man was over forty years old on whom this miracle of healing had been performed. (NKJV)*

**uneducated**
not trained by a recognized rabbi

The hands of the power brokers were tied. They couldn't discredit the evidence standing in front of them in the person of the healed beggar (Acts 4:14, 22). Their law said **"uneducated"** people could not be punished without at least one warning. They were in the precarious position of opposing what the majority of people were applauding (Acts 4:16).

what others say

**C. J. Klausner**

This was the first mistake which the Jewish leaders made with regard to the new sect. And this mistake was fatal. There was probably no need to arrest the Nazarenes, thus calling attention to them and making them "martyrs." But once arrested, they should not have been freed so quickly. The arrest and release increased the number of believers; for these events showed on the one hand that the new sect was a power which the authorities feared enough to persecute, and on the other hand they proved that there was no danger in being a disciple of Jesus.[8]

All they could do was order Peter and John never to speak Jesus's name in public again, threaten them with bodily harm if they did, and let them go (Acts 4:18, 21). But telling gung ho Christians to stop talking about Jesus is like telling the Mississippi River to go back to Minnesota! Peter and John had an irresistible urge to talk to everyone about Jesus. It turned out to be a bad day for Annas and his cronies.

## Taking Trouble Home

ACTS 4:23 *And being let go, they went to their own companions and reported all that the chief priests and elders had said to them. (NKJV)*

Where do you go when you've spent the night in jail and seventy of the nation's powerful have shaken their fists in your face, warning of dire consequences if you dare mention Jesus's name again? Peter and John knew. They returned to the refuge of "their own companions"—the caring community of Jesus's friends, the church.

**laying out**
Isaiah 37:16–20

**working out**
Romans 8:28

Chances are the brothers and sisters were together nearby, awaiting the outcome of "round one" with the city fathers. The church is not just a place to hear sermons; it's a place to share life's tough realities with supporting friends.

## Take It to the Lord in Prayer

ACTS 4:24–30 *So when they heard that, they raised their voice to God with one accord and said: "Lord, You are God, who made heaven and earth and the sea, and all that is in them, who by the mouth of Your servant David have said:*
*'Why did the nations rage,*
*And the people plot vain things?*
*The kings of the earth took their stand,*
*And the rulers were gathered together*
*Against the dd LORD and against His Christ.'*
*"For truly against Your holy Servant Jesus, whom You anointed, both Herod and Pontius Pilate, with the Gentiles and the people of Israel, were gathered together to do whatever Your hand and Your purpose determined before to be done. Now, Lord, look on their threats, and grant to Your servants that with all boldness they may speak Your word, by stretching out Your hand to heal, and that signs and wonders may be done through the name of Your holy Servant Jesus." (NKJV)*

After debriefing Peter and John, the Jesus people of Jerusalem prayed, <u>laying out</u> their situation before the Lord. First, they found Bible verses in Psalm 2:1–2 telling them opposition is normal for people identified with Christ ("God's Anointed") in a hostile world. In *The Message*, Eugene Peterson puts the Psalms passage this way: "Why the big noise, nations? Why the mean plots, peoples? Earth-leaders push for position, demagogues and delegates meet for summit talks, the God-deniers, the Messiah-defiers."[9]

Second, they confessed confidence God was in control, <u>working out</u> his plan.

Third, they didn't ask for an easier way or destruction of their enemies. They prayed for boldness to speak God's message. They asked for miracles to back up their testimony.

**William Barclay**

They had the conviction of the futility of man's rebellion. The word translated rage is used of the neighing of spirited horses. They may trample and toss their heads; in the end they will have to accept the discipline of the reins. Men may make their defiant gestures against God; in the end God must prevail.[10]

**Maude De Joseph West**

Herod . . . Pontius Pilate . . . the wily high priest and the people turned by his manipulation into a maniacal mob. . . . All these, living their own lives, scheming their own schemes, cruel, wicked, cunning, or weak, completely unaware of God Almighty, were nonetheless working out his perfect and inexorable will![11]

# Spiritual Booster Shot

ACTS 4:31 *And when they had prayed, the place where they were assembled together was shaken; and they were all filled with the Holy Spirit, and they spoke the word of God with boldness.* (NKJV)

Their prayer for signs and wonders (Acts 4:30) was answered in the surprising quality of spiritual and community life they experienced together.

First, the place was shaken and the Holy Spirit renewed his influence (filling). The first believers had been "filled with the Holy Spirit" at Pentecost (Acts 2:4 NKJV). Since then, whenever anyone puts his or her faith in Jesus, they "receive the gift of the Holy Spirit" (Acts 2:38 NKJV). This renewed "filling" was a "booster shot"—a fresh infusion of spiritual vitality to answer their prayer for courage.

Joseph, a Levite from Cyprus, whom the apostles called Barnabas (which means Son of Encouragement), sold a field he owned and brought the money and put it at the apostles' feet.

go to

**cheerfully**
2 Corinthians 9:7

# Normal Christianity

ACTS 4:32–37 *Now the multitude of those who believed were of one heart and one soul; neither did anyone say that any of the things he possessed was his own, but they had all things in common. And with great power the apostles gave witness to the resurrection of the Lord Jesus. And great grace was upon them all. Nor was there anyone among them who lacked; for all who were possessors of lands or houses sold them, and brought the proceeds of the things that were sold, and laid them at the apostles' feet; and they distributed to each as anyone had need. And Joses, who was also named Barnabas by the apostles (which is translated Son of Encouragement), a Levite of the country of Cyprus, having land, sold it, and brought the money and laid it at the apostles' feet. (NKJV)*

Spiritually energized, need and love combined for a unique adventure in fellowship: "They had all things in common." When somebody was needy, the group didn't shrug and say, "Tsk. Tsk. Too bad. We'll pray for you." They sacrificed to meet the needs. If you had money, the normal response was to <u>cheerfully</u> dig in and shell out. Surplus possessions were sold at the local swap meet to raise funds. When need could not be filled so simply, a "For Sale" sign was slapped on the forty acres near Bethany or the summer cabin on Lake Galilee.

Sharing was voluntary. Private ownership was not ended. People had possessions and owned homes (Acts 2:46; 4:32). The difference was, possessions were treated as community property. No one was without "family"—poor, hungry, lonely, crippled, blind, retarded, homeless—all found a home in the believers' fellowship. The first Christians took material as well as spiritual responsibility for each other.

The miracle is summed up in a single amazing line: "Nor was there anyone among them who lacked" (Acts 4:34 NKJV).

Wherever you went you found "grace"—mercy, kindness, acceptance, honesty, forgiveness, generosity (Acts 4:33). The way Jesus's followers lived together was powerful proof he was alive. This visible evidence added impact to the Christians' claim that Jesus had risen and was living in them.

### Ronald J. Sider

The costly sharing of the first church stands as a constant challenge to Christians of all ages. They dared to give concrete, visible expression to the oneness of believers.[12]

### Jim Wallis

The Spirit had shattered the normal assumptions of the economic order, and the early believers realized that the way of Christ militated against the private use and disposition of resources and led to the sharing of all resources as needs arose in the community. Material resources, no less than spiritual gifts, were to be shared and freely given for the good of the body and not for the personal gain and advantage of the one who possessed them. A whole new system of distribution had been created in God's new community with each person in a process of giving and receiving according to ability and need.[13]

### Billy Graham

It can be so easy at times to say we love people, and be completely honest and sincere in our expression. But so often we don't see the lonely person in the crowd, or the sick or destitute man or woman whose only hope of escape may be the love we can give through Christ.[14]

Was this amazing community of generosity and grace a fluke, a once-in-history happening never to be repeated? Or is it part of the promise of the gospel? The answer lies in the fact that the Jerusalem church lifestyle emerged in direct response to the teachings of Jesus—and those teachings are still to guide the lives and values of Christians today!

something to ponder

# Chapter Wrap-Up

- As Peter and John went to the Temple for prayer, they met a lame beggar asking for a handout. Peter grabbed the man's hand and pulled him to his feet. He was instantly healed and went into the Temple leaping and praising God. (Acts 3:1–10)

- A crowd gathered. Peter told them the man had been healed by faith in the name of Jesus. He urged them to listen to Jesus and quit their wickedness. (Acts 3:11–26)

- Upset because unlicensed apostles were teaching, temple officials arrested Peter and John. They were brought before the rulers to defend themselves. Peter told the rulers Jesus was their only hope of salvation. (Acts 4:1–22)

- The apostles were warned never to speak in Jesus's name and were released. They told the church. The church prayed for boldness to continue speaking and for God to provide miraculous proofs that Jesus was alive. (Acts 4:23–30)

- The Lord answered by shaking the church and renewing the Spirit's influence in their lives. Jesus's followers clung more closely to each other and shared so generously to meet each other's needs that there were no needy people among them! (Acts 4:31–37)

# Study Questions

1. What did the man at the Beautiful Gate ask for? What did Peter and John give him? Where did Peter say the power to do this miracle came from?

2. What does it mean to do something "in Jesus's name"?

3. What two reasons were given for the arrest of Peter and John? Why were the Sadducees upset about the apostles' telling that Jesus had risen from the dead?

4. How did Peter and John respond when they were ordered never again to speak or teach in the name of Jesus?

5. In what tangible ways did the Jerusalem Christians demonstrate their love for and solidarity with one another?

# Acts 5 The Perfect Church—Not!

**Chapter Highlights:**
- **The Ananias and Sapphira Affair**
- **The Purity-Power Connection**
- **Voice of Reason**

## Let's Get Started

Once he has his readers drooling over the delicious quality of together-life experienced by the first fellowship of Jesus's disciples, the author of Acts brings us back to reality with a dull thud. Nasty termites were chawing away at what on the surface looked like the ideal support group, the beginnings of a veritable "heaven on earth." Through the shockeroo reported in Acts 5 we discover there is a vital connection between honesty, discipline, accountability, pure motives, and spiritual power.

**go to**

**Son of Encouragement**
Acts 9:26–27;
11:22–24; 15:36–39

**Son of**
Hebrew prefix "Bar,"
indicates person's
character

**what others say**

**Charles Colson**

Fellowship is more than unconditional love that wraps its arms around someone who is hurting. . . . Too often we confuse love with permissiveness. . . . True fellowship out of love for one another demands accountability.[1]

## The Ananias and Sapphira Affair

ACTS 5:1–2 *But a certain man named Ananias, with Sapphira his wife, sold a possession. And he kept back part of the proceeds, his wife also being aware of it, and brought a certain part and laid it at the apostles' feet. (NKJV)*

Ironically, the loving act of a guy named Joe set the stage for one of the most shocking moments in early church life. Joe was a transplant from Cyprus. The Christians had nicknamed him "Barnabas" or "**Son of** Encouragement." The last sentence in Acts 4 tells the innocent part he played in the sordid Ananias and Sapphira affair: "Joses, . . . having land, sold it, and brought the money and laid it at the apostles' feet" (Acts 4:36–37 NKJV).

True to his reputation as encourager, Joe Barney sold land and contributed the proceeds for the needy. Others sold land and gave the proceeds too (see Acts 2:45; 4:34–35), but for some reason Joe Barney's gift was recorded. The gift was unusual not only because it

**not to own property**
Numbers 18:20;
Deuteronomy
10:8–9; 18:1–2

**sensed**
John 16:13

**basic satanic strategy**
John 8:44

was generous but also because he was a **Levite** and according to Mosaic law Levites were <u>not to own property</u> in the Promised Land. The land sale may not have been an act of loving generosity so much as an act of repentance for owning land contrary to the law. Joe Barney may simply have been relieving his conscience. Whatever the motive, it played a role in the tragic story that follows.

A Christian man, Ananias, and his beautiful wife, **Sapphira**, also sold some land. From the proceeds they made a generous, voluntary contribution. But there was a problem: They gave part of the money but gave the impression they were giving all. When Ananias came bearing his gift, Peter immediately <u>sensed</u> something was wrong, and instead of the oohs and ahs of approval that Ananias expected, Peter blew the lid off the deception.

Wrong motivation can spoil giving. Sometimes leaders, eager to fund "the Lord's work," appeal to exactly the kind of motives that got Ananias and Sapphira in trouble! Jesus had nothing good to say about such giving (see Matthew 6:1–4).

**Levite**
Israelite clan responsible to guide religious life

**Sapphira**
means "Beautiful"

**what others say**

**William Barclay**

This is one of the stories which demonstrate the almost stubborn honesty of the Bible. It might well have been left out because it shows that even in the early church there were very imperfect Christians.[2]

## The Label on the Pretender's Package

ACTS 5:3–4 *But Peter said, "Ananias, why has Satan filled your heart to lie to the Holy Spirit and keep back part of the price of the land for yourself? While it remained, was it not your own? And after it was sold, was it not in your own control? Why have you conceived this thing in your heart? You have not lied to men but to God."* (NKJV)

Ugly dishonesty stood exposed for all to see. The exposé reveals five startling facts.

1. A <u>basic satanic strategy</u> for robbing the church of its power is to infect it with dishonesty, hypocrisy.

2. It is possible for a Christian in the best of churches, surrounded by

people who are full of God's Spirit (Acts 4:31), to be "filled" (influenced) by Satan (Acts 5:3).

3. Satan's influence does not take away a person's responsibility for his or her choices (compare Acts 5:3 and 4).

4. New Testament giving is not an obligation but a free choice (Acts 5:4).

5. To lie to one's fellow believers is to lie to God (Acts 5:4).

**go to**

influenced
Luke 22:3;
John 13:27

**New Testament giving**
2 Corinthians
8:1–15; 9:1–15

dear children
Proverbs 3:11–12;
Hebrews 12:5–8

discipline
1 Peter 4:17;
1 Corinthians 11:30;
1 John 5:16–17

**discipline**
painful experiences
God allows to
cleanse believers
from sinful patterns

**what others say**

**Billy Graham**

We should be careful that any goodness the world may see in us is the genuine fruit of the Spirit and not a counterfeit substitute, lest we unwittingly lead someone astray. We must be constantly aware that Satan can take any human effort and twist it to serve his own purpose.[3]

## Dropping Dead in Church

ACTS 5:5–11 *Then Ananias, hearing these words, fell down and breathed his last. So great fear came upon all those who heard these things. And the young men arose and wrapped him up, carried him out, and buried him. Now it was about three hours later when his wife came in, not knowing what had happened. And Peter answered her, "Tell me whether you sold the land for so much?" She said, "Yes, for so much." Then Peter said to her, "How is it that you have agreed together to test the Spirit of the Lord? Look, the feet of those who have buried your husband are at the door, and they will carry you out." Then immediately she fell down at his feet and breathed her last. And the young men came in and found her dead, and carrying her out, buried her by her husband. So great fear came upon all the church and upon all who heard these things. (NKJV)*

Before the curtain came down on the sad scenario, the bodies of both Ananias and his wife were stretched out side by side in their family tomb near Jerusalem. Thank God, not everyone who lies in church drops dead. There might not be enough members left to keep cobwebs from collecting on the pews and pulpit!

The appalling passings of "Mr. and Mrs. A." were acts of a loving God correcting his dear children. And the **discipline** was not just for

**whole church**
1 Corinthians 12:26

**not the worst**
Philippians 1:21–23

**serious consequences**
1 Corinthians
11:27–32

**hot buttons**
Luke 9:57–62;
John 6:53–69

**Solomon's Porch**
John 10:23;
Acts 3:11; 5:12

the cheerless givers—but the <u>whole church</u>. The whole Christian community quickly developed "a healthy respect for God."[4]

## Was God Too Hard on Ananias and Sapphira?

Many of us reading this story tend to think what this hapless couple did was not that big a deal—a petty sin. I mean, who hasn't pretended to be more "Christian" or "honest" than they really are? Doesn't this incident make God look like an impatient, unreasonable tyrant? Where's the love? Where's the grace?

In the first place, death is <u>not the worst</u> thing that can happen to a Christian. Second, the world sees when Christians mishandle money. The Jesus movement cries for believers who live morally pure, consistent with Christ's teachings, refusing to play the sickening game of spiritual "let's pretend." Though the consequences of hypocrisy are not always as instantaneous, visible, and shocking as what happened to Mr. and Mrs. A., phony baloney spirituality always carries <u>serious consequences</u>. Discipline is part of God's love and grace.

**what others say**

**Charles Colson**

We need to know the fear of the Lord—the overwhelming, compelling awe and reverence of a holy God. The fear of the Lord is the beginning of wisdom: It provides the right perspective on God's sovereign rule over all creation. . . . For the church in the West to come alive, it needs to resolve its identity crisis, to stand on truth, to renew its vision . . . and, more than anything else, it needs to recover the fear of the Lord. Only that will give us the holy abandon that will cause us to be the church no matter what the culture around us says or does.[5]

Jesus, in his life and ministry, modeled the truth-telling style practiced in the early church. He never sugarcoated the gospel. He said things that pressed people's <u>hot buttons</u>. People were forced to face the truth and decide for or against him (John 3:19–21).

## The Purity-Power Connection

ACTS 5:12 *And through the hands of the apostles many signs and wonders were done among the people. And they were all with one accord in <u>Solomon's Porch</u>. (NKJV)*

What happened next demonstrates the spiritual impact of honesty and the death of hypocrisy. As the Jerusalem **church** shuddered with healthy fear after the Ananias and Sapphira catastrophe, new **signs** of power emerged. Until persecution made it impossible, Christians held large gatherings on the raised platform, called Solomon's Porch or the Colonnade, at the east end of the Temple's outer court (see Illustration #4).

## Purity-Power Product One: "Miraculous Signs and Wonders"

The early Christians were "supernaturalists"—they believed in miracles. Based on their experiences with Jesus, they believed that when it serves God's purpose he is willing and capable of setting aside natural laws or controlling them to accomplish his aims.

Two kinds of miracles demonstrate the presence of God in his church:

1. **Obvious miracles**—when God suspends natural laws.

*Bible example*—Opening the eyes of the blind (see John 9:32).

*Modern example*—Five-year-old Bobby has an oral tumor; surgery is scheduled. The little boy prays for healing. The tumor disappears.

**fulfilled prophecies**
Matthew 1:22–23;
2:5–6, 17–18; 3:3

**invasions**
Judges 3:7–8,
12–14; 4:1–3; 6:1–6

2. **Hidden miracles**—when God shapes and uses natural events and processes to accomplish his purposes (see Romans 8:28).[6]

*Bible examples*—<u>Fulfilled prophecies</u>; enemy <u>invasions</u> God used to turn Israel back to him.

*Modern example*—Our car's air conditioning breaks down in the heat of Arizona summer; childlike, Audrey prays, "Lord, please put that cloud over the sun until we get home." He does.

> **what others say**
>
> **Larry Richards**
>
> The naturalist insists that the material universe is all there is. Whatever happens must then be the result of natural laws, and miracles simply cannot happen. Reports of God's mighty acts in Old Testament times and of Jesus' miracles are either rejected out of hand, or some energy is expended trying to figure out reasonable natural causes to explain them away.
>
> The supernaturalist believes that there is a reality beyond our material universe. The Christian, basing his or her faith on God's self-revelation in Scripture, has confidence in the God who is Creator and Sustainer of the physical universe. . . . There is no uncrossable gulf fixed between the natural and the supernatural. God has bridged the gap often, and has shown that he is completely capable of acting in the material world.[7]

## Purity-Power Product Two: Meeting "Together"

The Greek word for *together* means "of one mind, flowing along together in harmony."

There is perhaps no greater miracle that serves as a sign—visible evidence of spiritual power and the presence of God—among Christians than the miracle of "togetherness" or unity—flowing along together in harmony. No other miracle gives such pure joy (see Psalm 133)!

## A Strange Formula for Church Growth

ACTS 5:13–14 *Yet none of the rest dared join them, but the people esteemed them highly. And believers were increasingly added to the Lord, multitudes of both men and women. (NKJV)*

## Miracles in the Book of Acts

**deacon**
one of seven
assigned to care
for poor

**apologist**
defender of the faith

**evangelist**
gospel preacher

| Accounts of Miracles | Scripture |
| --- | --- |
| Performed mainly by apostles | Acts 2:43; 3:1–10; 5:12; 9:33–34, 40–41; 13:9–11; 14:8–10; 16:16–18; 19:11–12; 20:9–10; 28:2–9 |
| Performed by Stephen the **deacon** **apologist** | Acts 6:8 |
| Performed by Philip the deacon-**evangelist** | Acts 8:6 |
| Performed by Ananias, an ordinary disciple | Acts 9:10, 17 |
| Miraculous answers to prayer by groups of Christians | Acts 12:5, 12–17; 14:19–20 |
| Miraculous signs help Jews and others believe in the Messiah | compare Acts 2:4–12 with Isaiah 28:11–12; see also 1 Corinthians 1:22 |
| Highest concentration of miracles took place among Jews and Samaritans | Acts 2–12 |
| Reports of miracles among Gentiles not so frequent as among Jews | Acts 13–28 |

After Ananias and Sapphira were carried out of church feetfirst, who, in their right mind, would want to be caught there harboring secret sin? Even with more people than ever skipping church, the believers' witness, the gracious lifestyle, the fresh purity were irresistibly attractive to people sick and tired of their culture of hypocrisy, materialism, and hatred. So their numbers grew. Most must have taken their spiritual temperature, making sure their sins were all confessed before heading for church.

When the church is clean, its leaders are respected. Healthy church growth requires discipline and accountability. Free from hypocrisy, the church attracts people hungry for reality.

## The Shadow of the Fisherman

ACTS 5:15–16 *so that they brought the sick out into the streets and laid them on beds and couches, that at least the shadow of Peter passing by might fall on some of them. Also a multitude gathered from the surrounding cities to Jerusalem, bringing sick people and those who were tormented by unclean spirits, and they were all healed.* (NKJV)

**like Jesus**
Matthew 4:23–24;
8:14–17

**healing**
Acts 2:43; 3:1–10;
4:30

**angel of the Lord**
Exodus 3:2; 14:19;
Isaiah 63:9

**angel of the Lord**
supernatural mes-
senger; sometimes
indicates the Lord's
personal presence

When the church acts with integrity its leaders are respected. The people's belief that Peter's shadow could heal people may or may not have been accurate. But the fact that many believed it shows their great respect for the apostles.

Facts about early Christian healing ministry are observed in this passage (Acts 5:12–16):

- <u>Like Jesus</u>, the early church gave high priority to <u>healing</u> the sick.
- Ministry to the sick was evidence (a "sign") God's power was at work.
- Healings were done through apostles.
- Healing ministry attracted needy people.

Caring for physically, spiritually, and mentally ill people—and helping them to heal—brings healthy church growth.

## God's "Get Out of Jail Free" Card

ACTS 5:17–21a *Then the high priest rose up, and all those who were with him (which is the sect of the Sadducees), and they were filled with indignation, and laid their hands on the apostles and put them in the common prison. But at night an angel of the Lord opened the prison doors and brought them out, and said, "Go, stand in the temple and speak to the people all the words of this life." And when they heard that, they entered the temple early in the morning and taught. (NKJV)*

The twelve apostle-ambassadors were becoming highly visible and commanding great respect both in and outside the group of disciples. The jealousy of the established religious authorities boiled over. The Twelve suddenly became "Jailbirds for Jesus"!

That night "an **angel of the Lord**" freed the jailbirds. The mysterious jailbreaker led them past the guards without being seen or opening doors! He instructed them to return to the Temple and keep telling people "all the words of this life." At sunrise, that's where they were.

Often in history, civil and religious authorities have thought they could stop the Jesus movement by removing its visible leaders. During the first three centuries, the Christians most likely to be martyred were bishops and other church leaders. It's a common error among enemies of the church to mistake apostles, pastors, and other leaders for the church's Head. Their removal has never stopped the movement, because the Head is Christ (see Ephesians 1:20–23). Leaders and rank-and-file disciples are his associates.

Then someone came and said, "Look, the men whom you put in prison are standing in the temple and teaching the people!" (Acts 5:25 NKJV). At that, the captain went with his officers and brought the apostles. They did not use force, because they feared that the people would stone them.

## Meanwhile, Back at the High Council

ACTS 5:21b–26 *But the high priest and those with him came and called the council together, with all the elders of the children of Israel, and sent to the prison to have them brought. But when the officers came and did not find them in the prison, they returned and reported, saying, "Indeed we found the prison shut securely, and the guards standing outside before the doors; but when we opened them, we found no one inside!" Now when the high priest, the captain of the temple, and the chief priests heard these things, they wondered what the outcome would be. So one came and told them, saying, "Look, the men whom you put in prison are standing in the temple and teaching the people!" Then the captain went with the officers and brought them without violence, for they feared the people, lest they should be stoned. (NKJV)*

At the Hall of Hewn Stone, the high priest convened the Sanhedrin and sent guards to bring the jailbirds for questioning. Finding the cell as bare as Mother Hubbard's cupboard, the guards returned empty-handed and chagrined. Just then, someone brought news the Twelve were at the Temple, preaching. The guardsmen rearrested them, very carefully, for fear of being stoned by temple-goers sympathetic to the apostles.

## Same Song, Second Verse

ACTS 5:27–28 *And when they had brought them, they set them before the council. And the high priest asked them, saying, "Did we not strictly command you not to teach in this name? And look, you have filled Jerusalem with your doctrine, and intend to bring this Man's blood on us!" (NKJV)*

**go to**

**run for their lives**
Mark 14:50

**crucifying**
Galatians 3:13

**Prince**
Isaiah 9:6

**Savior**
Matthew 1:21;
John 1:29

**right hand**
corulership with
God

**Prince**
Son of God,
Messiah

The high priest and his cronies had tried to stop this grassroots movement by threatening Peter and John with bodily harm if they mentioned Jesus's name in public again (see Acts 4:18, 21). That was after one lame beggar was healed. Now, not just one, but many people were being healed in the forbidden name! And belief in the Resurrection was spreading with "great power" (see Acts 4:33 NKJV). It was an angrier Sanhedrin this time. The high council's orders had been blatantly disobeyed. "You have filled Jerusalem with your doctrine!"

## The Bad News and the Good News

ACTS 5:29–32 *But Peter and the other apostles answered and said: "We ought to obey God rather than men. The God of our fathers raised up Jesus whom you murdered by hanging on a tree. Him God has exalted to His right hand to be Prince and Savior, to give repentance to Israel and forgiveness of sins. And we are His witnesses to these things, and so also is the Holy Spirit whom God has given to those who obey Him." (NKJV)*

The Twelve who had <u>run for their lives</u> when Jesus was arrested were changed men. Courage replaced cowardice. "We ought to obey God rather than men." Then, seizing the opportunity, even in this extremely hostile environment, they boldly stated the bad news and the good news.

*The bad news*—You people are guilty of killing Jesus by <u>crucifying</u> him.

*The good news*—The God of Israel raised Jesus from the dead and exalted him to his own **right hand**. Jesus, "**Prince** and <u>Savior</u>," offers Israel "the gift of a changed life and sins forgiven."[8]

We know these things because we've been changed and forgiven. The Holy Spirit verifies everything we are saying.

## A Voice of Reason in the Madness

ACTS 5:33–35 *When they heard this, they were furious and plotted to kill them. Then one in the council stood up, a Pharisee named Gamaliel, a teacher of the law held in respect by all the people, and commanded them to put the apostles outside for a little while. And he said to them: "Men of Israel, take heed to yourselves what you intend to do regarding these men. (NKJV)*

If you've read the <u>mob scenes</u> that led to the condemnation of Jesus, you're not surprised at the explosion of rage that erupted against the Twelve witnesses. Old men in priestly robes leaped to their feet and brandished angry fists. A **cacophony** of bitter voices demanded death to the Twelve. If not restrained, some would have gladly spilled their blood right there on the pavement in the Hall of Hewn Stone.

Into the midst of the near insanity, God sent a solitary voice of authority and reason. The man in the white hat, unexpected ally and all around cool dude was a **Pharisee**, known as "**Rabban** Gamaliel" or "Gamaliel the Elder," one of Israel's most respected teachers. Fellow teachers called him "the Beauty of the Law." His most famous student was Saul of Tarsus—the apostle Paul—(see Acts 22:3). He was, as far as we know, not a Christian, but God used him to rescue his people from a massacre.

## <u>"Give a Man Enough Rope, and He'll Hang Himself!"</u>

Acts 5:36–39 *For some time ago Theudas rose up, claiming to be somebody. A number of men, about four hundred, joined him. He was slain, and all who obeyed him were scattered and came to nothing. After this man, Judas of Galilee rose up in the days of the census, and drew away many people after him. He also perished, and all who obeyed him were dispersed. And now I say to you, keep away from these men and let them alone; for if this plan or this work is of men, it will come to nothing; but if it is of God, you cannot overthrow it—lest you even be found to fight against God." (NKJV)*

Gamaliel counseled the Sanhedrin to stop bugging the Christians. If their movement wasn't from God, it would fail. If it was from God, fighting Christians would be fighting God—a really stupid thing to do! It was just common, clod-kicking horse sense. And God used it to keep his ambassadors from becoming guests of honor at a first-century **necktie party**!

**go to**

**mob scenes**
Matthew 26:67;
Mark 14:65;
Luke 22:63–65

**cacophony**
harsh sound

**Pharisee**
member of a group that strictly kept Jewish religious traditions

**Rabban**
highly respected rabbi

**necktie party**
stoning, hanging—first-century Jewish death penalties

go to

lashes
2 Corinthians
11:23–25

Christ's disgrace
Matthew 10:17–22;
Mark 13:9–13;
Luke 12:11–12;
21:12–19

the Name
Jesus

what others say

**J. A. Findlay**

[Gamaliel's advice was based on] sound Pharisaic teaching: God is over all, and needs no help from men for the fulfilment of his purposes; all men must do is to obey, and leave the issue to him.[9]

Sometimes Christians are protected and even rescued from persecution and martyrdom by non-Christians who are sympathetic to their cause. Examples in Acts include Gamaliel (Acts 5:34–40); Gallio (Acts 18:12–15); the Roman commander (Acts 23:23–33); and the centurion (Acts 27:42–43).

The apostles left the Sanhedrin, rejoicing because they had been counted worthy of suffering disgrace for the Name.

## The Honor of Dishonor

**ACTS 5:40–41** *And they agreed with him [Gamaliel], and when they had called for the apostles and beaten them, they commanded that they should not speak in* **the name** *of Jesus, and let them go. So they departed from the presence of the council, rejoicing that they were counted worthy to suffer shame for His name.(NKJV)*

Even though Gamaliel's intervention averted a lynching, the punishment inflicted on the Twelve was harsh—thirty-nine lashes with a leather whip. As they emerged from the Hall of Hewn Stone, their backs were bloody but their hearts were full. They'd stared death in the face and demonstrated their loyalty to Jesus. Jesus told his followers to expect mistreatment by the religious establishment (Luke 21:12). They'd shared Christ's disgrace. That was reason enough for celebration!

what others say

**F. F. Bruce**

The apostles . . . found cause for joy in the thought that God had counted them worthy to endure this humiliation for the sake of Jesus' name. It was insignificant indeed when compared with the disgrace and anguish that Jesus had endured; but, as far as it went, it was a participation in his suffering, such as he had warned them to expect.[10]

## The Beat Goes On

ACTS 5:42 *And daily in the temple, and in every house, they did not cease teaching and preaching Jesus as the Christ. (NKJV)*

The disciples responded to this warning not to speak in Jesus's name as they had responded to the first one—with quiet defiance. Before the bruises healed they were back teaching in the temple court and from house to house. Jerusalem was being saturated with the good news about Jesus the Messiah.

what others say

### Maude de Joseph West

Sublime stubbornness, magnificent disobedience, matter-of-fact defiance! That comes close to making us "feel" for the high priest. In fact, we almost hope that he had access to the ancient world's equivalent for tranquilizer pills! Along about that time, he must have been Jerusalem's most frustrated citizen.[11]

The link between discipline and spiritual power is obvious. The Lord dealt with dishonesty in the early church in a way that created an aversion among Christians toward hypocrisy. Cleansed motives led to renewed commitment, and the Jerusalem Christian community became a conduit for God's power. Opposition opened the door for the good news to spread into the hallowed haunts of political power! When Christians walk together and before the world in obedience and purity without pretense, there's no telling what God's power can accomplish through them!

## Chapter Wrap-Up

- Ananias and Sapphira pretended to give all the proceeds of a land sale to the church. The Holy Spirit revealed their deception. Peter told them they'd lied to God. Both died. New respect for God swept the church. Hypocrisy vanished. (Acts 5:1–11)

- Christians met at Solomon's Porch. Miracles happened. Because of the Ananias and Sapphira affair, new people feared to join them, but still the church grew. They healed the sick and demon-possessed. (Acts 5:12–16)

- Success of the Christians filled religious leaders with jealousy. They arrested the apostles. An angel freed them, and they went on preaching. Some council members wanted to kill them, but Gamaliel talked them out of it. (Acts 5:17–40)

- The apostles were flogged and released. They rejoiced for the privilege of sharing Christ's disgrace, ignored the ban, and returned to preaching. (Acts 5:40–42)

## Study Questions

1. Who was behind the hypocrisy of Ananias and Sapphira? To whom did Peter say they had lied? Were they required to donate the proceeds of their land sale?

2. Explain the difference between "obvious" miracles and "hidden" miracles.

3. Identify three facts about the church's healing ministry observed in Acts 5:12–16.

4. Why did the priests and Sadducees put the apostles in jail? Who let them out? What did they do after being freed?

5. When members of the Sanhedrin wanted to kill the apostles, who spoke up in their behalf? What special title did his fellow teachers give him?

6. Why were the apostles so happy when they left the Sanhedrin?

# Acts 6-7 Opposition Adds Fuel to Faith's Fire

*Chapter Highlights:*
- **A Strategy for Servanthood**
- **The Magnificent Seven**
- **Stephen's Unusual Impact**
- **The Maddening Truth!**

## Let's Get Started

When you decide to take Jesus's instructions seriously, you are going to find yourself in some kind of <u>trouble</u>. As chapter 5 ends, the disciples, beat up and warned again not to speak the name of Jesus, returned to Solomon's Porch, where they shared the good news with <u>huge crowds</u>. (Estimates of church size at this time range from fifteen thousand to twenty thousand people.[1]) In addition to these illegal temple gatherings, they took the good news to small groups meeting in homes throughout the city (Acts 5:42). Opposition seemed to add fuel to faith's fire. The Jesus community kept growing and growing and growing.

And they kept doing the things Jesus had told them to do: Preach the good news. Heal the sick. Care for the poor. Obedience led to success. It also led right smack-dab into new trouble! The dynamite believers' fellowship of Jerusalem faced up to the problem, dealt with it in Jesus's spirit, kept on obeying his instructions, and discovered God is able to use even scary problems to strengthen his people.

**trouble**
James 1:2

**huge crowds**
Acts 2:41; 4:4; 5:14

## Too Big for the Mighty Twelve

> ACTS 6:1-2 *Now in those days, when the number of the disciples was multiplying, there arose a complaint against the Hebrews by the Hellenists, because their widows were neglected in the daily distribution. Then the twelve summoned the multitude of the disciples and said, "It is not desirable that we should leave the word of God and serve tables.* (NKJV)

In the midst of the most exciting time in its history a problem surfaced that could have torn the church apart—poor widows were overlooked in the distribution of food! Overlooked! It says, "You aren't important. You aren't loved." Given the church's public commitment to care for the poor, this was embarrassing—not the signal the church wanted to give.

# Discrimination in the "Perfect" Church?

To complicate matters, the overlooked widows were all part of the same ethnic group. Were they being neglected because they spoke with foreign accents? The original word translated "complaint" (Acts 6:1) means the Grecian Jews muttered indignant discontent, not openly but in behind-your-back whispers. To the widows waiting in vain for the first-century "meals on wheels" to arrive, it looked like a problem of prejudice and discrimination. In Jerusalem two major cultural groups existed side by side:

- Hebraic Jews, born and raised in the Jewish homeland and speaking **Aramaic.**

- **Grecian** Jews, born and raised in foreign countries and speaking **Greek**.

Homeland Jews often looked down on foreign Jews. Some felt that Grecian Jews were contaminated by pagan culture. Actually Grecian Jews were as **orthodox** as homeland Jews.

There is no evidence of intentional discrimination in the early church (Acts 4:32). Tearing down cultural barriers was part of the church's mission (see Acts 2:5–12, 39). Still, there is no reason to suppose every blind spot was instantly whisked away, turning early believers into perfect "saints" immediately. Such changes require the processes of growing up spiritually. That takes time.

In those days a woman whose husband died was often left destitute. She did not own property unless it was part of an inheritance from her father and he had no sons. Even then, she could keep the inheritance only if she married within the clan. The Bible gives special attention to the care of widows.

Caring for single women was a special concern among the original Christians. Many widows came to Jerusalem to live out their final years near the Temple, ran out of resources, and found themselves destitute. The church included them in its distribution of food to the poor. Some of these women had significant spiritual influence in the church.

# Development of Helping Ministry in the Early Church

The word early Christians used for helping others is *diakonia* (service, ministry, servanthood). Some form of it occurs 101 times in the New Testament. All Jesus's followers are called to be servants. The early church's serving ministry developed in at least five stages:

**go to**

Grecian
Acts 9:29

**growing up**
Ephesians 4:11–16

**care of widows**
Deuteronomy
24:19–21; 26:12–13;
Job 31:16–23;
Isaiah 1:17

**special concern**
James 1:27;
1 Timothy 5:3–16

**influence**
1 Timothy 5:9–10;
Titus 2:3–5

**Aramaic**
a derivative of
ancient Hebrew

**Grecian**
influenced by Greek
culture (Hellenistic)

**Greek**
"universal" language used
throughout the
Roman Empire

**orthodox**
conforming to
established
religious doctrine
and practice

## Five Stages of Ministry Development

| Stage | Scripture |
|---|---|
| 1. Jesus taught his disciples to serve. Christian servanthood reflects Jesus's willingness to give his life for others. | Acts 28:25–28 |
| 2. Spontaneous sharing occurred. With the Holy Spirit reminding them of Jesus's teachings, a kind of unorganized, ad-lib response to needs developed. | Acts 2:45; 4:34 |
| 3. Distribution was daily. Believers gathered daily for teaching, fellowship, bread breaking, and prayer. They ate together, and food was sent with the poor to keep them going till the next meeting. Care for the poor was patterned after Jewish practices. | Acts 6:1; Acts 2:42–46 |
| 4. The twelve apostles handled distribution. They received money and goods and, in addition to preaching, directed daily food distribution. | Acts 4:34–5:2; 6:2 |
| 5. Church growth demanded more organized care. As believers grew to fifteen or twenty thousand with numbers increasing daily, programless sharing developed more holes than Swiss cheese. A cry went up for a better game plan. | Acts 6:1 |

Godly growth always involves growth in love (Ephesians 4:16; Colossians 2:19). Church growth that reflects only statistical increases is not sufficient. If people who should be cared for are "overlooked" in the scramble for size, then, however exciting it seems, it isn't godly growth.

what others say

**Larry Richards**

The Jewish system of poor relief involved *tamhuy*, the "poor bowl," and *quppah*, the "poor basket." The first was a daily distribution of food provided for the homeless. The second was a weekly distribution of food and clothing provided for poor families. In both cases help was provided in goods, not in cash.[2]

## A Strategy for Servanthood

ACTS 6:3–5a *Therefore, brethren, seek out from among you seven men of good reputation, full of the Holy Spirit and wisdom, whom we may appoint over this business; but we will give ourselves continually to prayer and to the ministry of the word." And the saying pleased the whole multitude. (NKJV)*

**go to**

**God uses**
Romans 8:28

**wide diversity**
Romans 12:6–8;
1 Corinthians 12;
Ephesians 4:11–12;
1 Peter 4:10

**poor in spirit**
Matthew 5:3

**gifts**
abilities given by
God to help people
fulfill his purposes

The church did not for a minute consider copping out on care of the poor. It never entered their heads to choose between feeding hungry mouths and feeding hungry souls. Jesus said to do both! But it was clear that twelve mere men could not handle both (Acts 6:2). If church unity and outreach were to continue unhindered, the work must be shared.

Four things about the way they solved their problem are worth notice:

1. *No defensiveness.* Problems do not require finding someone to blame. <u>God uses</u> problems to help his church grow up.

> **what others say**
>
> **Keith Miller**
>
> God calls us to problems, not programs, in which we will find our ministries—problems which captivate our minds and imaginations and motivate us to give our lives to try to bring Christ's vision of wholeness to situations and people, as we begin to see them from his perspective.[3]

2. *Admission of human limitation.* Widow care was not just a leader problem—it was a problem for the whole church. Nobody can be everything the church needs. God's purpose is fulfilled by a <u>wide diversity</u> of people serving with their **gifts**.

> **what others say**
>
> **Sherwood Wirt**
>
> In my own life I have learned that a lot of [spiritual] growth consists simply of my getting out of God's way. It is actually shrinkage rather than growth. I am certain that God does not want me to develop into a spiritual giant in my own eyes, even if I could. He wants me to become a spiritual pygmy so he can handle me. He wants me <u>poor in spirit</u> so he can do something with me without his having to contend with my ever-present, darling ego.[4]

3. *Those chosen to serve met high spiritual qualifications.* The seven were not chosen because they were rich, popular, too dumb to say "No," or because they looked good in dark suits! Three qualifications for "table servers" were laid down: (1) They must be known

("men . . . whom everyone trusts"[5]); (2) full of (directed and controlled by) the Spirit; and (3) full of . . . wisdom ("good sense"[6]).

4. *They bent over backward to restore trust and peace.* All seven chosen represented the group that charged discrimination—all had Grecian names! The care of all the widows—Hebraic and Grecian—was entrusted to members of the neglected minority.

**go to**

**the seven**
Acts 21:8

**deacons**
men and women involved in practical "helping" ministries of the church

> ### what others say
>
> **Billy Graham**
>
> You have made your peace with God. . . . You now begin to see others through the eyes of Jesus. . . . Prejudices that you once held are beginning to slip away. Selfishness that was once characteristic of you in many areas of your life has now gone.[7]

As Leader of the church, Jesus does more than *talk* about how problems should be handled. He shows how by the way he himself handled problems in his life on earth. Part of knowing what Christ wants done is looking at his model and doing it his way.

## The Magnificent Seven

**ACTS 6:5b** *And they chose Stephen, a man full of faith and the Holy Spirit, and Philip, Prochorus, Nicanor, Timon, Parmenas, and Nicolas, a proselyte from Antioch,* (NKJV)

"The seven," they came to be called. They were emerging leaders in the Grecian Christian community. Beyond their qualifications to serve as "table servers" (Acts 6:2–3), Luke gives no details about Prochorus, Nicanor, Timon, and Parmenas. About Stephen he says he was "a man full of faith and the Holy Spirit" (Acts 6:5 NKJV) and "full of faith and power" (Acts 6:8 NKJV). Philip (not the apostle) became known as "Philip the evangelist" (Acts 21:8). Nicolas was a Gentile convert to Judaism.

They were never officially given the title **"deacons,"** though Christians often refer to them that way. They were prepared for service by six years of living in the growing Christian community. It takes time to grow honest, spiritual leaders with good common sense. The church grows in numbers and influence when there is harmony among Christians, the work is shared, and the needs of people are met.

something to ponder

**William Barclay**

It is extremely interesting to note that the first office-bearers to be appointed [in the church] were chosen not to talk but for practical service.[8]

According to New Testament teaching every Christian is gifted (see Romans 12:6–8; 1 Corinthians 12:4–11, 27–31; Ephesians 4:11; 1 Peter 4:8–11). What abilities do you have that can be used in service to others? What do you enjoy doing that might help the church?

**confirmed**
ratified, demonstrated approval

**blessing**
spiritual support, prayer for success

**identification**
oneness and equality

## The Laying on of Hands

ACTS 6:6–7 *whom they set before the apostles; and when they had prayed, they laid hands on them. Then the word of God spread, and the number of the disciples multiplied greatly in Jerusalem, and a great many of the priests were obedient to the faith.* (NKJV)

The early church used these steps in the selection process for the seven:

- The apostles clarified their spiritual and practical qualifications (Acts 6:3).

- The congregation selected the seven by consensus or mutual agreement (Acts 6:5–6).

- The apostles **confirmed** the congregation's choices by praying for them with the traditional laying on of hands (Acts 6:6). Laying on of hands was a Jewish tradition. It signified (1) **blessing** (see Genesis 48:13–30); (2) **identification** (see Leviticus 1:4; 4:4; 16:21); and (3) authority (see Numbers 27:22–23) for an assigned task.

The problem the seven were appointed to solve is never mentioned again. Evidently, these guys did a bang-up job.

Early Christians expected the Holy Spirit to guide them to solution of problems through the agreement (consensus) of leaders and people about a course of action (see Matthew 18:15–20; Acts 1:21–26).

key point

## Seven Habits of Highly Effective Churches

1. Listen to people.

2. End discrimination based on language, culture, or social distinctions.

3. Serve with your <u>gift</u>—don't do somebody else's work—and let others help.

4. Care for people and their needs, especially the poor.

5. Spread the Word of God.

6. Pray often and about everything.

7. Appoint spiritual leaders or servants—approve their ministry.

Results: People are pleased, hungry are fed, Word is spread, numbers increase, and priests believe.

go to

**gift**
Romans 12:6–8;
1 Corinthians
12:4–11;
Ephesians 4:11;
1 Peter 4:8–10

what others say

### Charles Colson

Harmony and oneness in spirit can be achieved only when Christians put aside their personal agendas and submit themselves to the authority of the Holy Spirit. . . . When the people of God, united in his name, proclaim the Word of God, they can turn their world upside down.[9]

## Stephen's Unusual Impact

**ACTS 6:8** *And Stephen, full of faith and power, did great wonders and signs among the people. (NKJV)*

Few Bible characters are described in as glowing terms as Stephen. A Grecian transplant, he was part of Jerusalem's foreign-born community. In the course of his food distribution work, Stephen had an unusual impact. He performed miracles and convinced many people in the Grecian Jewish community that Jesus is Messiah.

### Time Line of How the Church Grew

Illustration #5

# The Frame-Up

**go to**

**death penalty**
Leviticus 24:10–23

**destroy**
John 2:19;
Matthew 26:59–61;
Mark 15:29–30;
Luke 21:5–6

**respect for the Temple**
John 2:14–17;
Matthew 21:12–16

**Law**
Matthew 5:17–20;
Romans 13:8;
Galatians 3:24

**synagogues**
480 Jewish gathering places for study and prayer in Jerusalem

**blasphemous words**
slander; misuse of God's name

**Judaism**
Jewish religious system

ACTS 6:9–14 *Then there arose some from what is called the Synagogue of the Freedmen (Cyrenians, Alexandrians, and those from Cilicia and Asia), disputing with Stephen. And they were not able to resist the wisdom and the Spirit by which he spoke. Then they secretly induced men to say, "We have heard him speak blasphemous words against Moses and God." And they stirred up the people, the elders, and the scribes; and they came upon him, seized him, and brought him to the council. They also set up false witnesses who said, "This man does not cease to speak blasphemous words against this holy place and the law; for we have heard him say that this Jesus of Nazareth will destroy this place and change the customs which Moses delivered to us." (NKJV)*

Stephen distributed food to the poor in the **synagogues** of Greek-speaking Jews like himself, including the Freedmen synagogue. Freedmen were liberated slaves. They were usually very poor. So it was natural that his relief work would bring Stephen into their community.

In the Freedmen's synagogue Stephen found himself in red-hot debate with unbelieving Jews. The debate revolved around what Stephen believed about the Temple and Jewish religious traditions. These small-minded men were no match for Stephen's "wisdom and the Spirit by which he spoke" (Acts 6:10 NKJV). (In other words, they lost the debate!) So they attacked Stephen on two other fronts.

*Slander*—In a first-century version of "being tried in the press," they stirred up the people. Stephen was guilty of speaking "**blasphemous words** against Moses and God," they said.

*Formal charges*—They officially accused Stephen before the Jewish High Court on two counts. Count 1: Blasphemy against the Temple and the Law (Acts 6:13). Conviction carried the <u>death penalty</u>. Count 2: Plotting destruction of **Judaism** by claiming Jesus would <u>destroy</u> the Temple (Acts 6:14).

## Did the Christians Plan to Tear Down the Temple?

It was a lie. Christians were not plotting to destroy the Temple. Jesus and his disciples had great <u>respect for the Temple</u> and the <u>Law</u>. But some Christian beliefs were twisted by their enemies to form a condemning accusation of Stephen. Christians believe the following:

- The Temple is not the only place to meet God. People can meet God anywhere (see Matthew 18:20; John 4:21–24; Acts 17:24).
- The Law and temple services are **fulfilled** in Christ (see Matthew 5:17).
- God writes his Law on people's hearts and minds by the Holy Spirit (see Jeremiah 31:33; Hebrews 8:10).
- God's grace is not exclusively for Jews; it's for Gentiles too (see Matthew 28:19; Acts 2:39).

These beliefs were misinterpreted as a threat to traditional Jewish religion.

**glowing face**
Exodus 34:29–35

**fulfilled**
spiritual transactions pictured in Law and temple worship have become reality

## The Intimate Presence of Jesus

> ACTS 6:15–7:2 *And all who sat in the council, looking steadfastly at him, saw his face as the face of an angel. Then the high priest said, "Are these things so?" And he said, "Brethren and fathers, listen: The God of glory appeared to our father Abraham when he was in Mesopotamia, before he dwelt in Haran, . . . (NKJV)*

Jews associated a <u>glowing face</u> with a person close to God. Stephen, on trial for his life, experienced the intimate presence of Jesus (Matthew 28:20). He addressed his judges with respect (Acts 7:2). But before his defense rested, he would charge them with the very crimes for which they accused him.

## The Defense Calls Its Only Witness—History!

**the big picture**

**Acts 7:3–43**

Stephen used the examples of Israel's forefathers Abraham, Joseph, and Moses in his defense. He gave his listeners a star-studded history lesson.

Stephen marshaled case histories from the Old Testament to prove four points:

1. God's presence and work are not confined to the geographical boundaries of Israel.

**Abraham**
Genesis 12:1–25:11

**Promised Land**
Genesis 12:7

**Joseph**
Genesis 37–48

**dreams**
Genesis 37:5, 9, 19

**defied the decree**
Exodus 2:1–10;
Hebrews 11:23

**Moses**
Exodus 1–40

**Promised Land**
Palestine, land
promised to
Abraham and his
descendants

**circumcision**
removal of the fore-
skin of the penis as
a symbol of faith
and belonging to
God's Old
Testament people
(not required of
Christians)

**pharaoh**
title of Egyptian
kings

**Hebrews**
Israelites, Jews

2. Meeting God is not limited to a man-made house of worship or any "holy place."

3. True faith does not need "holy places" or visible structures to thrive; it only needs the presence and Word of God.

4. Israel had a history of rejecting God by rejecting his representatives and idolizing man-made structures.

God revealed himself to <u>Abraham</u>, revered father of the Hebrew nation, when he was a pagan in Mesopotamia, far from the **Promised Land**. Acting on "the bare word of God,"[10] Abraham followed the Lord not knowing where he would be led. He never owned a square foot of the Promised Land, but believed God's promise to give it to his offspring. He received **circumcision** as a symbol of confidence in God's promise.

Three generations later jealous brothers (Israel's founding "fathers") sold <u>Joseph</u> into slavery. But exile from the Promised Land did not separate him from God. He had nothing to hang on to but promises God made in his <u>dreams</u>. From slavery he rose to rule Egypt under a grateful pharaoh. When famine struck, his brothers found themselves at the mercy of the brother they'd rejected. As God's representative, Joseph forgave and rescued them. He brought his whole family to live in Egypt where they flourished.

A later Egyptian **pharaoh** forgot Joseph's role in Egypt's survival and turned the **Hebrews** into slaves. He decreed that Hebrew new-born babies should be thrown out like garbage and allowed to die of exposure. Moses's parents <u>defied the decree</u> and protected their infant son for three months. When they could hide him no longer, they set him afloat in a special basket on the Nile River. An Egyptian princess found the infant in the basket, fell in love with the unusual baby, and raised <u>Moses</u> as her son. He was educated in Pharaoh's palace (right under ol' Pharaoh's nose!).

As an adult, Moses threw in his lot with the Hebrew slaves and offered himself as their deliverer (Acts 7:23–25). They would have nothing to do with him. He escaped to Arabia (Midian) where he spent the next forty years herding sheep. There, in Gentile territory, 250 miles across the desert from the temple site, God met Moses in a burning bush and called it "holy ground" (Acts 7:33 NKJV). (All it takes to make a holy place is God's holy presence!)

To make a long story short (the <u>unabridged version</u> is four volumes in the Old Testament!): God heard the cries of the slaves down in Egypt land—far from any holy place (Acts 7:34). He sent Moses back to Egypt to lead them to freedom amid Fourth of July fireworks courtesy of God (Acts 7:36)!

Fifty days later, God met Moses on **Mount Sinai**. The mountain shook with God's presence. God presented Moses "living oracles to give" to the Hebrews (Acts 7:38 NKJV)—the <u>Ten Commandments</u> and the Law. Moses's faith did not depend for a millisecond on a holy place. He knew he had the presence and living Word of God.

While Moses was on Sinai's summit getting God's words, the Hebrews were in the foothills slapping together a hasty, nasty golden **calf** (Exodus 32:4)—something tangible to believe in. No matter that their mooless moo-cow was nothing but a chunk of cold metal. For a lifeless little bull they turned their backs on the living words of God! Tragically, this was only the beginning of their idolatry (Acts 7:42–43).

go to

**unabridged version**
Exodus, Leviticus, Numbers, Deuteronomy

**Ten Commandments**
Exodus 20:1–17

**tabernacle**
Exodus 25–31

**Mount Sinai**
volcanic mountain in southern Arabia

**calf**
bull; Egyptian fertility god some Hebrews worshiped while in slavery

**tabernacle**
tent, temporary dwelling

## Blueprint for the Tabernacle

ACTS 7:44–45a *"Our fathers had the tabernacle of witness in the wilderness, as He appointed, instructing Moses to make it according to the pattern that he had seen, which our fathers, having received it in turn, also brought with Joshua into the land possessed by the Gentiles, (NKJV)*

On Sinai God gave Moses the blueprint for the <u>tabernacle</u>, a temporary place for Israel to meet God (see Illustration #6). It was designed with these features:

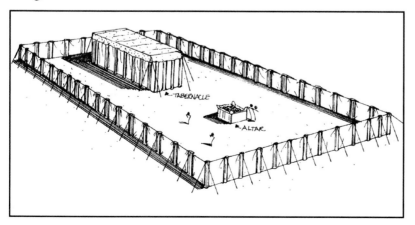

TABERNACLE

ALTAR

**Illustration #6**
Wilderness Tabernacle—God designed each feature of this portable tent or church that the Israelites carried with them. It was called a tabernacle.

**go to**

shadowy pictures
Hebrews 9, 10

dreamed
Psalm 132:2–5

a descendant
Luke 1:26–33

Solomon built
2 Chronicles 2–7

- Its furnishings were <u>shadowy pictures</u> of **spiritual transactions** that would later be part of a relationship with God through Jesus Christ (Hebrews 8:5; 10:1).

- It could be folded up and moved at a moment's notice, so Israel could choose to believe God was among them wherever they went (Acts 7:45).

## No Dream House for God

ACTS 7:45b–47 *whom God drove out before the face of our fathers until the days of David, who found favor before God and asked to find a dwelling for the God of Jacob. But Solomon built Him a house.* (NKJV)

Stephen continued his history lesson: Years later King David <u>dreamed</u> of replacing the collapsible chapel with a permanent house for God. The Lord slammed on the brakes, telling David he didn't need a house and never asked anyone to build him one!

**spiritual transactions**
prayer, intercession, new birth, forgiveness, salvation

**descendant**
Messiah, Christ

One day, God promised, <u>a **descendant**</u> of David would build the spiritual house God really wanted (1 Chronicles 17:3–14). David's son <u>Solomon built</u> the first, most magnificent Jewish temple. And God met with his people there (1 Kings 8:10–11). But even as he prepared to build it, Solomon acknowledged that no man-made building could ever contain God: "Who is able to build Him [God] a temple, since heaven and the heaven of heavens cannot contain Him?" (2 Chronicles 2:6 NKJV).

## God Doesn't Live in a Man-Made House

ACTS 7:48–50 *However, the Most High does not dwell in temples made with hands, as the prophet says:*
*"Heaven is My throne,*
*And earth is My footstool.*
*What house will you build for Me? says the LORD,*
*Or what is the place of My rest?*
*Has My hand not made all these things?"* (NKJV)

Stephen stood accused of blasphemy for suggesting the Temple is not essential. This was not true. His defense strategy was to explain what he and the other Christians did believe and he quoted from Isaiah 66:1–2. The Temple had served a purpose. But even temple worshipers must understand—the house is not God and God "does not dwell in temples made with hands."

Pagans think temples <u>contain gods</u> and to threaten a temple is to <u>threaten a god</u>. But it's not a biblical idea. It makes God out to be small and distorts people's perception of him, confusing him with religious institutions, "sacred" places, and man-made traditions. God is none of these "religious" things. He is the Most High—too great to be stuck in a man-made structure. Not even the universe can contain him, for heaven's sake!

**contain gods**
1 Kings 8:27

**threaten a god**
Acts 19:27

**forever**
Revelation 21:2–4

**direction of angels**
Galatians 3:19;
Hebrews 1:4; 2:2

## God's New "Temple"

As caregiver working among the people of the early church, Stephen saw God building a new kind of temple. This unique, new "holy place" was rising amid the rubble of ruined religion. The old Temple would be destroyed (not by Christians, but pagan Romans, in AD 70). But the new living temple would be <u>forever</u>! New Testament writers describe it this way:

- 1 Corinthians 3:16—"Do you not know that you are the temple of God and that the Spirit of God dwells in you?" (NKJV).

- Ephesians 2:22—"In whom you also are being built together for a dwelling place of God in the Spirit" (NKJV).

- 1 Peter 2:5—"You also, as living stones, are being built up a spiritual house, a holy priesthood, to offer up spiritual sacrifices acceptable to God through Jesus Christ" (NKJV).

With Jesus as their foundation, his followers are the lively, flesh-and-blood house of God. Their love, loyalty, and care are focused less and less on religious structures, like the gold and marble building that dominated Jewish life, and are becoming refocused on the living, breathing family bonded together by their common connection to Christ.

# <u>The Maddening Truth!</u>

ACTS 7:51–54 *"You stiff-necked and uncircumcised in heart and ears! You always resist the Holy Spirit; as your fathers did, so do you. Which of the prophets did your fathers not persecute? And they killed those who foretold the coming of the Just One, of whom you now have become the betrayers and murderers, who have received the law by the <u>direction of angels</u> and have not kept it." When they heard these things they were cut to the heart, and they gnashed at him with their teeth. (NKJV)*

**go to**

resistance
Isaiah 63:10

gnashing of teeth
Psalm 35:16;
Luke 13:28

freshly infused
Acts 4:8, 31

laying his life
Mark 8:35

guarantees
1 John 2:1–2

**Just One**
Messiah, Christ

**gnashing of teeth**
sign of rage

**infused**
permeated,
controlled

Stephen ended his defense with an in-your-face indictment of not only Israel past but the arrogant Sanhedrin itself. They accused Stephen of slander against God, Moses, the Law, and the Temple. But it is they who slandered Moses and God and destroyed the Temple. Stephen pronounced them guilty on four counts:

- *Count 1*—Persistent <u>resistance</u> against the Holy Spirit (Acts 7:51).

- *Count 2*—Persecution and martyrdom of the prophets (Acts 7:52).

- *Count 3*—Betrayal and murder of the **Just One** (Acts 7:52).

- *Count 4*—Disobedience of the Law they claim to defend (Acts 7:53).

The room erupted with rage verging on insanity. Powerful politicos reacted with bestial **gnashing of teeth**.

## Hero's Welcome for the Faithful Witness

ACTS 7:55–56 *But he [Stephen], being full of the Holy Spirit, gazed into heaven and saw the glory of God, and Jesus standing at the right hand of God, and said, "Look! I see the heavens opened and the Son of Man standing at the right hand of God!" (NKJV)*

<u>Freshly</u> **infused** with the Holy Spirit, Stephen was given a rare glimpse into the heavenly world. He saw Jesus standing at God's right hand. Usually, Jesus is pictured as seated. Here he stands to welcome a faithful witness <u>laying his life</u> on the line for his Lord's sake. Jesus's place at God's right hand <u>guarantees</u> Stephen's salvation.

Jesus stands by his people as they do what he has sent them to do. They never face suffering or death alone. He stands with them, strengthening, seeing them through it, welcoming them with his affirming, "Well done!" (See Matthew 25:21, 23; Luke 19:17.)

## The Rock of Execution

ACTS 7:57–60 *Then they cried out with a loud voice, stopped their ears, and ran at him with one accord; and they cast him out of the city and stoned him. And the witnesses laid down their clothes at the feet of a young man named Saul. And they stoned Stephen as he was calling on God and saying, "Lord Jesus, receive my spirit." Then he knelt down and cried out with a loud voice, "Lord, do not charge them with this sin." And when he had said this, he fell asleep.* (NKJV)

go to

**stoning**
Leviticus 20:27;
Deuteronomy
17:5–7;
Joshua 7:25

The judges heard Stephen's description of Jesus at **God's right hand** as the ultimate blasphemy. Law-trained, robed jurists stuffed their fingers in their ears and yelled to drown out the voice of the witness. The tribunal entrusted with justice and order, became a pack of junkyard dogs. The Law's provisions for justice were trampled under furious feet in a rush to snuff out Stephen's life.

Stoning was the capital punishment prescribed by the Law of Moses for blasphemy. According to legal rules, after a fair trial with witnesses and careful deliberation (a death sentence required overnight consideration), the convicted person was taken out of the city to an eleven-foot-deep pit known as "The Rock of Execution." On the way he was urged to confess his guilt, with the promise of "a share in the age to come" if he did. He was stripped, bound hand and foot, and pushed headfirst into the pit. If he died from the fall, the execution was ended. If not, the **witnesses** against him led others in throwing heavy stones down on him until he died.

There is no indication that any of the "proper" procedures were followed in Stephen's case. In fact, the Sanhedrin had no legal right to execute anyone without permission from Roman authorities. Their rage blinded them to the risks.

A young man named Saul witnessed the execution. He guarded the **executioners'** clothes and applauded (Acts 7:58; 8:1). Just what every lynch mob needs—a cheerleader!

Stephen was the first Christian martyr. Thousands in every generation have died for their loyalty to Jesus. In Kenya, East Africa, in 1950 hundreds of African Christians who agreed with the goal of national freedom but refused to join Mau Mau fighters in their campaign of murder were strangled or hacked to death with machetes in their homes. When government authorities offered them guns to protect themselves, their answer was, "No. We love you and we love our Kikuyu brothers as well. How can we tell them about the love of God if we are holding guns?" They continued to testify . . . as they died.[11]

**God's right hand**
coruler with God the Father

**witnesses**
accusers, those who testified against him at the trial

**executioners**
witnesses against the accused led the stoning

# A Spirit Stones Could Never Crush

**ACTS 7:59–60** *And they stoned Stephen as he was calling on God and saying, "Lord Jesus, receive my spirit." Then he knelt down and cried out with a loud voice, "Lord, do not charge them with this sin." And when he had said this, he fell asleep.* (NKJV)

As the stones of death fell, Stephen mirrored Jesus on the cross.

Jesus prayed: "Father, into Your hands I commit My spirit" (Luke 23:46 NKJV). Stephen prayed: "Lord Jesus, receive my spirit" (Acts 7:59 NKJV).

Jesus prayed: "Father, forgive them" (Luke 23:34 NKJV). Stephen prayed: "Lord, do not charge them with this sin" (Acts 7:60 NKJV).

## Why Did Stephen Die?

| Reasons for Stephen's Death | Scripture |
| --- | --- |
| He suggested the Temple was no more holy than any place God meets people. | Verses 2, 9, 30–34, 38, 44 |
| He insisted God does not live in man-made institutions or traditions. | Verses 48–50 |
| He accused religious officials of resisting and rejecting God. | Verses 51–52 |
| He accused the Law's "champions" of failure to obey the Law. | Verse 53 |
| He placed Jesus on the same level as God. | Verses 55–56 |

Religious people will kill for "sacred" buildings and institutions. Jesus's people will die for him, with shining faces and forgiving hearts.

# Chapter Wrap-Up

- As the young church grew, its care of the poor developed gaps. Greek-speaking widows were overlooked in the food distribution. Complaints of neglect and discrimination surfaced. The solution was to share the work. (Acts 4:34–5:2; 6:1–4)

- Seven spiritually mature, practical-minded men were chosen from the Grecian community to care for the distribution to the church's poor. The apostles prayed and laid hands on the men selected and turned the work over to them. (Acts 6:5–7)

- Stephen, one of the seven, was a whiz at proving Jesus was the Messiah. When enemies of Christ couldn't win an argument with him, they hatched a plot to bring him before the Sanhedrin on trumped-up charges. (Acts 6:8–14)

- As he defended himself, Stephen's face glowed. He showed from history how God is not confined to any "holy place" but meets people when and where he chooses. He traced Israel's history of rejection. (Acts 6:15–7:45)

- David wanted to build a house for God, but God said "No." Solomon built the Temple. But building a house to contain God is impossible, Stephen said. (Acts 7:44–50)

- Stephen ended his defense with an indictment of the Sanhedrin. When he described his vision of Jesus at God's right hand, infuriated council members dragged him out and stoned him. As he died, he asked the Lord to forgive them. (Acts 7:51–60)

# Study Questions

1. What specific qualifications did the apostles tell the church to look for in the people chosen to care for the poor?

2. What Christian beliefs may have been twisted by Stephen's enemies to charge that he spoke against the Temple and conspired to destroy the Temple and Judaism?

3. Of what four things did Stephen say his accusers were guilty?

4. What two prayers did Stephen pray while being stoned to death? What two prayers did Jesus pray at his death?

# Part Two
# THE ZEAL OF THE
# NEW CHRISTIANS

# Acts 8 Scattergun!

## Let's Get Started

Stephen was the first to die for Jesus. He met Christ's enemies' mindless rage with a shining face. Even as the boulders of death crushed his body, somewhere inside Stephen found superhuman strength to forgive his killers (Acts 7:54–60).

A young man named Saul was there. He threw no stones. He held the killers' coats (Acts 7:58). He could not have known that from that moment on his destiny would be bound together with the Christians.

## Who Was Saul?

> ACTS 8:1a *Now Saul was consenting to his death.* (NKJV)

Who was this Saul guarding the killers' cloaks? His participation in Stephen's execution suggests three "may haves":

- He may have been a member of the Sanhedrin.
- He may have acted as *praeco*, the official herald who announced the crime for which the condemned man was executed.[1]
- He may have been one of the rabbinical students who attended Sanhedrin meetings to learn.

## Saul's All-Out Campaign

> ACTS 8:1b–3 *At that time a great persecution arose against the church which was at Jerusalem; and they were all scattered throughout the regions of Judea and Samaria, except the apostles. And devout men carried Stephen to his burial, and made great lamentation over him. As for Saul, he made havoc of the church, entering every house, and dragging off men and women, committing them to prison.* (NKJV)

Saul was convinced traditional Judaism and the faith of Jesus could never coexist. To preserve the ancient religion, the new sect must be smashed—and he was just the guy to do it! The Sanhedrin's approach

**not to speak**
Acts 4:18; 5:40

**high esteem**
Acts 2:47; 4:21; 5:13

of ordering Jesus's partisans <u>not to speak</u> in their founder's name had failed.

The day Stephen died, Saul, with approval of the Sanhedrin (Acts 9:2), launched an all-out campaign to wipe the name of Jesus from his followers' lips and to drive faith in him from their hearts (Acts 8:1, 3; 22:4). Saul was an equal opportunity persecutor—targeting both men and women. Some paid with their lives (Acts 22:4).

His goal was to destroy the church! (The Greek word for "destroy" means ferocious, animal-like devastation.)

Until Saul's onslaught, the young church had been held in <u>high esteem</u> by the citizens of Jerusalem. Now believers ran for their lives! The Twelve stayed in town (wearing dark glasses, hats pulled down, and collars pulled up—as we say in the spy business: "incognito"). Facing danger with their brothers and sisters was an act of courage.[2] Among the first to lay their lives on the line for Jesus were women (Acts 8:3). Just as Christian women witnessed, so they suffered and died.

Saul's was the first general persecution of the church. Over the next 250 years, ten imperial Roman persecutions, plus hundreds of local incidents of arrest, beating, and lynching, would try to force Christians to renounce their faith. But it is estimated that more Christians have been killed for their faith in the last fifty years than in the first three centuries of the church![3]

**what others say**

**Henry Halley**

Saul . . . laid waste the church, dragging men and women to prison, beating them that believed, putting many to death, making havoc of the church beyond measure.[4]

## Scurrying to Fulfill Their Mission

ACTS 8:4 *Therefore those who were scattered went everywhere preaching the word. (NKJV)*

Had it not been for Saul, the first disciples might have hung around enjoying the lively Jerusalem fellowship indefinitely. But the world was waiting. The first disciples had been "witnesses . . . in Jerusalem" for seven or eight years. Phase two of the Jesus revolution—"in all Judea and Samaria" (Acts 1:8 NKJV)—WAS like a racehorse in the gate, stomping, snorting, champing at the bit for a gallop on the open track.

In a sweet irony, the searing pain of Saul's hot breath on their necks sent reluctant disciples scurrying to fulfill their <u>commission</u>. With the help of this little Pharisee crazy with <u>misdirected zeal</u>, the faith of Jesus broke out all over Judea and leaped the walls of prejudice to ignite Samaria.

Behind the scenes, the Lord of the church is at the controls of his movement. He uses the "disaster" of persecution to spread his message. An early Christian, Tertullian, wrote, "The blood of the martyrs is the church's seed." Early believers had spent several years in the faith-building environment of the Jerusalem Christian community. Now the faith that had been built must be taken out to a world waiting for the good news, and as director of world events, Jesus saw to it that it was (see Illustration #7).

## The Scattering Church

Did the early Christians—those paragons of spiritual love and power—really have to be kicked out of the nest to get them to get on with God's work?

Early Christians apparently had the same problems modern Christians do. They clung to the status quo too long. Now, as then, willingness to risk sharing one's faith outside the security of the believers' circle sometimes requires a hefty shove!

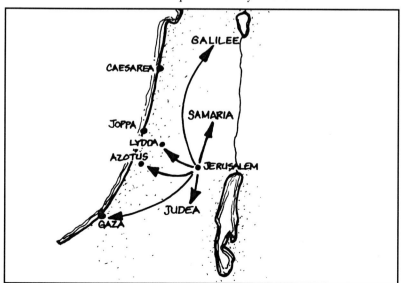

go to

**commission**
Matthew 28:19–20

**misdirected zeal**
Philippians 3:6;
1 Timothy 1:12–15

**Illustration #7**
Map of the Scattering Church—When Paul's persecution of the church began, Christians ran for their lives in all directions. They took the Gospel with them from Jerusalem to Joppa in Samaria, where Peter had his vision (Acts 9:32–10:48); to Caesarea, the home of Cornelius (Acts 9:32–10:48); and to Judea and Gaza when Philip met the Ethiopian (Acts 8:26–39).

**go to**

Sychar
John 4:4–42

**transplants**
2 Kings 17:24–28

**anticipation**
Deuteronomy
18:15–19;
John 4:25

**down**
Jews leaving
Jerusalem always go
"down"; it's in the
mountains and high
in their hearts

what others say

### Robert E. Coleman

Jesus . . . [foresaw] the day when the Gospel of salvation in his Name would be proclaimed convincingly to every creature. Through that testimony his church militant would someday be the church universal even as it would become the church triumphant. It was not going to be an easy conquest. Many would suffer persecution and martyrdom in the battle. Yet no matter how great the trials through which his people would pass, and how many temporal skirmishes were lost in the struggle, the ultimate victory was certain. His church would win in the end (Matthew 16:18).[5]

### Billy Graham

Again we face a dark time in the history of God's people. In spite of some encouraging signs, the forces of evil seem to be gathering for a colossal assault on the work of God in the world. . . . Our world needs to be touched by Christians who are Spirit-filled, Spirit-led, and Spirit-empowered. Are you that kind of Christian?[6]

## <u>The Greater Samaria Miracle Crusade</u>

Acts 8:5–8 *Then Philip went **down** to the city of Samaria and preached Christ to them. And the multitudes with one accord heeded the things spoken by Philip, hearing and seeing the miracles which he did. For unclean spirits, crying with a loud voice, came out of many who were possessed; and many who were paralyzed and lame were healed. And there was great joy in that city. (NKJV)*

Philip, highly visible in Jerusalem as one of the seven who cared for the poor (Acts 6:5), hightailed it north across the Samaritan border. He stopped in an unnamed town—perhaps a Greek-speaking city, where a language barrier wouldn't hinder sharing the gospel—perhaps <u>Sychar</u> where Jesus met the woman at the well.

Samaritans were a people of mixed ancestry—a combination of poor northern Israelites and <u>transplants</u> from other conquered nations. Their religion was a corrupted form of Judaism. They accepted as Scripture only the first five books of the Old Testament. They shared the Jews' <u>anticipation</u> of the Messiah. "Pure" Jews never accepted Samaritans as real Jews. In turn, Samaritans despised Jews for their rejection.

Philip introduced Jesus to the Samaritans as their Messiah (Acts 8:5). The Holy Spirit authenticated his preaching with miracles (Acts 8:6). Hundreds believed, and there was joy all over town (Acts 8:8)!

## No Tricks and No Illusions

**sorcerer**
Exodus 7:11–12;
Acts 13:4–12

> ACTS 8:9–13 *But there was a certain man called Simon, who previously practiced sorcery in the city and astonished the people of Samaria, claiming that he was someone great, to whom they all gave heed, from the least to the greatest, saying, "This man is the great power of God." And they heeded him because he had astonished them with his sorceries for a long time. But when they believed Philip as he preached the things concerning the kingdom of God and the name of Jesus Christ, both men and women were baptized. Then Simon himself also believed; and when he was baptized he continued with Philip, and was amazed, seeing the miracles and signs which were done. (NKJV)*

**Magus**
practitioner of illusions, sorcery, and quackery

**occult practices**
incantations calling for action or influence by supernatural (demonic) powers

**sorcerer**
person who uses drugs to produce "magical" effects

The town's most notorious celebrity was a sleight-of-hand artist named Simon—early Christian literature calls him "Simon **Magus**." He wowed the local citizens with illusions ("magic" tricks) and sorceries. Sorcery involved **occult practices** and, often, drug-induced "magical" effects. ("Just snort a little of this white powder and voila! you're off to la-la land!" One "trip" and you're convinced the drug dealer is "God's man of faith and power"!) When this first-century magician saw Philip's miracles—paralytics walking, demon-harassed people restored to sanity (Acts 8:7)—he was impressed. These were not illusions! No tricks, no drugs, no hallucinations.

Simon's skills as an illusionist and <u>sorcerer</u> convinced the Samaritans he had a pipeline to God (Acts 8:10). Simon "believed," and Philip baptized him (Acts 8:13 NKJV). His faith appeared to be sincere. After his baptism Simon followed Philip everywhere, like a wizard's apprentice, trying to figure out the evangelist's "magic."

### what others say

**William Barclay**

Simon was by no means an unusual type in the ancient world. There were many astrologers and soothsayers and magicians, and in a credulous age they had great influence. . . . Even the twentieth century has not risen above fortune-telling and astrology, as almost any popular newspaper or magazine can

**spiritual gifts**
Romans 12:6–8;
1 Corinthians
12:7–11, 28–30;
Ephesians 4:11

**spiritual life**
1 John 5:12

**discernment**
1 Corinthians 12:10;
Hebrews 5:14

**discernment**
ability to distinguish
between good and
evil

witness. It is not to be thought that Simon and his fellow-practitioners were all conscious frauds. Many of them had deluded themselves before they deluded others and believed in their own powers.[7]

# Spirit Link

ACTS 8:14–17 *Now when the apostles who were at Jerusalem heard that Samaria had received the word of God, they sent Peter and John to them, who, when they had come down, prayed for them that they might receive the Holy Spirit. For as yet He had fallen upon none of them. They had only been baptized in the name of the Lord Jesus. Then they laid hands on them, and they received the Holy Spirit. (NKJV)*

Big guns from Jerusalem, Peter and John, were dispatched to check out what was happening in Samaria. Philip was a "new kid on the block." He needed help. Many Samaritans believed and were baptized in Jesus's name, but something was missing: "As yet He [the Holy Spirit] had fallen upon none of them" (Acts 8:16 NKJV). Usually, the gift of the Spirit came with believing in Jesus (Acts 2:38; 10:44). What tipped the evangelist and apostles off that the Holy Spirit had not yet been given to the Samaritans?

It may have been the absence of visible <u>spiritual gifts</u>—speaking in new languages, sharing spiritual insights, caring for one another, etc.

It may have been the absence of <u>spiritual life</u>—liveliness of spirit—eagerness for spiritual things, thirst for fellowship, worship, knowledge of Christ.

It may have been confusion left over from the Samaritans' involvement in the occult, drugs, and other deceptions of Simon's magic—things Peter exposed in Acts 8:20–23.

It may have been special knowledge or insight given by the Holy Spirit—the "gift of **discernment**"—that tipped the leaders off to what was missing.

what others say

**Audrey I. Girard**

When God's Spirit resides within us, he communicates to us an antsy feeling when other people's spirits are not in tune with his. That's the time to pray. Being insightful (discerning) is a gift from God to make us knowing and caring.[8]

## The Full Influence of the Spirit

Peter and John's dual task was to bring believing Samaritans under the full influence of the Spirit and to establish a solid connection between the new Samaritan church and the "mother" church in Jerusalem. Three things were unique about the Holy Spirit's coming at Samaria:

**faith based on miracles**
John 2:23–24; 4:48; 7:3–5

**grace**
unearned, unmerited favor

1. The Spirit came when the apostles prayed for them (Acts 8:15).

2. There was a waiting period between believing and receiving the Spirit (Acts 8:16).

3. The Spirit's coming coincided with the apostles' touch (Acts 8:17).

### what others say

**F. F. Bruce**

It was one thing for them to be baptized by a freelance evangelist like Philip, but not until they had been acknowledged and welcomed by the leaders of the Jerusalem church did they experience the signs which confirmed and attested their membership in the Spirit-possessed society.[9]

## Confused About Power

> ACTS 8:18–19 *And when Simon saw that through the laying on of the apostles' hands the Holy Spirit was given, he offered them money, saying, "Give me this power also, that anyone on whom I lay hands may receive the Holy Spirit."* (NKJV)

Philip had not hesitated to accept the magician's confession of faith as real. But Simon's faith was shallow. Instead of adopting the thinking and lifestyle of Jesus, he continued to be dazzled by Philip's miracles and the apostle's ability to influence people (Acts 8:13, 18). Faith based on miracles and signs isn't trustworthy. Simon's faith had more holes than a fishnet:

1. *He was confused about grace.* He thought he could buy God's favor (Acts 8:18–20).

**hell**
place of the dead;
eternal punishment;
Satan's domain

**right**
straight, true, honest

*2.* *He was confused about power.* He couldn't see the difference between the power of the occult, magic, and superstition and the power of the Holy Spirit.

*3.* *He was confused about ministry.* He saw the work of the apostles as another kind of showmanship (Acts 8:21). If he had the formula, he could do it too!

*4.* *He was confused about the Holy Spirit's work.* His entrepreneurial mind saw it as a way to get rich, influence people, and satisfy his ego.

True Christian churches are always founded on apostolic teaching and authority.

When they had testified and proclaimed the word of the Lord, Peter and John returned to Jerusalem, preaching the gospel in many Samaritan villages.

## Inner Change Needed

ACTS 8:20–25 *But Peter said to him, "Your money perish with you, because you thought that the gift of God could be purchased with money! You have neither part nor portion in this matter, for your heart is not right in the sight of God. Repent therefore of this your wickedness, and pray God if perhaps the thought of your heart may be forgiven you. For I see that you are poisoned by bitterness and bound by iniquity." Then Simon answered and said, "Pray to the Lord for me, that none of the things which you have spoken may come upon me." So when they had testified and preached the word of the Lord, they returned to Jerusalem, preaching the gospel in many villages of the Samaritans. (NKJV)*

Peter blows the lid off Simon's mixed-up priorities. The idea that God's gifts go to the highest bidder is so corrupt it could only come straight from **hell**! J. B. Phillips translates Peter's response in Acts 8:20, "To hell with you and your money!"[10] Although he confessed faith in Christ, Simon's heart was not **right**. He was up to his pointy wizard's hat in spiritual trouble: He needed inner change—repentance.

Simon's "prayer request" was a magician's illusion. Sources outside the Bible report[11] he continued to chase his badly motivated dream of spiritual authority. After this, he moved to Rome where he became a hero of heretics whose ideas created disunity in the church for centuries. Non-Christian Romans honored him with a statue inscribed, *Semoni Sancto Deo*, "To Simon the holy god."

Christians rightly rejoice whenever a public figure or celebrity confesses faith in Christ and becomes identified with the Jesus movement. But fame and notoriety should not be confused with spiritual maturity. New Christians need time to grow in their faith and understanding of God's grace and Christ's way of life before they are pushed forward as spokesmen for the gospel or leaders in the church.

## Holy Hitchhiker

ACTS 8:26–29 *Now an angel of the Lord spoke to Philip, saying, "Arise and go toward the south along the road which goes down from Jerusalem to Gaza." This is desert. So he arose and went. And behold, a man of Ethiopia, a **eunuch** of great authority under Candace the queen of the Ethiopians, who had charge of all her treasury, and had come to Jerusalem to worship, was returning. And sitting in his chariot, he was reading Isaiah the prophet. Then the <u>Spirit said</u> to Philip, "Go near and overtake this chariot." (NKJV)*

As Peter and John returned to Jerusalem, the Lord gave Philip new orders: "Take a hike!" Obedient, Philip headed back into dangerous Judean territory where Saul was still harassing Christians. He hadn't gone far when the entourage of an important **Ethiopian** government official came down the road, headed home after a pilgrimage to the Holy City. He was the treasurer and personal attendant of Queen Candace (pronounced "kan-da-kee"), and a worshiper of Israel's God.

Jesus is the church's strategist. He puts people where he needs them if they listen to his voice.

**Spirit said**
1 Kings 19:12–13;
Isaiah 30:21

**Head**
Ephesians 4:15–16

**eunuch**
castrated male servant

**Ethiopian**
person from African kingdom on the Nile River near modern Sudan

**Head**
title for Christ emphasizing his role as CEO of the church

what others say

**Watchman Nee**

Divine work must be divinely initiated. A worker may be called directly by the Spirit, or indirectly through reading the Word, through preaching, or through circumstances; but whatever the means God uses to make known his will to a man, his must be the Voice heard through every other voice. He must be the One who speaks, no matter through what instrument the call may come. . . . It is from the **Head** that all our direction comes.[12]

## Seeker's Question: Who's the Lamb?

ACTS 8:30–35 *So Philip ran to him, and heard him reading the prophet Isaiah, and said, "Do you understand what you are reading?" And he said, "How can I, unless someone guides me?" And he asked Philip to come up and sit with him. The place in the Scripture which he read was this:*

*"He was led as a sheep to the slaughter;*
*And as a lamb before its shearer is silent,*
*So He opened not His mouth.*
*In His humiliation His justice was taken away,*
*And who will declare His generation?*
*For His life is taken from the earth."*

*So the eunuch answered Philip and said, "I ask you, of whom does the prophet say this, of himself or of some other man?" Then Philip opened his mouth, and beginning at this Scripture, preached Jesus to him.* (NKJV)

As he traveled, the African read aloud from the scroll of Isaiah 53:7–8. Philip ran to the chariot and asked if the Ethiopian understood what he was reading. "Come and ride with me," the man said. "Explain it to me."

Philip simply told the man what he knew: Isaiah was talking about Jesus bearing the injustice of the cross to save people from their sins. No sales pitch. No pulpit pounding. He just told the man what he knew.

## A Statement of Faith

ACTS 8:36–40 *Now as they went down the road, they came to some water. And the eunuch said, "See, here is water. What hinders me from being baptized?" Then Philip said, "If you believe with all your heart, you may." And he answered and said, "I believe that Jesus Christ is the Son of God." So he commanded the chariot to stand still. And both Philip and the eunuch went down into the water, and he baptized him. Now when they came up out of the water, the Spirit of the Lord caught Philip away, so that the eunuch saw him no more; and he went on his way rejoicing. But Philip was found at Azotus. And passing through, he preached in all the cities till he came to Caesarea.* (NKJV)

From what happened next, we can guess Philip, in his conversation with the African, included something like what Peter said at Pentecost: "Repent, and let every one of you be baptized in the name of Jesus Christ for the remission of sins" (Acts 2:38 NKJV).

rose with Christ
Romans 6:1–4

The entourage approached a desert stream, and the man got the idea to be baptized.

It was a statement of faith. So together, Philip and the eager-beaver believer splashed into the water. Philip baptized the man while his royal troupe watched. As they came out of the water, the Spirit whisked Philip away to his next assignment, and a dripping Ethiopian went home to tell the story and lay the foundation for the Ethiopian Christian church.

**what others say**

**William Barclay**

To the early Christians baptism was, whenever possible, by immersion and in running water. It symbolized . . . cleansing. . . . It marked a clean break. . . . [It] was a real union with Christ. As waters closed over a man's head he seemed to die with Christ and as he emerged he <u>rose with Christ</u>.[13]

When things got hot in Jerusalem, Philip and other Christians didn't stand around waiting to get clobbered! As they fled they talked about Jesus. Whatever happens, wherever Jesus's follower goes, he or she is there as Christ's witness—a storyteller of the good news. Contrary to what my sixth-grade teacher Ms. Anderson told me, neatness does not always count. The storyteller doesn't have to look good or be eloquent. He or she simply tells what he or she knows. And the news spreads!

Driving witnesses out of Jerusalem through Saul's persecution seems drastic. But as head of the church, Jesus Christ knew best what it would take to get his message out.

**Acts 8 Scattergun!**                                                           103

# Chapter Wrap-Up

- The day Stephen died, Saul launched a crusade to destroy the church. Men and women were jailed for the crime of following Jesus. Many escaped to the outlying villages, telling the Jesus story wherever they went. (Acts 8:1–4)

- Philip went to Samaria, where he preached and performed miracles. Many Samaritans believed in Jesus. One who believed and was baptized was a magician named Simon, who some people thought was some sort of god. (Acts 8:5–13)

- Peter and John were sent from Jerusalem to help establish the Samaritan church. They touched people, and the people received the Holy Spirit. (Acts 8:14–17)

- Simon the magician was impressed when he saw what happened when the apostles touched people. He offered to buy the ability to do what they were doing. Peter was outraged. (Acts 8:18–24)

- An angel told Philip to take a hike down the Gaza Road where he thumbed a ride with an African official on his way home after a visit to Jerusalem. The African believed on Jesus and was baptized. (Acts 8:25–40)

# Study Questions

1. What did God use to get Christians to leave Jerusalem and take the message of Christ to Judea and Samaria?

2. What happened in Samaria when Philip proclaimed Christ? Who was his most notable "convert"?

3. Identify three things that were different about the Holy Spirit's coming to the Samaritans. Why was it important for the apostles to be there?

4. Simon's attempt to buy the power to give people the Holy Spirit showed his confusion. Identify at least three areas of his confusion.

# Acts 9 Saul's Astonishment at Christian's Joy

## Let's Get Started

Saul of Tarsus could not erase the memory of Stephen's shining face. Stephen's last words, "Lord Jesus, receive my spirit" (Acts 7:59 NKJV), played over and over in Saul's mind like a broken record. "Lord, do not charge them with this sin" (Acts 7:60 NKJV). Lord Jesus . . . Lord Jesus . . . Lord Jesus.

He tried to drown the images by persecuting more people. Again and again, the zealous persecutor was secretly astonished at the serenity—even joy—with which these men and women met danger and death.

**what others say**

**Bishop Festo Kivengere**

I remember [a former Mau Mau fighter who had turned to Christ] . . . he said, "I was one who led a group of fighters to attack a Christian family at night. We were ordered to do it because they were 'hard-core resisters.' But to my surprise, that man loved us. He said he was not at all afraid to die, for he would immediately be with Jesus. Then he pleaded with us, not for his life, but for ours, that we awake and repent while there was still time. We killed him, but he died praying, 'Father, forgive them and give them time to turn about.' We went back to the forest, but the face of that man and his love never left me. At last his Jesus has found me, and now I want to tell everyone about him."

How do you destroy Christians like that? You beat them; they love you. You put them to shame; they think you have given them an opportunity to be creative. You kill them and they win you![1]

## Blind Fury

ACTS 9:1–2 *Then Saul, still breathing threats and murder against the disciples of the Lord, went to the high priest and asked letters from him to the synagogues of Damascus, so that if he found any who were of the Way, whether men or women, he might bring them bound to Jerusalem. (NKJV)*

**kill**
Acts 22:4; 26:10

**the Way**
John 14:6;
Acts 18:25–26; 19:9,
23; 22:4; 24:14, 22

**Gamaliel**
Acts 5:34–39

**expert**
Philippians 3:5–6

**zeal**
Philippians 3:6

**the Way**
nickname emphasizing Christianity as a distinct style of living

**extradition**
surrender of an accused person in one state to be tried by another state

**Tarsus**
important Roman city three hundred miles north of Jerusalem

Self-appointed champion of traditional religion, Saul boasted publicly of his intent to <u>kill</u> Christians if they did not renounce Jesus. The religious establishment gave his campaign of terror its approval. When harassed disciples fled, spreading the message of the Messiah as they went, Saul and the high priest agreed the campaign against **the Way** (Acts 9:2) should be taken beyond the walls of the Holy City.

In the Roman Empire the various peoples were governed by the laws of their own nations. According to Jewish law, the Sanhedrin in Jerusalem had authority over the six million Jews scattered throughout the Roman world. **Extradition** of escapees back to Jerusalem for punishment required authorization from the high priest. The "letters" Saul carried would be honored by both the secular government and the synagogue officials in Damascus.

## Profile of a Persecutor

From references in Acts—mostly what the man says about himself—we develop the following profile of this obsessed man Saul—later called Paul. He was

- a "young man" (see Acts 7:58)—meaning he was between twenty-four and forty years of age;

- a Jew, born a Roman citizen in **Tarsus** (see Acts 21:39; 22:3, 25–29);

- fluent in Greek, Aramaic, and Hebrew (see Acts 21:37, 40; 22:2);

- raised in Jerusalem (see Acts 22:3);

- a disciple of the respected Pharisee, <u>Gamaliel</u>, under whom he received a superior rabbinical education that probably began at age thirteen (see Acts 22:3);

- an <u>expert</u> in Jewish law (see Acts 22:3); and

- motivated in his persecution of Christians by <u>zeal</u> for God (see Acts 22:3).

"The rest of the story" of Saul of Tarsus is the subject of most of the rest of the book of Acts.

**shekinah**
Exodus 14:19–20;
24:15–18;
2 Chronicles 7:1

**from Jesus's face**
Luke 9:28–32;
2 Corinthians 4:6

## The Road to Truth

As Saul and his entourage of temple police reached a high point on the trail over Mount Hermon, suddenly spread out below them lay a white city on a green plain—like "a handful of pearls in a goblet of green."[4] **Damascus**, one of the oldest cities in the world, is 150 miles north of Jerusalem. Ten thousand Jews lived there. Consequently, there were many synagogues from which to flush out Christians to drag back to Jerusalem in chains. The trip took a week—time for the Holy Spirit to penetrate Saul's dark fury with questions.

Within sight of Damascus, the questions raised by his encounters with Christians were answered. Acts records three accounts of this moment—this one in Acts 9 and two first-person accounts in Acts 22 and 26 (see also 1 Corinthians 15:8–10; Galatians 1:13–17; and 1 Timothy 1:12–14).

## Smack Down!

**ACTS 9:3–4** *As he journeyed he came near Damascus, and suddenly a light shone around him from heaven. Then he fell to the ground, and heard a voice saying to him, "Saul, Saul, why are you persecuting Me?" (NKJV)*

It was high noon (see Acts 22:6; 26:13). A flash of light brighter than the sun knocked Saul flat! Some people think a mountain thunderstorm broke over the travelers, striking Saul with a lightning bolt and the Lord spoke to him out of the storm. Others suggest Saul was dazzled by what the Old Testament calls the **shekinah**, the radiance of God's personal **glory**, shining from Jesus's face.

**Damascus**
capital of modern Syria

**shekinah**
Hebrew for the special, visible presence of God

**glory**
splendor, radiance

**saw Jesus**
Acts 9:17, 27;
26:15–16;
1 Corinthians 9:1; 15:8

# The Last Appearance of Christ

> ACTS 9:5 *And he said, "Who are You, Lord?" Then the Lord said, "I am Jesus, whom you are persecuting. It is hard for you to kick against the goads."* (NKJV)

In that blazing light Saul saw something that changed him forever. Prostrate in dirt and camel dung on the Damascus Road, Saul <u>saw Jesus</u>—not a dream or vision of Jesus, but Jesus in person—the crucified, risen-again Christ (Acts 9:17, 27). Jesus spoke the persecutor's name, "Saul, Saul, why are you persecuting Me?" (Acts 9:4 NKJV).

Saul did not recognize his confronter. But he had sense enough to realize that whoever knocked him down and was talking to him was the Boss!

"I am Jesus, whom you are persecuting" (Acts 9:5 NKJV).

Talk about a whack upside the head! A swift kick in the convictions! A bop on the belief system! Judaism's "hero" fighting the influence of a dead Nazarene whose claims he thought could be dismissed, suddenly, in a flash of insight, realized that while he'd been chasing Christians, the Nazarene was alive and well and taking it all very personally!

---

**what others say**

**John R. W. Stott**

To begin with, we must hear his voice. . . . Sometimes we hear his voice through the prickings of the conscience, sometimes through the gropings of the mind. Or it may be a moral defeat, or the seeming emptiness and meaninglessness of our existence, or an inexplicable spiritual hunger, or a sickness, bereavement, pain or fear, by which we become aware that Christ is . . . speaking to us. Or his call may come through a friend, a preacher or a book. Whenever we hear, we must listen.[5]

---

# Three Blind Nights

> ACTS 9:6–9 *So he, trembling and astonished, said, "Lord, what do You want me to do?" Then the Lord said to him, "Arise and go into the city, and you will be told what you must do." And the men who journeyed with him stood speechless, hearing a voice but seeing no one. Then Saul arose from the ground, and when*

*his eyes were opened he saw no one. But they led him by the hand and brought him into Damascus. And he was three days without sight, and neither ate nor drank. (NKJV)*

"Go into town and wait for instructions." The light disappeared. The avenger of Judaism blinked his eyes. He was blind as a bat! His traveling companions saw the light and Saul's tumble, heard a strange sound (unintelligible to them), listened to Saul's side of the conversation, but had not the foggiest idea of what had just happened.

At Judas's Bed-and-Breakfast, Saul skipped breakfast. He spent three days and nights in the dark, fasting—no food, no drink—the radical sort of fasting reserved for urgent repentance and seeking God. He prayed. While he waited Saul had a **vision** of someone named Ananias coming to touch and heal him.

**go to**

**vision**
Genesis 46:2;
Daniel 10:7;
Luke 1:22;
Acts 10:3, 9–23;
18:9

**vision**
a revelation from God, often received when the person is in a dreamlike state

> **what others say**
>
> **William Barclay**
>
> There is all of Christianity in what the Risen Christ said to Paul, "Go into the city, and you will be told what to do." Up to this moment Paul had been doing what he liked, what he thought best, what his will dictated. From this time forward he would be told what to do. The Christian is a man who has ceased to do what he wants to do and who has begun to do what Christ wants him to do.[6]

## Reluctant Gofer

> **the big picture**
>
> **Acts 9:10–16**
>
> Meanwhile, in Damascus a disciple named Ananias had a vision in which God told him to go to the house of Judas on Straight Street and ask for a man from Tarsus named Saul. God told Ananias that Saul had a vision that Ananias would come, place his hands on him, and restore his sight. Ananias was willing to go, but he'd heard all about Saul's murderous mission. Ananias wondered if God knew what he was doing. God said, "Go, he is a chosen vessel of Mine."

Ananias was a well-respected, law-abiding member of the Jewish community in Damascus (see Acts 22:12) and a Christian disciple—follower of Christ—(Acts 9:10). He was listening for the Lord's voice.

His first response (before he knew the assignment) was "Here I am, Lord." When the Lord told him what he wanted him to do on Straight Street (see Illustration #8), Ananias began to make like a motorboat—"But-but-but-but . . ." (Acts 9:13). Saul was at the bottom of Ananias's list of people he was dying to meet. In his imagination, he could hear dungeon doors clanging shut behind him!

"Hold the phone, Lord! Me, 'reach out and touch' the Christian-hater of all time? That's like sending Chicken Little to lay hands on the Big Bad Wolf!" (Acts 9:13–14).

But the Lord insisted. "Go, for he is a chosen vessel of Mine to bear My name before Gentiles, kings, and the children of Israel" (Acts 9:15 NKJV).

Ananias did as he was told. By the time he reached the Straight Street Hotel, confidence and acceptance replaced suspicion. His first word to Saul, the sightless spiritual upstart, was "Brother" (Acts 9:17 NKJV).

what others say

**William Barclay**

In Christ, Paul and Ananias, the men who had been the bitterest of enemies, came together as brothers.[7]

**Illustration #8**
Map of Damascus—This map of Damascus shows Straight Street, the main east-to-west thoroughfare, which is called Darb al Mustaqim today. Ananias was sent to see Paul at the house of Judas on this street.

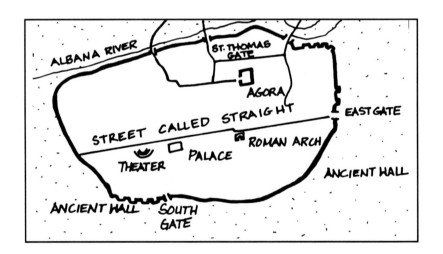

The Smart Guide to the Bible

# Transformation of the Troublemaker

**go to**

**personal suffering**
2 Corinthians
11:23–29

**nothing to deserve**
Ephesians 2:8–9;
1 Timothy 1:16

**light on**
2 Corinthians 4:6

*Acts 9:17–19 And Ananias went his way and entered the house; and laying his hands on him he said, "Brother Saul, the Lord Jesus, who appeared to you on the road as you came, has sent me that you may receive your sight and be filled with the Holy Spirit." Immediately there fell from his eyes something like scales, and he received his sight at once; and he arose and was baptized. So when he had received food, he was strengthened. Then Saul spent some days with the disciples at Damascus. (NKJV)*

Saul's spiritual **metamorphosis** wasn't complete until Ananias came. He emerged from his three-day encounter with the risen Jesus with four fundamental certainties, which became the driving force in his life:

**metamorphosis**
scientifically—process by which larva becomes butterfly; spiritually—rebirth, awakening

1. Jesus is Lord (Acts 9:5–6).

2. Gentiles and Jews alike must be told about Jesus (Acts 9:15).

3. Saul was God's chosen representative to take the message to the Gentiles (Acts 9:15).

4. This calling would be costly in terms of <u>personal suffering</u> (Acts 9:16).

## Saul's Process of Spiritual Reconstruction

The miracle of spiritual rebirth involved five important processes for Saul:

1. A personal encounter with Jesus (Acts 9:3–6). Jesus initiated it. Saul did <u>nothing to deserve</u> it. Like a hound on the scent of a coon Jesus pursued him and turned the <u>light on</u> in his rebellious, self-righteous brain so Saul could see him.

2. He surrendered to Jesus as Lord of his life (Acts 9:5).

3. Other Christians played an important role in Saul's conversion (Acts 9:10–19, 27–28). They forgave him for harm he'd done and accepted him as "brother" (Acts 9:17 NKJV).

4. Saul was filled with the Holy Spirit (Acts 9:17–18).

**5.** Saul's conversion was personal but not private. He (a) was baptized—public confession of his faith in Jesus (Acts 9:18); (b) was commissioned as Christ's ambassador-witness (Acts 9:15); and (c) became part of the believers' fellowship (Acts 9:19).

> what others say
>
> ### Billy Graham
>
> Conversion occurs when we repent and place our faith in Christ. But what is the process like as we approach the point of conversion? . . . The key word is variety. . . . The night I came to Christ there were several people around me weeping. I had no tears at all and wondered if my act of commitment was genuine. . . . Conversion is no less real to quiet people than to the more expressive or dramatic ones. . . . Jesus described the conversion experience like the movement of the wind (John 3:8). Wind can be quiet, gentle, or it can reach cyclone proportions. So it is with conversion, sometimes easy and tender, and other times a tornado which alters the entire landscape.[8]

## Bible Terms for Conversion

| Term | Definition | Scripture |
|------|-----------|-----------|
| Conversion | Turn to Christ; change beliefs, attitudes, behavior | Acts 15:3; 16:13–15; Romans 16:5; 1 Thessalonians 1:9; 1 Timothy 3:6 |
| Renewal | Restore spiritual life and relationship with God | Titus 3:5; Jeremiah 31:23–34 |
| Born again | Become a child of God by receiving Christ | John 1:12–13; 3:3, 5; 1 John 3:9 |
| Resurrection | Become alive to God; end separation caused by sin | Ephesians 2:1–7; Philippians 3:10–11 |
| New creation | Become a new person, one of God's new people | 2 Corinthians 5:17; 1 Peter 2:9–10 |
| Receive Christ | Actively welcome Christ into one's life | Romans 5:10–11; 2 Corinthians 5:16–21 |
| Reconciliation | Restoration of harmony with God | Romans 5:10–11; 2 Corinthians 5:16–21 |
| Saved | Rescued from sin's consequences | John 3:16; Romans 10:9–10 |
| Decision | Choice, commitment to follow Christ | Matthew 16:24; Joshua 24:15 |

# Maddening Metamorphosis

disciples
sympathizers, friends

## the big picture

### Acts 9:20-24

After his encounter with the Lord, Saul told the story of his conversion in the synagogues, announcing that Jesus is God's Son, the Messiah. The change in Saul shocked his hearers, who knew he had been sent to Damascus to arrest Christians. An assassination plot developed.

At first, Saul was welcomed as a respected traveling teacher. His letters from the high priest (Acts 9:2) opened the door. But the story he told was different from the one they expected to hear. He had changed 180 degrees. And the change drove the enemies of Jesus crazy!

A group of overzealous Jews decided Saul must be terminated! So they posted assassination squads at the town gates to rub the "turncoat" out if he ventured outside the city. Saul's past now mirrored his future. The fulfillment of Ananias's prophecy had begun (Acts 9:16).

## The Principle of Interdependence

ACTS 9:25 *Then the **disciples** took him by night and let him down through the wall in a large basket. (NKJV)*

Meanwhile, back at the church, the very people Saul had been sent to arrest became his spiritual family. He soon discovered how absolutely essential other Christians were to his physical as well as spiritual survival. When his would-be assassins hatched their plot, it became clear Paul had to make himself scarce if he was going to see sunrise. In the middle of the night his Christian friends sneaked him out a hole in the city wall, letting him down in a basket. He escaped into the night, headed for Jerusalem.

From the start, Saul learned the vital principle of mutual dependence by which the healthy Christian community functions. First, he found his way into the city after being blinded only with the help of his traveling companions. Then, his information about God's plan for his life came through Ananias. Then came his escape through the wall—if not for his Christian brothers, his career would have ended in Damascus, with an assassin's knife.

**teamed up**
Acts 11:25–26;
13:2–3

The Lord's instructions often come to us through others. It is essential that we learn the principle of interdependence: We need each other. Direct revelation from God can sometimes lead to independence, individualism, spiritual pride, and separation from others in the community of faith. The Lord arranged for Saul to learn this principle early.

## Barnabas Convinced of Truth of Saul's Conversion

ACTS 9:26–27 *And when Saul had come to Jerusalem, he tried to join the disciples; but they were all afraid of him, and did not believe that he was a disciple. But Barnabas took him and brought him to the apostles. And he declared to them how he had seen the Lord on the road, and that He had spoken to him, and how he had preached boldly at Damascus in the name of Jesus. (NKJV)*

Another lesson in dependence on other Christians waited for Saul in Jerusalem. When he left for Damascus, he had been "breathing threats and murder against the disciples of the Lord" (Acts 9:1 NKJV). He'd done a pretty good job of wrecking the Jerusalem church (see Acts 8:1, 3). And his name was definitely not on the top of the Christians' "Most Desirable Dinner Guest List"! When he tried to make contact with them on his return from Damascus, they prudently slammed the door in his face. They were sure it was a scheme to infiltrate the believers' circle to destroy it. Nobody would let him get close enough to tell his story.

Until Barnabas. Barnabas (see Acts 4:36) took the risk of listening to Saul's story and became convinced his conversion was real. He became Saul's access into the wary Jerusalem fellowship. Later Saul and Barnabas <u>teamed up</u> for ministry.

## Agitator, Go Home!

ACTS 9:28–30 *So he was with them at Jerusalem, coming in and going out. And he spoke boldly in the name of the Lord Jesus and disputed against the Hellenists, but they attempted to kill him. When the brethren found out, they brought him down to Caesarea and sent him out to Tarsus. (NKJV)*

In Jerusalem, Saul took up where Stephen left off, ministering among the <u>Grecian Jews</u>, as if the former persecutor felt driven to continue the martyr's unfinished work. The reaction was a rerun. Stephen's killers added Saul to their hit list. Once again, Saul's Christian brothers saved his neck, whisking him out of town and sending him packing to Tarsus, his boyhood home.

It is impossible to imagine the spread of the Christian gospel throughout the Roman Empire apart from Saul's conversion and ministry. As the Lord's "chosen vessel" (Acts 9:15 NKJV), Saul devoted the rest of his life, including all his material and physical resources, to the service of Christ the Lord who surprised him on the Damascus road.

Once we see who Jesus is, we are never the same again. We too become his "chosen vessels." Whether the vision comes in dramatic Damascus road fashion or through quiet interaction with the Bible and the Spirit, the only reasonable response is to <u>give ourselves</u>, including all our energies and material resources, to serving him.

**Grecian Jews**
Acts 6:1, 8–10

**give ourselves**
Romans 12:1–2

**saints**
Acts 9:13, 32, 41;
26:10

**saints**
"holy ones";
Christians, God's
people

## Peter Visits Communities Outside Jerusalem

**ACTS 9:31–32** *Then the churches throughout all Judea, Galilee, and Samaria had peace and were edified. And walking in the fear of the Lord and in the comfort of the Holy Spirit, they were multiplied. Now it came to pass, as Peter went through all parts of the country, that he also came down to the **saints** who dwelt in Lydda. (NKJV)*

After Saul the converted troublemaker—whose capacity for causing a ruckus wherever he went is legendary—left Jerusalem, there was a little window of peace for the early Christians.

Peter used the window to visit Christian communities outside Jerusalem. During his trip to the country two miracles powerfully impacted the Judean coastal area along the Mediterranean Sea.

## The First Miracle

**ACTS 9:33–35** *There he found a certain man named Aeneas, who had been bedridden eight years and was paralyzed. And Peter said to him, "Aeneas, Jesus the Christ heals you. Arise and make your bed." Then he arose immediately. So all who dwelt at Lydda and Sharon saw him and turned to the Lord. (NKJV)*

**go to**

**Joppa**
Joshua 19:46;
2 Chronicles 2:16;
Ezra 3:7;
Jonah 1:3

**used her material resources**
Proverbs 31:20, 31;
Matthew 5:16

**Joppa**
seaport for
Jerusalem

**Tabitha**
means "gazelle,"
a small, graceful
antelope with soft,
bright eyes

The first miracle took place at the junction between two trade routes—the Egypt to Babylon road and the Joppa to Jerusalem highway—at the town of Lydda. A man named Aeneas had been disabled for eight years. Peter said, "Jesus the Christ heals you." Aeneas got up; his paralysis vanished. He went around showing people what had happened, and people turned to the Lord.

**what others say**

**Mother Basilea Schlink**

Cures, which are effected in the name of Jesus, reveal to people that the stream of divine life is continually flowing from the One who is life. His strength is given not only to revive soul and spirit, but also to heal the bodies of sick people and to awaken new life.[9]

## Down-to-Earth Witness for Christ

ACTS 9:36–38 *At Joppa there was a certain disciple named Tabitha, which is translated Dorcas. This woman was full of good works and charitable deeds which she did. But it happened in those days that she became sick and died. When they had washed her, they laid her in an upper room. And since Lydda was near Joppa, and the disciples had heard that Peter was there, they sent two men to him, imploring him not to delay in coming to them.* (NKJV)

Eleven miles from Lydda in the Mediterranean coastal city of **Joppa** (now part of Tel Aviv) lived a Christian woman named **Tabitha**, noted for the lovely way she used her material resources and sewing skills to help the poor. In that mixed community of Aramaic- and Greek-speaking peoples, this woman was a byword in both cultures for kindness and caring. Tabitha died. Her body was prepared for burial, which, according to Jewish custom, would take place before sundown the day of her death.

Christian women like Tabitha used their skills and talents to help the poor in Jesus's name. Their down-to-earth witness for Christ had a powerful impact on the people they helped.

# "Tabitha, Arise!"

**go to**

**almost exactly**
Mark 5:40–41

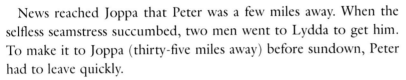

**the big picture**

### Acts 9:39–43

Peter went to Joppa. He prayed and then commanded Tabitha to get up. She did. When people saw the miracle Peter had performed through God's power, many became believers.

News reached Joppa that Peter was a few miles away. When the selfless seamstress succumbed, two men went to Lydda to get him. To make it to Joppa (thirty-five miles away) before sundown, Peter had to leave quickly.

Peter had seen Jesus raise the dead. So when they took him upstairs to where Tabitha's body lay in state, he did <u>almost exactly</u> what he'd watched Jesus do—even down to the words he said. He sent the mourners out, prayed, and said to the dead woman, "Tabitha, arise" (Acts 9:40 NKJV) Then he called the teary-eyed mourners back and presented her to them . . . alive!

The impact was powerful—all over Joppa people "believed on the Lord" (Acts 9:42 NKJV). Miracles and answers to prayer convince people to put their faith in Jesus.

Biblical church growth is measured in (1) impact in the lives of people, (2) encouragement or hope, (3) additions to the community of faith, and (4) the extent to which believers' lives honor the Lord (Acts 9:31).

**key point**

**what others say**

### Ajith Fernando

Can this [raising of the dead] happen today too? Jesus did it, the apostles did it, and there is no prohibition to Christians in later ages praying for the dead. We must, of course, remember that death is God's gateway to ultimate triumph, and many wonderful Christians, like Stephen and James in Acts, were not spared "untimely" deaths. Therefore, we must have considerable discernment and sensitivity before praying for the raising of the dead. But submission to Scripture prohibits me from saying that we should never pray this way.[10]

## Chapter Wrap-Up

- When Christians escaped Saul's persecution in Jerusalem, he pursued them to Damascus. On the way, Jesus appeared to him and turned his life around. (Acts 9:1–6)

- Saul was left blind and waiting for the Lord's instructions. Ananias came. The Holy Spirit filled Saul, healed his eyes, and disclosed God's plan for him. (Acts 9:7–18)

- Saul immediately preached Christ in Damascus. Enemies plotted to kill him. Christian friends helped him escape. In Jerusalem, Christians were afraid of him. Barnabas believed in him and convinced them his conversion was real. (Acts 9:19–31)

- After Saul left for Tarsus, the church in Judea, Galilee, and Samaria experienced a time of peace and growth. Peter visited the Christians in the Judean countryside, where two notable miracles convinced many to believe in Jesus. (Acts 9:31–43)

## Study Questions

1. With what question did Jesus confront Saul on the road to Damascus? What spiritual principle did this question reveal concerning Jesus and his followers?

2. Identify four of the five important spiritual processes involved in Saul's spiritual reconstruction or conversion.

3. What happened when Saul first came back to Jerusalem, and who helped him become accepted among the believers?

4. What resulted from the healing of Aeneas and the raising of Tabitha from the dead?

# Acts 10–11 Challenging Phase of the New Revolution

**Chapter Highlights:**
- The God-Fearer
- Peter and the Three Men
- Concerned Jewish Christians
- Fugitives on Mission
- The First "Christians"

## Let's Get Started

Peter and his sidekick John were in Samaria when the Samaritans, a mixed breed of **"impure Jews,"** received the Holy Spirit and became followers of Jesus (Acts 8:25). Acceptance of the Samaritans into the church was a big stretch even for fully informed Christian Jews like Peter and John. It went against lifelong anti-Samaritan prejudice. But Jesus <u>always accepted</u> Samaritans. What else could his followers do?

Even with inclusion of the Samaritans, however, Christianity remained mostly a Jewish thing. But the young church's CEO had bigger plans! He'd outlined his strategy in Acts 1:8—"You shall receive power when the Holy Spirit has come upon you; and you shall be witnesses to Me in Jerusalem, and in all Judea and Samaria, and to the end of the earth" (NKJV). With the Jerusalem campaign going strong and new churches popping up "throughout all Judea, Galilee, and Samaria," the movement took a deep breath (Acts 9:31 NKJV). The most challenging phase of the revolution was just around the next bend in the road.

The importance of what happened next is underscored by the amount of space given to it by Luke—the story is repeated <u>three times</u> in Acts! The dramatic revelation to the young church that non-Jews were to be accepted as full participants was a major turning point.

**go to**

**always accepted**
John 4:4–42

**three times**
Acts 10; 11:4–17;
15:7–9

**impure Jews**
Samaritans were a
mix of Jew and
Gentile parentage

## The God-Fearer

ACTS 10:1–2 *There was a certain man in Caesarea called Cornelius, a centurion of what was called the Italian Regiment, a devout man and one who feared God with all his household, who gave alms generously to the people, and prayed to God always.* (NKJV)

Thirty-five miles up the coast from Joppa was Caesarea, center of Roman occupational government in Judea and a showplace of

go to

**centurion**
Matthew 27:54;
Acts 23:17; 27:43

**God-fearers**
Acts 13:26, 50;
17:4, 17

**short of circumcision**
Acts 11:3

Roman culture. The city was built by **Herod the Great** and named for Emperor Caesar Augustus. Its citizens included both Jews and **Gentiles**. A military officer named Cornelius was stationed there. Cornelius was a Roman. He was a **centurion**, like a captain today (see Illustration #9), assigned to the **Italian Regiment**. He and his family were "**God-fearers**," a term for Gentiles attracted to Judaism who attended the synagogue, prayed to God, and lived by Jewish moral principles, but were not fully converted to Judaism because they stopped short of circumcision.

**Illustration #9**
Centurion—
Cornelius was a
Roman centurion.
He would have worn
a ceremonial helmet
and carried a battle
shield.

**Herod the Great**
"King" of Judea
when Jesus was
born

**Gentiles**
non-Jews

**centurion**
commander of one
hundred soldiers

**Italian Regiment**
detachment of sol-
diers recruited in
Italy

**God-fearers**
Jews called them
"Proselytes of the
Gate"—almost Jews

## Roman Military Structure

| Roman Military Designation | Definition | Modern Equivalent |
|---|---|---|
| Legion | Six thousand men | Division |
| Cohort | Each legion divided into ten cohorts of 600 men | Battalion |
| Centuries | Each cohort divided into six centuries of 100 men | Company |
| Centurions | Each century commanded by a centurion; centurions were called "the backbone of the Roman army."[1] | Captain |

what others say

### Maude De Joseph West

Cornelius . . . was a good man, a devout man, a generous man, but he was still a Gentile and no Jew would have eaten at table with him any more than you would get down on the floor and drink milk from a dish with your cat.[2]

### John Kennedy

In the heyday of Greek and Roman culture the Jewish way of life had a definite appeal to many [Gentiles]. . . . Proselytes (to Judaism) were of two orders, "Proselytes of Righteousness" and "Proselytes of the Gate." The former were obliged to undergo the rite of circumcision and baptism, undertook to obey all the observations of Jewish law, and received all the privileges of a born Jew. . . . The latter had a much looser, yet none the less vital attachment to the Jewish community. They were not circumcised, and probably not baptized, neither were they bound by the ceremonial observances of the law, but they worshipped regularly in the synagogue, and were bound by the moral precepts of the law which the Jews regarded as binding on all mankind. In the Acts of the Apostles these people are referred to as "devout men" or those that "fear God."[3]

## Your Prayers Are Answered!

ACTS 10:3–8 *About the ninth hour of the day he saw clearly in a vision an angel of God coming in and saying to him, "Cornelius!" And when he observed him, he was afraid, and said, "What is it, lord?" So he said to him, "Your prayers and your alms have come up for a memorial before God. Now send men to Joppa, and send for Simon whose surname is Peter. He is lodging with Simon, a tanner, whose house is by the sea. He will tell you what you must do." And when the angel who spoke to him had departed, Cornelius called two of his household servants and a devout soldier from among those who waited on him continually. So when he had explained all these things to them, he sent them to Joppa. (NKJV)*

God did not wait for Jewish Christians to reach out to the Gentiles. (He might still be waiting!) Captain Cornelius was a **devout**, generous Gentile seeking God. An angel appeared to this noble Roman during observance of evening prayers. God had observed his devotion and generosity. The angel's terminology is straight out of the Jewish worship manual: Cornelius's prayers and

**go to**

**memorial**
Joshua 4:7;
Exodus 12:14;
Luke 22:19;
1 Corinthians
11:24–25

**3 p.m.**
Acts 3:1

**prayer time**
Psalm 55:17;
Daniel 6:10

**no-no list**
Leviticus 11

gifts to the poor had "come up" to God like the aroma of a pleasing sacrifice. God accepted his devotion and generosity as a "memorial" (Leviticus 2:2), an act of gratitude for God's **grace**.

Captain Cornelius longed for God. As a pagan he was sick of the **multiplicity** of immoral and powerless pagan deities. "The answer to your spiritual hunger is nearby," the angel told him.

(The angel might have added: "If the wind is blowing in from the sea, just follow your nose to the tanner's house!" Tanning hides is a smelly business.)

Cornelius wasted no time. Even though it was after 3 p.m., he dispatched three men to Joppa (about thirty-five miles away) with orders to bring back Peter (Acts 10:7–8).

## What's for Lunch?

ACTS 10:9–13 *The next day, as they went on their journey and drew near the city, Peter went up on the housetop to pray, about the sixth hour. Then he became very hungry and wanted to eat; but while they made ready, he fell into a trance and saw heaven opened and an object like a great sheet bound at the four corners, descending to him and let down to the earth. In it were all kinds of four-footed animals of the earth, wild beasts, creeping things, and birds of the air. And a voice came to him, "Rise, Peter; kill and eat."* (NKJV)

It was midday at Simon the Tanner's odoriferous cottage by the sea—prayer time, not mealtime. Jews ate two meals a day—a light meal in mid-morning and a more substantial meal in late afternoon. Peter was on the roof of the house, where he could catch the Mediterranean breezes. He was praying. He was hungry.

His rooftop experience is called *ekstasis* (Acts 10:10). As Peter saw the huge tablecloth being lowered from the sky and spread before him containing animals, reptiles, and birds—all on the Jewish no-no list of "**unclean**" creatures to be avoided—he was shocked! A voice told Peter to get up, kill something to eat, and dig in.

## Start the Revolution Without Me!

ACTS 10:14–16 *But Peter said, "Not so, **Lord**! For I have never eaten anything common or unclean." And a voice spoke to him*

**grace**
loving-kindness,
mercy

**multiplicity**
a great number

**ekstasis**
"a displacement of
the mind from its
ordinary state and
self-possession, an
ecstasy, a trance"[4]

**unclean**
prohibited by Old
Testament laws of
ritual purity

**Lord**
God the Father,
Jesus, and the Holy
Spirit are all
addressed this way
in Acts

*again the second time, "What God has cleansed you must not call common." This was done three times. And the object was taken up into heaven again. (NKJV)*

**go to**

commitment to God
Leviticus 11:43–44

The sight before him and the instruction to "kill and eat" left Peter dumbfounded. As a moderately orthodox Jew he'd carefully observed the Jewish prohibitions against contact with anything impure—and what was "impure" was carefully spelled out in the Mosaic Law. These laws of ritual purity were so deeply ingrained in his psyche he was even willing to debate God!

## what others say

### Lawrence O. Richards

In the Old Testament community of faith, <u>commitment to God</u> was demonstrated by isolation from anything or anyone that was ritually unclean. Laws of ritual purity touched on every phase of a person's life—from conception and birth to clothing that might be worn, food that might be eaten, and treatment of the dead. The intent of these laws of separation was to constantly remind the Jewish people that they were set apart to God, and that they were to honor God in every aspect of their lives.[5]

## Clean and Unclean Animals[6] According to Leviticus 11

| Category | Classification Principle | Examples |
|---|---|---|
| Land animals | If it has a split hoof and chews the cud it is clean. Animals with paws or that travel in any other way are unclean. | Camel, badger, pig, weasel, rat, lizards of all types are unclean. Cattle, goats, sheep, deer are clean. |
| Water creatures | If it has fins and scales it is clean. | Catfish, eels, shellfish are unclean. |
| Birds | Specific birds are restricted. Birds of prey and carrion eaters are unclean. | Eagles, vultures, hawks, ravens, owls, cormorant, osprey, storks, heron, hoopoe, bats are unclean. |
| Insects | Flying insects that walk, except those with jointed legs, are unclean. | Locusts, katydids, crickets, grasshoppers are clean. |

Christ's word is final on all matters of faith and practice. In Peter's case, the Spirit of Jesus made it clear that arbitrary Old Testament prohibitions had ended. The New Testament way of relating to God would not be by keeping rules, but by responding to the Spirit.

*key point*

**voice**
1 Kings 19:11–13;
Isaiah 30:21

**voice of the Spirit**
inward conviction;
sense of the right
thing; silent, per-
sonal message from
God perceived in
back of one's mind

While Peter was still thinking about the vision, the Spirit said to him, "Go down and go with them, doubting nothing; for I have sent them" (Acts 10:20 NKJV).

## Peter and the Three Men

ACTS 10:17–20 *Now while Peter wondered within himself what this vision which he had seen meant, behold, the men who had been sent from Cornelius had made inquiry for Simon's house, and stood before the gate. And they called and asked whether Simon, whose surname was Peter, was lodging there. While Peter thought about the vision, the Spirit said to him, "Behold, three men are seeking you. Arise therefore, go down and go with them, doubting nothing; for I have sent them."* (NKJV)

Peter had never "done lunch" like this before! He wrestled with the meaning of what he'd just experienced. As the disquieting smorgasbord faded from view, he heard foreign voices. They were at the tanner's front gate asking for Peter. At this point the voice in the vision became a personal, inner voice. The **voice of the Spirit** told him to go downstairs, meet the visitors, and not to hesitate to go with them. The Spirit added, "I have sent them."

> what others say
>
> **Mother Basilea Schlink**
>
> Every morning I ask [the Holy Spirit] for his leading and guidance. Then it is as if there were someone standing beside me and speaking to me, and yet I hear no voice. . . . What a gift! We can trust in the Holy Spirit and leave the guidance to him.[7]

## Breakthrough!

ACTS 10:21–22 *Then Peter went down to the men who had been sent to him from Cornelius, and said, "Yes, I am he whom you seek. For what reason have you come?" And they said, "Cornelius the centurion, a just man, one who fears God and has a good reputation among all the nation of the Jews, was divinely instructed by a holy angel to summon you to his house, and to hear words from you."* (NKJV)

All his life Peter had been taught to see Gentiles as impure. He would not enter a Gentile's house for fear of touching something "unclean." Contact with anything unclean required a process of ritual cleansing before one could participate in worship. Israel must be a "separated" people, **consecrated** to God.

But it was time for change. The old rules of separation must be scrapped if the Jesus movement was to take the next step toward world conquest: witness "to the end of the earth" (Acts 1:8 NKJV). If not, the Jesus revolution would end before it had scarcely begun because it would be forever trapped behind the growth-stifling walls of Judaism. For the good news of salvation through Jesus Christ to be offered to "whoever" (John 3:16; Acts 2:21), the barriers between Jews and Gentiles had to come down.

### Eating with Gentiles

Specifically the voice in the vision told Peter to eat what is unclean. That very day and in the days following he would find himself eating with "unclean" Gentiles (Acts 10:23; 11:2). But food wasn't really the issue, although scrapping the outdated food laws was necessary if Jewish and non-Jewish believers were to eat together. Acceptance and fellowship were the issues.

<u>Eating together</u> is an act of fellowship and acceptance. It's why Christians often "break bread" (share meals and celebrate the Lord's Supper) together. But at issue in Peter's mind-altering vision was God's plan for the church to open its doors (and hearts) to believing Gentiles and accept them as <u>part of Christ's body</u> . . . without reservations.

**go to**

**eating together**
Acts 1:4; 2:42, 46

**part of Christ's body**
1 Corinthians 12:13

**consecrated**
set apart for a holy purpose

## <u>Jump of Faith</u>

key point

### the big picture
#### Acts 10:23–33

Peter invited the men at the gate to be his overnight guests. The next day he and six Jewish Christian men from Joppa headed for Caesarea. The centurion had invited his Gentile relatives and friends to meet Peter. Peter told how God had dealt with him about his prejudice toward Gentiles and asked Cornelius why he'd sent for him. Cornelius told about the angel's visit.

Peter the brash was not one to let grass grow under his feet when it came to acting on orders from the Lord. Ignoring his personal discomfort and tossing aside the risk of censure by fellow Jews, he went

**angel's visit**
Acts 10:1–8

**kosher**
suitable for Jews
to eat

down to meet the men from Caesarea. The light began to dawn: "Unclean" animals in the vision were metaphors for people he had been seeing as "unclean." Peter's actions and words show in four ways that he got the message and broke through to a new way of seeing people:

1. Peter welcomed as guests the Gentile messengers who stood at the gate not expecting to be invited into a Jewish home (Acts 10:23). It was an easy first step. It didn't involve eating anything that wasn't **kosher**.

2. Peter returned with Cornelius's men—no questions asked (Acts 10:23, 29). Anticipating the need for witnesses to stand with him when the inevitable storm of criticism struck, he took along six Christian brothers from Joppa (Acts 11:12).

3. When Peter arrived Captain Cornelius met him at the door, wondering if he would cross the threshold into a Gentile's house. Peter walked right in (Acts 10:25, 27).

4. The house was full of people—Gentile people—Cornelius's friends and relatives. Peter told them about his change of mind: "You know how unlawful it is for a Jewish man to keep company with or go to one of another nation. But God has shown me that I should not call any man common or unclean. Therefore I came without objection as soon as I was sent for" (Acts 10:28–29 NKJV).

## Gentile God-Fearers Gain the Gospel

> *the big picture*
>
> **Acts 10:34–43**
>
> Peter talked to the Gentiles at Cornelius's house about Jesus, his anointing with the Holy Spirit, his goodness and healing, how God was with him, his death on the cross and resurrection from the dead, and how trusting him brings forgiveness.

When Cornelius told about the <u>angel's visit</u> and his instructions to send for Peter (Acts 10:30–32), Peter responded with a declaration of the gospel's inclusiveness: "In truth I perceive that God shows no partiality. But in every nation whoever fears Him and works righteousness is accepted by Him" (Acts 10:34–35 NKJV).

Like Cornelius, the friends and relatives gathered to hear Peter "feared God" (Acts 10:2, 35)—Gentiles who, though not converts to Judaism, prayed to Israel's God, and gave money to the synagogue and the poor. They were not in the dark about Jesus—they'd heard the Christian message (Acts 10:36–38). They only needed to be reminded of the facts and told the good news was for them.

Peter's talk clues us in to the things early Christians shared when they witnessed to non-Jewish people:

- Jesus is Lord of all people, sent by God to bring the good news of peace with God (Acts 10:34–36).
- Jesus was empowered by the Holy Spirit to do good, heal, and free people from the devil's bondage (Acts 10:37).
- Jesus was crucified (Acts 10:39).
- God raised him from the dead; many saw him alive (Acts 10:40–41).
- Christians are witnesses to the reality of his resurrection life (Acts 10:41).
- God has appointed Jesus to judge all the world's people (Acts 10:42).
- Everyone who believes in Jesus receives forgiveness through **his name** (Acts 10:43).

Then Peter said, "Can anyone forbid water, that these should not be baptized who have received the Holy Spirit just as we have?" (Acts 10:47 NKJV). So he ordered that they be baptized in the name of Jesus Christ. Then they asked Peter to stay with them for a few days.

## Pardon the Glorious Interruption!

the big picture

**Acts 10:44–48**

While Peter was still speaking these words, the Holy Spirit came on all who heard the message. The circumcised believers who had come with Peter were astonished that the gift of the Holy Spirit had been poured out even on the Gentiles. For they heard them speaking in tongues and praising God.

**filled**
Acts 2:4;
Ephesians 5:18

**new languages**
Acts 2:4; 19:6;
1 Corinthians 12–14

**objections**
Acts 8:36; 11:17

The crowd of God-fearers was ready to take the plunge. Before Peter could end his sermon his listeners were *all* <u>filled</u> with the Holy Spirit and spoke in <u>new languages</u>! Turning to the Jewish Christians who'd come with him, Peter asked if there were any <u>objections</u> to these Gentiles being baptized as Christians. No objection was heard, and all were baptized, declaring their faith in Jesus (Acts 10:44–48).

Peter and his Jewish compadres stayed a few more days to teach and help establish the new church at Cornelius's house in Caesarea.

The barriers of culture and race began to crumble. The door to the Gentiles was flung open. It was just the beginning of God's strategy for broadcasting the gospel. Within a few decades, what began at Cornelius's house expanded to encompass the entire Roman world. Paul, soon to be known as "the apostle to the Gentiles," expressed the principle involved: "There is neither Jew nor Greek, there is neither slave nor free, there is neither male nor female; for you are all one in Christ Jesus" (Galatians 3:28 NKJV).

**what others say**

### F. F. Bruce

The descent of the Spirit on those Gentiles was outwardly manifested in much the same way as it had been when the original disciples received the Spirit at Pentecost: they spoke with tongues and proclaimed the mighty works of God (see Acts 2:4, 11). Apart from such external manifestations, none of the Jewish believers present . . . would have been so ready to accept the reality of the spirit's coming on them. . . . As in Peter's vision the voice of God overruled food restrictions . . . so now the act of God in sending the Spirit overruled the sacred tradition which forbade association with Gentiles.[8]

## <u>Concerned Jewish Christians</u>

**ACTS 11:1–3** *Now the apostles and brethren who were in Judea heard that the Gentiles had also received the word of God. And when Peter came up to Jerusalem, those of the circumcision contended with him, saying, "You went in to uncircumcised men and ate with them!"* (NKJV)

Peter's extended time with Cornelius's family and friends at Caesarea did two things. First, it gave time for news of what Peter had done to reach Jerusalem and be discussed over the back fence and down at the fish market before he returned from his trip to the country. Second, the fact that he spent several days living and (especially) eating with Gentiles intensified the anxiety and ire of concerned Jewish Christians in Jerusalem.

## The Concern of the Circumcised

The whole church heard the gossip (Acts 11:1). Most disturbed was a group called "those of the circumcision." Actually, all Jewish males were circumcised, but this phrase designated a group of Christian Jews who were especially concerned that Gentiles should submit to the rite of circumcision (in other words, become Jews) before being fully accepted into the church. Today's English Version calls them "those who were in favor of circumcising Gentiles."[9]

Of course, these folks had seen no vision nor heard the Lord's voice sweeping away the old prohibitions. They'd not been there when the Spirit came to the Gentiles. The very idea of Peter going in to ceremonially unclean homes and eating nonkosher food with ceremonially unclean people made the hair stand up on the back of their sanctified necks!

the big picture

### Acts 11:4-17

Peter told about his rooftop vision, the trip to Caesarea, the conversation with Cornelius, and the coming of the Holy Spirit on the Gentiles just as the Spirit had come on the disciples at Pentecost.

## "The Spirit Made Me Do It!"

Peter simply reported what had happened. The six brothers from Joppa were there to back up his story (Acts 11:12). Having had a little time since the Cornelius incident to reflect on it, Peter also shared his interpretation:

1. The episode at Caesarea was a fulfillment of Jesus's promise to baptize believers with the Holy Spirit (Acts 1:5; 11:16).

2. God's acceptance of the Gentiles was verified by the exact same gift he'd given the 120 on the day of Pentecost—the gift of his Spirit (Acts 2:38–39; 11:17).

**3.** Besides—"What do you want me to do? Pick a fight with God?" (Acts 11:17). Peter tried that on the roof of the tanner's scented seaside domicile. God had the last word then. Peter wasn't about to try to talk him out of it now.

## The Miracle of Acceptance

ACTS 11:18 *When they heard these things they became silent; and they glorified God, saying, "Then God has also granted to the Gentiles repentance to life." (NKJV)*

Considering they had all grown up indoctrinated in prejudice, the ease with which the other disciples accepted Peter's conclusions was nothing short of miraculous! No sullen grumbling, muttering under their breath, or opposition. They praised God!

Peter was convicted and changed, never to go back. But not everyone's experience was long lasting. Some of the people were filled with praise at first, but they saw things differently later on when they realize just how many Gentiles joined the church.

As believers in the twenty-first century, we are also called to a radical acceptance of others. The world sees and judges people on the basis of race, background, occupation, age, and appearance. But we are to see others as fellow believers or as people who need the Lord. It is not easy learning to accept others; the early Christians are proof of that. But it is one of the changes followers of Jesus Christ are called to make. With whom do you associate that no minister would normally contact?

Gentiles have always been included in the Lord's plan to restore people to fellowship with God. When the time was right, he cut through the barriers of human prejudice, reluctance, and fear and drew them to himself. It was so clearly an act of God that even the mouths of the detractors were shut for a while.

## Fugitives on Mission

ACTS 11:19 *Now those who were scattered after the persecution that arose over Stephen traveled as far as Phoenicia, Cyprus, and Antioch, preaching the word to no one but the Jews only. (NKJV)*

The persecution following Stephen's martyrdom had sent Jesus's followers scurrying to the hills (Acts 8:1). As they fled they shared the good news all over Judea and Samaria (Acts 8–10). Even so the faith of Christ spread no farther than a 100-mile radius of Jerusalem. But some fugitives kept going—to places like Phoenicia (150 miles), Cyprus (250 miles), and Antioch (300 miles) (Acts 11:19). Those who escaped beyond the 100-mile limit were mostly Greek-speaking Jews. Raised outside the **Holy Land** (Acts 11:20), they were at home in foreign places.

**Holy Land**
Israel

**Eusebius**
early church historian

**Jerome**
early church theologian

## The Queen of the East

ACTS 11:20 *But some of them were men from Cyprus and Cyrene, who, when they had come to Antioch, spoke to the Hellenists, preaching the Lord Jesus.* (NKJV)

A few persecution-escapees stopped when they reached the free Roman city of Antioch on the Orontes, third largest city in the Roman Empire, with a population of 500,000. Antioch was one of the most beautiful cities in the empire, often called "Antioch the Beautiful" or "Queen of the East." Its balmy air was fragrant with the scent of roses from which rare Antiochene perfumes were made. It was a cosmopolitan town. From all over the empire people moved there to share the prosperity. Among the migrants were many Jews. Jews were well treated in Antioch. The synagogue there was considered the second most beautiful on earth. Gentile converts to Judaism and "God-fearers" were numerous.

Antioch was a pagan city filled with temples. At the foot of Mount Silpius, south of the city, was a huge rock formation that looked like a faceless human head. Pagan mythology said this was the head of Charon, the god in charge of transporting dead souls to the underworld. Nearby was the Grove of Daphne, worship center for Apollo, Artemis, Astarte, and other gods. Worship at the grove featured ritual prostitution. "The morals of Daphne" was a worldwide expression for sexual immorality.

### Luke's Hometown?

Early Christian writers (**Eusebius** and **Jerome**) state that Luke, author of Acts, was a native of Antioch. He may have been one of the Greeks who came to Christ during the spiritual awakening of

Acts 11. From this point, much of what is reported is based on the author's eyewitness accounts.

## Revolutionizing the Revolution

**ACTS 11:21** *And the hand of the Lord was with them, and a great number believed and turned to the Lord.* (NKJV)

Everywhere the fugitives went they preached Christ . . . to Jews. But when they got to Antioch, a metropolis oozing with spiritual hunger and open to new ideas, a few—some from the Island of Cyprus and some from Cyrene, North Africa (Acts 11:20)—began to talk about Jesus to **Greeks** too. Luke's terminology indicates they made a noteworthy adjustment in their approach: Instead of talking about Jesus as Messiah, a Jewish term non-Jews would not relate to, these smart witnesses emphasized the good news about the <u>**Lord**</u> Jesus (Acts 11:20). "Lord" was a familiar term in the religious culture of Antioch. Many searched in various cults for a "lord" and "savior" who could guarantee salvation and life after death. Greeks turned to the Lord in great numbers! This was revolutionary. Unnerving. Jewish witnesses soon found themselves surrounded by "pagan believers."[10]

## Barnabas's First Apostolic Mission

**ACTS 11:22–23** *Then news of these things came to the ears of the church in Jerusalem, and they sent out Barnabas to go as far as Antioch. When he came and had seen the grace of God, he was glad, and encouraged them all that with purpose of heart they should continue with the Lord.* (NKJV)

By this time the leaders of the church at Jerusalem should have been accustomed to the relentless efforts of the Holy Spirit to widen the circle of the church. With each leap of the faith <u>outside</u> the comfortable confines of Jewish orthodoxy, they had <u>carefully checked</u> to verify that what was happening was the work of God. This time they sent Barnabas—on his first apostolic assignment. Barney was the right man for the job.

## All-Around Great Guy

**ACTS 11:24–26a** *For he was a good man, full of the Holy Spirit and of faith. And a great many people were added to the Lord.*

go to

**Lord**
John 20:28;
Philippians 2:6–11;
Ephesians 1:21–23;
1 Peter 3:22

**outside**
Acts 8, 10

**carefully checked**
Acts 8:14–17;
11:1–18

**Greeks**
Gentiles, not just people from Greece, but anyone influenced by Greek culture

**Lord**
title emphasizing Jesus's deity and authority

*Then Barnabas departed for Tarsus to seek Saul. And when he had found him, he brought him to Antioch. So it was that for a whole year they assembled with the church and taught a great many people. (NKJV)*

**evangelism**
introducing new people to Christ

**discipled**
trained, helped grow in knowledge of Christ and spiritual maturity

Barnabas had a nickname based on his spiritual giftedness: Son of Encouragement. He lived up to his name (see Acts 4:36; 9:27; 11:23). A Cypriot Jew, he was born on an island 150 miles west of Antioch. His native language was Greek. Barnabas was a Levite, the clan from which priests were chosen, hence he was well trained in the Scriptures. If anyone was "sold out" for Jesus Christ, it was this man (see Acts 4:36–37). He had experienced the daily life of the original community of believers (see Acts 2:41–47; 4:32–35; 9:26–27). An apostle and a good man, he lived by faith, under the Holy Spirit's influence.

Barnabas accomplished four things in Antioch:

1. He affirmed God was at work (Acts 11:23).

2. He participated in successful **evangelism** (Acts 11:24).

3. He linked up with Saul (Paul) to create an effective spiritual leadership team (Acts 11:25–26).

4. He and Saul successfully **discipled** the new converts for a year (Acts 11:26).

## That Wild and Crazy Church

Jewish followers of Christ had their churches in Jerusalem, Judea, and Galilee. Believing Samaritans had theirs. Since Peter's visit, a church of Gentile God-fearers was meeting at Cornelius's house in Caesarea. But not until Antioch was there a church where believing Jews steeped in the law met regularly with Gentile believers who'd grown up entirely outside the influence of Judaism. These former pagans knew nothing of the strict moral and social discipline of the Ten Commandments.

The spiritual explosion going on among Antiochene Gentiles happened so fast the Jewish believers quickly gave up making an issue of circumcision, purification ceremonies, and other traditional observances. The Antioch church's meetings were probably roughly mod-

**go to**

**ate together**
Acts 2:42, 46;
Galatians 2:11–13

eled after synagogue meetings, but the flood of untutored Gentiles made a shocking difference. Manners, clothing styles, and hair lengths, so important to Jews, had to be overlooked for the sake of fellowship around Christ.

Most shocking of all to Jewish sensibilities was the sharing of meals with the Gentile believers. Christians <u>ate together</u>. In Antioch, Jews and Gentiles shared meals in ways strict Jews considered uncouth and irreverent. By choosing to build fellowship on the simple basis of mutual faith in the Lord Jesus, the Jewish pioneers in Antioch blazed a trail for the acceptance of Gentiles by the whole church.

**what others say**

**Gene Edwards**

[The Gentile believers at Antioch] were so rowdy and noisy! "Reverence" was not part of their experience. They were completely uninhibited. As they ate (no Jew could ever overlook this), they did so with dirty hands. No Jewish prayer. . . . Just eating and rejoicing in the Lord. Their clothes were not like Jewish clothing. Nor did they seem as clean. . . . The length of their hair, by Jewish standards, was an abomination. And, to top it off . . . [none of them] had ever been circumcised![11]

## The First "Christians"

ACTS 11:26b *And the disciples were first called Christians in Antioch. (NKJV)*

It may be significant that the watching world first recognized disciples of Jesus as "Christians" after the walls of separation fell, and Jews and Gentiles were observed living together in harmony in the same community of faith. "Christians" is not the name Jesus's followers usually chose for themselves. Only two other verses in the New Testament use that term (Acts 26:28; 1 Peter 4:16).

They usually call themselves:

- "brethren" (Acts 1:16)
- "believers" (Acts 5:14)
- "disciples" (Acts 6:7)
- "saints" (Acts 9:32)
- the "Way" (Acts 22:4)

Their Jewish enemies derided them as "Galileans" (Acts 2:7), "Nazarenes" (Acts 24:5), or "this sect" (Acts 28:22).

"Christians" may have been a nickname of ridicule—as "Puritan," "Quaker," or "Methodist" first were. But hiding in the nickname was a spark of respect. The Greek word is *Christianous*, which can mean "members of Christ's party," "belonging to Christ," "Christ-people," or "little Christs."

**heterogeneous**
mixed

**accommodated**
adjusted, accepted
diversity

## The Grace-People

When Barnabas arrived to check out the spiritual revolution in Antioch, he saw in this **heterogeneous** group "the grace of God" (Acts 11:23 NKJV). "Grace" is a Bible word for "God's free and spontaneous action taken to meet human need, especially in providing salvation."[12] Attitudes and actions of the Antioch disciples were visible proof of God's grace:

- They were willing to cross racial, cultural, and social barriers to share Jesus with others (Acts 11:20). This was hugely successful (Acts 11:21, 24).

- They displayed a refreshing spirit of unity as diverse people from diverse cultures (Jews and Gentiles) **accommodated** one another in order to be together.

- They were eager to learn and willing to actively pursue spiritual growth (Acts 11:26).

- They responded generously to needs of their fellow Christians when they heard about them (Acts 11:28–30).

You could get a picture of "grace" by looking at the way Antioch believers were together. Acceptance, harmony, gratitude, teachableness, enthusiasm, willingness to risk, accommodation, fellowship, joy, caring, generosity—do you suppose these might be reasons their neighbors called them "Christians"? Do others think of you as a Christian? If so, what do you think convinces them?

*something to ponder*

**what others say**

**Maude De Joseph West**

It was the pagans who gave the adherents of the new religion the title which set them apart from Jews. The disciples were called Christians first at Antioch. A title of pious respect and regard? Hardly! An epithet hurled at a group of wild-eyed

**prophet**
Acts 15:32; 19:6;
Romans 12:6;
1 Corinthians 14:3,
29–39

**prophet**
speaker for God,
preacher, exhorts
believers, some-
times foretells the
future

fanatics? Possibly. A distinct term, matter-of-factly distinguish-
ing the strange new sect from proselytes of the Jewish religion? Quite likely. In any event, it is the name which Christ's
followers have worn from that day onward, sometimes to his
glory and sometimes, alas, to his embarrassment.[13]

## Three You'll Hear from Again

ACTS 11:27–30 *And in these days prophets came from
Jerusalem to Antioch. Then one of them, named Agabus, stood
up and showed by the Spirit that there was going to be a great
famine throughout all the world, which also happened in the
days of Claudius Caesar. Then the disciples, each according to
his ability, determined to send relief to the brethren dwelling in
Judea. This they also did, and sent it to the elders by the hands of
Barnabas and Saul. (NKJV)*

Keep the names of three people in mind: Barnabas, Saul, and
Agabus. Barnabas and Saul (Acts 11:25–26) spent a year at Antioch.
Then they were sent out as an apostolic team to plant churches in
other Gentile cities (Acts 13:3). Agabus (Acts 11:27–28) was a traveling **prophet** who predicted "severe famine" in the Roman Empire
and a food shortage in Jerusalem. He appears again in Acts 21:10. A
thirteen-year drought (AD 41–54) had already begun when Agabus
prophesied in AD 44.

# Chapter Wrap-Up

- Cornelius, a God-fearing Gentile in Caesarea, was told by an angel to send for Peter. Peter, in Joppa, saw a vision that confronted his prejudice against Gentiles and prepared him to go to Cornelius. (Acts 10:1–20)

- When Peter arrived at Cornelius's house, he shared the gospel with a group of Gentiles who, while listening, believed on Jesus and were filled with the Spirit. (Acts 10:21–48)

- Peter was called on the carpet by Jewish Christians to explain his interaction with Gentiles and eating nonkosher food. When they heard the facts and how the Holy Spirit had come on the Gentiles, they praised God. (Acts 11:1–18)

- Some Christians who escaped Saul's persecution ended up in Antioch, where they began sharing Jesus with Greeks. Many Antiochenes turned to the Lord. Barnabas was sent from Jerusalem to check it out. (Acts 11:18–21)

- Barnabas saw God's grace at work in the mixed fellowship of Jewish and Gentile believers. He got Saul to join him, and for a year they discipled a throng of newly converted Antiochenes. (Acts 11:22–30)

# Study Questions

1. What did Peter see in his vision on the roof of the tanner's house? What did the voice tell him to do? When he protested, what did the voice say?

2. Name three of the five things Peter did to show he had gotten the message of the vision and changed his mind.

3. What revolutionary thing did Christian witnesses do in Antioch that was not usually done?

4. Identify three of the four things Barnabas accomplished in Antioch.

5. Identify three of the four visible proofs that may have caused Antiochenes to refer to disciples of Jesus as "Christians."

# Acts 12 King of Hot Air and Maggots

*Chapter Highlights:*
- Here a Herod, There a Herod
- Peter Arrested
- Peter Knocks at the Garden Gate

## Let's Get Started

Jesus didn't sugarcoat anything. He never hid the fact that people who linked up with him would suffer the same rejection and persecution he did . . . which finally got him killed. Jesus said, "If the world hates you, you know that it hated Me before it hated you. . . . If they persecuted Me, they will also persecute you. . . . These things I have spoken to you, that you should not be made to stumble. . . . The time is coming that whoever kills you will think that he offers God service. And these things they will do to you because they have not known the Father nor Me. But these things I have told you, that when the time comes, you may remember that I told you of them" (John 15:18, 20; 16:1–4 NKJV).

Secular authorities mostly ignored the Jesus movement as just another Jewish internal squabble, and of no concern to the Roman occupation government—the real government. Ridiculing disciples in Antioch as "Christians" (Acts 11:26) was the church's worst trouble from the secular world.

Secular government's hands-off policy ended with events reported in Acts 12. Religious and civil authorities began to combine their efforts to stop the Jesus movement. The first foray of government into the anti-Christian cause was also short-lived. It did some damage. But in the long run its greatest accomplishment was to affirm the principle that though believers suffer and die in the battle for God's kingdom, the ultimate outcome is assured. Victories are won through the prayers of God's people. The proud and powerful anti-God-players are brought down. In the process God's truth captures more territory and captivates more minds and hearts.

## Here a Herod, There a Herod, Everywhere a Herod

ACTS 12:1 *Now about that time Herod the king stretched out his hand to harass some from the church.* (NKJV)

**Herod the Great**
Matthew 2:1–20;
Luke 1:5

**Antipas**
Matthew 14:1–11;
Mark 6:14–29;
Luke 3:1, 19;
13:31–33; 23:7–12;
Acts 4:27

**Archelaus**
Matthew 2:22

**Philip**
Luke 3:1

**dynasty**
succession of rulers
from one family line

**Bethlehem**
Judean town where
Jesus was born

**Tetrarch**
ruler of a minor
province

**Ethnarch**
ruler of a country

This is the first mention in Acts of the New Testament's notorious succession of puppet rulers bearing the title "Herod." Here's the whole Herod **dynasty** in the order of their appearance in the New Testament:

- Herod the Great—King of Judea from 37 to 4 BC. Rebuilt the Temple. Slaughtered the babies of **Bethlehem** in an attempt to destroy the baby Messiah, Jesus.

- Herod Antipas—**Tetrarch** of Galilee and Perea, 4 BC–AD 39. Beheaded John the Baptist. Jesus stood trial before him on his way to crucifixion.

- Herod Archelaus—**Ethnarch** of Judea, Samaria, and Idumea, 4 BC–AD 6. So cruel, ineffective, and universally hated, the Romans replaced him with a governor.

- Herod Philip—Tetrarch of Iturea and Trachonitis, 4 BC–AD 34. Founder of Caesarea-Philippi, where Jesus spent some time.

- Herod Agrippa I—King of Judea, AD 37–44. "King Herod" of Acts 12. Grandson of Herod the Great by his Jewish queen Mariamne.

- King Herod Agrippa II—Son of Agrippa I (Acts 25–26).

### Get Agrippa Yourself, Man!

Herod Agrippa I was a "puppet" king answerable to Rome. He was a savvy politician and realized the effectiveness of his reign depended on maintaining a good relationship with the Jewish leaders. The fact that his grandmother was a Jew helped. Many Jews liked him because he kept the Jewish law and all the Jewish holy days. His attack against the church was pure politics.

## Political Correctness Turned Deadly

ACTS 12:2 *Then he [Herod Agrippa I] killed James the brother of John with the sword. (NKJV)*

Earlier Christian leaders were held in such high esteem by the people it had been unwise to attack them directly (Acts 5:26). By Acts 12 public opinion (always fickle) had turned against them. Agrippa, reading the political winds, decided his popularity in the polls would get an upward kick with an attack against the church—especially targeting its high-profile leaders. So he arrested several Christians, including the apostle James.

The recorded details of James's martyrdom are scant. He was hacked to death with the sword (beheaded), the first apostle martyred for his faith in Jesus. Several New Testament characters have the name James. This one is James, son of Zebedee, the brother of John. Jesus nicknamed him and his brother "Sons of Thunder." He was one of Jesus's inner circle of confidants. Jesus once predicted that James would drink the same cup of suffering and experience the same "baptism" as he. Thanks to Herod, he did.

James was martyred with the sword. Another prominent New Testament character, Paul, would face the same fate in Rome. In modern times, Christians are killed for their faith in the same way. China is one such place. In 1934, John and Betty Stam of China Inland Mission were put to death with the sword by Chinese communists.[1] In 1966–1976, the Chinese Cultural Revolution forced religious activity underground, destroyed most Bibles, looted Christians' homes, and imprisoned or executed many Christians.[2]

**go to**

**Sons of Thunder**
Mark 3:17

**inner circle**
Luke 9:28; 22:8

**same cup**
Mark 10:39

**religious establishment**
Jewish leaders and supporters, not the people in general

### what others say

**Samuel Rutherford**

Through many afflictions we must enter into the kingdom of God. . . . It is folly to think to steal to heaven with a whole skin.[3]

**Billy Graham**

It is never easy to be a Christian. The Christian life can still bring its own loneliness, unpopularity, and problems. It is human nature to dislike, resent, or regard with suspicion anyone who is "different." . . . To suffer for the faith is not a penalty; it is a privilege. In doing so, we share in the very work and ministry of Christ. If we are united with Christ and his sufferings, we shall also be united with Christ in his resurrection.[4]

## Peter Arrested

ACTS 12:3–4 *And because he saw that it pleased the Jews, he proceeded further to seize Peter also. Now it was during the Days of Unleavened Bread. So when he had arrested him, he put him in prison, and delivered him to four squads of soldiers to keep him, intending to bring him before the people after Passover. (NKJV)*

The **religious establishment** rejoiced to see James's head roll. A good politician knows the expediency of pleasing the special inter-

**dim view**
Mark 14:2

**Fortress Antonia**
Acts 21:31–22:29

**united**
Matthew 18:19–20

**Fortress Antonia**
Roman "barracks"
adjacent to the tem-
ple area

**night watches**
four watches of
three hours each[5]

ests, so when what he did to James got good press, Agrippa decided to nab another apostle, Peter.

Agrippa decided not to terminate the Big Fisherman until after the twin festivals of Passover and Unleavened Bread. The festival schedule that year was carefully planned to go like this:

*Thursday*—Search and destroy all yeast (leaven).

*Friday noon*—Sacrifice Passover lambs at the Temple.

*Friday after sundown*—Eat Passover meal with family and guests.

*Next seven days*—Celebrate Israel's escape from Egypt. Eat only unleavened bread.

*Day after the festival*—Chop off Peter's head!

The Jews took a <u>dim view</u> of executions during this high holy season. One must operate by certain priorities, you understand: First, we must take a few days off to worship God. Then we can get back to killing Christians! So, in the spirit of the holidays, Peter "celebrated" in prison (probably at the Roman **Fortress Antonia**), guarded by four relays of four soldiers each—one squad for each of the **night watches**. This was unusually heavy security, reserved for the most dangerous felons.

what others say

**William Barclay**

The great tragedy of this particular wave of persecution was that it was not due to any man's principles, however misguided; it was due simply to Herod's bid to gain popular favor with the people.[6]

## The Miracle of Uncertain Praying

**ACTS 12:5** *Peter was therefore kept in prison, but constant prayer was offered to God for him by the church. (NKJV)*

What were the Christians doing while Peter was "on holiday" in the slammer? They grabbed their most potent weapon—prayer—and aimed it at the powers-that-be. The original Greek word Luke uses to describe their praying indicates considerable energy was exerted; their praying was intense, fervent, and extended. They prayed all night (Acts 12:6, 12). They were <u>united</u>—"constant prayer was offered to God for him by the church." James had been killed. Unless God rescued him, Peter was next. It was time for serious prayer.

Theirs was, we shall soon discover, imperfect prayer. But it was enough to unleash the power of Almighty God.

## Dreamy Escape

ACTS 12:6–11 *And when Herod was about to bring him out, that night Peter was sleeping, bound with two chains between two soldiers; and the guards before the door were keeping the prison. Now behold, an angel of the Lord stood by him, and a light shone in the prison; and he struck Peter on the side and raised him up, saying, "Arise quickly!" And his chains fell off his hands. Then the angel said to him, "Gird yourself and tie on your sandals"; and so he did. And he said to him, "Put on your garment and follow me." So he went out and followed him, and did not know that what was done by the angel was real, but thought he was seeing a vision. When they were past the first and the second guard posts, they came to the iron gate that leads to the city, which opened to them of its own accord; and they went out and went down one street, and immediately the angel departed from him. And when Peter had come to himself, he said, "Now I know for certain that the Lord has sent His angel, and has delivered me from the hand of Herod and from all the expectation of the Jewish people." (NKJV)*

Here's the picture. It's the night before Peter is to stand trial before King Herod; the church is up all night, praying, dreading the worst. The two guards to whom Peter is chained wrist-to-wrist are at attention. The two guards at the cell door are on high alert against any plot to "spring" the prisoner. Everybody—Christians, soldiers— is tense, vigilant, on the job.

Peter? It's the night before his almost certain death sentence. What's he doing? Ho-hum. He's taking a siesta—sawing logs! He's resting like a baby in its mother's arms! His conscience is clear. He's

**life or death**
Philippians 1:20

**another vision**
Acts 10:9–16

**Mark**
Acts 13:5, 13;
15:37–40;
Colossians 4:10;
2 Timothy 4:11;
1 Peter 5:13

**Mark**
author of the Gospel
of Mark

confident of God's sovereign control—whether it means <u>life or death</u>. He's in dreamland.

Suddenly the dream changes. Whack! Somebody slaps him on the side. He opens his eyes. His cell is full of light. Someone is there who isn't dressed like a Roman soldier. "Quick, get up!" the dream visitor says. Suddenly the chains fall off Peter's wrists, clattering to the cell floor. The guards are still at attention, looking straight ahead, chained to nobody, unaware their prisoner is loose. "Get dressed and put on your shoes," the bright intruder says. "Don't forget your coat (it's cold outside). Follow me."

Peter follows like an obedient puppy, past the two guards in the cell and the two at the entrance. Nobody notices. They come to the front gate of the fortress. It swings open. Out on the cobblestones they walk till the street dead-ends. "Wow!" Peter thinks, "I'm having <u>another vision</u>!"

Suddenly he's alone. Reality hits him: He's awake, busted out of jail . . . and it's no dream! "God has rescued me!" he says. God controls circumstances and answers our prayers according to his purposes.

**what others say**

**Charles Wesley**

Long my imprisoned spirit lay

Fast bound in sin and nature's night;

Thine eye diffused a quick'ning ray,

I woke; the dungeon flamed with light.

My chains fell off, my heart was free,

I rose, went forth, and followed thee.[8]

## Peter Knocks at the Garden Gate

ACTS 12:12–17 *So, when he had considered this, he came to the house of Mary, the mother of John whose surname was **Mark**, where many were gathered together praying. And as Peter knocked at the door of the gate, a girl named Rhoda came to answer. When she recognized Peter's voice, because of her gladness she did not open the gate, but ran in and announced that Peter stood before the gate. But they said to her, "You are beside yourself!" Yet she kept insisting that it was so. So they said, "It is* *his angel." Now Peter continued knocking; and when they opened the door and saw him, they were astonished. But motioning to them with his hand to keep silent, he declared to them how the Lord had brought him out of the prison. And he said, "Go, tell these things to James and to the brethren." And he departed and went to another place. (NKJV)*

go to

**mountain-moving faith**
Matthew 17:20;
21:21

**guardian angel**
Matthew 18:10

The first thing Peter had to do was let the Christians know of his escape. Next, he had to head for cover—Agrippa was sure to be after him. From the fortress he went directly to Mary's house where a group was praying through the night. Her home was the meeting place of one of Jerusalem's early **house churches** (see Illustration #10).

Peter knocked on the entrance. Rhoda, a servant girl, part of the praying group, went to the gate. Peter identified himself. She recognized his voice, and in her excitement she left him standing in the street while she rushed back inside with the incredible news.

Not all the reactions show evidence of "mighty, <u>mountain-moving faith</u>."

Rhoda was overjoyed. But others said, "You're nuts!" (Too many sleepless nights of prayer, perhaps, had driven the sensitive young thing over the edge!) Another theory: "It's his angel." (Many believed a person's <u>guardian angel</u> could take on the appearance of the person under his care.)

When they stopped arguing about who or what was at the gate and opened it, they saw Peter and "went wild!"⁹ He waved his hand to calm them down, "Shh! You'll wake the neighbors!" He stayed only long enough to ask them to report his escape to James (another James—brother of Jesus, now a leader among Jewish Christians). Then he disappeared into the night. He left Judea, possibly for Antioch or someplace in **Asia Minor** (Galatians 2:11; 1 Peter 1:1), beyond Herod's jurisdiction.

Even though their reactions to Peter's knock at the door reveal they weren't at all sure God was going to answer their prayers, the disciples prayed anyway. It was the right thing to do. It was the only thing to do! They prayed because they cared. They prayed because Jesus taught them to pray. They prayed because God uses prayer in his war against the powers of this world. And, even though their prayers were not perfect and their faith was shaky, God heard them.

**house churches**
Jerusalem church was divided into groups that met in homes

**Asia Minor**
modern Turkey

something to ponder

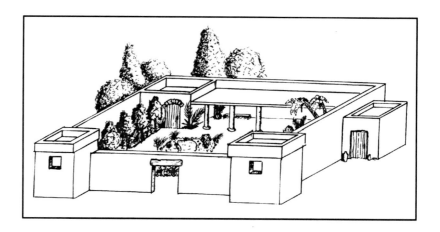

**Illustration #10**
Typical House Church—Christians in Jerusalem gathered at homes of wealthy believers. Most homes had an inner courtyard, such as the one shown here, that could accommodate large groups. A gate, not shown, opened from the street onto the courtyard leading to the living quarters.

Two Christian women of different social rank play important roles in this incident: (1) Mary, Mark's mom, hosts and perhaps leads a church in her home and (2) Rhoda, a simple, believing servant girl recognizes that the answer to their prayers has arrived.

something to ponder

This story contains a mystery: Why should James be martyred while Peter escapes martyrdom? It's a question for which only the Lord has the answer. F. F. Bruce reminds us this scenario "has been repeated countless times in the history of the people of God." By faith, says Hebrews, some "escaped the edge of the sword" (11:34 NKJV); and by faith others "were slain with the sword" (11:37 NKJV). Go figure!

## King of Hot Air and Maggots

ACTS 12:18–19 *Then, as soon as it was day, there was no small stir among the soldiers about what had become of Peter. But when Herod had searched for him and not found him, he examined the guards and commanded that they should be put to death. And he went down from Judea to Caesarea, and stayed there. (NKJV)*

go to

**thousand years**
1 Kings 5:9–12

Herod suspected Peter's jailbreak was an "inside job" and the guards had been bribed. Roman military law required punishment of guards who let a prisoner escape to match the punishment the prisoner would have received. In this case, the sentence was death (Acts 12:18–19). If all the guards watching Peter were held responsible, sixteen men were sacrificed on the altar of Herod's political ambitions that day!

Frustrated, Herod Agrippa retreated to the town founded by his grandfather. He was soon to discover there is no retreat from the justice of God. God was not finished answering his people's prayers.

## All Dressed Up and No Place to Go!

ACTS 12:20–21 *Now Herod had been very angry with the people of Tyre and Sidon; but they came to him with one accord, and having made Blastus the king's personal aide their friend, they asked for peace, because their country was supplied with food by the king's country. So on a set day Herod, arrayed in royal apparel, sat on his throne and gave an oration to them. (NKJV)*

The people of Tyre and Sidon, on the Phoenician seacoast west of Galilee, depended on good relations with Herod to maintain the flow of food supplies from Galilee on which they had depended for a <u>thousand years</u>. Somehow they had offended Herod Agrippa. To keep from starving, they decided to seek peace. Perhaps with a well-placed bribe they secured the support of Blastus, one of Herod's advisers, who arranged a peace conference.

what others say

**Flavius Josephus**

[Agrippa] entered the theater at daybreak. There the silver, illuminated by the touch of the first rays of the sun, was wondrously radiant and by its glitter inspired fear and awe in those who gazed upon it. Straightway his flatterers raised their voices from various directions—though hardly for his good—

> addressing him as a god. "May you be **propitious** to us," they added, "and if we have hitherto feared you as a man, yet henceforth we agree that you are more than mortal in your being!"[12]

## Dances with Worms

ACTS 12:22–23 *And the people kept shouting, "The voice of a god and not of a man!" Then immediately an angel of the Lord struck him, because he did not give glory to God. And he was eaten by worms and died. (NKJV)*

The citizens of Tyre and Sidon believed flattery will get you anything! In his arrogance, Agrippa accepted their cheers. His willingness to usurp God's place spelled his doom. Agrippa the "god" died from being "eaten by worms" (Acts 12:23). Possible medical diagnosis: intestinal roundworms. Roundworms can grow to sixteen inches long, clog the intestines, and cause extreme pain, vomiting, and death (all of which makes James's beheading sound like a walk in the park!).

what others say

### Maude De Joseph West

[Agrippa] was seized with agonizing pains in his belly. His wondrous silver garment was nothing more than extra weight upon his outraged flesh as he was carried back to his palace. There, five days later, he died of the same loathsome disease which had claimed the life of his grandfather, Herod the Great. . . . Josephus describes in graphic and revolting detail the illness which killed Herod's grandfather. Oh, yes indeed, there were worms—lots of worms![13]

## Our God Is Marching On

ACTS 12:24–25 *But the word of God grew and multiplied. And Barnabas and Saul returned from Jerusalem [to Antioch] when they had fulfilled their ministry, and they also took with them John whose surname was Mark. (NKJV)*

With the demise of the great god-pretender, the Romans appointed a governor to rule Judea. All that was left was for Luke to contrast Agrippa's miserable end with the unstoppable progress of the Word of God.

Herod Agrippa I was not the first nor would he be the last tyrant to try to stomp out Christian faith. Add to the list Nero, Diocletian, Hitler, Stalin, Mao, Idi Amin, and a thousand others who set themselves against the church. All are dead. The gospel of Jesus lives on.

God personally oversees the spread of his Word. When Christians are left at peace, their witness spreads and numbers grow. When they are martyred, their blood sprouts new believers anyway.

Check out these lessons on prayer from the church at Mary's house:

- The church prayed together (Acts 12:5; also, Matthew 18:19).
- The prayer group was inclusive—rich and poor; men and women; servants, masters (Acts 12:12–13).
- Their prayer was "constant" (Acts 12:5).
- They prayed over an extended time—eight days (Acts 12:2, 4–5).
- They prayed "to God" (Acts 12:5).
- They prayed all night (Acts 12:12).
- They prayed in spite of their doubts and were surprised when Peter escaped (Acts 12:15–16).
- With prayer, they used common sense. Not waiting to be rearrested, Peter left town (Acts 12:17).
- God did more than they prayed for. Herod's fraud was exposed and he died (Acts 12:23–24).

Worldly circumstances and forces can seem all-powerful. It is easy to forget God is at work in everything. How does this chapter help you put world leaders and events in perspective?

# Chapter Wrap-Up

- King Herod arrested several Christians at Jerusalem and killed the apostle James. When he saw this pleased the religious leaders, he arrested Peter and placed him under heavy guard at Fortress Antonia. (Acts 12:1–4)

- While Peter was in jail awaiting certain execution, the people of the church gathered to pray for his release. The night before his trial and execution, an angel came into the prison, woke Peter up, and led him past the guards to freedom. (Acts 12:5–11)

- When he realized he hadn't dreamed the escape, Peter went to Mary's house where a group was praying. At first, they couldn't believe it was him. After welcoming him, he talked with them, and they sent him off to a safe place. (Acts 12:12–17)

- Herod met his deserved end after he allowed the Phoenicians to call him a god. After his death, the church experienced another spurt of growth. (Acts 12:18–25)

# Study Questions

1. How was the apostle James martyred? What was different about this persecution?

2. What did the church do to get Peter out of prison? Where did they do this?

3. What happened as a result of what the believers did? What does this reveal about who holds the real power—secular authorities or the Lord of the church?

4. When Peter knocked at the door of Mary's house, who did members of the group think was really out there? What would you have said if you were there? What do these responses reveal about the prayers of the group?

5. What did Herod Agrippa do that showed him to be the fraud he was?

# Part Three
# FILLED WITH GOD'S SPIRIT

# Acts 13–14 World Ambassadors

*Chapter Highlights:*
- **Proconsul Believes Despite Interference**
- **Paul Goes to Antioch to Recover**
- **Watering Baby Plants**

## Let's Get Started

Meanwhile, back in Antioch, Cilicia, Jesus's followers continued to develop the faith-based community that was about to become the bridge over which the good news of Jesus could cross from the Holy Land to the rest of the world. Antioch's uniqueness was its disturbingly glorious mix of people from all sorts of religious, racial, and social roots drawn together around the risen Jesus without the hang-ups of Judaism's fellowship-inhibiting religious rules or society's class structure.

Give Antioch fellowship a blue ribbon! It was the first place Jews freely shared the good news with pagans (Acts 11:20). It was the first place large numbers of non-Jews believed and were welcomed into the church (Acts 11:23). It was the first place Jesus's disciples were called "Christians" (Acts 11:26). It was the first church to send humanitarian aid to hungry Jerusalem Christians (Acts 11:28–30). It was the first church to recognize the partnership of Barnabas and Saul (Acts 11:30), who had just returned from delivering the aid package (Acts 12:25).

Antioch's destiny as a launching pad for Christian ambassadors was about to become clear.

**gifted**
Ephesians 4:11

**shepherds**
pastors

**prophecy**
communication of
God's message

**teaching**
explanation of the
meaning and application of God's message

## Dream Team

> ACTS 13:1 *Now in the church that was at Antioch there were certain prophets and teachers: Barnabas, Simeon who was called Niger, Lucius of Cyrene, Manaen who had been brought up with Herod the tetrarch, and Saul. (NKJV)*

A committed group of **shepherds** watched over development of the Antioch church. This team was spiritually <u>gifted</u> to provide two things needed to help people grow up in relationship to Jesus Christ: **prophecy** and **teaching**. The leadership team at Antioch included these men:

**disciple**
Matthew 28:19–20

**equip converts**
Ephesians 4:11–16

**prophetic insight**
1 Corinthians
12:8, 10

- *Barnabas*—"Son of encouragement," a good man, full of the Holy Spirit and faith (Acts 11:24).
- *Simeon*—Nickname: "Niger" (Latin for "dark-skinned" or "black"), probably an African.
- *Lucius*—A North African from Cyrene (modern Libya).
- *Manaen*—His name means "comforter," a man with aristocratic connections.
- *Saul*—A trained rabbi, former persecutor of Christians, brought to Antioch by Barnabas to help **disciple** and <u>equip converts</u> (Acts 11:25–26).

Antioch's spiritual leadership team was as racially and socially varied as the people they served. Many challenges that keep today's Christians apart were met and overcome in that ancient fellowship. This "wild and crazy," racially mixed church was the Holy Spirit's choice for a bridge over which to reach the world.

**disciple**
(verb) teach and
train to live as fol-
lowers of Christ

**fasting**
skipping meals to
concentrate on spiri-
tual things—mostly
prayer

# Barnabas and Saul Called to Wider Mission

> ACTS 13:2–3 *As they ministered to the Lord and fasted, the Holy Spirit said, "Now separate to Me Barnabas and Saul for the work to which I have called them." Then, having fasted and prayed, and laid hands on them, they sent them away.* (NKJV)

These prophets and teachers were doing two things together: (1) worshiping the Lord and (2) **fasting**. In this context they sensed the Holy Spirit was calling Barnabas and Saul to a wider mission and that the Antioch church should send them out with their support.

How did the Spirit communicate his desires? No self-destructing cassette tape outlined an "impossible" mission. No mysterious cat brought tomorrow's newspaper today. The word probably came through a gift of <u>prophetic insight</u>. The group reached a place of harmony when the five found themselves with a single persistent conviction. All (including Barnabas and Saul) agreed the Spirit was speaking.

**what others say**

**Oswald Chambers**

The key to the missionary problem is not the key of common sense, nor the medical key, nor the key of civilization or education or even evangelization. The key is prayer.

> "Pray ye therefore the Lord of the harvest, that he will send forth workers into his harvest" (Matthew 9:38). Naturally, prayer is not practical, it is absurd . . . from the ordinary common-sense point of view.[1]

From the Antioch experience we discover that the head of the church guides and communicates his will to his people best when they are (1) worshiping—expressing their love and respect for him; (2) setting aside their own wants and desires—fasting; (3) experiencing spiritual harmony—unity amid diversity—with each other; (4) listening for his voice; (5) responding as they understand what he wants them to do; and (6) willing to support each other in doing God's will.

## Boldly Go Where No One Has Gone Before

ACTS 13:4–5 *So, being sent out by the Holy Spirit, they went down to Seleucia, and from there they sailed to Cyprus. And when they arrived in Salamis, they preached the word of God in the synagogues of the Jews. They also had John as their assistant. (NKJV)*

The Christians at Antioch surrounded Barnabas and Saul and John Mark, the young man who would go with them, touching them in a show of love and support, sending them on their way.

John Mark, the third member of the missionary team, was Barnabas's cousin (Colossians 4:10). John Mark was an eyewitness, unlike Barnabas and Saul, of Jesus's life and death. He was raised in a godly home. His mother's house was a gathering place for Christians in Jerusalem (Acts 12:12). Later, he authored the first "Life of Christ" ever published—the Gospel of Mark.

The church's sending act was significant for three reasons. First, Christ's ambassadors were sent out not as independents but connected to the sending church. Second, the laying on of hands symbolized the congregation's support. Third, the church's willingness to deny itself the ministry of two of its valued leaders in order to share the good news with strangers demonstrates a spirit of liberality.

Barnabas , Saul, and John Mark trekked the fifteen miles down the Orontes River to Seleucia, Antioch's seaport, and boarded a ship for the sixty-mile sail to the island of Cyprus, their first stop (see illustration below). For Saul, later called Paul, it was the first sixty miles of a ministry itinerary that would consume the rest of his life and take him a total of more than seventeen thousand miles—more than halfway around the world.[2]

Examine Acts 13 and 14 for the seven-point strategy this missionary group used for planting new churches:

1. Go where the gospel has not been heard.

2. Concentrate on population, governmental, and commercial centers.

3. First, share the good news with Jews and God-fearers at the synagogue.

4. Stay a short time teaching new believers and establishing the church.

5. Move on, trusting new believers to the Holy Spirit and each other.

6. Revisit young churches to encourage believers and confirm leaders.

7. Return to home base (the sending church) and report.

**Illustration #11**
Paul's First Missionary Journey—The first missionary journey of Paul, formerly called Saul, began at Seleucia, near Antioch. Arrows show the route he took from there.

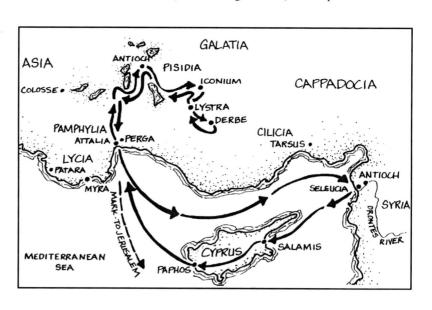

# Proconsul Believes Despite Interference

**sorcerer**
Acts 8:9–13, 18–24

**Paphian**
Syrian version
of the Greek
god Aphrodite

**proconsul**
provincial governor,
a judicial and mili-
tary position

> ACTS 13:6–8 *Now when they had gone through the island to Paphos, they found a certain sorcerer, a false prophet, a Jew whose name was Bar-Jesus, who was with the proconsul, Sergius Paulus, an intelligent man. This man called for Barnabas and Saul and sought to hear the word of God. But Elymas the sorcerer (for so his name is translated) withstood them, seeking to turn the proconsul away from the faith. (NKJV)*

The island of Cyprus was a Roman province famous for copper mining and shipbuilding. The team landed at the Greek city of Salamis and preached in synagogues across the island. Acts 11:19 says that Christian fugitives escaped to Cyprus and told the story of Jesus. The team may have run into Barnabas's relatives—Cyprus was his home turf (Acts 4:36).

The last stop was the provincial capital, Paphos, a pagan city notorious for immorality connected with worship of the love-goddess, "the **Paphian**." When the **proconsul**, Sergius Paulus, got wind of what Barnabas and Saul were teaching, he wanted to hear more.

Their attempts to share the good news with him were opposed by Bar-Jesus Elymas, a Jewish <u>sorcerer</u>, who pulled every trick in the book to keep the proconsul from believing in Jesus. In that superstitious first-century culture it was common for government officials to employ sorcerers, fortune-tellers, and wizards as advisers. With his boss on the verge of becoming a Christian, Elymas saw his source of income evaporating before his beady, greedy, lying, drug-glazed eyes!

Immediately mist and darkness came over him, and he groped about, seeking someone to lead him by the hand. When the proconsul saw what had happened, he believed, for he was amazed at the teaching about the Lord.

# Holy Spirit Energizes Paul

> ACTS 13:9–12 *Then Saul, who also is called Paul, filled with the Holy Spirit, looked intently at him and said, "O full of all deceit and all fraud, you son of the devil, you enemy of all righteousness, will you not cease perverting the straight ways of the Lord? And now, indeed, the hand of the Lord is upon you, and you shall be blind, not seeing the sun for a time." And immediately a dark mist fell on him, and he went around seeking some-*

**go to**

**evaluation of wizards**
Leviticus 19:26, 28,
31; 20:6;
Deuteronomy
18:9–14;
Isaiah 8:19–20;
Malachi 3:5

**his own case**
Acts 9:8–12

**Paul**
Saul's Greek name

*one to lead him by the hand. Then the proconsul believed, when he saw what had been done, being astonished at the teaching of the Lord.* (NKJV)

It was a critical moment for Sergius Paulus and Cyprus. The governor's spiritual restoration and that of many islanders hung in the balance. It was no time for tolerance. The Holy Spirit energized **Paul**. His eyes blazed with anger as he stared Elymas straight in the eye and, in the presence of the governor, confronted the anti-Christ wizard with a point-by-point exposé of his spiritual rottenness. What Paul said to the bogus "Jesus" of Paphos expresses fairly well the Bible's <u>evaluation of wizards</u>, witches, and practitioners of black and white magic, spiritualism, and the occult:

- You are no son or follower of Jesus—you're a "son of the devil" (Acts 13:10 NKJV).

- You are the "enemy of all righteousness" (13:10 NKJV).

- You are "full of all deceit and all fraud" (13:10 NKJV).

- You never stop making right seem wrong and wrong seem right.

- The Lord is against everything you stand for.

Here is your sentence from the Lord himself, Paul added, "You shall be blind, not seeing the sun for a time" (Acts 13:11 NKJV). Immediately "Dr. Know-It-All"[3] found himself groping in the dark, begging for somebody to take his hand and show him the way out. The blindness would be temporary.

As for Sergius Paulus, as the misty darkness fell on his "adviser," he believed in Jesus and stepped into God's sunlight.

## what others say

**Venerable Bede**

Remembering <u>his own case</u>, [Paul] knew that by the darkening of the eyes the mind's darkness might be restored to light.[4]

**Billy Graham**

It is the Spirit-filled Christian who knows when to have "righteous indignation" and when to be patient, and who knows when long-suffering becomes an excuse for inaction or a crutch to hide a defect of character.[5]

### Alias, Paul

In Acts 13:9 the author sneaks the information about Saul's name change into the narrative without explanation. From then on, except when telling the story of his conversion, Saul is Paul. Saul is his Jewish name. His parents, members of the tribe of Benjamin (Philippians 3:5), named their son after Israel's first king, Saul, a Benjamite. Like many Jews, especially those living outside the Holy Land, they also gave him a Greek name. "Paul" (Paulus) is Greek for "little."

When working with Gentiles he used his Greek name. The first time it's noticed is when he shares the gospel with his namesake, Governor Sergius Paulus of Cyprus.

**go to**

**radical change**
Acts 9:1–29

**leader**
Acts 11:25–26, 30;
12:25; 13:1–2, 7

**Pamphylia**
Roman province on the south coast of Asia Minor (Turkey)

> ### what others say
> **Walter Wangerin**
>
> To indicate the <u>radical change</u> within himself, [Saul] changed his name to Paul, and . . . began to tell the story—in Greek, to the Greeks.[6]

## Paul Takes the Lead

> ACTS 13:13a *Now when Paul and his party set sail from Paphos, they came to Perga in **Pamphylia**; (NKJV)*

Until the incident at Sergius Paulus's palace in Paphos, Barnabas had been the <u>leader</u> of the apostolic expedition; his name is listed first. After Cyprus, Barnabas and Paul were still the inseparable one-two gospel punch, but Paul was named first, indicating a subtle change in team leadership. To his credit, Barnabas (the encourager) was okay with this.

> ### what others say
> **William Barclay**
>
> Without his name being mentioned this verse (Acts 13:13) pays the greatest of all tributes to Barnabas. . . . There is from him no word of complaint. He was a man prepared to take second place so long as God's work was done.[7]

## John Goes Home

> ACTS 13:13b *and John, departing from them, returned to Jerusalem. (NKJV)*

**reference**
Galatians 4:13

**pattern Jesus used**
Matthew 13:54;
Luke 4:16

**tailored his message**
1 Corinthians
9:19–23

John Mark, the team's young helper (Acts 13:5), left the mission at Perga and returned to Jerusalem. We're not told why. Guesses include: (1) the confrontation with Elymas shook him up; (2) he resented Paul replacing cousin Barnabas as team leader; (3) he had second thoughts about preaching to Gentiles; (4) he was homesick and needed his mommy; or (5) your guess is as good as mine!

## Paul Goes to Antioch to Recover

ACTS 13:14a *But when they departed from Perga, they came to Antioch in Pisidia, (NKJV)*

No preaching was done in Perga. A <u>reference</u> in his letter to the Galatians suggests Paul became sick in the coastal lowlands and headed to higher altitude to recuperate. After Mark sailed for Jerusalem, Paul and Barnabas climbed the rugged and dangerous trail across the Taurus Mountains to the city of Antioch, Pisidia (see Illustration #11), on a plateau 3,600 feet above sea level. Antioch was a common town name. Sixteen first-century towns had that name. This one was in Pisidia province. The team would return and preach in Pamphylia later (Acts 14:24–25).

## Paul Exhorts the People

ACTS 13:14b–16 *and went into the synagogue on the Sabbath day and sat down. And after the reading of the Law and the Prophets, the rulers of the synagogue sent to them, saying, "Men and brethren, if you have any word of exhortation for the people, say on." Then Paul stood up, and motioning with his hand said, "Men of Israel, and you who fear God, listen: (NKJV)*

In first-century synagogues, distinguished visitors were often asked to speak. For the apostle-ambassadors this represented a wide-open door to present the good news about the Messiah. It was a <u>pattern Jesus used</u>. Paul <u>tailored his message</u> to communicate to his Jewish audience.

# Judaism and Christianity Are One

**go to**

**God promised**
Psalm 2:7;
Isaiah 55:3;
Psalm 16:10;
Acts 13:33–37

**anyone**
John 3:16;
Acts 2:21;
Romans 1:16

**the big picture**

## Acts 13:17–41

Paul traced the history of God's involvement with Israel from the patriarchs to King David. David was special because he was willing to do whatever God wanted. Jesus, David's descendant, was sent by God to be Israel's Savior. John the Baptist announced him. The people and leaders at Jerusalem rejected Jesus, and Pilate executed him. Jesus rose from the dead, and many people saw him. His resurrection fulfilled Old Testament prophecies. People who believe in Jesus are forgiven and **justified** before God.

**justified**
declared righteous, acceptable to God

**Savior**
Rescuer from sin's control and consequences; Redeemer

In this message Paul does something very important. He shows how Judaism and Christianity are not different religions. Both are part of a single, wonderful, loving process by which God reveals himself to human beings and makes it possible for the estrangement caused by sin to be taken away so God and people can live together in peace.

Here's the gist of Paul's sermon in a few sound bites:

- *Sound bite 1*—Israel has always been the object of God's special care (Acts 13:17–19).

- *Sound bite 2*—God gave Israel Canaan as their homeland and great leaders—judges, kings—especially King David, "a man after [God's] own heart" (Acts 13:16–22).

- *Sound bite 3*—God promised to send David's descendant to rescue both Jewish children of Abraham and Gentile friends of God. He's here! He's the "**Savior**—Jesus" (Acts 13:23–26).

- *Sound bite 4*—The people and their leaders in Jerusalem failed to recognize the Savior. He was crucified and buried, but God raised him from the dead. Everything <u>God promised</u> Israel is fulfilled in the resurrected Jesus (Acts 13:27–37).

- *Sound bite 5*—Here's what it comes down to: <u>Anyone</u> may be forgiven of his or her sins and justified (judged "not guilty" and "okay") before God through Jesus and what he accomplished. The Law of Moses could never do that! This leaves you with a choice: Trust Jesus, or play the cynic and refuse to believe (Acts 13:38–41).

Judaism is the root from which Christianity grows. Christianity is the tree Judaism was always destined to become.

# Paul Gets Heckled

**go to**

story hidden
Acts 14:1–5; 17:1–5;
18:5–8; 19:8–10

appointed
chosen by God

**the big picture**

## Acts 13:42–45

The people of the synagogue urged Paul and Barnabas to continue teaching the following Sabbath. Next Sabbath a large crowd gathered to hear about Jesus. Synagogue leaders were jealous and spoke abusively against Paul's teaching.

Many who listened to the apostles' message accepted God's offer of grace (forgiveness and justification—Acts 13:38–39). That's the often-unnoticed success story hidden in the reports of negative responses in synagogue after synagogue. During the next week Paul and Barnabas spent many hours encouraging those who chose to follow Jesus as their Messiah to continue in their newfound freedom (Acts 13:42–43).

The word got around, and the following Saturday "almost the whole city came together to hear the word of God" (Acts 13:44 NKJV).

When regular synagogue-goers arrived, they found strangers sitting in their pews! (I hate it when that happens!) Leaders and unbelieving rank-and-file Jews, consumed with jealousy, heckled Paul, making it impossible for him to speak.

## Casting Pearls Before Appreciative Pagans

ACTS 13:46–49 *Then Paul and Barnabas grew bold and said, "It was necessary that the word of God should be spoken to you first; but since you reject it, and judge yourselves unworthy of everlasting life, behold, we turn to the Gentiles. For so the Lord has commanded us:*
*'I have set you as a light to the Gentiles,*
*That you should be for salvation to the ends of the earth.'"*
*Now when the Gentiles heard this, they were glad and glorified the word of the Lord. And as many as had been* **appointed** *to eternal life believed. And the word of the Lord was being spread throughout all the region.* (NKJV)

Paul and Barnabas cited Isaiah's prophecy about how God expected the Jews to be a saving "light to the Gentiles" (Isaiah 49:6 NKJV). They left the synagogue to focus on non-Jewish townspeople who were thrilled to hear the news of forgiveness and justification through Jesus.

The apostolic strategy was the same in every city: Take the good news of Messiah Jesus to the Jews first. God loves the Jewish people. He sent the Messiah to reveal his plan of salvation to them first. They were the ones to whom the ancient messianic promises and prophecies were given. They anticipated Christ's arrival. The invitation to receive Christ was offered to them before anyone else. Many—an estimated one-third of first-century Jews—believed and welcomed Jesus as Messiah. Tragically twice as many chose to turn him away. And often for such a tawdry substitute—jealousy (Acts 13:45)!

The early church grew rapidly when it gave up trying to convince hard-hearted religious people and targeted the people who'd never heard of Jesus.

**go to**

**shook off the dust**
Luke 10:10–11

**shook off the dust**
traditional Jewish declaration of separation and warning of judgment

**what others say**

### J. R. Dumelow

God desires the salvation of all men (1 Timothy 2:4; 4:10, etc.), but inasmuch as he foresees that some (in the expression of their free will) will actually repent and believe, while others will refuse to do so, he ordains the former to eternal life, and the latter to eternal death (Romans 8:28–30, etc.).[8]

## The People Join in the Attack Against the Apostles

ACTS 13:50–52 *But the Jews stirred up the devout and prominent women and the chief men of the city, raised up persecution against Paul and Barnabas, and expelled them from their region. But they shook off the dust from their feet against them, and came to Iconium. And the disciples were filled with joy and with the Holy Spirit. (NKJV)*

As the green-eyed monster flexed its muscles and flapped its lying lips, unbelieving synagogue leaders convinced some leading women and the town fathers to join their attack against the apostles. When last seen, Paul and Barnabas were headed east-southeast, waving to a joyful bunch of new Christians who'd come to the city limits to see them off. As they passed a dour-faced collection of synagogue officials, "Tiny" (Paul) and Barney paused for a moment, pulled off their sandals, and, in a defiant gesture, **shook off the dust** of Antioch's streets in the faces of the religious high mucky-mucks.

The story of the Jewish reaction at Antioch, Pisidia, is repeated again and again in Acts. Some believed in Jesus as Messiah; others

**go to**

**free gift**
Ephesians 2:8–9

**messianic**
belonging to the
Messiah, Christ

refused. Believing Jews joined believing Gentiles to become part of the **messianic** movement sweeping the world. Unbelieving Jews went back to their traditions, but it was never the same. God had visited them, eternal life had been within their reach, but out of fear, jealousy, or blindness, they had said "No" to their destiny.

## Power and Poison

ACTS 14:1–7 *Now it happened in Iconium that they went together to the synagogue of the Jews, and so spoke that a great multitude both of the Jews and of the Greeks believed. But the unbelieving Jews stirred up the Gentiles and poisoned their minds against the brethren. Therefore they stayed there a long time, speaking boldly in the Lord, who was bearing witness to the word of His grace, granting signs and wonders to be done by their hands. But the multitude of the city was divided: part sided with the Jews, and part with the apostles. And when a violent attempt was made by both the Gentiles and Jews, with their rulers, to abuse and stone them, they became aware of it and fled to Lystra and Derbe, cities of Lycaonia, and to the surrounding region. And they were preaching the gospel there.* (NKJV)

Ninety miles east of Pisidian Antioch, on the east–west road from Syria to Ephesus was Iconium (modern Konya, Turkey). "As usual" the apostle-ambassadors began their work at the synagogue. Luke describes their preaching as "the word of [God's] grace"—the news that God loves people and has provided salvation as a <u>free gift</u> to those who put their faith in Jesus (Acts 14:3). Their witness was punctuated with healing miracles.

Real love is too much for some people to handle. They are more comfortable with hate. So as usual the good news led to division. Some believed. Some refused and poisoned the minds of others against the missionaries. An assassination plot developed. Paul and Barnabas managed to avoid the conspirators for a while, but the time came when getting out of town fast was the only sensible thing to do. On to the twin cities of Lystra and Derbe!

Verbal abuse and slander are favorite weapons of the enemies of Christ. First-century Christians were (falsely) accused of atheism, cannibalism, child-sacrifice, incest, worship of an ass's head and human sex organs, illegal assembly, arson, and hatred of the human race. During the 1950s in China, Christian leaders were routinely accused of hostility to Communist government policies, womanizing, counter-revolutionary activities, poisoning water supplies, and espionage, among other things. Many Chinese Christians were sentenced to long prison terms based on such charges.

# Get Real!

ACTS 14:8–13 *And in Lystra a certain man without strength in his feet was sitting, a cripple from his mother's womb, who had never walked. This man heard Paul speaking. Paul, observing him intently and seeing that he had faith to be healed, said with a loud voice, "Stand up straight on your feet!" And he leaped and walked. Now when the people saw what Paul had done, they raised their voices, saying in the **Lycaonian** language, "The gods have come down to us in the likeness of men!" And Barnabas they called Zeus, and Paul, Hermes, because he was the chief speaker. Then the priest of Zeus, whose temple was in front of their city, brought oxen and garlands to the gates, intending to sacrifice with the multitudes. (NKJV)*

Who could have anticipated such a devilish turn of events! Instead of giving glory to God for the healing of the believing lame man, the people's appreciation turned to idolatry—a complete misunderstanding of the truth—a lie!

In this case it was a lie based on fear (as most idolatry is). A local legend held that two of the gods, **Zeus** and **Hermes**, had once assumed human form and visited the town of Lystra. Only an old man and woman offered them hospitality. The two gods became angry and destroyed the town, wiping out the entire population, except for the old couple! The Lystrans were determined not to make the same mistake again. This led to the bizarre incident with Paul and Barnabas.

Religious fervor, powered by sheer terror, escalated out of control. Paul and Barnabas, not understanding the local language, did not realize at first what was happening. The priest of Zeus, whose job it was to keep the gods happy, brought bulls to sacrifice to the visiting "deities."

# Apostles Tear Their Clothes

ACTS 14:14–18 *But when the apostles Barnabas and Paul heard this, they tore their clothes and ran in among the multi-*

**go to**

**patient God**
Acts 17:30;
Romans 2:4;
2 Peter 3:9

**crops and food**
Genesis 8:22;
Psalm 4:7;
Ecclesiastes 9:7;
Isaiah 25:6;
Acts 2:46

**testimony**
Psalm 19:1–4;
Acts 17:24–28;
Romans 1:19–20

**reject the exalted**
Matthew 23:8–12

*tude, crying out and saying, "Men, why are you doing these things? We also are men with the same nature as you, and preach to you that you should turn from these useless things to the living God, who made the heaven, the earth, the sea, and all things that are in them, who in bygone generations allowed all nations to walk in their own ways. Nevertheless He did not leave Himself without witness, in that He did good, gave us rain from heaven and fruitful seasons, filling our hearts with food and gladness." And with these sayings they could scarcely restrain the multitudes from sacrificing to them. (NKJV)*

The apostles' drastic action barely managed to stop the sacrifices. They tore their clothes to rags and plunged into the crowd of would-be "worshipers," yelling, "We also are men with the same nature as you"! Half naked, they forced the people to touch and look and see that they were mere flesh.

Not only did Paul and Barnabas expose themselves as humans to a crowd determined to make them gods, but they dared call this "great honor" a "useless thing." In fact, the entire pagan system of worship is a useless thing from which people must turn to find the real God.

The real God is

- the *living* God (Zeus and Hermes were lifeless figments of human imagination!),
- the Creator who made everything in heaven, earth, and sea,
- the <u>patient God</u> who "allowed all nations to walk in their own ways" (Acts 14:16 NKJV), waiting for them to turn to him, and
- the kind God who provides rain and <u>crops and food</u> that bring joy to human hearts.

To people who pay attention, the created universe, rain, and food, are visible <u>testimony</u> in every generation to the existence, power, and goodness of God. A starting place for witness is to show people God's work in creation and his supply of human needs.

The authenticity of Christian leaders demands they <u>reject the exalted</u> positions people build for them. In Lystra there could be no mistake about the fact that, even though they were God's messengers, Paul and Barnabas were nonetheless ordinary humanity. Their vulnerability nearly cost Paul his life (Acts 14:19)!

what others say

**Oswald Chambers**

There is no room for . . . the crank or the fanatic in missionary work. A fanatic is one who has forgotten he is a human being. Our Lord never sent out cranks and fanatics, he sent out those who were loyal to his domination. He sent out ordinary men and women . . .[9]

go to

**battered Paul**
2 Corinthians 11:25;
Galatians 6:17

## Down but Not Out

ACTS 14:19–20 *Then Jews from Antioch and Iconium came there; and having persuaded the multitudes, they stoned Paul and dragged him out of the city, supposing him to be dead. However, when the disciples gathered around him, he rose up and went into the city. And the next day he departed with Barnabas to Derbe.* (NKJV)

Embarrassed and feeling foolish, the Lystran crowd was an easy target for clever enemies of the gospel who used the confusion to create a riot. The attack focused on Paul, since he was the main speaker. Stones flew. Paul went down. To hide what they had done from Roman authorities (who would strongly disapprove of such a riot), they dragged what they thought was Paul's dead body out of the city and dumped it. Christians—Barnabas, the healed lame man, and other believers—gathered around the <u>battered Paul</u>, who revived and went back into the city with them.

what others say

**William Barclay**

It was John Wesley's advice, "Always look a mob in the face." There could be no braver thing than Paul's going straight back amongst those who had tried to murder him. A deed like that would have more effect than a hundred sermons. Men were bound to ask themselves where a man got the courage to act in such a way.[10]

## Watering Baby Plants

ACTS 14:21–25 *And when they had preached the gospel to that city and made many disciples, they returned to Lystra, Iconium, and Antioch, strengthening the souls of the disciples, exhorting them to continue in the faith, and saying, "We must through many tribulations enter the kingdom of God." So when they had*

**go to**

**elders**
1 Timothy 3;
Titus 1;
1 Peter 5

**Spirit had gifted**
Ephesians 4:11

**servant-leadership**
Matthew 20:25–28

**leader**
Ephesians 5:23;
Colossians 1:18

**strengthened**
literally, "confirmed
the minds of"

**elders**
Greek:
*presbuteros*—over-
seers, pastors, spiri-
tually mature leaders

*appointed elders in every church, and prayed with fasting, they commended them to the Lord in whom they had believed. And after they had passed through Pisidia, they came to Pamphylia. Now when they had preached the word in Perga, they went down to Attalia. (NKJV)*

Next, the church planters headed for Derbe, sixty miles southeast on the border of Galatia. The good news had good success there.

From Derbe they returned for a brief visit to each place where they had left a knot of believers, a baby church. In most places, their first visit had been cut short by the pressing necessity to "get outta Dodge" quickly to keep from being killed. On these return visits the apostles did four things:

1. They **strengthened** the disciples (Acts 14:22), instructing them further concerning the Christian way.

2. They encouraged them to remain true to the faith (Acts 14:22). The little flocks of believers in each place faced the same persecution and pressure as the apostles.

3. They appointed <u>elders</u> in each church (Acts 14:23). They helped believers in each place to recognize people the Holy <u>Spirit had gifted</u> for <u>servant-leadership</u>.

4. They commended them to the Lord (Acts 14:23). The most effective leaders and committed people cannot make church happen as it is intended. The church, like the Christian life, requires a walk of faith—a dependence on Christ to function as Savior and <u>leader</u> of his church, his body.

## Full Circle

**ACTS 14:26–28** *From there they sailed to Antioch, where they had been commended to the grace of God for the work which they had completed. Now when they had come and gathered the church together, they reported all that God had done with them, and that He had opened the door of faith to the Gentiles. So they stayed there a long time with the disciples. (NKJV)*

Back at "home base" in Antioch on the Orontes, the "sending church" waited and prayed for the return of their favorite sons. When Barnabas and Paul returned after two-plus years on the campaign trail, that whole wild and crazy, gung-ho-for-Jesus group came together to hear the report of what God was doing among the Gentiles. Why shouldn't they? They had been there at every turn in the road in their hearts and prayers.

**Moravians**
Protestant denomination arising in fifteenth-century Bohemia and Moravia

what others say

**Paul Billheimer**

The **Moravians** . . . carried on a chain of prayer day and night which continued uninterrupted for 100 years. This was the beginning of the modern missionary movement.[11]

## Chapter Wrap-Up

- A group of spiritually powerful prophets and teachers met, fasted, and prayed in Antioch. The Holy Spirit communicated his desire that Barnabas and Saul be sent out to take the message of Jesus into the Gentile world. (Acts 13:1–3)

- The team sailed to Cyprus, where they preached in the synagogues. At Paphos, the governor wanted to hear the gospel, but a Jewish sorcerer kept him from it. In an outburst of power, Paul stopped the sorcerer and struck him blind. (Acts 13:4–12)

- From Cyprus the team traveled to Antioch, Pisidia. Paul showed how Christianity grew from Judaism's roots. When synagogue leaders opposed them, they shared Jesus with Gentiles. Many believed. When a persecution started, they left. (Acts 13:13–52)

- The apostolic team had an effective ministry in Iconium until a campaign of slander turned many against them and a plot developed to stone them to death. They found out about the plot and headed for Lystra and Derbe. (Acts 14:1–7)

- At Lystra, a lame man was healed. People thought Paul and Barnabas were gods. The apostles tore their clothes and dived into the crowd to show they were human, then told them to turn to the real God. Paul was stoned and left for dead. (Acts 14:8–20)

• After preaching at Derbe, the team revisited the towns where they'd preached. They confirmed the believers' faith, encouraged them, and appointed elders in each city. Then they returned to their home base in Antioch on the Orontes. (Acts 14:21–28)

## <u>Study Questions</u>

1. Identify and describe two types of ministry the leaders at Antioch used to help people grow up in relationship to Jesus?

2. What two things did the prophets and teachers do when they got together as a team? What did the Spirit tell them to do?

3. Identify three of the five things Paul said to Elymas the sorcerer which express the Bible's evaluation of wizards, witches, and practitioners of magic, spiritualism, and the occult (Acts 13:9–11).

4. After the lame man's healing, who did the people of Lystra think the apostles were? What did Paul and Barnabas do to show they were human?

5. What "testimony" to his reality and kindness has God given to all people?

# Acts 15 Outsiders Crash the Christian Party

**Chapter Highlights:**
* The Council of Jerusalem, AD 50
* Yes! to the Revolution
* Risk-Takers Deliver Liberating Letter

## Let's Get Started

To some early Christians it seemed the gospel had leaped out of its corral and was galloping across the world landscape like a herd of mustangs—beyond control, free, and wild. Wonderful things were happening among non-Jewish people.

Strict Jews who believed in Jesus were happy when the first Gentiles found the Lord. But then they watched as changes took place that made them extremely uncomfortable. From childhood it had been drilled into them that circumcision was the symbol separating God's people from pagans. Naturally, they expected believing Gentiles to start acting like Jews!

This set up a showdown that led to another important turning point in early Christianity. The shoot-out at the Jerusalem Council lets us observe a fine example of creative conflict resolution.

## Jewish Believers Decide to "Enlighten" Gentile Believers

> ACTS 15:1 *And certain men came down from Judea and taught the brethren, "Unless you are circumcised according to the custom of Moses, you cannot be saved."* (NKJV)

Gentiles would soon outnumber Jews in the church. No one in leadership seemed to be raising the all-important circumcision issue. Everyone danced around the subject of the sacred surgery. Paul and Barnabas's two-year mission brought a quadrillion more non-Jews into the church without telling them they had to obey Jewish rules!

To some Hebrew Christians this was unacceptable. Two questions bugged them:

1. How can non-Jews be saved and considered the people of God if they don't observe the Law of Moses (Acts 15:1)?

**justified**
right with God,
accepted

2. How can Christians who keep the traditions of Judaism "break bread" with ceremonially unclean Gentiles who ignore Moses's rules about the "right" food and the "right" way to prepare it (see Acts 11:3) and who don't get circumcised?

Some concerned Jewish believers decided that if their leaders weren't going to deal with these issues they'd have to. They packed their bags and headed for Antioch to "enlighten" the Gentile believers there.

## Paul and Barnabas Challenge Suppositions

ACTS 15:2–4 *Therefore, when Paul and Barnabas had no small dissension and dispute with them, they determined that Paul and Barnabas and certain others of them should go up to Jerusalem, to the apostles and elders, about this question. So, being sent on their way by the church, they passed through Phoenicia and Samaria, describing the conversion of the Gentiles; and they caused great joy to all the brethren. And when they had come to Jerusalem, they were received by the church and the apostles and the elders; and they reported all things that God had done with them. (NKJV)*

Intense argumentation followed as Paul and Barnabas challenged the erroneous suppositions of the legalist teachers. Since these Pharisaic "evangelists" claimed to represent the Jerusalem church, it was decided the Jerusalem church and the apostles should be brought into the controversy. So Antioch dispatched Paul and Barnabas and others to powwow with the apostles and elders at Jerusalem. The churches along the way were glad to hear of Gentiles coming to Christ. When the duo arrived, the Jerusalem church treated the two missionaries like conquering heroes.

This debate had to happen because it raised questions that were at the heart of the Christian message: First, can a person be good and law abiding enough to earn God's favor, or must he simply admit his helplessness and humbly throw himself on God's mercy and grace? Second, what must a person do to be saved—work or believe?

In his letter to the Galatians, Paul states the principle behind his and Barnabas's contention that Gentiles must be accepted into full fellowship in the church without being required to be circumcised and practice the Old Testament ceremonies: "Knowing that a man is not **justified** by the works of the law but by faith in Jesus Christ. . . . for by the works of the law no flesh shall be justified" (Galatians 2:16 NKJV).

key point

Some issues are so essential to the good news they cannot be compromised! The truth that salvation is by <u>faith not works</u> is one of those issues.

The apostles and elders met to consider this question.

## The Council of Jerusalem, AD 50

> **Acts 15:5–6** *But some of the sect of the Pharisees who believed rose up, saying, "It is necessary to circumcise them, and to command them to keep the law of Moses." Now the apostles and elders came together to consider this matter.* (NKJV)

In case you haven't heard, conflict is not foreign to the church. Never has been. Here we are taken inside an early church business meeting called to consider an issue so crucial, if not dealt with correctly, it could have created a gigantic roadblock to the progress of the gospel at a time when it was just beginning to penetrate the world at large. It gives us our best view of the early church's approach to corporate problem solving.

### Who Was There?

It was an open meeting. The decision would affect the whole church (Acts 15:4, 22). So grassroots members were there along with the church's leaders. Two types of leaders are identified (Acts 15:2, 4, 6, 22, 23):

1. *Apostles*—Members of the original Twelve still in Jerusalem, plus Paul and Barnabas. James had been martyred (see Acts 12:2). Peter was on the lam but, at considerable personal risk, came back for this meeting (see Acts 12:19; 15:7).

2. *Elders*—Spiritual leaders (shepherds) appointed for pastoral care of the local congregation in Jerusalem. This local leadership team is first mentioned in Acts 11:30. James, Jesus's brother, is recognized as the leader of this pastoral team (see Acts 12:17; 15:13; 21:18).

The debate was set up by Christian **Pharisees**. Pharisees in the New Testament are <u>not usually</u> pro-Jesus. But these exceptional Pharisees were followers of Jesus and part of the church. They kept philosophical ties with the legalistic Pharisee party. Their argument:

go to

**faith not works**
John 6:28–29;
Galatians 5:6;
Ephesians 2:8–9

**not usually**
Matthew 3:1–12;
9:1–13; 12:12–14;
23:23–24

**Pharisees**
meticulously
observed the Law of
Moses and ceremo-
nial rules developed
by rabbis

"Gentiles must be circumcised and required to obey the law of Moses."

## Principles of Church Decision-Making

Thorough discussion of all viewpoints and willingness to listen (Acts 15:7, 12) are essential to turn division into unity. The Greek words the author of Acts uses to describe the debate tell how thorough the discussion was:

- Acts 15:2—"no small dissension and dispute" (Greek: "not a little discord and questioning")
- Acts 15:7—"much dispute" (Greek: "seeking, discussion, debate, controversy")

Howard Marshall calls it "a general free-for-all."[1] Eugene Peterson's interpretation of Acts 15:7 says, "The arguments went on and on, back and forth, getting more and more heated."[2]

The early church historian Luke doesn't give the arguments of those in favor of demanding that Gentiles live under Jewish law. Focus is on statements that carried the day and led to the harmonious conclusion.

Two basic Christian beliefs guided the discussion:

key point

1. Christians believe Jesus is personally involved with them in the affairs of the church, through his Holy Spirit (Acts 15:28; see Matthew 18:20; 28:20).

2. Christians believe agreement among themselves carries great power and authority (Acts 15:22, 25; see Matthew 18:17–19).

## Gentiles Invited by God

ACTS 15:7–12 *And when there had been much dispute, Peter rose up and said to them: "Men and brethren, you know that a good while ago God chose among us, that by my mouth the Gentiles should hear the word of the gospel and believe. So God, who knows the heart, acknowledged them by giving them the Holy Spirit, just as He did to us, and made no distinction between us and them, purifying their hearts by faith. Now therefore, why do you test God by putting a yoke on the neck of the disciples which neither our fathers nor we were able to bear? But we believe that through the grace of the Lord Jesus Christ we shall be saved in the same manner as they." Then all the multitude kept silent and listened to Barnabas and Paul declaring how many miracles and wonders God had worked through them among the Gentiles. (NKJV)*

**go to**

**impossible burden**
Romans 7:7–25;
Galatians 3:10–14

Peter, the apostle with a price on his head, stood to remind them what God did in the Captain Cornelius affair—an incident still fresh in their minds. His arguments were simple and convincing, as the following chart shows:

**multifarious**
diverse, great
variety

## God Chose the Gentiles As Well As the Jews

| Paul's Argument | Scripture |
| --- | --- |
| God initiated the outreach to the Gentiles. | Acts 15:7; 10:3–20; 11:17 |
| God verified his acceptance of Gentiles by giving them the Holy Spirit, just like he did us Jewish believers. | Acts 15:8; 10:44; 11:15–17 |
| God makes no distinction between Jews and Gentiles. The hearts of both are purified on the basis of faith in Jesus. | Acts 15:9 |
| To lay the burden of Moses's Law on people God has accepted amounts to questioning God's judgment. | Acts 15:10; 11:17 |
| If lifelong Jews have found the Law an impossible burden, what sense does it make to expect Gentiles to bear it. | Acts 15:10 |
| The Law never saved anyone. Jews and Gentiles alike are saved through the grace (undeserved favor) of the Lord Jesus. | Acts 15:11 |

To buttress Peter's arguments, Paul and Barnabas related their experiences, reporting visible evidence of God at work among the Gentiles in Asia Minor (Acts 15:12). The assembly fell silent, listening. The facts had a calming effect.

**what others say**

**William Barclay**

The attempt to obey the Law's **multifarious** commands and so to earn salvation was a losing battle which left every man in default. There is only one way—the acceptance of the free gift of the grace of God in an act of self-surrendering faith.

Peter went right to the heart of the question. . . . Can a man earn the favor of God? Or must he admit his own helplessness and be ready in humble faith to accept what the grace of God gives? In effect, the Jewish party said, "Religion means earn-

## Yes! to the Revolution

ACTS 15:13 *And after they had become silent, James answered,
saying, "Men and brethren, listen to me: (NKJV)*

After the arguments had been heard, a respected member of the
local church leadership team offered a decision he felt was consistent
with the facts and on which he felt the body could agree. Who was
this "James," and why should the church listen to him?

James was Jesus's biological brother (Mark 6:3). He'd seen Jesus
after his resurrection (2 Corinthians 15:7). He'd become acknowledged leader of the Jerusalem church because of his mature Christian
character and spiritual giftedness. He was nicknamed "Old Camel
Knees" because he spent so much time on his knees in prayer. He
was known and respected both in and outside the church as a faithful observer of the Law of Moses.

what others say

### William Barclay

[James's] leadership was not a formal office; it was a moral
leadership conceded to him because he was an outstanding
man.[4]

## The Last Argument

ACTS 15:14–18 *Simon has declared how God at the first visited
the Gentiles to take out of them a people for His name. And with
this the words of the prophets agree, just as it is written:*
  *'After this I will return*
  *And will rebuild the tabernacle of David, which has
    fallen down;*
  *I will rebuild its ruins,*
  *And I will set it up;*
  *So that the rest of mankind may seek the LORD,*
  *Even all the Gentiles who are called by My name,*
  *Says the LORD who does all these things.'*
*Known to God from eternity are all His works. (NKJV)*

Though James was a committed keeper of Jewish religious law, he could see only one direction for the church to take. Two things convinced him:

go to

**eat together**
Acts 1:4; 2:42, 46; 6:1–2; 11:3

**idolatry**
Exodus 20:4–6

**eating blood**
Genesis 9:4; Leviticus 17:10; Deuteronomy 12:23–25

1. *God's actions* (Acts 15:14). No believer would suggest God goofed in gathering "a people for His name" from the Gentiles (as reported by Peter, Paul, and Barnabas).

2. *God's Word* (Acts 15:15–18). A prophecy from the book of Amos convinced him it had always been God's plan for Gentiles to be welcomed into the church as Gentiles—not forced to become Jews! (See Amos 9:11–12.)

## Consensus for Freedom and Fellowship

**consensus**
what the group can agree on

**sacrificed to idols**
food in Gentile markets was often offered to an idol before being sold

ACTS 15:19–21 *Therefore I judge that we should not trouble those from among the Gentiles who are turning to God, but that we write to them to abstain from things polluted by idols, from sexual immorality, from things strangled, and from blood. For Moses has had throughout many generations those who preach him in every city, being read in the synagogues every Sabbath."* (NKJV)

The facts were obvious: (1) God accepts Gentiles on the basis of faith (Acts 15:8); and (2) Judaism's ceremonial laws hinder the gospel's growth among non-Jews and create barriers to fellowship between true believers (Acts 15:10–11). Confronted by the facts and the group's expressed concerns, James pulled together a **consensus** and proposed it be communicated to the churches.

1. *No roadblocks to faith* (Acts 15:19). The church should not make it difficult for Gentiles to turn to God. Circumcision isn't mentioned, but the intent is Gentiles are off the hook. No Jewish rituals are required, including circumcision.

2. *No roadblocks to fellowship* (Acts 15:20). Gentiles should make accommodations to their Jewish friends so they can eat together freely. Two things Jews find especially repulsive are idolatry (anything to do with idols) and eating blood. Non-Jewish believers can make it easier for Jews to break bread with them if they stop serving food **sacrificed to idols** or unbled meat.

3. *The moral high road* (Acts 15:20). Guarding against sexual sin of all kinds must have high priority. Lust, sexual sin, and marital unfaithfulness destroy fellowship.

4. *No anxiety about Moses* (Acts 15:21). Pharisees wanted Gentiles to live under Moses's influence. They feared erosion of his authority if new believers didn't keep the Law. Not to worry! "Moses has had throughout many generations those who preach him in every city, being read in the synagogues every Sabbath" (Acts 15:21 NKJV). Christians will always be influenced by Moses. (James was right.) Christians love the Old Testament. Moses still speaks to Christians!

The "requirements" of the Jerusalem Council were aimed at removing the main barriers to fellowship between Jewish and Gentile Christians.

**what others say**

**F. F. Bruce**

Idolatry, fornication, and murder were the three cardinal sins in Jewish eyes; avoidance of these was held to be binding on the whole human race.[5]

**Maude De Joseph West**

It comes as a shock to most of us that the sin of gross immorality was mentioned in the same breath with dietary customs. Among Gentiles, chastity was not something to be cherished, nor impurity a sin to be avoided. They simply did not know any better. How could they have known? Their very religions were filthily immoral.

We know better. Nonetheless, we are moving swiftly toward that abyss of immorality from which those Gentiles were rescued by the grace of our Lord and Savior, Jesus Christ.[6]

When the letter was composed reporting the decision to the Gentile churches, it read: "It seemed good to the Holy Spirit, and to us . . ." (Acts 15:28 NKJV). The Holy Spirit had this great idea, and we all agreed. In this case, the Spirit of Jesus, the church's Head, led his people through the processes involved in consensus making.

**Lawrence O. Richards**

In many ways the first church council can serve as a model for resolving disputed issues today. We note especially that:

1. The issue was clearly defined.

2. The issue was brought to the entire leadership for open discussion and debate.

3. Differing positions were actively argued.

4. Evidence from what God was currently doing was considered.

5. The interpretation of what God was doing was tested for harmony with Scripture.

6. Special concern was shown for the sensibilities of those who "lost" the debate.

7. The "winners" were asked to surrender some of the rights they had won in view of some of the convictions of the "losers."

. . . We cannot expect everyone to surrender convictions which are wrong, however clear the voice of God through church and Scripture. What we can do is seek to hear the Holy Spirit's voice through our brothers and the Word of God. And, as we debate, remember always that we are one family in Christ, and that those who differ from us remain brothers and sisters whom we have a duty to love.[7]

The Lord leads his church in practical matters through consensus (agreement, harmony). Keys to consensus are dependence on the Holy Spirit to guide the process, commitment to unity rather than "winning," valuing each other personally, and willingness to listen to each other's concerns.

key point

# Risk-Takers Deliver Liberating Letter

**Acts 15:22–35**

The apostles and elders and the Jerusalem church sent Paul and Barnabas back to Antioch accompanied by Judas and Silas. They carried a letter restating the decision to free believing Gentiles from Jewish rules. The Antioch Christians welcomed the liberating letter. Judas and Silas returned to Jerusalem. Paul and Barnabas continued to teach and preach in Antioch.

Four men were dispatched with the letter from Jerusalem to "the brethren who are of the Gentiles" in Antioch and the provinces of Syria and Cilicia (Acts 15:23 NKJV). Acts 15:26 identifies Paul and Barnabas as "men who have risked their lives for the name of our Lord Jesus Christ" (NKJV). Judas Barsabas and Silas, two members of Jerusalem's leadership team (Acts 15:22), both prophets (Acts 15:32), were sent along to authenticate and explain the letter.

The straight-talking letter repudiated the unauthorized teachers who'd caused such angst in Antioch, freed Gentiles from Judaism's religious rituals, and encouraged a "Just say No!" attitude toward sexual sin and things that strain cross-cultural Christian fellowship.

## Coming Apart at the Teams

ACTS 15:36–39a *Then after some days Paul said to Barnabas, "Let us now go back and visit our brethren in every city where we have preached the word of the Lord, and see how they are doing." Now Barnabas was determined to take with them John called Mark. But Paul insisted that they should not take with them the one who had departed from them in Pamphylia, and had not gone with them to the work. Then the contention became so sharp that they parted from one another. (NKJV)*

At this strategic moment in the history of the church, when it began to radically change from a movement within Judaism to a predominantly Gentile movement, two of its most important visionaries could no longer see eye to eye and parted company—never to work together again.

## The Devil in the Details

Luke gives so few details that we can only guess why the conflict between Paul and Barnabas could not be resolved. Here's what we know:

They agreed to revisit the churches they'd planted. But Mark, Barnabas's younger cousin, became the focus of a "contention . . . so sharp" that they parted (Acts 15:39 NKJV). The original word means "an angry dispute." A fight.

In this corner, wearing white trunks and weighing 200 pounds: BARNABAS THE ENCOURAGER—the "people person," <u>champion of young believers</u> no one else wants to help. He wanted to take Mark with them even though he'd jumped ship on the first voyage (Acts 13:13). "Come on, Paul, give the kid another chance!"

In this corner, wearing purple trunks and weighing 190 pounds: PAUL THE PERFECTIONIST—the "do or die person," the <u>get up and keep punching</u> guy, intense, concerned for success of the mission. Mark had blown his chance, leaving them shorthanded on the first trip.

"The kid's not dry behind the ears! A quitter! Excess baggage!"

**go to**

**champion of young believers**
Acts 9:26–27; 11:23

**get up and keep punching**
Acts 14:19–20

## Breaking Up the Old Gang

ACTS 15:39b–41 *And so Barnabas took Mark and sailed to Cyprus; but Paul chose Silas and departed, being commended by the brethren to the grace of God. And he went through Syria and Cilicia, strengthening the churches. (NKJV)*

The original missionary team split in two:

- Team Cyprus: Barnabas and Mark
- Team Europe: Paul and Silas

Who was right, and who was wrong? The song says, "It takes two to tango!" As in every rancorous split-up, there was no doubt plenty of blame to go around.

Barnabas turned out to be right in his assessment of Mark. After a few more years of discipling with the "son of encouragement," early church tradition says Mark ministered with Peter and wrote a New Testament Gospel. According to 2 Timothy 4:11, even Paul changed his mind about Mark. Paul continued to esteem Barnabas as an equal in commitment and sacrifice for the Gospel (1 Corinthians 9:6).

**go to**

**breakup**
Acts 15:37–39

**Silvanus**
2 Corinthians 1:19;
1 Thessalonians 1:1;
2 Thessalonians 1:1

**Jesus's teaching**
Matthew 20:25–28

**worked good**
Romans 8:28

After the <u>breakup</u> of the original missionary team, Paul chose Silas and headed for Asia Minor to follow up the young churches there. It was rebuilding time for Paul's team. His new partner, Silas a.k.a. <u>Silvanus</u>, was an elder in the Jerusalem church, sent with Paul and Barnabas to explain the decision of the Jerusalem Council freeing Gentiles from Jewish religious rules. He was a preacher or speaker for God with an effective ministry with the Gentiles in Antioch (see Acts 15:32). Like Paul, he was a Roman citizen (see Acts 16:37–38).

<u>Jesus's teaching</u> and example suggest that bringing along weak, failing individuals is high on the list of Christian leadership priorities. His patience with the weak and failing is legendary. Look what he put up with from those twelve deficient disciples closest to him!

God <u>worked good</u> from the conflict. Two teams went two directions sharing the good news. New Testament readers are left with the comforting assurance that God uses people in his work who are very, very human.

## what others say

### Larry Richards

Was Paul a hypocrite? He urged others to reconcile their differences but became so angry with Barnabas that he broke up with his friend. Paul . . . was a fallible human being. None of us are without weakness; all of us are susceptible to sin. . . . Later Mark . . . became reconciled to Paul, who wrote to Timothy to, "get Mark and bring him with you, because he is helpful to me in my ministry" (2 Timothy 4:11). This tacit admission that he was wrong clears Paul of the charge of hypocrisy but (worked good) not of acting foolishly in breaking up with Barnabas over giving Mark a second chance.[9]

Division between Christians can have disastrous results. But the Lord is able to use (and often has used) division to get his people to move in new directions which fulfill his goals. One thing is certain: Division cannot stop the spread of the good news.

# Chapter Wrap-Up

- The Gentile-Jewish fellowship at Antioch was disrupted by teachers who insisted Gentiles must be circumcised. Paul and Barnabas debated them. The church sent them to discuss the issue with elders and apostles in Jerusalem. (Acts 15:1–4)

- The first world church council met to discuss the issue. Christian Pharisees insisted Gentiles come under Moses's Law. Peter, with Paul and Barnabas's support, told how God accepted Gentiles on the same basis as Jews—by faith in Jesus. (Acts 15:5–12)

- James, leader of the Jerusalem church, proposed freeing Gentile believers from the Law and called for them to adjust to their Jewish brothers and sisters by a couple of dietary changes and to avoid sexual sin. Church leaders agreed. (Acts 15:13–22)

- Two local leaders, Judas and Silas, were sent to Antioch with Paul and Barnabas and a letter outlining the council's decision. The Gentile believers were overjoyed with the decision freeing them from the obligation of circumcision. (Acts 15:22–34)

- Paul and Barnabas made plans to go on another missionary journey, but got into an argument about whether John Mark should go along again. The disagreement became so intense, the team split up. (Acts 15:35–41)

# Study Questions

1. When unauthorized teachers from Jerusalem came to Antioch insisting that Gentile believers had to be circumcised in order to be saved, how did Paul and Barnabas respond? What was the real issue?

2. In his argument before the apostles and elders at Jerusalem, Peter stressed six points. Identify three of them.

3. What two things convinced James that the Gentiles should be accepted into the church as Gentiles and not expected to become Jews?

4. What two things did James feel Gentiles should do to make fellowship with their Jewish counterparts easier?

5. What was the issue that led to the breakup of Paul and Barnabas?

# Acts 16 Penetration into the Roman World

Chapter Highlights:
- Rebuilding the Dream Team
- River Sisters
- Red Carpet for the "Bad Guys"

## Let's Get Started

The decision by the Jerusalem Council (see Acts 15) to release Gentiles from the Law of Moses kicked into motion a time of transition for the young church. Christians were no longer merely another Jewish sect. The Jesus movement was rapidly becoming a predominantly Gentile movement. The story, as told in Acts, shifts attention to the gospel's penetration deep into the Roman world and to the widening ministry of Paul.

**spiritually valuable abilities**
gifts of the Holy Spirit

## Rebuilding the Dream Team

ACTS 16:1 *Then he [Paul] came to Derbe and Lystra. And behold, a certain disciple was there, named Timothy, the son of a certain Jewish woman who believed, but his father was Greek.* (NKJV)

Paul regrouped with Silas, his new partner, and left on another missionary journey (see Illustration #12). When Paul and Barnabas visited Lystra five years earlier, Paul was nearly killed by a crowd of "adoring fans" who suddenly turned violent and stoned him (Acts 14:8–21). He was left for dead outside the city. Out of that pile of bloody stones rose not only a battered-but-unbowed Paul but also a Christian church. And out of that church emerged a gifted young man named Timothy who was to become one of Paul's most trusted coworkers and dearest friends.

### "God-Honoring" Timothy

Timothy was the son of a Jewish Christian mother and a Greek father. His name means "God honoring." He was a lifelong student of the Bible (see 2 Timothy 3:14–15) but was not raised a strict Jew. His mother, Eunice, and grandmother Lois were excellent spiritual models (see 2 Timothy 1:5). Tim possessed **spiritually valuable abilities**, but needed encouragement to use them (see 1 Timothy 4:14; 2 Timothy 1:6). Even so, he was respected by fellow Christians who commissioned him for Christian ministry (see Acts 16:2; 2 Timothy 4:14).

**Illustration #12**
Paul's Second Missionary Journey—Paul's second missionary journey began at Antioch, north of Jerusalem. Paul's travels with Silas are shown. The dashed line shows where Barnabas and Mark left Paul and headed for Cyprus.

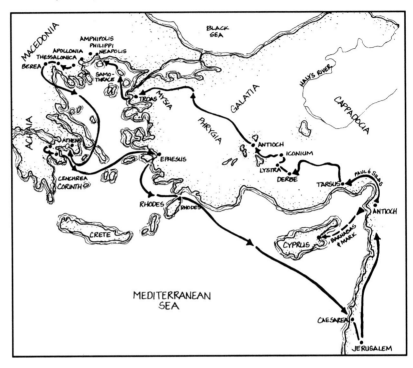

go to

**mind of Christ**
1 Corinthians
2:9–16;
2 Corinthians 10:5

**serendipities**
unexpected, delightful discoveries and experiences

## The Wondrous Wisdom of Holy Inconsistency

ACTS 16:2–3 *He [Timothy] was well spoken of by the brethren who were at Lystra and Iconium. Paul wanted to have him go on with him. And he took him and circumcised him because of the Jews who were in that region, for they all knew that his father was Greek. (NKJV)*

What's this? Paul, the champion of spiritual freedom who argued successfully for liberation of Gentiles from the necessity of circumcision, who was in Lystra to pass that good news to the church there, now does a 180 by circumcising Timothy. What's wrong with the picture? What was Paul doing?

Some people accuse Paul of inconsistency. Perhaps. But "foolish consistency," wrote R. W. Emerson, "is the hobgoblin of little minds."[1] Paul's was no "little mind." He was never as committed to the wisdom of the Jerusalem Council as to the <u>mind of Christ</u> and the day-to-day leadership of the Holy Spirit. No set of rules can cover all the surprises and **serendipities** involved with the Holy

something to ponder

Spirit's personal leading. In circumcising Timothy, Paul acted according to higher principles than the principles of freedom, personal preference, or doing the least the church demands. Far more important to him were the following things:

- The principle of personal obedience to Christ (see 2 Corinthians 10:5)

- The principle of living by the spirit not the letter of the law (see 2 Corinthians 3:6)

- The principle of accommodation on **nonessentials** in order to communicate the gospel to diverse people (see 1 Corinthians 9:19–23)

- The principle of love (see 1 Corinthians 13:4–8)

### Why Did Timothy Let Paul Perform "the Surgery"?

There were two main reasons Tim Terrific chose this elective surgery. Both are "because of the Jews" (Acts 16:3 NKJV), and both have to do with the team's priority of taking the gospel to the Jews in every city first (Acts 13:5, 14; 14:1; 16:13; 17:2, 10, 17; 18:4; Romans 1:16). First, Tim wanted to assure Jews that following Christ did not mean they had to stop being Jewish. Second, he wanted all the credibility he could get with the Jews they would be trying to reach.

Timothy did not have to submit to circumcision to be accepted by God or the church. But because he loved the Jewish people, he <u>surrendered</u> his rights in order to serve them.

## <u>Following the Holy Spirit Around</u>

> **the big picture**
>
> **Acts 16:4–10**
>
> Paul and his friends delivered the Jerusalem apostles' decision, and the churches grew. The Holy Spirit kept Paul from preaching in Asia and from entering Bithynia. Paul had a vision of a man asking him to come to Macedonia, so he went.

Christian workers' movements are a blend of strategic planning and sensitivity to the Spirit. Acts 16:6–10 describes four ways the team experienced the Lord's step-by-step leadership:

**surrendered**
Matthew 20:27–28

**nonessentials**
religious practices, preferences, and opinions not required for salvation

**prophecy**
1 Timothy 4:14

**uneasiness**
Colossians 3:15

**closed doors**
circumstances making a course of action impossible or impractical

1. *Spiritual roadblocks.* "They were forbidden by the Holy Spirit" from preaching in Asia province (Acts 16:6 NKJV). How the Spirit did this we're not told. <u>Prophecy</u>? <u>Uneasiness</u> about a planned action?

2. *Adverse conditions and physical limitations.* The Spirit of Jesus "did not permit them" to go north toward Bithynia (Acts 16:7 NKJV). Perhaps Paul became sick and needed a doctor. So they went to Troas where their friend, Dr. Luke, was. Paul's sickness was the Lord's way of denying permission to visit a place not on the divine itinerary.

3. *Vision (Acts 16:9):* "A vision . . . in the night" (literal translation). The same mental picture came to Paul repeatedly that night: A Macedonian stood pleading for Paul and the team to cross the Aegean Sea to Europe and "help us."

4. *Team agreement.* When Paul shared his vision, the team—Paul, Silas, Timothy, and Luke—started packing, "concluding" the vision was a call from God (Acts 16:10 NKJV). The whole team agreed the vision was God communicating his will.

"**Closed doors**" and circumstances had kept them moving west-northwest to Troas. There, with their toes in the Aegean, the orders they'd been listening for came in an all-night vision and team consensus.

## Dr. Luke Signs On

At Troas (Acts 16:10), so quietly the average reader may miss it, another member joined the team aboard the ship for Macedonia and would stick with Paul like flypaper until the last chapter of Acts. He doesn't wear a nametag. The subtle insertion of the little two-letter first-person plural pronouns, "we" and "us" (Acts 16:10 and ninety-six other verses in Acts), reveals that the author of Acts had signed on. Most of what he writes from this point on is eyewitness recall.

Luke was a Greek. Paul calls him, "Luke the beloved physician" (Colossians 4:14 NKJV). Unconfirmed early church stories about Luke suggest these intriguing possibilities:

- He was Theophilus's slave, (see Acts 1:1) freed after he restored his master's health.[2]

- He was a "charter member" of the Antioch church.[3]

- He was in Troas waiting to sign on as a ship's doctor.[4]

- He joined the team as personal physician to the frequently ailing Paul.[5]

**Roman colony**
citizens dressed
Roman, spoke Latin,
lived by Roman law

# Europe Calls!

ACTS 16:11 *Therefore, sailing from Troas, we ran a straight course to Samothrace, and the next day came to Neapolis,* (NKJV)

At last, the Spirit said, "Go!" The team headed for the dock with "Europe or bust!" stickers on their luggage. Their first port o' call on the way to Macedonia was Samothrace, a mountain island rising five thousand feet above the sea. The next day passengers and cargo were unloaded at Neapolis (modern Kavalla, Greece), seaport for Philippi.

what others say

### John Pollock

They did not think of themselves as passing from the continent of Asia to Europe. [These] terms were in use, but the Aegean was Greek on either side. They had, instead, the excitement of approaching a new province, bringing them nearer Rome. They knew that beyond Macedonia they could reach Achaia and Italy, and the vast lands of Gaul, Spain, Germania, even the mist-bound island of Britain lately added to the empire: all save Rome untouched by the Good News. They were not bringing force of arms or a political program: just four men—and Another, invisible. . . .[6]

# River Sisters

ACTS 16:12–13 *and from there to Philippi, which is the foremost city of that part of Macedonia, a colony. And we were staying in that city for some days. And on the Sabbath day we went out of the city to the riverside, where prayer was customarily made; and we sat down and spoke to the women who met there.* (NKJV)

Philippi was a **Roman colon**y and commercial center on the Via Ignatia, the main overland route between the Aegean and Adriatic Seas. It was named for Philip of Macedon, father of Alexander the Great. Much of the population was retired military personnel.

**Lord opened**
John 6:44

**freed-woman**
liberated female
slave

**household**
family, servants,
slaves, and other
dependents

The Jewish population of Philippi was too small for a synagogue, which required a minimum of ten men. Jews gathered at the riverside for Sabbath prayers. At the River Gangites the apostles found a group of Jewish and God-fearing Gentile women and told them about Jesus. The Philippian church began with a group of praying women. As Christianity spread in the Roman Empire, women greatly outnumbered men among early converts.

## Lady in Purple

ACTS 16:14–15 *Now a certain woman named Lydia heard us. She was a seller of purple from the city of Thyatira, who worshiped God. The Lord opened her heart to heed the things spoken by Paul. And when she and her household were baptized, she begged us, saying, "If you have judged me to be faithful to the Lord, come to my house and stay." So she persuaded us.* (NKJV)

Macedonian women were noted for their independence. Under Roman law a freeborn woman with three children or a **freed-woman** with four children had the right to own property and enter into legal transactions without the consent of a husband or father. Many Macedonian women became highly influential.

One such woman was Lydia, a God-fearing Gentile who heard Paul preach at the riverside prayer meeting. She conducted a successful business in purple cloth dyed with the secretions of a rare Mediterranean shellfish. So rare and costly was this dye only the wealthy could afford the cloth. Trading in this exquisite fabric had made Lydia wealthy. And she was head of her own household.

The <u>Lord opened</u> Lydia's heart, and she believed in Jesus, becoming the first person on the European continent to turn to Christ. After she and her entire **household** were baptized she persuaded the team to stay at her home.

Women were attracted to early Christianity because within the Christian community women enjoyed higher status and security than among their pagan neighbors. By contrast to pagan women, who were married very young (often before puberty), Christian women had more freedom to decide if and when they would marry. Christian husbands could not easily divorce their wives. Marital faithfulness was expected of both Christian husbands and wives.

# The Case of the Unfortunate Fortune-Teller

> ACTS 16:16 *Now it happened, as we went to prayer, that a certain slave girl possessed with a spirit of divination met us, who brought her masters much profit by fortune-telling.* (NKJV)

The second European impacted by the good news came from the opposite end of the social spectrum from Lydia. She was a slave, physically and spiritually. She was mentally ill, tormented by an evil spirit Luke describes as *pneuma pythona*—the spirit of **Python**—which controlled her speech. "The ancient world had a strange respect for mad people because, they said, the gods had taken away their wits in order to put the mind of the gods into them."[7] The Philippians believed this girl was clairvoyant—that she could tell the future. Her owners charged high fees for her services as a fortune-teller.

**devil tells the truth**
Mark 1:23–26

**Python**
mythical snake guarding ecstatic speeches of the god Apollo

# Fortune-Teller Gets a Future

> ACTS 16:17–18 *This girl followed Paul and us, and cried out, saying, "These men are the servants of the Most High God, who proclaim to us the way of salvation." And this she did for many days. But Paul, greatly annoyed, turned and said to the spirit, "I command you in the name of Jesus Christ to come out of her." And he came out that very hour.* (NKJV)

When this tormented girl followed Paul and the others around announcing that they were God's servants telling "the way of salvation," Paul did not take it as a compliment. This continued several days. Paul became "annoyed." (That's putting it mildly. The Greek word means strongly irked, provoked, and "worked up" with anger or grief.) The tortured girl told the truth, but when the <u>devil tells the truth</u>, the effect is always confusion.

Finally, Paul whirled around and, in Jesus's name, commanded the evil spirit to come out of her. Instantly, the mental anguish ended and the slave girl was free from her spiritual bondage! Luke doesn't say she became a Christian. Likely she did.

# The Gospel—a Pain in the Pocketbook!

> ACTS 16:19–24 *But when her masters saw that their hope of profit was gone, they seized Paul and Silas and dragged them into the marketplace to the authorities. And they brought them to the magistrates, and said, "These men, being Jews, exceed-*

**go to**

**loss of revenue**
Acts 19:23–27

**beaten**
2 Corinthians 11:25

**exorcised**
expelled, gotten rid of

**property**
Romans referred to slaves as "living tools"

**anti-Semitic**
against the Jews

*ingly trouble our city; and they teach customs which are not lawful for us, being Romans, to receive or observe." Then the multitude rose up together against them; and the magistrates tore off their clothes and commanded them to be beaten with rods. And when they had laid many stripes on them, they threw them into prison, commanding the jailer to keep them securely. Having received such a charge, he put them into the inner prison and fastened their feet in the stocks. (NKJV)*

When they realized their profits had flown the coop along with the evil spirit, the girl's owners hit the ceiling! (Luke uses the same Greek word in verse 18 for departure of the evil spirit as in verse 19 for departure of the owners' profits. Their ill-gotten gain was literally **"exorcised"** along with the tormenting spirit!) Typical of people whose bottom line is money, they had no concern for the girl's welfare and no gratitude for her healing. She was, after all, **property**. By healing her Paul violated their property rights!

The owners played on the crowd's **anti-Semitic** sentiments. Their charges never mentioned the real reason for their ire, their <u>loss of revenue</u>. They accused Paul and Silas of being anti-Roman. (If the truth won't sell, try hogwash!)

Without investigating the charges, the magistrates ordered Paul and Silas <u>beaten</u> and jailed. The jailer was ordered to "guard them carefully." He locked them in the local jail's maximum-security cell and clamped their feet in stocks.

The economic effects of Christians' commitment to help people can trigger animosity. During AD 257–258 in Rome, Laurence, a deacon of the church at Rome, was ordered to hand over the treasures of the church to the head of the empire's pagan religion. Laurence promised to comply. Next day he gave all the money to the city's poor. (The church cared for 1,500 Roman widows and orphans at the time.) When officials asked where the treasures were, Laurence pointed to the poor. "These are the treasure of the church!" he said. He was beheaded for his disobedience.[8]

In the 1990s in suburban Phoenix, Arizona, a church ministering to the homeless came under attack by neighbors who claimed the presence of the homeless people was causing their property values to drop. City government intervened and ordered the church to stop its outreach to the homeless.

# Rejoicing and Singing in Prison

> ACTS 16:25–26 *But at midnight Paul and Silas were praying and singing hymns to God, and the prisoners were listening to them. Suddenly there was a great earthquake, so that the foundations of the prison were shaken; and immediately all the doors were opened and everyone's chains were loosed. (NKJV)*

**rejoicing**
Matthew 5:10–12;
Acts 5:41

Philippi's maximum-security cell was no Holiday Inn. It was colder than a witch's elbow and blacker than the ace of spades and smellier than road tar. The stocks were ingeniously designed to immobilize the feet and legs for maximum discomfort (see Illustration #13). This torture was often used on early Christians. Such were the accommodations enjoyed in the Philippian stockade.

Backs bruised and torn, punished illegally for an act of mercy, these crazy Christian fanatics had no time for self-pity. Rejoicing was the order of the evening! About midnight the stockade echoed with the sound of two Jewish-accented male voices singing hymns! As a kid in church, I remember an old fire-and-brimstone preacher saying, "Paul sang tenor, Silas sang baritone, and God joined in with a thundering bass that shook the prison so violently stocks fell off, locks shattered, doors flew open, and the prisoners' chains fell away!" All might have escaped, but none did.

In the dungeon dark, the Lord Jesus touched people who could be reached no other way. "The [other] prisoners were listening" (Acts 16:25 NKJV). Their chains broke too. They could have escaped but didn't. The jailer found Jesus. The other prisoners got a taste of the gospel.

# Jailer Reprieve

> ACTS 16:27–28 *And the keeper of the prison, awaking from sleep and seeing the prison doors open, supposing the prisoners had fled, drew his sword and was about to kill himself. But Paul called with a loud voice, saying, "Do yourself no harm, for we are all here." (NKJV)*

The jailer knew, according to Roman military law, that if prisoners had escaped he would be given the punishment the fugitives would have received. An executed criminal's property would be confiscated. To protect his family from loss of their property, he grabbed his sword to take his own life. Just in the nick of time, Paul shouted, "Don't do it! We are all here!"

## The Million-Dollar Question

> ACTS 16:29–30 *Then he called for a light, ran in, and fell down trembling before Paul and Silas. And he brought them out and said, "Sirs, what must I do to be saved?"* (NKJV)

"What must I do to be saved?" As a Roman and a pagan, did the jailer understand what he was asking?

- He may have heard the fortune-teller say these men came to tell people how to be saved (Acts 16:17).
- He'd felt supernatural power in the earthquake and believed Paul and Silas were connected with it.
- He'd been on the brink of suicide—perhaps he was asking how he could escape his superior's punishment (Acts 16:27, 29).
- His response to the answer shows he understood his need for spiritual restoration and sincerely wanted to know how to get it (Acts 16:33–34).

## The Million-Dollar Answer

> ACTS 16:31–32 *So they said, "Believe on the Lord Jesus Christ, and you will be saved, you and your household." Then they spoke*

*the word of the Lord to him and to all who were in his house. (NKJV)*

The answer was that there was nothing the jailer needed to do. Everything necessary for his salvation had been done for him by Christ. All that was required was to believe in Jesus! Furthermore, the same offer was extended to everyone in his house. It's a familiar pattern in Acts: The head of the house trusts Jesus, and the rest of the family follows, believing and being baptized (Acts 10:2; 16:14–15, 33–34). All are included in God's promise of salvation. Each must simply make his or her personal decision to believe.

**rejoiced**
Isaiah 55:1–2, 10–13

**word of the Lord**
the good news about Jesus

**spurious**
illegitimate, falsified origin

## Was the Jailer "Saved"?

**ACTS 16:33–34** *And he took them the same hour of the night and washed their stripes. And immediately he and all his family were baptized. Now when he had brought them into his house, he set food before them; and he rejoiced, having believed in God with all his household. (NKJV)*

Luke reports four evidences of the authenticity of the jailer's conversion:

1. *Making amends*—he nursed Paul's and Silas's wounds.

2. *Baptism*—he and his family confessed their faith and were baptized.

3. *Table fellowship*—he shared a meal with Paul and Silas in his home.

4. *Joy*—he and his family <u>rejoiced</u> over their new faith in God.

what others say

**William Barclay**

Unless a man's Christianity makes him kind it is not real. Unless a man's professed change of heart is guaranteed by his change of deeds it is a **spurious** thing.[9]

## Red Carpet for the "Bad Guys"

**ACTS 16:35–39** *And when it was day, the magistrates sent the officers, saying, "Let those men go." So the keeper of the prison*

**persecution**
Philippians 1:27–30

*reported these words to Paul, saying, "The magistrates have sent to let you go. Now therefore depart, and go in peace." But Paul said to them, "They have beaten us openly, uncondemned Romans, and have thrown us into prison. And now do they put us out secretly? No indeed! Let them come themselves and get us out." And the officers told these words to the magistrates, and they were afraid when they heard that they were Romans. Then they came and pleaded with them and brought them out, and asked them to depart from the city. (NKJV)*

At daybreak officers came with orders to release the prisoners. To their chagrin the prisoners refused to leave! Paul and Silas demanded the magistrates who had plunked them in the pokey illegally and unjustly come, apologize for their gross negligence, and personally escort them out. "They have beaten us openly, uncondemned Romans," said Paul. Oops! A shiver of alarm ran up and down the magistrates' collective spines! By law, Roman citizens could not be executed, beaten, tortured, or placed in stocks without a public hearing.

When the judges showed up to escort the apostles to freedom, it was with a markedly more conciliatory tone than when they ordered their incarceration. They did, however, politely suggest the apostles leave town!

Paul and Silas did not hesitate to use their rights as Roman citizens to protect themselves and others from unjust and arbitrary treatment. Philippian Christians would soon face <u>persecution</u>. The apostles' protest may have helped protect some.

**what others say**

**Lawrence O. Richards**

Christians do have a dual citizenship. We owe total allegiance to heaven. Yet even as we live by the laws of our earthly nation, so we can claim all the rights granted us here as well.[10]

## The Church at Lydia's House

ACTS 16:40 *So they went out of the prison and entered the house of Lydia; and when they had seen the brethren, they encouraged them and departed. (NKJV)*

A small cadre of Christian believers gathered at Lydia's villa for final exhortations. A baby church was beginning. Its membership spanned the social spectrum: an upper-class seller of expensive fabric, a slave girl, a middle-class jailer, and others you can read about in Paul's letter to the Philippians. At this point Luke, the author, switches to third-person pronouns ("they," "them"). The good doctor stays behind to help deliver the baby church. Good choice. Philippi was a medical center.[11]

# Chapter Wrap-Up

- After the breakup with Barnabas, Paul chose Silas as his partner and headed for Asia Minor. At Lystra, Timothy was added to the team. (Acts 16:1–5)

- By various hindrances, circumstances, and sensitivities, the Holy Spirit led the team to Troas. There Paul had a vision revealing God's will for them to take the gospel to Europe. Dr. Luke joined them at Troas. (Acts 16:6–11)

- At Philippi, a group of women met at the river to pray. When Paul shared the gospel, Lydia, a Philippian businesswoman, believed and was baptized. (Acts 16:12–15)

- Paul expelled an evil spirit from a clairvoyant slave girl. The apostles were arrested, beaten, and jailed. At midnight they sang. An earthquake broke chains and opened prison doors. The jailer and his family received the Lord. (Acts 16:16–34)

- Paul and Silas refused to leave jail until the judges apologized for mistreating them. When they left Philippi, a new church was meeting at Lydia's house. (Acts 16:35–40)

# Study Questions

1. Since the Jerusalem Council (Acts 15) agreed that Gentiles need not be circumcised to be Christians, what four "higher principles" may have guided Paul in circumcising Timothy?

2. What are two reasons Tim was willing to submit to "the surgery"?

3. What finally convinced Paul and the missionary team that it was God's will to go to Europe? Who joined the team at this point? How do we know this?

4. Stories of three people whose lives were touched by the gospel are told in Acts 16. Who were they? What were their occupations? Where were they on the social scale?

5. When the jailer asked Paul and Silas, "What must I do to be saved?" (Acts 16:30 NKJV), what was the answer? What four things did the jailer do to show he had been converted to Christ?

# Acts 17 Junkyard of the Gods

## Let's Get Started

Everyone is **religious**—even those who pretend not to be. All people **worship** something. It may be a decorated stick in the forest, statue of a potbellied Eastern philosopher, world leader, teacher, river, mountain, science, success, sports, music, "fun," a cause—their own glands—even their own face in the mirror. They may not call it "god." But they ascribe supreme worth to it and expend their best energies for it. They expect the god to give them meaning and comfort—maybe even immortality.

Some say, or hope, God does not exist. Others don't know. Or if he exists they insist there's no way to know for sure. I have a friend who calls himself a "devout agnostic." He's devoted to (in other words quite religious about) not knowing God. Still others claim to know there's a living God, but have all but lost him in a maze of lifeless religious trappings, ceremonies, and rules.

John wrote, "No one has seen God at any time. The **only begotten Son**, who is in the bosom of the Father, He has declared Him" (John 1:18 NKJV). As early Christian witnesses fanned out across the world, they were confronted with humanity's vast ignorance about God. They met people whose struggle to know (or avoid) God had caused them to create thousands of deities to whom they looked for good fortune, protection, and something to fill the emptiness inside. The Christian challenge was how to share with such people the good news of Jesus, whom Christians believe is the only One who reveals God as he really is.

## World-Class Troublemakers

> **ACTS 17:1–4** *Now when they had passed through Amphipolis and Apollonia, they came to Thessalonica, where there was a synagogue of the Jews. Then Paul, as his custom was, went in to them, and for three Sabbaths reasoned with them from the Scriptures, explaining and demonstrating that the Christ had*

**religious**
devoted to an ultimate reality or deity

**worship**
regard with great respect, honor, or devotion

**only begotten Son**
God's Son, Jesus Christ

*to suffer and rise again from the dead, and saying, "This Jesus whom I preach to you is the Christ." And some of them were persuaded; and a great multitude of the devout Greeks, and not a few of the leading women, joined Paul and Silas. (NKJV)*

Sixty-two miles west of Philippi was Thessalonica, the most important city in Macedonia. Paul, Silas, and Timothy followed the same strategy there as in other towns—they went first to the synagogue and shared their message with the Jews and the **Proselytes of the Gate** who met there. Paul showed from the Old Testament the necessity for the death and resurrection of Jesus, and declared that he was the promised Messiah. Some Jews and Greeks became convinced and "**joined** Paul and Silas."

## Let's Start a Ruckus!

ACTS 17:5–9 *But the Jews who were not persuaded, becoming envious, took some of the evil men from the marketplace, and gathering a mob, set all the city in an uproar and attacked the house of Jason, and sought to bring them out to the people. But when they did not find them, they dragged Jason and some brethren to the rulers of the city, crying out, "These who have turned the world upside down have come here too. Jason has harbored them, and these are all acting contrary to the decrees of Caesar, saying there is another king—Jesus." And they troubled the crowd and the rulers of the city when they heard these things. So when they had taken security from Jason and the rest, they let them go. (NKJV)*

Trouble from synagogue leaders was not triggered by desire to protect the traditional faith so much as plain mud-ugly, yellowbellied, green-eyed jealousy! In Thessalonica synagogue leaders found some disreputable characters hanging around the market itching to make a lot of noise and beat somebody up. Unable to find Paul and Silas, they grabbed Jason and some other believers and hauled them off to the **politarchs**.

They trumped up charges against the Christians: (1) they were world-class troublemakers—this riot was their fault; (2) they defied Caesar's decrees; and (3) they promoted a king to replace Caesar. All pure hogwash. But shrewdly calculated to turn superpatriotic Romans into a tizzy.

It worked. The crowd and officials went into orbit! But since there was no real evidence the charges were true, Jason and the others were released after they had **"taken security,"** guaranteeing Paul and Silas would leave town and never come back. To protect Jason and the others, Paul and Silas slipped out of town after sundown and did not return. Paul kept in touch with <u>letters</u>.

**go to**

**letters**
1 Thessalonians and
2 Thessalonians

**taken security**
posted bond; put up
bail money

**what others say**

### Howard Marshall

The Jews were "jealous" because here as elsewhere Paul won over the "devout Greeks," those already attracted to Judaism—the very people they themselves hoped to win as converts.[2]

Of what "crime" were the Christians accused? "These who have turned the world upside down have come here too" (Acts 17:6 NKJV). Is it true? The original Greek statement from which this is translated can be interpreted several ways. Check out these translations and verses:

- *"Christians turn the world upside down"* (King James Version). It's true. Jesus changes people. Examples: Luke 19:1–10; Acts 9:1–20; Acts 19:18–20; 1 Corinthians 6:9–11.

- *"Christians upset the civilized world"* (William Barclay's translation).[3] It's true. Jesus's values conflict with society's values. See Matthew 5:3–10; Luke 6:20–36; Luke 16:15; Luke 18:14.

- *"Christians subvert the whole world"* (F. F. Bruce's translation).[4] It's true. When the gospel gets into people they become part of a secret force seeking to undermine and overturn the unjust, immoral principles and practices on which godless culture is founded. See Matthew 13:33; Luke 17:20–21; John 19:36; Romans 12:1–21; 1 Corinthians 13:1–13.

- *"Christians cause trouble all over the world"* (New International Version). It's true. Christ's teachings do not please people who don't want their selfish lifestyles disturbed. Christ's claims and ideas are often met with discomfort and rage, which leads to trouble. See Luke 12:49–53; John 15:18–16:4.

what others say

**Billy Graham**

Jesus Christ . . . was the greatest of all revolutionaries, and he seeks true revolutionaries today who have been transformed by the power of his gospel and who are prepared to row against the mainstream, to go through the straight gate and follow the narrow way (see Matthew 7:13–14). This way may be filled with suffering, hardships, ridicule, and ostracism from the group. It is difficult to follow Jesus Christ. The problem of applying his teachings to our lives is often confusing; that is why it is so important to rely upon the Scripture and upon the Holy Spirit.[5]

## Searching the Bible for God

ACTS 17:10–12 *Then the brethren immediately sent Paul and Silas away by night to Berea. When they arrived, they went into the synagogue of the Jews. These were more fair-minded than those in Thessalonica, in that they received the word with all readiness, and searched the Scriptures daily to find out whether these things were so. Therefore many of them believed, and also not a few of the Greeks, prominent women as well as men.* (NKJV)

After the fierceness of opposition in Thessalonica, Berea was a breath of fresh air. The message of Jesus Christ sounded no less strange to Berean ears than to Thessalonian ears. But the Bereans did their homework. They compared what Paul was saying with Old Testament Scripture. The final word, for them, was the written Word of God. When they realized the missionaries were telling the truth, they embraced it. Wise listeners check the Bible to see if a preacher or teacher is telling the truth.

## Mail Order Riot

ACTS 17:13–14 *But when the Jews from Thessalonica learned that the word of God was preached by Paul at Berea, they came there also and stirred up the crowds. Then immediately the brethren sent Paul away, to go to the sea; but both Silas and Timothy remained there.* (NKJV)

Back in Thessalonica synagogue leaders got wind that Paul was preaching in Berea. Zealous "Keepers of the Ancient Ways,"[6] they made the fifty-mile trip to Berea to start another riot, which led to another hasty hiatus for Paul.

It was too late to stop the Lord's work. A group of eager Bible students was already being drawn together around Jesus. Timothy and Silas stayed to get the church founded, while Paul hightailed it to the coast.

## Junkyard of the Gods

go to

**behind every shrine**
1 Corinthians 8:4–6;
10:18–20

**idol**
any object one
shapes or uses as an
object of worship[7]

ACTS 17:15–16 *So those who conducted Paul brought him to Athens; and receiving a command for Silas and Timothy to come to him with all speed, they departed. Now while Paul waited for them at Athens, his spirit was provoked within him when he saw that the city was given over to idols.* (NKJV)

For Paul, Athens was culture shock! A common saying was that there were more **idols** in Athens than in all the rest of Greece combined! Others—artists, tourists—might have noted the skill of the sculptors, the costliness of the rare collection of statuary and fine art. Paul saw it differently. He was overwhelmed by a sense of tragedy that a city so noted for intellectual brilliance could be so abysmally ignorant and confused about God!

Behind every shrine, temple, and altar, the sensitive spirit of Christ's apostle saw a sinister spirit—a demon committed to stupefying brilliant minds. The great intellects of Athens soared among the stars, but their shriveled spirits crawled like oversized infants groping for God in a junkyard of "sacred" toys!

what others say

### Howard Marshall

The apostle Paul was a strategist. He campaigned in the great cities of the Roman World. He selected centers on trade routes, seaports, places where there was much coming and going. From these centers the message could run like fire far and wide. . . . So he came . . . to Athens, a city with 1000 years of history . . . founder of democracy, home of . . . the greatest university of the world, center of philosophy, literature, science and art—but hard ground for the gospel.[8]

## A New Slant on God

ACTS 17:17–18 *Therefore he reasoned in the synagogue with the Jews and with the Gentile worshipers, and in the marketplace daily with those who happened to be there. Then certain*

pantheistic
belief that imper-
sonal forces and
laws of nature are
gods

*Epicurean and Stoic philosophers encountered him. And some said, "What does this babbler want to say?" Others said, "He seems to be a proclaimer of foreign gods," because he preached to them Jesus and the resurrection. (NKJV)*

The Athenian marketplace was crowded with people haggling over produce and goods. Mixed with the businesspeople were philosophers, politicians, and teachers "haggling" over the latest philosophical and political ideas. Paul dived into this mix with both feet. Among those who listened to him were Epicurean and Stoic philosophers.

• *Epicureans*—Disciples of Epicurus (341–271 BC). They believed pleasure (happiness) is "the chief end of life." The most worthy pleasure is to be pain-free. Intellectual pleasure is superior to sensual pleasure. Matter is eternal. Existence ends when the body dies—there is no resurrection. The gods have no interest in human affairs.

• *Stoics*—Disciples of Zeno (340–265 BC). They were **pantheistic**—"The Force be with you!" and all that jazz. Life's goal is harmony with nature and its laws and strict control of all human passions, emotions, and affections. Duty is more important than love. Suicide is recommended as a means of escape from a life that can no longer be sustained with dignity.

When the philosophers called Paul a "babbler" (Acts 17:18 NKJV), the word they used literally meant "seed-picker." Their first impression was that Paul was a hawker of secondhand scraps of learning. The name they called him reveals an overblown view of their own wisdom. Some thought Paul was promoting two new foreign gods—one named Iasous (Jesus) and the other named Anastasis ("Resurrection") (Acts 17:18). Why not listen? The streets of Athens were overloaded with gods from all over the world. What could it hurt to add a couple more to the gaudy crowd?

## The Mars Hill Society

ACTS 17:19–21 *And they took him and brought him to the Areopagus, saying, "May we know what this new doctrine is of which you speak? For you are bringing some strange things to our ears. Therefore we want to know what these things mean." For all the Athenians and the foreigners who were there spent their time in nothing else but either to tell or to hear some new thing. (NKJV)*

For centuries this small hill in Athens, called the **Areopagus**, had been the location for a court that heard criminal cases. In Paul's day it had become a center for the discussion of philosophical ideas among local and foreign experts in history, philosophy, and religion. This "thinkers' club" had taken on the name of the hill, Mars Hill. Nothing got their intellectual juices flowing like a hot new idea.

## The God Nobody Knows

A CTS 17:22–23 *Then Paul stood in the midst of the Areopagus and said, "Men of Athens, I perceive that in all things you are very religious; for as I was passing through and considering the objects of your worship, I even found an altar with this inscription:*

*TO THE UNKNOWN GOD.*

*Therefore, the One whom you worship without knowing, Him I proclaim to you: . . ." (NKJV)*

Six hundred years BC the city of Athens was in the grip of a terrible plague. Hundreds died. The town fathers consulted with a **Pythian** priestess to find out the source of the plague and why their sacrifices to the gods were having no effect. They were told the city was under a curse because of the treachery of King Megacles, who had promised amnesty to a group of people if they would surrender. When they did, the king broke his word and killed them all!

Athenians had sacrificed to every god they could think of, but the plague persisted. The priestess said there was another god who held the city accountable for their king's crime. Problem: She couldn't tell them his name!

The priestess received an **oracle** instructing the town council to send a delegation to the island of Crete to bring back a prophet named Epimenides who would be able to tell them how to appease the unknown deity.

Epimenides instructed the council members to bring to the Areopagus (where the council held its meetings) a flock of hungry sheep—half of them white and half, black. Stonemasons should also be brought along with a supply of stones and mortar.

At dawn the flock was released on the grassy hill. Epimenides prayed a humble prayer, acknowledging their pitiful ignorance of his name and asking the unknown God to look with compassion and forgiveness on the city. He prayed that this God would reveal his

**Pythian**
Acts 16:16

**Areopagus**
Hill of Ares, Greek god of war (Roman: Mars)

**Pythian**
possessed with the serpent-spirit who guarded the oracles of Apollo

**oracle**
message from God

willingness to help by causing the sheep that pleased him—black or white—to lie down on the grass instead of grazing. Each sheep that laid down was sacrificed to the unknown God on an altar constructed on the spot where the animal laid down. Some of these altars bore the inscription *agnosto theo*—"to an unknown God" (see Illustration #14).

According to Greek storytellers,[9] the plague began to lift the very next day! Within a week, the sick had recovered and Athens was praising Epimenides' "unknown God." But after six centuries, all they knew of this God was that he had forgiven Athens and removed its plague.[10]

All creation and God's continuing forgiveness, healing, protection, and supply of daily human needs make it clear to all but the most closed minds that there exists a good and powerful Being who cares for his creatures and provides a place for them to live. Even so, to most people he continues to be the Unknown God. It's hard to find God in an information vacuum! To know God requires his personal self-disclosure. He does this through his written Word (the Bible), his Holy Spirit, and his messenger-witnesses.

**Illustration #14**
Altar to an Unknown God—This drawing depicts the type of altar to an unknown God that was built in Athens.

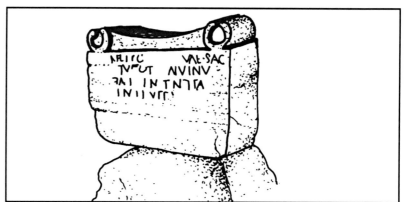

## The God Who Wants to Be Known

the big picture

### Acts 17:24–31

"God, who made the world and everything in it, since He is Lord of heaven and earth, does not dwell in temples made with hands," Paul said. He proceeded to introduce the philosophers to this Creator God.

The nameless God of Athens had a name! Introducing him to the Athenian intellectuals, Paul called him by the Greek name Theos. The name rang a bell with his educated listeners because it was the name the great Greek philosophers had used when writing about the supreme God in whose existence they believed. Drawing his information from the Bible, Paul unmasked their "unknown" Theos-God with these facts:

1. Theos-God made the world and everything in it (Acts 17:24; Genesis 1).

2. Theos is Lord of heaven and earth, sky and land—too great to be confined to a man-made temple or altar (Acts 17:24; 1 Kings 8:27; Isaiah 66:1–2).

3. Theos is not dependent on people to meet his needs or run his errands. Au contraire! People are dependent on him for "life, breath, and all things" (Acts 17:25 NKJV).

4. Theos created all nationalities, beginning with one man (Acts 17:26; Genesis 1:27; 2:7). (Athenians believed they "sprang from the soil of their native [Greece],'" and were superior to other races and nationalities. Paul punctures their balloon!)

5. Theos planned specific times and places for people to live and created an inhabitable planet before putting them on it (Acts 17:26; Genesis 1:1–26).

6. Theos provided everything needed for life and security so people could see what he's done and reach out to him (Acts 17:27). (If God remains "unknown," it is because humans suppress the truth about him visible in the created universe [Romans 1:18–23].) He wants people to know him. "He is not far from each one of us!" (Acts 17:27 NKJV).

7. Theos doesn't play hide-and-seek. In fact, we "can't get away from him!"

8. Theos originated humans. It makes no sense to think he could be a statue chiseled by a human sculptor from gold, silver, or stone (Acts 17:29; Isaiah 44:9–20)!

**overlooked**
Acts 14:15–17;
Romans 3:25

**judged**
Romans 6:23; 14:12;
2 Corinthians 5:10;
Revelation 20:11–15

**mention of
resurrection**
Matthew 27:62–66;
28:11–12;
Acts 4:2; 23:6–8

9. Theos <u>overlooked</u> Athenian ignorance about him in the past, but no more! Now they must turn from unknowing and know God (Acts 17:30).

10. Theos has set a time for the world to be <u>judged</u> (Acts 17:31; Psalms 9:8; 96:13; Hebrews 9:27). The identity of the presiding judge has been revealed: He's the man God raised from the dead (Acts 17:31; John 5:25–27; Romans 1:4)!

To make his point, Paul quotes two poets familiar to his listeners.

- Epimenides, 600 BC, wrote of Theos: "In Him we live and move and have our being" (Acts 17:28 NKJV).

- Aratus, 300 BC, wrote: "We are also His offspring" (Acts 17:28 NKJV).

**what others say**

**Epimenides (in the poem from which Paul quotes)**

They fashioned a tomb for thee O holy and high one—
The Cretans always liars, evil beasts, idle bellies!
But thou art not dead; thou livest and abidest forever.
For in thee we live and move and have our being.[13]

**Michael Green**

To the cultured [pagans] . . . the Christians seek to establish the fact that there is one God, discredit idolatry and through the light of natural revelation (God the Creator and Sustainer) to prepare the way for the special revelation of God contained in Christ.[14]

## Intellectuals Believe

ACTS 17:32–34 *And when they heard of the resurrection of the dead, some mocked, while others said, "We will hear you again on this matter." So Paul departed from among them. However, some men joined him and believed, among them Dionysius the Areopagite, a woman named Damaris, and others with them.* (*NKJV*)

At <u>mention of resurrection</u> the Mars Hill Society disintegrated into cynical laughter. To Epicureans and others, end-time judgment and resurrection were absurd. According to legend, when Athena, patron goddess of the city, founded the Areopagus, the god Apollo said: "Once a man dies and the earth drinks up his blood, there is no resurrection."[15] Stoics did not believe in resurrection but believed in continuing existence after this life. Perhaps they were the ones who said they'd like to hear more.

Some listeners believed. Two are named: Dionysius, a member of the Mars Hill Society, and Damaris. The Society had no women members, so Damaris may have been a bystander listening to the discussion or a street woman plying her trade in the market. She made history as a charter member in the tiny infant church at Athens.

filthy rags
Isaiah 64:6

feeding on husks
Luke 15:16

Parthenon
temple to the goddess Athena, built on the Acropolis at Athens

## what others say

### Maude De Joseph West

Paul did not gain many converts among the Greek intellectuals. It is so even today. Men, wise in their own conceits, smug in their self-sufficiency, are not easily persuaded that their souls are wearing filthy rags and feeding on husks. God is only for the weak and the stupid, and they, the intelligentsia, have absolutely no need of him.[16]

### John Pollock

Athens had rejected (Paul). He could not know that his speech would go down to posterity . . . as one of the greatest speeches of Athens. He could not know that whole books would be written about it or that in a few hundred years the **Parthenon** would become a Christian church; and that nineteen centuries on, when Greece after long suppression became once more a sovereign state, the national flag which flies beside the ruins of the Parthenon would be lowered to half-mast each Good Friday, and raised on Easter Day in honor of Christ's resurrection.[17]

## Chapter Wrap-Up

- Paul's team preached in Thessalonica. Jews and God-fearing Greeks (including prominent women) became persuaded Jesus was the Messiah. Jealous synagogue leaders accused Christians of being troublemakers. (Acts 17:1–9)

- Bereans received the message about Jesus after carefully studying Old Testament Scripture to see if what they were hearing was true. Enemies from Thessalonica came to Berea and stirred up trouble. Paul went on to Athens. (Acts 17:10–15)

- Athenians' idolatry distressed Paul. Sabbaths, he taught in the synagogue; weekdays, he preached to pagan philosophers in the marketplace. (Acts 17:16–21)
- Speaking at the Areopagus, Paul revealed the identity of the "Unknown God" whose altar he found there. (Acts 17:22–31)
- When Paul told them about the resurrection of Jesus, the Epicureans made jokes about it. A few people said they wanted to hear more. A few Greeks—Dionysius and Damaris and a few other intellectuals—believed in the Lord. (Acts 17:32–34)

## Study Questions

1. Of what three "crimes" did enemies accuse the Christians in Thessalonica?

2. How did the Berean Jews respond to the message of Christ?

3. What did Paul use as a starting place for his teaching about God at the Areopagus (Mars Hill Society) in Athens?

4. Using Paul's Mars Hill teaching (Acts 17:24–31 NKJV), fill in the blanks:

   a. People are dependent on God for "_____, _____, and all things."

   b. God is "not far from ____ ____ ____ ____."

   c. "In Him we ____ and move and ___ ___ _____."

   d. "We are also His _____."

5. What did Paul say that made some of the Areopagus members sneer?

# Acts 18 Sin City Saints

## Let's Get Started

From the frying pan of intellectual, idolatrous Athens, Paul leaped into the fire of sex-saturated, materialistic Corinth. Traveling alone, he approached Corinth through the five-hundred-year-old **Isthmian wall** that spanned the five-mile Corinthian **isthmus**. He may have wondered if this hotbed of **hedonism** could possibly be convinced to respond to the invitation of the pure and selfless Nazarene he had come to introduce.

**Isthmian wall**
twenty-five feet high

**isthmus**
narrow strip of land connecting northern and southern Greece

**hedonism**
belief that pleasure is the most important good in life

## The Swinging City of Aphrodite and Apollos

ACTS 18:1 *After these things Paul departed from Athens and went to Corinth. (NKJV)*

Corinth was famed as "the Bridge of Greece." Situated on the Corinthian Isthmus, the narrow neck of land that keeps southern Greece from being an island, its geographical position made it a key commercial center. The only overland trade route between northern and southern Greece passed through Corinth. It had two seaports, one on the Aegean Sea and one on the Adriatic Sea. Small ships were carried from one port to the other across the isthmus on a tramway, saving two hundred miles of treacherous sea travel. Its strategic location gave Corinth potential as a center from which the news of Jesus could spread in all directions.

### For the Love of Sport

The first thing Paul saw as he passed through the Isthmian wall was the huge stadium where the Isthmian Games were held. This biennial sporting event was second only to the Olympics in importance. The games began with a sacrifice to Poseidon, the sea god, followed by athletic, equestrian, and musical competitions. The Isthmian games were notoriously corrupt. Athletes broke training rules and sold themselves to the highest bidder. Magicians and for-

**to illustrate**
1 Corinthians
9:24–27;
Colossians 4:12;
1 Timothy 4:7–9;
2 Timothy 2:5; 4:7–8

**Acropolis**
Greek city's fortified
high ground; moun-
tain overlooking the
city

tune-tellers bilked the gullible. Every sort of huckster hawked his wares. Philosophers gathered to argue. It was just the kind of carnival atmosphere where a brash evangelist like Paul would be found declaring the news of Jesus Christ. His letters reveal he was somewhat of a "sports fan" and often used sports <u>to illustrate</u> spiritual truth.

## To "Act the Corinthian"

Six miles south of the stadium was the city of 100,000 to 700,000 (depending on who you asked). A city of sailors, traveling salesmen, and government officials—"everybody" was from someplace else!

Fifteen hundred feet above the city atop the Acrocorinth (Corinthian **Acropolis**) was the town's most impressive feature, the Temple of Aphrodite, goddess of love and Poseidon's coruler of the sea. Every night a thousand prostitute-priestesses descended from the temple to the town to engage its male citizens and visitors in "worship" of the goddess.

In the first-century world, to be called a "Corinthian" did not necessarily mean you came from Corinth—it meant you were hooked on pleasure and sexual excess. Prostitutes were called "Corinthian girls." To "act the Corinthian" meant to engage in sex outside of marriage. And when a Corinthian was portrayed in a play, he was always drunk.

**what others say**

**John Pollock**

In the city itself, the archaic Temple of Apollo . . . also glorified sex as well as music, song, and poetry, for Apollo was the ideal of male beauty. The temple's inner recesses held nude statues and friezes of Apollo in various poses of virility. . . . If the love of Christ Jesus could take root in Corinth, the most populated, wealthy, commercial-minded, and sex-obsessed city of eastern Europe, it must prove powerful anywhere.[1]

## What's a Nice Jewish Boy Doing in a Place Like This?

Though born in the pagan city of Tarsus, Paul was brought up Jewish. He cut his teeth on the Ten Commandments. He trained in Jerusalem to be a rabbi. Since his conversion (see Acts 9) he was a committed follower of the lofty moral teachings of Jesus.

As he moved about Corinth, at the games, the Forum, the market, and in the neighborhoods, he was surrounded by prostitutes and their customers, practicing homosexuals, cheating business people, drunks, and addicts. It was not unusual to be accosted by a harlot. Everyday conversation was filled with lust and moral filth, cursing and slander (see 1 Corinthians 6:9–10). The town lived for money, pleasure, wine, gambling, sports.

The Christian mind is <u>trained</u> by Scripture and the Holy Spirit to be sensitive, repulsed by sin, saddened by immorality. The realization that so many were trapped in destructive lifestyles seems to have nearly overwhelmed Paul. As his ministry in Corinth began, he experienced a deep sense of "weakness, . . . fear, and . . . much trembling" (1 Corinthians 2:3 NKJV).

## Soul Mates

> **ACTS 18:2** *And he found a certain Jew named Aquila, born in Pontus, who had recently come from Italy with his wife Priscilla (because Claudius had commanded all the Jews to depart from Rome); and he came to them. (NKJV)*

Paul did not like to work alone. It wasn't simply a matter of personal preference—spiritual <u>teamwork</u> was the principle on which the early church nearly always operated. Jesus set the <u>pattern</u>.

Silas and Timothy had stayed in Berea to help the young church get on its feet (Acts 17:15).

Corinth had a significant Jewish colony. Following his usual pattern, Paul went to the synagogue. There he met a Christian couple, newly arrived from Rome—a man named Aquila and his wife, Priscilla. The three of them became close friends and coworkers for Christ.

Aquila and Priscilla moved easily around the Roman Empire (see Illustration #15). Aquila was a Jew. Priscilla may also have been Jewish, but some scholars speculate she was from the aristocratic Roman family Prisca. <u>Prisca</u> is the formal name Paul sometimes uses to refer to her in his letters. Luke uses her familiar name, Priscilla. Before Corinth, they lived in Rome and were part of the church there. They were forced to leave Rome in AD 49 when Claudius Caesar issued an order banishing Jews from the capital city.

**go to**

**trained**
2 Timothy 3:14–17;
Hebrews 5:14

**teamwork**
Acts 2:14; 6:3–6;
8:14; 11:25–26;
13:1, 4–5; 15:39–40

**pattern**
Matthew 10:5;
Luke 9:28; 10:1

**Prisca**
2 Timothy 4:19

**go to**

**accepted gifts**
Philippians 4:10–19

**the right**
1 Corinthians 9

**cardinal**
primary, basic, chief

**cilicium**
cloth made of goat
hair from Paul's
home province of
Cilicia

The **cardinal** principle for function in the church is interdependence (1 Corinthians 12:21–27). Church leadership as seen in Acts follows that cardinal principle. No apostle, elder, deacon, or pastor is called to "go it alone" or to be a "Lone Ranger" running everything. (Even the Lone Ranger had his Tonto!)

# Paul Continues to Make His Living As a Tradesman

**ACTS 18:3** *So, because he was of the same trade, he stayed with them and worked; for by occupation they were tentmakers.* (*NKJV*)

One of the things that first linked Aquila, Priscilla, and Paul was their common trade. The original word for "tentmakers" literally means "leather workers." They made leather tents from goatskin and wove goat fleece into waterproof cloth called **cilicium**, which was used to make tents and cloaks.

**Illustration #15**
Aquila and Priscilla's
Travels—The lines
and numbers on this
map indicate the
mobility of Aquila
and Priscilla. They
(1) came from
Pontus, (2) lived in
Rome, (3) met and
worked with Paul in
Corinth, (4) moved
to Ephesus, and (5)
and later moved
back to Rome.

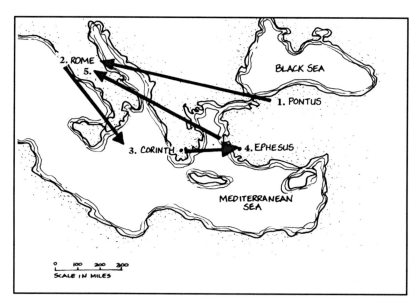

Paul sometimes <u>accepted gifts</u> in order to spend full time in ministry (he taught that the minister has <u>the right</u> to be supported by those he or she serves). But in Corinth and as a general policy he chose to earn his living and that of his fellow team members by working as a tentmaker. In his rabbinical training he'd been taught it was improper to demand payment for teaching the Scriptures.

"He who makes a profit from the crown of the **Torah** shall waste away," said Rabbi Hillel.[2] Rabbi <u>Gamaliel</u> said, "All study of the Torah which is not combined with work will ultimately be futile and lead to sin."[3]

Paul was always careful to avoid the impression that the gospel was just another way to make a buck! His motive for preaching was not profit (2 Corinthians 2:17). Besides, working with his hands put Paul side by side with the ordinary working stiffs of Corinth—people he wanted to reach with the good news about Jesus.

### what others say

**Bernard of Clairvaux**

Learn the lesson that, if you are to do the work of a prophet, what you need is not a scepter but a hoe.[4]

Read the following passages to discover why Paul continued to make his living doing ordinary, non-religious work while engaged in ministry, instead of being a "full-time" minister:

- Acts 20:33–35
- 1 Corinthians 9:13–19
- 2 Corinthians 2:17
- 2 Corinthians 11:7–12
- 1 Thessalonians 2:9
- 2 Thessalonians 3:7–10

## Try Gentile Persuasion!

ACTS 18:4–6 *And he reasoned in the synagogue every Sabbath, and persuaded both Jews and Greeks. When Silas and Timothy had come from Macedonia, Paul was compelled by the Spirit, and testified to the Jews that Jesus is the Christ. But when they opposed him and blasphemed, he shook his garments and said to them, "Your blood be upon your own heads; I am clean. From now on I will go to the Gentiles." (NKJV)*

**Gamaliel**
Acts 5:34–39; 22:3

**Thessalonians**
1 Thessalonians 3:6–10

**Philippians**
2 Corinthians 11:9; Philippians 4:16

**Torah**
Old Testament Scripture

On Sabbath days Paul was given opportunity to teach at the synagogue. Silas and Timothy completed their work with the young churches of Macedonia and rejoined him. Hearing how well the <u>Thessalonians</u> and Bereans were doing gave the apostle a shot in the arm. The <u>Philippians</u> sent a gift which freed Paul to lay aside tent-making to concentrate on a last-ditch effort to convince his Jewish brothers to welcome Jesus as their Messiah.

**announcement**
Luke 9:5; 10:1;
Acts 13:51

**all his household**
Acts 10:2, 44; 16:15,
31–34

**host**
Romans 16:23

History repeated itself in Corinth when Jewish resistance became so intense there was nothing to do but to leave the synagogue and take the gospel to pagans. Paul's shaking his clothes was a dramatization the Jewish congregation would have understood as an <u>announcement</u> of futility and separation, and warning of judgment. A strict Jew returning to Israel from a pagan land would shake the dust of that land from his clothing so as not to bring pagan contamination into Israel.

"You've made your bed," Paul was saying, "Now lie in it!"

## "Somewhere, God Always Opens a Window!"[5]

ACTS 18:7–8 *And he departed from there and entered the house of a certain man named Justus, one who worshiped God, whose house was next door to the synagogue. Then Crispus, the ruler of the synagogue, believed on the Lord with all his household. And many of the Corinthians, hearing, believed and were baptized.* (NKJV)

As synagogue doors slammed shut, the house next door, the home of a Gentile named Justus, opened its doors to welcome the Christian messengers. The greatest shock waves felt in the Jewish community must have been when its leading citizen, Crispus, with <u>all his household</u>, joined the Christian meeting next door!

These verses read like a Who's Who in Corinth. Justus, also known as "Gaius," was a wealthy Roman God-worshiper who attended the synagogue. One of the few people in Corinth whom Paul personally baptized (see 1 Corinthians 1:14), his home was spacious enough to <u>host</u> "the whole church" at Corinth.

Crispus was synagogue president, an ordained rabbi, and trained in the Law. As president he was in charge of congregational life, arranged Scripture readers and speakers, and presided at meetings. Paul's teaching would have been cleared through him. He and all his household believed in Jesus as Messiah. Paul personally baptized him (see 1 Corinthians 1:14).

## The Undiscovered Church

ACTS 18:9–11 *Now the Lord spoke to Paul in the night by a vision, "Do not be afraid, but speak, and do not keep silent; for I am with you, and no one will attack you to hurt you; for I have many people in this city." And he continued there a year and six months, teaching the word of God among them.* (NKJV)

Paul had faced opposition in every city—mob violence, stoning, beating, imprisonment, sickness, threats, ridicule, rejection, hatred, and verbal and personal abuse. In Corinth he was confronted with sin so open and glamorized, morally degenerate lifestyles so foreign, that his mind went into overload. He may have been tempted to move on before the Lord's work in Corinth was solidly established.

At that crucial moment, Jesus spoke to Paul in a vision, telling him to keep talking without fear (Acts 18:9–10 NKJV). The Lord gave three reasons he shouldn't cut and run:

- The Lord's presence: "I am with you."

- The Lord's protection: "No one will attack you to hurt you."

- The Lord's people: "I have many people in this city."

Paul stayed a year and a half, teaching God's Word to anyone who would listen. One of the greatest churches in the New Testament emerged. A burgeoning fellowship of previously lost souls came to Christ out of the depths of moral and spiritual darkness.

"Here's what some of you were," wrote Paul in a letter after he left, "fornicators, idolaters, adulterers, homosexuals, sodomites, thieves, covetous, drunkards, revilers, extortioners!" "But," he added, "you were **washed**, you were **sanctified**, you were **justified** in the name of the Lord Jesus and by the Spirit of our God!" (see 1 Corinthians 6:9–11 NKJV). The church at Corinth was a fellowship of people whose lifestyles were turned right side up through the straightforward telling of Jesus's story—especially his death on the cross and what it means (see 1 Corinthians 2:1–5; also 1:18–25).

While in Corinth, Paul wrote two letters to the Christians in Thessalonica. These **two letters** became part of the New Testament.

The amazing thing about this story is that before the Corinthian church existed, the Lord looked at this infamously wicked city and saw something wonderful even the visionary apostle Paul could not see. "I have many people in this city!" The church was there, waiting to be discovered not only among the nice, moral folks, but among the druggies, prostitutes, gays and lesbians, cheats and jailbirds. Jesus loves and wants to rescue all kinds of people!

**washed**
forgiven, cleansed from past sins, kept clean

**sanctified**
set apart for God's service, useful to God

**justified**
declared "not guilty," right with God

**two letters**
First and Second Thessalonians

something to ponder

# Christians Win a Round in Court

the big picture

**Acts 18:12–16**

Jewish leaders in Corinth brought Paul up on charges before the Roman provincial official, Gallio. Gallio ruled in favor of Paul and the Christians.

The Lord promised Paul protection (Acts 18:10). That protection came from an unexpected source. In summer, AD 51, a noble Roman named Gallio was appointed **proconsul** of the province of **Achaia**. Gallio was a son of the famous Roman orator Seneca and brother of the Stoic philosopher Seneca (Junior). He was known for kindness and fairness. His brother wrote: "No man was ever as sweet to one as Gallio is to all."[6]

Paul's enemies thought they could buffalo the new proconsul into silencing Paul and the Christians. Judaism was a protected religion under Roman law. By charging that Paul "persuades men to worship God contrary to the law" (Acts 18:13 NKJV), they hoped to convince Gallio that Christianity was not Jewish and could not be included in the protections the government granted Judaism. Gallio, however, ruled that what Paul was doing was no crime against Roman law. He saw the whole case as nothing but a fuss among rival Jews over theology, and he had no intention of getting the government involved in it (Acts 18:14–15).

what others say

**F. F. Bruce**

Gallio's ruling meant in effect that Paul and his associates, so long as they committed no breach of public order, continued to share the protection which Roman law granted to the practice of Judaism. . . . It meant that for the next ten or twelve years . . . [until Nero reversed this policy] the gospel could be proclaimed in the provinces of the empire without fear of coming into conflict with Roman law.[7]

# Poor Sosthenes

ACTS 18:17 *Then all the Greeks took Sosthenes, the ruler of the synagogue, and beat him before the judgment seat. But Gallio took no notice of these things. (NKJV)*

Gallio ejected the accusers from his court. Then he sat there with a disinterested look on his face while the Greeks beat the stuffing out of Sosthenes, the synagogue president! Sosthenes was the successor to Crispus, who lost his job as synagogue officer when he became a Christian (see Acts 18:8). Quite possibly he is the same Sosthenes who coauthored Paul's first letter to Corinth (see 1 Corinthians 1:1), which would mean he too became a Christian.

## A Haircut, a Vow, and a Trip

**ACTS 18:18** *So Paul still remained a good while. Then he took leave of the brethren and sailed for Syria, and Priscilla and Aquila were with him. He had his hair cut off at Cenchrea, for he had taken a vow. (NKJV)*

After Gallio's favorable decision, Paul stayed a while longer in Corinth. Then he left, headed for . . . ? Luke skimps on the why's and wherefore's and doesn't tell how much time it took to do this or that, so we are left to make "educated" guesses. Here's the itinerary I'm guessing (with the scholars' help) Paul took:

1. He packed his bags and hiked to Cenchrea, Corinth's Aegean seaport. Before embarking he went to Ye Olde Tonsorial Shoppe for a haircut, because "he had taken a **vow**." When Jews were especially thankful they "took a vow" promising to demonstrate their gratitude to God publicly. Paul had entered Corinth with fear and trembling. By God's mercy he'd survived the dangers of the wicked city unscathed, leaving behind a gifted, growing church. Getting a haircut was his Jewish way of saying "Thanks!"

2. His final destination was the Roman province of Syria, which included both Antioch—his home church—and Jerusalem—everybody's "mother" church (Acts 18:18).

3. Priscilla and Aquila traveled with him as far as Ephesus (Acts 18:19). Anxious to get on his way, Paul left, promising to return, "God willing" (Acts 18:21).

4. He boarded a ship to Caesarea, Jerusalem's nearest seaport. In Jerusalem he "greeted the church" (Acts 18:22). For some reason only his mother knows for sure, Luke doesn't mention Jerusalem.

**go to**

**vow**
Deuteronomy
23:21–23

**vow**
promise made to
God

**Lamb**
sacrifice to take
away the world's sins

His use of "up" and "down" tells us Paul went there. Jews always went "up" to Jerusalem no matter where they came from and "down" no matter where they were going when they left.

5. From Jerusalem Paul went "down" to Antioch, his home base (Acts 18:22).

6. After time in Antioch he took another "missionary journey" (see Illustration #16). No details are given here (Acts 18:23).

## Silver-Tongued Stranger

*the big picture*

**Acts 18:19-28**

Priscilla and Aquila got involved in the life of the synagogue. Their quiet infiltration of the Ephesian Jewish community contributed to Paul's success when he returned. One person this dynamic duo influenced was a silver-tongued Egyptian Jew named Apollos. Apollos was of great help to believers and was a good debater for Christ.

Apollos was a native of Alexandria, Egypt, where a million Jews lived. Highly educated, he knew his way around the Old Testament. He believed in Jesus through the teachings of John the Baptist. A skilled orator, he was a fiery, courageous preacher.

As a student of John the Baptist, Apollos knew the basics about Jesus, but lacked important facts needed to effectively communicate the good news.

- He knew Jews demonstrated readiness to receive Christ by repentance and baptism (see Luke 3:3–14).

- He knew Jesus was the Savior—John called him "**Lamb** of God" (see John 1:29–34).

- He knew Christ would baptize people with the Holy Spirit (see Luke 3:16).

- He "had been instructed in the way of the Lord" (Acts 18:25 nkjv)—the way of life modeled by Jesus.

He was probably in the dark about the church's decision to accept Gentiles without requiring them to live under Jewish law (see Acts 15:28–29). Also Alexandrian Jews tended to interpret the Bible

**allegorically** rather than literally—perhaps Apollos needed correction at that point. Priscilla and Aquila took him under their wing and "explained to him the way of God more accurately" (Acts 18:26 NKJV).

After that Apollos was an unstoppable **apologist** for Christ (Acts 18:27–28). He went to Europe and developed an appreciative following at <u>Corinth</u>.

**Corinth**
1 Corinthians 1:12;
3:4–9

**allegorically**
seeing questionable hidden meanings in straightforward Bible passages

**apologist**
defender of the faith, debater

> what others say
>
> **William Barclay**
> One of the commonest titles in Acts is The Way (see Acts 9:2; 19:9, 23; 22:4; 24:14, 22); and that title shows us at once that Christianity means not only believing certain things but putting them into practice.[8]

## Aquila and Priscilla Served Christ Together

- *Acts 18:3*—Worked together to earn a living
- *Acts 18:3*—Opened their home to Paul
- *Acts 18:3–4*—Helped start the church at Corinth
- *Acts 18:18–19*—Moved to Ephesus to help start another new church
- *Acts 18:24–25*—Spotted potential in Apollos as a Christian communicator
- *Acts 18:26*—Opened their home to Apollos, corrected, filled gaps in his knowledge of the gospel
- *Acts 18:2, 18–19, 26*—Ministered together without concern about whose ministry got noticed. (In the beginning Aquila is named first, and later Priscilla is mentioned first, probably indicating her gifts were more prominent; still, they were inseparable in ministry.)
- *Romans 16:3–4*—Impacted churches in Corinth, Ephesus, and Rome with their risking-everything, apostolic-style ministry.
- *Romans 16:5*—Opened their home to a house church in Rome (and probably in Ephesus).

After Acts 18:2, Priscilla's name is nearly always listed before Aquila's. When Paul greets the two in his letters, he mentions

Priscilla first (see Romans 16:3; 2 Timothy 4:19). She probably was the more prominent of the two. In a culture that tended to put women down, the Christians valued the special contribution of its women to God's work.

# Chapter Wrap-Up

- Corinth was a hotbed of hedonism, sports fanaticism, and sexual excess disguised as religion. Paul's need for support was filled by Aquila and Priscilla, with whom he worked as a tentmaker. (Acts 18:1–3)

- Some Jews, including the synagogue president and his family, embraced Jesus as their Messiah. But opposition forced Paul to take his teaching outside the synagogue to the home of Titius Justus, a Gentile believer. (Acts 18:4–8)

- Paul felt a great sense of inadequacy as he ministered in Corinth. The Lord assured him in a vision that he had many people in the city. If Paul kept speaking in spite of his fears he would find them. The Lord would protect him. (Acts 18:9–11)

- Enemies accused Paul before the Roman governor Gallio, who ruled in favor of the Christians. (Acts 18:12–17)

- As Paul left Corinth with Aquila and Priscilla he demonstrated thankfulness to God with a vow. He left Aquila and Priscilla in Ephesus and went on to Jerusalem and Antioch. (Acts 18:18–23)

- When Apollos, an educated Alexandrian Jew and student of John the Baptist, arrived in Ephesus and taught in the synagogue, Priscilla and Aquila took him in and filled the gaps in his theology. He went on to Europe and became a highly successful Christian apologist. (Acts 18:24–28)

# Study Questions

1. Who did Paul link up with in Corinth? What did he have in common with them?

2. Where did Paul go to preach when he could no longer preach in the synagogue? What important person followed him there? How did the Corinthians respond?

3. What three reasons did the Lord give for Paul to stay in Corinth and continue to courageously preach the gospel?

4. What Egyptian Jew was influenced by Aquila and Priscilla, and what were his strengths related to Christian ministry?

# Acts 19 Freedom and Fury in the City of the No-Gods

**Chapter Highlights:**
- **The Long Road to Ephesus**
- **The Key to the City**
- **Faith Incompatible with Magic**

## Let's Get Started

Ephesus was a deceptively beautiful metropolis. The magnificent temple to the fertility goddess Artemis—one of the seven wonders of the first-century world—dominated its skyline and religious, social, and economic life. No sensual pleasure was denied. It was a world financial center. Dreams of material success and affluence captivated the minds and consumed the energies of the people. All the happiness money could buy was at their fingertips. Life for the Ephesians should have been "the good life."

But when the early Christians looked at Ephesus, they saw something very different. They saw a culture of fear scarcely veiled by the architectural, artistic, and sensual beauty on display. Christ's followers saw a half-million souls trapped in a devil-dominated world of **necromancy**, **occultism**, witchcraft, and useless worship of a lifeless, powerless goddess. Magic symbols and **incantations** failed to give them control over their world. Worship failed to connect them with the living God. Nearly the entire populace lived on a treadmill of **superstition**, confusion, and terror.

Into this environment went Paul.

## The Long Road to Ephesus

**ACTS 19:1a** *And it happened, while Apollos was at Corinth, that Paul, having passed through the upper regions, came to Ephesus. (NKJV)*

Ephesus was an evangelistic prize that had eluded Paul. Twice before, the city and its surrounding province had been on his planned itinerary. Twice, the Lord overruled his plans. The first detour occurred on the second apostolic foray into Asia Minor when Paul and his companions "were forbidden by the Holy Spirit to preach the word in **Asia**" (Acts 16:6 NKJV). Instead, the team was sent to <u>Macedonia</u> (Acts 16:10).

go to

**Macedonia**
Acts
16:11–18:18

**necromancy**
contact with spirits of the dead

**occultism**
belief in, influence by, involvement with supernatural powers

**incantations**
spells and verbal charms

**superstition**
trust in magic, chance, or false ideas of cause

**Asia**
Roman state where Ephesus was the largest city; today—western Turkey

**no superhero**
1 Corinthians 2:3;
2 Corinthians
12:7–10

Paul's heart again drew him to Ephesus after a fruitful ministry in Corinth. This time he went there, accompanied by Aquila and Priscilla, and preached in the synagogue. The synagogue congregation was responsive. But Paul had been antsy. He couldn't stay. He left for Antioch, Syria, with a stopover at Jerusalem (see Acts 18:18–22 and illustration below).

Luke, the early church historian, doesn't tell how long this detour took. Paul rejoined Aquila and Priscilla in Ephesus after he had spent some time in Antioch and then took an overland trip to churches he and Barnabas had planted in Galatia and Phrygia—in the Asia Minor interior (Acts 18:23).

**Illustration #16**
Paul's Third Missionary Journey—This map shows the route of Paul's third missionary journey, which began in Antioch, Syria, north of Jerusalem. From there he traveled overland toward Ephesus.

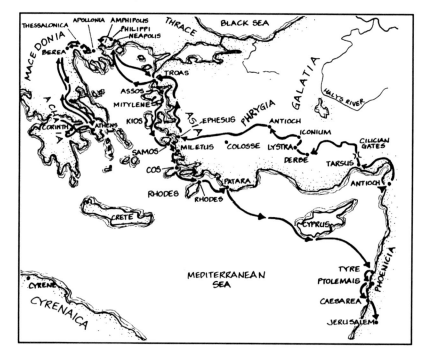

Why did Paul keep skirting Ephesus? Paul was <u>no superhero</u>. Ephesus represented a new kind of challenge. Never had he encountered a city so completely given over to the occult. As a mere man, he may have needed time to get his soul and mind ready for the fierce spiritual warfare he knew he'd face inside the Ephesian city limits.

## The Key to the City

go to

**in a person**
1 Corinthians 12:3;
Galatians 3:2;
1 Thessalonians 1:5–7;
Hebrews 6:4

**with faith**
Acts 2:38;
Romans 8:9

ACTS 19:1b–2 *And finding some disciples he said to them, "Did you receive the Holy Spirit when you believed?" So they said to him, "We have not so much as heard whether there is a Holy Spirit." (NKJV)*

Finally, Paul arrived in the great city. The Lord provided a welcome mat. In a special encounter the Holy Spirit handed Paul the "key to the city."

He had not been in Ephesus long before he bumped into a small group of disciples. Luke, the early church historian, reserves that term for followers of Jesus. These men believed. They'd been baptized. They talked and looked like Christians. Their faith appeared to be the real McCoy. But Paul had an uneasy feeling. Something was missing.

"Did you receive the Holy Spirit when you believed?" Paul asked (Acts 19:2 NKJV). (Good question. The New Testament doesn't recognize the possibility of being a real Christian unless the Spirit comes to live <u>in a person</u>. The Holy Spirit comes in the package <u>with faith</u>.)

"We have not so much as heard whether there is a Holy Spirit," was the incredulous response (Acts 19:2 NKJV).

**unregenerate**
not Christian; lacking Christ's inner life

what others say

### John Kennedy

There is no detailed description given whereby we may know God's people. . . . It may be difficult to explain in terms that would satisfy the **unregenerate** man how children of God recognize one another, but the witness of the Spirit is a reliable guide.[1]

## The Unheard-of Spirit

ACTS 19:3–4 *And he said to them, "Into what then were you baptized?" So they said, "Into John's baptism." Then Paul said, "John indeed baptized with a baptism of repentance, saying to the people that they should believe on Him who would come after him, that is, on Christ Jesus." (NKJV)*

Paul quizzed them about baptism. Turns out they'd been baptized by John the Baptist or one of his followers.

**references**
Genesis 1:2;
Numbers 11:16–17;
Isaiah 63:10–11;
Joel 2:28–32

**fulfilled**
Acts 1:5; 2:4; 2:38

Their professed ignorance about the Holy Spirit cannot mean they'd never heard of him. John's disciples knew the Old Testament, which is loaded with <u>references</u> to the Holy Spirit. What's more, they knew John the Baptist. John clearly prophesied that Christ's main work would be to baptize people with the Holy Spirit (see Matthew 3:11; Luke 3:16; John 1:33).

What these disciples most likely meant was that they didn't know the prophecy about Christ baptizing people with the Holy Spirit had been <u>fulfilled</u>. They hadn't heard about Pentecost, the day the Holy Spirit came to live in people who believe in Jesus.

## Double Dip

**ACTS 19:5** *When they heard this, they were baptized in the name of the Lord Jesus. (NKJV)*

The Ephesian "disciples" also didn't seem to know John had identified Jesus as Messiah and told people to put their trust in him (see John 1:29–35). When they heard this, they believed and were baptized "in the name of the Lord Jesus."

This is the only place in the New Testament where anyone is said to have been rebaptized. It highlights the fact that there was a huge difference between John's baptism and baptism into Jesus Christ.

John's baptism was a ceremonial bath of repentance. It represented a commitment to a radical life-change[2] and an announcement of intent to live a better life in preparation to receive Christ when he arrived (see Luke 3:3–14; John 1:6–9, 14).

Jesus's baptism is a dramatized declaration in which believers in Jesus are dipped in water (or have it poured or sprinkled on them) to announce they believe in Jesus, have welcomed him into their lives as Savior and Lord, and are united with him and everything he has done and stands for (see Romans 6:1–11).

In the Bible, to act "in" or "in the name of" someone means to act depending on and consistent with the character, values, and accomplishments of the person whose name is used.

Authentic Christian faith does not depend on saying the right words or doing the right religious rituals, but on the character and faithfulness of Jesus Christ.

# The Energizer Enters

ACTS 19:6–7 *And when Paul had laid hands on them, the Holy Spirit came upon them, and they spoke with <u>tongues</u> and <u>prophesied</u>. Now the men were about twelve in all.* (NKJV)

When Paul placed his hands on the "Ephesian Twelve," it symbolized acceptance into Christian fellowship. The Holy Spirit's coming to them at their baptism points up the most important difference between John's and Jesus's ministries. John could bring people to the point of readiness to change. But only Jesus, coming to live in them in the person of his Holy Spirit—spiritually baptizing them—could make it possible for people to live changed lives.

**what others say**

**Billy Graham**

The filling of the Holy Spirit should not be a once-for-all event, but a continuous reality every day of our lives. It is a process. We must surrender ourselves to him daily, and every day we must choose to remain surrendered. In every situation involving conflict between self and God's will, we must make our decisions on the basis of our constant submission to Christ.[3]

# Paul Leaves Synagogue for School of Tyrannus

ACTS 19:8–9 *And he went into the synagogue and spoke boldly for three months, reasoning and persuading concerning the things of the kingdom of God. But when some were hardened and did not believe, but spoke evil of the Way before the multitude, he departed from them and withdrew the disciples, reasoning daily in the school of Tyrannus.* (NKJV)

The aggressive and relentless preaching and teaching of Paul, combined with Jesus's "<u>yeast-in-dough</u>" principle, produced amazing results in Ephesus and the surrounding province. For three months the synagogue **pulpit** was open. Many Jews were persuaded to believe in Jesus. At the same time some hardened their hearts. Inevitably the opposition became too disruptive for Paul to continue. When the synagogue door slammed shut, Paul took the believers with him and moved his base of operations to the lecture hall or school of **Tyrannus** where **daily** he shared the good news of Jesus with all comers.

**tongues**
Acts 2:4–11, 17; 10:44–46

**prophesied**
Acts 4:31, 33; 9:17–20; 10:44–46

**yeast-in-dough**
Matthew 13:33

**pulpit**
Hebrew: *migdalez*—desk where Torah scrolls were read

**Tyrannus**
philosopher whose hall Paul rented

**daily**
11 a.m.–4 p.m.—siesta time for Professor Tyrannus's students[4]

**seven churches**
Revelation 2–3

**healing ministry**
Acts 14:3, 6–10;
Romans 15:17–19;
2 Corinthians 12:12

**Sefer ha-Rasim**
Book of Mysteries

# The Incredible Statistic

ACTS 19:10 *And this continued for two years, so that all who dwelt in Asia heard the word of the Lord Jesus, both Jews and Greeks.* (NKJV)

During Paul's two years at Tyrannus's hall, the seven churches mentioned in Revelation were probably founded. Paul taught, then he and his colleagues fanned out across the province sharing what they were learning of Jesus.[5] Paul spent a total of three years in Ephesus (see Acts 20:31). His coworkers included Aquila, Priscilla, Silas, Timothy, Erastus, Gaius, Aristarchus, Luke, the "Ephesian Twelve," believers from the synagogue, and others (see Acts 18, 19). Little knots of believers sprang up throughout the area. And everyone—can you believe it?—everyone in the province heard the good news from someone (Acts 19:10)!

## Faith Versus the Boogie Man

In spite of its grand emphasis on religion, philosophy, and material acquisition, the culture of Ephesus displayed glaring evidence that none of these met the spiritual needs of the people. The literature of early Ephesus contains much evidence that the study and practice of occultism and magical arts was pervasive. "Witches came out of the woodwork!"[6] Superstition substituted for faith. Famous parchments, called "Ephesian Letters," contained incantations of secret names and words guaranteed to bring safe travel, fertility, and success in business or love.

Even Jews who lived there dabbled in the forbidden stuff. A book of first-century Jewish magic, *Sefer ha-Rasim*, lists names of angelic beings used in casting good and evil spells.[7]

# Sweaty Hankies and Healing Power

ACTS 19:11–12 *Now God worked unusual miracles by the hands of Paul, so that even handkerchiefs or aprons were brought from his body to the sick, and the diseases left them and the evil spirits went out of them.* (NKJV)

In the witchy atmosphere of Ephesus, God worked in mysterious ways. Paul's healing ministry took a bizarre twist: Handkerchiefs (the Greek word means "sweat rags") and aprons worn by Paul in his tentmaking work were taken to sick and mentally ill people and they got well! But keep the story straight:

1. God did the miracles, not Paul.

2. The healing power was in God, not sweat-soaked rags Paul wore around his head or goat-oil-stained aprons he wiped his hands on.

3. Paul's dirty laundry was a visual aid to help people make the leap into faith in God.

Some people need visual aids. Healing people who needed to touch Paul's cast-off clothing before they could believe (even though, in reality, such things are unnecessary) was a loving God's gracious way of meeting people where they were.

## Some Visual Aids in the New Testament

| Reference | Visual Aid | What Happened |
|---|---|---|
| Mark 5:27–34; 6:56 | Touched edge of Jesus's cloak | Woman and all who touched were healed. |
| John 9:6–7 | Mud on blind man's eyes, washing | Blindness healed. Man converted. |
| Acts 2:38, 41 | Baptism | Spirit received. Believers added to church. |
| Acts 5:15–16 | Passed by Peter's shadow | Sick, tormented people healed. |
| Acts 19:11–12 | Touched Paul's hankies and aprons | Illnesses cured. Evil spirits left. |
| 1 Corinthians 11:23–26 | Lord's Supper, bread and wine | Remember Jesus. Proclaim his death. |

## It Takes One to Know One

**ACTS 19:13–16** *Then some of the itinerant Jewish exorcists took it upon themselves to call the name of the Lord Jesus over those who had evil spirits, saying, "We exorcise you by the Jesus whom Paul preaches." Also there were seven sons of Sceva, a Jewish chief priest, who did so. And the evil spirit answered and said, "Jesus I know, and Paul I know; but who are you?" Then the man in whom the evil spirit was leaped on them, overpowered them, and prevailed against them, so that they fled out of that house naked and wounded. (NKJV)*

A troupe of professional exorcists billed as "the seven sons of Sceva" claimed to exorcise those who had "evil spirits." They heard about Paul's success casting out evil spirits in Jesus's name and decided to add the name of Jesus to their bag of tricks and incantations.

**go to**

**confessed**
1 John 1:9

One day Sceva's boys were hired to cast out an evil spirit. To their surprise, when they intoned the name of Jesus over the harassed soul, the evil spirit yelled back, "Jesus I know, and Paul I know, but who are you?" At which point the demon attacked the exorcists, and they were last seen "streaking" out of the house and down the street, leaving a trail of bloody footprints!

> **what others say**
>
> **Mark Galli**
>
> Jews and pagans had their own exorcism prayers and rituals . . . long before Christianity arrived. But Christian exorcism was impressive in that it used no elaborate invocations or rituals—just prayer, Scripture, and the name of Jesus.[8]

Jesus's name is not a "magic" word to use to make a profit or get fame for yourself. Jesus's name represents a mighty person whose power is for making the name and character of his Father God known and for doing his will.

## Faith Incompatible with Magic

ACTS 19:17–20 *This became known both to all Jews and Greeks dwelling in Ephesus; and fear fell on them all, and the name of the Lord Jesus was magnified. And many who had believed came confessing and telling their deeds. Also, many of those who had practiced magic brought their books together and burned them in the sight of all. And they counted up the value of them, and it totaled fifty thousand pieces of silver. So the word of the Lord grew mightily and prevailed.* (NKJV)

News of the Sceva boys' fiasco got around quickly—probably accompanied by a lot of loud laughing. Not everyone thought it was funny. The incident became the epicenter of a spiritual earthquake. Jesus's name was suddenly known and respected all over town. Misuse of it could send you to the emergency room!

Christians awoke to the fact that faith in Jesus and magic incantations and spells are totally incompatible. Dependence on charms, secret names, and occult practices is sinful. Many confessed their secret evil deeds openly. Many Christians who had secretly hung on to some of their old superstitions after believing in Jesus took dramatic and costly steps to sever the old evil connections. They brought magical scrolls, "Ephesian Letters," lists of angelic names, and occult paraphernalia and, as Ephesus watched, these once-prized items valued at fifty thousand days' wages—several million dollars—went up in holy smoke!

The power of the Word of God was demonstrated most dramatically when the Ephesian believers confessed their evil practices and burned the other books and sources to which they looked for wisdom and hope. They burned their bridges behind them and gave themselves in exclusive allegiance to Christ. What are some things you hesitate to "burn" in order to be really honest and committed to the Lord? What would it cost to let them go?

In the twenty-first century wholehearted, no-strings-attached surrender to Jesus still sets people free and gives them real joy.

**go to**

**the collection**
Romans 15:25–28;
1 Corinthians
16:1–4;
2 Corinthians
8, 9

*something to ponder*

## Missionary Eyes

> ACTS 19:21–22 *When these things were accomplished, Paul purposed in the Spirit, when he had passed through Macedonia and Achaia, to go to Jerusalem, saying, "After I have been there, I must also see Rome." So he sent into Macedonia two of those who ministered to him, Timothy and Erastus, but he himself stayed in Asia for a time.* (NKJV)

**the Way**
Christianity, the
unique way of life

Watching the bonfire of proof that the gospel was taking root in Ephesus, Paul's squinty missionary eyes got that faraway look. "I must visit Rome!" He would stay on a little longer to direct "mopping up" operations in Ephesus. Timothy and Erastus headed for Macedonia and Corinth to urge <u>the collection</u> of financial aid for hard-pressed Christians in Israel. Paul would take the money to Jerusalem, then head for Rome.

## Ephesus and the Temple of Diana

> ACTS 19:23–24 *And about that time there arose a great commotion about **the Way**. For a certain man named Demetrius, a silversmith, who made silver shrines of Diana, brought no small profit to the craftsmen.* (NKJV)

Ephesus was the capital, not only of occultism and witchcraft, but of idolatry. The city's greatest claim to fame was the temple of Diana (alias: Artemis or Aphrodite), goddess of love, fertility, and nourishment (see illustration #17). The magnificent structure was larger than a football field. Its roof was supported by 127 sixty-foot-high stone columns. Scores of priests and prostitute-priestesses served worshipers and tourists from all over the world. The temple was the center of everything in Ephesus, including religion, the arts, and banking.

If you were a true Diana-worshiper, the goddess was the most beautiful relic in the world. Her temple contained an image of her "which fell down from Zeus" (see Acts 19:35 NKJV)—a meteorite resembling, to believing eyes, the form of a many-breasted woman. To clearer eyes she was an old, cold, black rock, full of lumps and crannies where spiders spun their webs.

## Monthlong Festival of Diana

ACTS 19:25 *He called them together with the workers of similar occupation, and said: "Men, you know that we have our prosperity by this trade. (NKJV)*

The "lusty month of May" brought the annual monthlong Festival of Diana, honoring the goddess. Nearly the whole province converged on Ephesus to worship, compete, and have a high old time! It was the State Fair, Olympics, World Series, Miss America Pageant, and Mardi Gras rolled into one.

It was a time of high religious fervor, and it was a time to spend money. Souvenir manufacturers and merchants depended on Artemisia for their year's profits (a lot like Christmas!). Thousands bought trinkets and medals to remember the occasion. Especially popular were wooden, silver, or gold images of the goddess and the temple.

## Man-Made Statues Are "Not Gods"

ACTS 19:26–28 *Moreover you see and hear that not only at Ephesus, but throughout almost all Asia, this Paul has persuaded and turned away many people, saying that they are not gods which are made with hands. So not only is this trade of ours in danger of falling into disrepute, but also the temple of the great goddess Diana may be despised and her magnificence destroyed, whom all Asia and the world worship." Now when they heard this, they were full of wrath and cried out, saying, "Great is Diana of the Ephesians!" (NKJV)*

It is possible the riot of the silversmiths erupted at the Festival of Diana. In his speech, Demetrius, president of the local brotherhood of silversmiths, quoted Paul as saying that man-made gods are "not gods" (Acts 19:26 NKJV)! The "magnificence" (Acts 19:27 NKJV) of their dear old space-rock maiden was at stake. Demetrius touched a most sensitive nerve by pointing out that, with the shrinkage of the silver shrine and trinket business, Christianity was also becoming a royal pain in the pocketbook.

The smiths and salesmen ran into the streets shouting the cult cry voiced by worshipers in the temple: "Great is Diana of the Ephesians!" (Acts 19:28 NKJV).

The screaming smithies of Ephesus represent all who oppose spirituality, morality, or justice when profit margins are threatened. In our modern world, there is ample evidence that <u>idolatry of the bottom line</u> is alive and well.

**idolatry of the bottom line**
Colossians 3:5

# Riot in Ephesus

**go to**

**Gaius**
Romans 16:23;
1 Corinthians 1:14

**Aristarchus**
Acts 20:4; 27:2;
Colossians 4:10;
Philemon 24

**Alexander**
2 Timothy 4:14–15

**officials**
ten-member council
called "Asiarchs"

## the big picture

### Acts 19:29–41

When the craftsmen took their demonstration to the streets, many citizens joined them. Paul's friends Gaius and Aristarchus were seized. Provincial **officials** friendly to Paul urged him not to confront the mob. When the Jews pushed Alexander forward to speak, they shouted him down. For two hours in the city stadium they shouted, "Great is Diana of the Ephesians!" The riot ended when the town clerk took charge, warned the crowd of repercussions from Rome, and dismissed the assembly.

Shoppers in the marketplace joined the demonstration. The mob rushed into the twenty-five-thousand-seat, open-air theater. Many had not the foggiest idea what all the fuss was about (Acts 19:32), but it was exciting and everybody was doing it—so they joined in. They didn't want to miss whatever was happening.

Unable to find Paul, the crowd nabbed a couple of his team members, Gaius and Aristarchus. Paul, never one to run from a chance to share the gospel, wanted to face the mob. But cooler heads convinced him to stay away (Acts 19:30–31).

Jewish leaders, concerned the demonstration might turn anti-Semitic, pushed Alexander, a Jewish metalworker, into the theater, to explain the difference between Jews and Christians.

Finally, the city clerk, executive officer of the town council, quieted the crowd with a somber warning.

"This meeting is adjourned!" the clerk said.

Repeatedly in Acts and in church history since that time to the present, the Lord has used honest judges and government officials to protect his people who are under attack.

**key point**

## what others say

### William Barclay

[The town clerk] saved Paul and his companions but he saved them because he was saving his own skin. . . . Paul wished to face the mob but they would not let him. Paul was a man without fear. For the silversmiths and the town clerk it was safety first; for Paul it was always safety last.[9]

# Chapter Wrap-Up

- At Ephesus, Paul met twelve men who appeared to be Christians. They were disciples of John the Baptist, who had never experienced Christ coming in to live in them. When Paul baptized them in Jesus's name, the Holy Spirit came into their lives. (Acts 19:1–7)

- Paul taught in the Ephesian synagogue until opposition against the gospel hardened. Then he took his base of operations to the lecture hall of Tyrannus. From there, the message of Jesus was taken to people all over the city and province. (Acts 19:8–10)

- Strange things happened in Ephesus as the gospel spread. Items of Paul's clothing brought healing. Unbelievers using Jesus's name were attacked by a demon they tried to exorcise. Occult books were burned in a huge bonfire. (Acts 19:11–20)

- Christianity had such a powerful impact in Ephesus it threatened to bankrupt craftsmen and sellers of pagan artifacts. The metalworkers demonstrated against Paul. This led to a riot that was finally quelled by the town officials. (Acts 19:21–41)

# Study Questions

1. What was missing in the faith and experience of the twelve disciples Paul discovered in Ephesus (Acts 19:1–5)?

2. Why did Paul stop teaching in the synagogue and move his meeting to Tyrannus's hall? What happened while Paul taught there?

3. What unusual and costly thing did the new Christians at Ephesus do to break free from their old superstitious and sinful life patterns and to demonstrate their commitment to Christ? What was the result?

4. What were Demetrius and the silversmiths so mad about? What form of modern "idolatry" do they represent?

# Acts 20 The Vulnerable Ambassador

*Chapter Highlights:*
- **Man in Motion**
- **Paul Calls for the Elders of the Church**
- **The Visible Church Leader**

## Let's Get Started

Even before the wild demonstration at the Ephesian festival of Artemis, Paul's eyes were already fixed on Rome, capital of the world (see Acts 19:21–22). Beyond Rome he hoped to go to Spain and plant churches in the western Mediterranean area (see Romans 15:24–28). He took a roundabout route to reach his goal. And as Luke tells it, every stop Paul made, everything he said and did on the way to Rome, had a ring of finality.

**revisiting**
Acts 14:21–25;
15:36, 40; 16:4–5;
18:23

## Man in Motion

> **ACTS 20:1** *After the uproar had ceased, Paul called the disciples to himself, embraced them, and departed to go to Macedonia.* *(NKJV)*

The riot of the silversmiths had shown Paul his continued presence in Ephesus would create more problems for the young Ephesian church. After three years (see Acts 20:31) it was time to move. He called the believers together, encouraged them to keep the faith, and said his final adios.

## Bolstering the Brotherhoods

> **ACTS 20:2–3a** *Now when he had gone over that region and encouraged them with many words, he came to Greece and stayed three months.* *(NKJV)*

From the start of his apostolic ministry, Paul had followed the pattern of <u>revisiting</u> churches he'd helped establish. On these return visits he did six things:

1. *He talked a lot* (Acts 20:2). "Many words" in Greek indicates more than quantity. It means breadth and fervor. He fine-tuned their theology and built a fire under their faith.

2. *He encouraged them* (Acts 20:2). "Encouragement" in Greek is

persuasion, cheer, and comfort. Paul lifted their spirits in the face of the persecutions and pressures and gave them solid reasons to keep on believing.

3. *He strengthened them* (see Acts 18:23). "Strengthened" means Paul validated and invigorated their faith, taught them to rest confidently in the Lord.

4. *He appointed elders for them* (Acts 14:23). He identified spiritually mature people and gave them authority to shepherd the Christian flock.

5. *He prayed for them* (see Acts 14:23; 20:36; Ephesians 1:15–23).

6. *He commended them to the Lord* (see Acts 14:23; 20:32). "Commended" means Paul handed control and care of each church to the Lord. He would travel on but Jesus would be their Leader and Savior.

The Lord's leadership strategy includes giving the church gifted, spiritually mature people who help keep it on track. "He Himself [Christ] gave some to be apostles, some prophets, some evangelists, and some pastors and teachers, for the equipping of the saints for the work of ministry, for the edifying of the body of Christ" (Ephesians 4:11–12 NKJV). These people do not do the church's work for it; they prepare and encourage the church to do its work.

what others say

**Audrey I. Girard**

Every individual and church has the responsibility to seek God's guidance by praying, reading the Bible and listening for that inner conviction that the Holy Spirit promises (see John 16:13).[1]

## Never Go It Alone

ACTS 20:3b–5 *And when the Jews plotted against him as he was about to sail to Syria, he decided to return through Macedonia. And Sopater of Berea accompanied him to Asia—also Aristarchus and Secundus of the Thessalonians, and Gaius of Derbe, and Timothy, and Tychicus and Trophimus of Asia. These men, going ahead, waited for us at Troas. (NKJV)*

The early church practiced the principle of spiritual teamwork Jesus had taught his disciples. Paul never traveled alone. At least eight men made the trip to Jerusalem with him:

sharing themselves
2 Corinthians 8:1–5

- *Sopater*—Alias: Sosipater. Home church: Berea. Paul's relative (see Romans 16:21).

- *Aristarchus*—Home church: Thessalonica. Paul's coworker (see Acts 19:29). Was with him in prison and on the voyage to Rome (see Acts 27:2).

- *Secundus*—Home: Thessalonica.

- *Gaius*—Home church: Derbe. Probably became a Christian when Barnabas and Paul first visited there (see Acts 14:20–21).

- *Timothy*—Home church: Lystra (see Acts 16:1). Paul's spiritual "son" (see 1 Timothy 1:2). Permanent member of Paul's team.

- *Tychicus*—Home: Asia province. Carried messages from Paul to the churches (see Ephesians 6:21–22; Colossians 4:7–8).

- *Trophimus*—Home: Asia. Focus of controversy in Jerusalem that led to Paul's arrest (see Acts 21:29).

- *Luke*—His presence is revealed by references to "us" and "we" (Acts 20:5–6).

These men represented Gentile churches that raised relief money for struggling Jewish believers. They apparently linked up with Paul in Corinth (where he'd spent three months), intending to travel from there to Antioch (Syria) and then on to Jerusalem, in time for the Jewish Passover. There are good reasons why such an entourage should make this particular trip with Paul:

1. The cash they carried was enough to tempt many a robber. A corps of burly Christian men could better assure its safe arrival than a scrawny rabbi (Paul) traveling alone.

2. Christian giving is not merely a transfer of money. It's a response of loving hearts <u>sharing themselves</u>. Each church wanted its contribution to have a face.

## Don't Take Unnecessary Risks

The assassination plot was discovered just as Paul and the others were about to sail from Greece to Syria. A ship carrying Jewish pil-

The early church practiced the principle of spiritual teamwork Jesus had taught his disciples. Paul never traveled alone. At least eight men made the trip to Jerusalem with him:

**no help**
Philippians 1:20–26;
Psalm 6:4–5

grims to Jerusalem for the Passover would have provided the ideal opportunity to get rid of the man some considered "Public Enemy Number One" by simply throwing him overboard. "Paul was a man who always walked with his life in his hands."[2]

Discovering the plot, Paul gave up his plans to get to Jerusalem for Passover. He did not board the ship but, taking Luke with him, hoofed it overland to Philippi. The other men, serving as decoys, boarded the original ship and got off at Troas to wait for Paul and Luke (Acts 20:5). The assassins assumed Paul was with them. By the time they discovered otherwise, they were at sea.

Paul risked his life for Jesus again and again. But martyrdom was not something he courted. He was willing to die for his faith but avoided death as long as he possibly could. The Lord had given him a job to do, and his first priority was to finish that job (see Acts 20:24). He'd be no help to anyone if he were dead!

> **what others say**
>
> **William G. Bixler**
> The early church did not advocate voluntary martyrdoms . . . Jesus himself . . . advised fleeing when persecution was imminent.[3]

The early church encouraged flight to escape persecution and warned against rushing into voluntary martyrdom.[4] Paul escaped from Damascus (Acts 9:25); Peter, from Herod (Acts 12:17). Paul used Roman citizenship to avoid assassination (Acts 25:1–11).

## Plan B: Jerusalem by Pentecost

ACTS 20:6 *But we sailed away from Philippi after the Days of Unleavened Bread, and in five days joined them at Troas, where we stayed seven days. (NKJV)*

According to the revised plan, Paul and Luke sailed from Philippi after the Feast of Unleavened Bread. In AD 57, the twin feasts of Passover and Unleavened Bread were celebrated in Jerusalem on April 7–14. The next big festival would be Pentecost, six weeks later. Paul celebrated Passover in Philippi. From there he and Luke took a ship to Troas to rejoin the team.

# Sunday-Go-to-Meeting in the Early Church

ACTS 20:7–8 *Now on the first day of the week, when the disciples came together to break bread, Paul, ready to depart the next day, spoke to them and continued his message until midnight. There were many lamps in the upper room where they were gathered together. (NKJV)*

first day
1 Corinthians 16:2

Luke's record of this visit gives a rare glimpse of a regular early church meeting. It looks more like a family gathering than a formal "worship service." That's as it should be. After all, Jesus promised his followers more than to be part of an audience. He said they'd have a family—brothers and sisters, parents and children (see Mark 10:29–30). In the face of life's pressures, only a family can meet the Christian's need for support.

- *They met on Sunday.* This is the first New Testament reference to the <u>first day</u> as the regular meeting time for Christians.

- *They ate together.* Early Christians celebrated the Lord's Supper (Holy Communion) as part of a potluck meal (love feast).

- *They met at night.* This was probably to accommodate slaves who could only come when the day's work was done.

- *They met three floors up* (Acts 20:9). Early church meetings were held in the homes of members. Wealthy homes often had a third-story loft. Many people also lived in three-story concrete tenements in which poorer families occupied the third floor.

- *The length of the meeting was not regulated by the clock* (Acts 20:7, 11). More important issues were in focus. This was the last chance to hear from the apostle Paul.

## what others say

### John O. Gooch

In the first century, the Lord's Supper included not only the bread and the cup but an entire meal. As part of the meal, neighbors who had quarreled made peace again. . . . When worship was ended, Christians took home the consecrated bread so that those who couldn't attend worship could partake of the Lord's Supper. In North Africa, Christians took home the bread so they could celebrate the sacrament every day with their families.[5]

# Sleeping in Church Can Be Dangerous

go to

**Elijah-like**
1 Kings 17:21–23

**ACTS 20:9–12** *And in a window sat a certain young man named Eutychus, who was sinking into a deep sleep. He was overcome by sleep; and as Paul continued speaking, he fell down from the third story and was taken up dead. But Paul went down, fell on him, and embracing him said, "Do not trouble yourselves, for his life is in him." Now when he had come up, had broken bread and eaten, and talked a long while, even till daybreak, he departed. And they brought the young man in alive, and they were not a little comforted. (NKJV)*

Young Eutychus may have put in a hard day's work before coming to the meeting. The place was lit with smoky oil lamps (Acts 20:8). The atmosphere was stuffy. Sometime after midnight, Eutychus fell asleep and fell out the window! He landed on the stone pavement three stories down! Dr. Luke may be the one who pronounced him dead.

Elijah-like, Paul stretched himself over the lad's body. "He's alive!" he announced. They all went back upstairs and ate together. Paul started talking again and didn't stop till the sun came up! (And you thought your pastor's sermons were long!)

In a family gathering, neatness doesn't count much. Setting tables, eating, doing dishes, wiping up spilled food, changing diapers, handling tough questions, rescuing young men who fall out the window! It's very likely Paul's teaching was not an all-night lecture. (That'd be enough to put a whole congregation to sleep!) He taught in the Jewish style—the style of Jesus—interspersing teaching with questions and interaction. What counts when Christians gather is to meet God, remember Jesus, yield to the Spirit, build relationships, and leave better equipped to live the life and share the story.

In this life difficulties are bound to occur, and there's nothing like a Eutychus falling out the window now and then to keep a congregation in touch with reality!

something to ponder

## what others say

**Philip Yancey**

Anyone can form a club; it takes grace, shared vision, and hard work to form a community. The Christian church was the first institution in history to bring together on equal footing Jews and Gentiles, men and women, slaves and free. . . .

> Church is one place . . . that brings together generations: infants still held at their mother's breasts, children who squirm and giggle at all the wrong times, responsible adults who know how to act appropriately at all times, and senior citizens who drift asleep if the preacher drones on too long.[6]

**go to**

**elders**
Titus 1:5–9

**overseers**
1 Timothy 3:1–7

## Paul Calls for the Elders of the Church

ACTS 20:13–17 *Then we went ahead to the ship and sailed to Assos, there intending to take Paul on board; for so he had given orders, intending himself to go on foot. And when he met us at Assos, we took him on board and came to Mitylene. We sailed from there, and the next day came opposite Chios. The following day we arrived at Samos and stayed at Trogyllium. The next day we came to Miletus. For Paul had decided to sail past Ephesus, so that he would not have to spend time in Asia; for he was hurrying to be at Jerusalem, if possible, on the Day of Pentecost. From Miletus he sent to Ephesus and called for the elders of the church. (NKJV)*

The Acts storyteller, Luke, obviously kept a log or diary of each day's travels. The morning after the all-night meeting, Paul stayed in Troas when the rest of the team set sail. The ship would stop at Assos, a twenty-mile hike from Troas (Acts 20:13–14). He'd catch up there. He probably wanted to check on Eutychus before he left or get rejuvenated by some aerobic walking.

Here we learn of Paul's desire to reach Jerusalem before Pentecost. Because of limited time and because his name was still "mud" in some Ephesian circles, Paul called for leaders of the Ephesian church to join him for a farewell muster at Miletus, thirty miles from Ephesus. The ship on which Paul had booked passage would be anchored at Miletus for a few days. Luke's minutes of the meeting provide the only example in Acts of Paul's preaching to Christians.

Paul uses three terms in his message to identify church leaders. In the first century, all three "titles" refer to the same local church office.

1. *Elders* (Acts 20:17). This was the traditional term for Jewish community and religious leaders. It emphasizes the need for church leaders to be spiritually mature.

2. *Overseers* (Acts 20:28). This emphasizes the leaders' role as guides

**shepherds**
Ephesians 4:11;
1 Peter 5:1–3

**shows**
Luke 6:39–40

and protectors watching over God's people to guard them from spiritual danger. Synonym: guardian.

3. *Shepherds* (Acts 20:28). The Greek word means "one who feeds, pastures, tends a flock"; "shepherd" or "herdsman." It emphasizes a leader's role as caregiver. Synonym: pastor.

## The Visible Church Leader

ACTS 20:18 *And when they had come to him, he said to them: "You know, from the first day that I came to Asia, in what manner I always lived among you,* (NKJV)

In his "farewell address" to the Ephesian elders, Paul did not explain a Bible passage or offer insights into the meaning of some pithy Greek word. He did not appeal to their intellects or list ten rules for effective church leadership. He took the risk of talking about himself, his record, his ministry, his fears and tears and hopes. He believed and demonstrated a very important principle that distinguishes Jesus-style leadership from all others: The Christian leader does not merely tell people the way they should live, but in the way he himself lives, he *shows* them the way.

If the shepherd-overseers of Ephesus wanted to know how to live and work, they needed to remember how Paul lived and worked. Paul was sure enough of himself to dare to say, "Follow me!"

what others say

**Audrey I. Girard**

Let the beauty of your Grace be reflected in our face
And let no one doubt to Whom we belong.[7]

## The Way I Was

ACTS 20:19–21 *serving the Lord with all humility, with many tears and trials which happened to me by the plotting of the Jews; how I kept back nothing that was helpful, but proclaimed it to you, and taught you publicly and from house to house, testifying to Jews, and also to Greeks, repentance toward God and faith toward our Lord Jesus Christ.* (NKJV)

As the visible, vulnerable Christian leader he was not cold, aloof, or distant. He got down and dirty, up close and personal, where they could see and know him . . . warts and all!

- In the face of personal danger he did the Lord's work with humility and intensity (Acts 20:19).

- No matter the cost in <u>lost reputation</u> and <u>public outrage,</u> he didn't hesitate to tell people what they needed to hear (Acts 20:20).

- He pursued his evangelistic and teaching ministry everywhere anyone would listen—both "publicly and from house to house" (Acts 20:20 NKJV).

- He invited people, regardless of ethnic and cultural background, to leave their sins, turn to God, and put their faith in Jesus as Lord (Acts 20:21).

**go to**

**lost reputation**
Acts 19:9

**public outrage**
Acts 19:23–31

**God's watchman**
Ezekiel 33:1–9

## "Bound in the Spirit"

ACTS 20:22–27 *And see, now I go bound in the spirit to Jerusalem, not knowing the things that will happen to me there, except that the Holy Spirit testifies in every city, saying that chains and tribulations await me. But none of these things move me; nor do I count my life dear to myself, so that I may finish my race with joy, and the ministry which I received from the Lord Jesus, to testify to the gospel of the grace of God. And indeed, now I know that you all, among whom I have gone preaching the kingdom of God, will see my face no more. Therefore I testify to you this day that I am innocent of the blood of all men. For I have not shunned to declare to you the whole counsel of God. (NKJV)*

This was good-bye. Paul had spent seven or eight years establishing churches on both sides of the Aegean Sea. He had done his job. He would never return.

The statement "I am innocent of the blood of all men" was Paul's very Jewish way of saying he had faithfully carried out his spiritual responsibility. He'd explained the saving plan of God completely. If people of Ephesus chose to reject the gospel and be lost from God, the guilt was theirs, not his! As God's <u>watchman</u>, he had not failed to sound the alarm.

**go to**

**wolves**
1 Timothy 1:3–7;
4:1–3;
2 Timothy 3:6–9;
4:3–4;
1 Peter 5:8–9

**bought and paid**
1 Corinthians
6:19–20; 7:23;
Revelation 5:9

**redeeming**
buying people's
freedom from sin

**Howard Marshall**

As the watchman who warns people faithfully of the coming of an enemy is not guilty if they choose to ignore the warning, so it is with Paul as a preacher of the gospel. Paul's assurance was derived from his confidence that he had faithfully preached the gospel in every particular; he had dealt with the whole of God's plan of salvation.[8]

In Acts 20:22 Paul uses a phrase that shows how the Lord Jesus reveals the direction he wants his people to go and the things he wants them to do: "bound in the spirit" (NKJV). In the original Greek this means the Spirit of Christ (Holy Spirit) living in the Christian provides the moral motivation to do the right thing, the thing Jesus wants us to do. Christians are not forced by outward rules and regulations or expectations, but "the compelling motivation for our choices comes from within."[9]

## What Every Church Needs Is a Good Sheepdog!

ACTS 20:28–31 *Therefore take heed to yourselves and to all the flock, among which the Holy Spirit has made you overseers, to shepherd the church of God which He purchased with His own blood. For I know this, that after my departure savage wolves will come in among you, not sparing the flock. Also from among yourselves men will rise up, speaking perverse things, to draw away the disciples after themselves. Therefore watch, and remember that for three years I did not cease to warn everyone night and day with tears. (NKJV)*

Sometimes elders, overseers, shepherds of the church would be better described as "sheepdogs." There are dangers out there. "Savage <u>wolves</u>" eager to decimate the flock. Leaders must guard themselves and the church against the ravages of faith destroyers. Here's Paul's argument:

1. You didn't choose your job—you're an overseer because the Holy Spirit "made you" one (Acts 20:28 NKJV).

2. God <u>bought and paid</u> for the church with "His own blood." (Jesus's death was God **redeeming** his people.) The church flock belongs to God, not the shepherds (Acts 20:28 NKJV).

3. Some people (some hearing Paul say these words!) want to possess the church for themselves. They will push themselves forward and speak "perverse things" to get the flock to follow them instead of God (Acts 20:29–30 NKJV).

4. This persistent danger calls for impassioned watchfulness and warnings (Acts 20:31).

to God
Acts 14:23

help the weak
1 Corinthians 9:22

Healthy church growth not only involves adding disciples, leaders, and locations but also subtracting harmful influences, attitudes, and teachings.

## You're in Good Hands with the Almighty

ACTS 20:32–35 *So now, brethren, I commend you to God and to the word of His grace, which is able to build you up and give you an inheritance among all those who are sanctified. I have coveted no one's silver or gold or apparel. Yes, you yourselves know that these hands have provided for my necessities, and for those who were with me. I have shown you in every way, by laboring like this, that you must support the weak. And remember the words of the Lord Jesus, that He said, 'It is more blessed to give than to receive.'" (NKJV)*

Paul again reminds the Ephesian pastors of the example of his life and ministry:

- He did not micro-manage the churches. He trusted the well-being, protection, and progress of the church <u>to God</u>, his Word, and his grace. He did not depend on his own efforts to produce change and mature Christians. He trusted God's grace at work in his people.

- He served without the thought of material gain.

- He wasn't afraid to get his hands dirty to support himself and others.

- He worked hard to <u>help the weak</u>.

- He got joy and fulfillment from a giving-rather-than-receiving lifestyle.

Everyone who accepts Jesus's invitation to follow him is called to full-time Christian living, fully developed Christian character, and wholehearted commitment to the Lord. If Paul was called to lay his life on the line for the witness of God's grace through Jesus, so are we.

### Ruth Bell Graham

Pashi, from India, was a college student. When he was presented with the claims of Christ, Pashi told me, "I would like to believe in Christ. But we have never seen a Christian who was like Christ." . . .

I asked . . . Dr. Akbar Haqq, a brilliant Christian who had been president of a school of Islamic studies in India . . ."How would you answer Pashi? What would you say?"

"That is simple," he answered decisively. "I would tell Pashi, 'I am not offering you Christians. I am offering you Christ.'"[10]

## Bon Voyage!

ACTS 20:36–38 *And when he had said these things, he knelt down and prayed with them all. Then they all wept freely, and fell on Paul's neck and kissed him, sorrowing most of all for the words which he spoke, that they would see his face no more. And they accompanied him to the ship.* (NKJV)

This is all too personal! These are not dutiful employees waving good-bye to a respected boss and mentor. There's too much emotion—too much personal pain at seeing Paul go. It's another indication that Paul's leadership style was not to run things from above or to demand obedience in order to fulfill the boss's personal goals. Paul had involved himself personally in their lives, given himself to them, in such a self-revealing, honest, caring way that it lifted their relationship with him to a much higher, closer, more personal level.

When Paul left with the announcement that they would never see him again, they broke down and cried! Paul was no scary "authority figure." He was their spiritual father and a friend with whom their lives had become interwoven in a rich tapestry of love.

Jesus said those who learn from him become like him (see Luke 6:40). New Testament leadership follows this pattern. It is not merely a matter of transmission of facts and principles and motivating people by a system of rewards and pressures. It is the passing of a quality of life from the leader to those he or she leads.

# Chapter Wrap-Up

- Paul left Ephesus for Macedonia where he encouraged the Christians. With several companions, he planned to travel to Jerusalem with a gift for needy Jewish believers. A plot against his life delayed his departure until after the Passover. (Acts 20:1–6)

- At a stopover in Troas, Paul went to the Sunday gathering of the local church and preached till midnight. A youth named Eutychus fell to his death from the third-story window. Paul revived him and preached on till the sun came up. (Acts 20:7–12)

- At a stopover in Miletus, Paul gathered the leaders of the Ephesian church together for a final farewell. (Acts 20:13–17)

- He told the Ephesian elders to follow his example. He talked about his willingness to die for the gospel. He warned the Ephesian church of coming trouble for them and reminded them of their responsibility to protect God's flock. (Acts 20:18–31)

- Paul committed them to God's care, reminded them of his unselfish, giving lifestyle while among them, and quoted a saying from Jesus found nowhere else in the Bible. They saw him off with hugs, kisses, and tears. (Acts 20:32–38)

# Study Questions

1. Identify the five characteristics of the church meeting in Troas.

2. Who fell asleep and fell out the window?

3. Identify three "titles" for local church leaders used in Acts 20:17–38, and tell what aspect of Christian leadership each emphasizes.

4. Let's play "Who Wants to Be a Church Leader?" according to Acts 20:28–31:

   - The $1,000 question: Who really chooses a church leader for his or her job?

     a. The congregation

     b. The leader himself or herself

c. The leader's wife

d. The Holy Spirit

- The $10,000 question: Who owns the church and why?

    a. The pastor because of his position

    b. The congregation because it gives money

    c. God because he shed his blood

    d. The bank because it holds the mortgage

- The $100,000 question: Because of danger from people who distort the truth to get people to follow them instead of God, what's a church leader to do?

    a. Be on guard

    b. Don't rock the boat

    c. Resign and move to another church

    d. Warn people of the danger

# Part Four
# CHAINED WITNESS

# Acts 21:1–22:29 Staring Down Danger

## Let's Get Started

The Ephesian church leaders wept openly as they escorted Paul to the ship and kissed him good-bye (see Acts 20:37–38). Jerusalem was calling him like a Star Trek tractor beam. Paul loved the Holy City. No other place on earth held such attraction to Jews or inspired such yearning and intense loyalty.

For Paul this trip to <u>Mount Zion</u> held more danger and at the same time more opportunity than any before in his life. He knew (see Acts 20:23) he would probably leave Jerusalem in chains—possibly even in a coffin! But he felt compelled to go there—no matter the risks!

**Mount Zion**
Psalm 48:2

## Don't Go, Paul, Don't Go!

ACTS 21:1–6 *Now it came to pass, that when we had departed from them and set sail, running a straight course we came to Cos, the following day to Rhodes, and from there to Patara. And finding a ship sailing over to Phoenicia, we went aboard and set sail. When we had sighted Cyprus, we passed it on the left, sailed to Syria, and landed at Tyre; for there the ship was to unload her cargo. And finding disciples, we stayed there seven days. They told Paul through the Spirit not to go up to Jerusalem. When we had come to the end of those days, we departed and went on our way; and they all accompanied us, with wives and children, till we were out of the city. And we knelt down on the shore and prayed. When we had taken our leave of one another, we boarded the ship, and they returned home.* (NKJV)

Luke's logbook records the voyage from Miletus, site of Paul's farewell meeting with the Ephesian elders, to Caesarea, the seaport nearest Jerusalem. Incidents at two of the stops along the way tested Paul's commitment to face what lay ahead and assured him his fellow Christians cared.

**produced**
Galatians 5:22–23

**gifts**
Romans 12:6–8;
1 Corinthians
12:1–11, 27–31

**daughters**
Acts 2:17–18

**prominence to women**
Acts 1:14; 6:1–7;
9:36–42; 16:15;
18:18–19

**gifts**
abilities, sensitivities,
graces enabling
people to do God's
work

**prophetesses**
women gifted to
speak God's
message

The first incident took place at the Phoenician seaport town of Tyre. The disciples, "through the Spirit," urged Paul not to go to Jerusalem.

"Through the Spirit" does not mean the Spirit said, "Don't go!" In Acts 20:22 Paul specifically says he went "bound in the spirit." The Holy Spirit in his fellow Christians made them sensitive to his danger and <u>produced</u> the love they had for him. Awareness and concern were expressed through special **gifts** of the Spirit. But going to Jerusalem in the face of danger was Paul's personal response to the clear directions from the Lord for which he alone must answer.

# A Family of Preacher-Girls

*ACTS 21:7–9 And when we had finished our voyage from Tyre, we came to Ptolemais, greeted the brethren, and stayed with them one day. On the next day we who were Paul's companions departed and came to Caesarea, and entered the house of Philip the evangelist, who was one of the seven, and stayed with him. Now this man had four virgin daughters who prophesied. (NKJV)*

The team's host in Caesarea was Philip, one of the seven appointed twenty years earlier to feed Jerusalem's poor (Acts 6:1–6). What a reunion this was! The last time Paul and Philip were mentioned in the same paragraph, Philip was running for his life with Paul (then called Saul), the Christian-hater, in hot pursuit! After preaching around the country, Philip settled in Caesarea and raised four <u>daughters</u> who were "**prophetesses**." Philip's preacher-daughters later moved with their father to the Ephesus area where they lived to old age and were valued by the second-century church as sources of information about early Judean Christianity.

## what others say

### Ajith Fernando

Luke's mention of Philip's daughters highlights the fact that people not regarded as being of high status did have positions of prominence in the church. The breaking of human barriers is one of the main subthemes of Acts. Luke has given <u>prominence to women</u> in different ways. . . . The present passage records single women exercising what the New Testament regards as a key gift for the church (Acts 21:9). . . . Acts teaches us that women, especially women marginalized by society, have a prominent role in fulfilling the agenda of the kingdom.[1]

# Detour! There's a Muddy Road Ahead

ACTS 21:10–11 *And as we stayed many days, a certain prophet named Agabus came down from Judea. When he had come to us, he took Paul's belt, bound his own hands and feet, and said, "Thus says the Holy Spirit, 'So shall the Jews at Jerusalem bind the man who owns this belt, and deliver him into the hands of the Gentiles.'"* (NKJV)

Luke reports the arrival in Caesarea of the Christian prophet <u>Agabus</u> with a message for Paul. Agabus, fresh from Jerusalem, knew the atmosphere in the Holy City. In the <u>style of Old</u> Testament prophets, he pantomimed his prophecy, tying his own hands and feet with Paul's **belt** and forecasting that in Jerusalem the owner of the belt would be tied up and turned over to godless people.

### Lawrence O. Richards

In Acts 20:22 Paul confessed to being in the dark about what would happen to him in Jerusalem. . . . But then came a word of prophecy! Paul would face hostility. He would be bound. But he would survive to be handed over to the Gentiles, and so ultimately fulfill his mission to that world. A warning? No, a word of grace, and a reminder that even men of great faith, like Paul, need encouragement from the Lord. As do we all.[2]

# "I'd Rather Die on My Feet Than Live on My Knees!"

ACTS 21:12–14 *Now when we heard these things, both we and those from that place pleaded with him not to go up to Jerusalem. Then Paul answered, "What do you mean by weeping and breaking my heart? For I am ready not only to be bound, but also to die at Jerusalem for the name of the Lord Jesus." So when he would not be persuaded, we ceased, saying, "The will of the Lord be done."* (NKJV)

The scene that followed Agabus's prophecy was emotional. Paul's friends begged him to avoid Jerusalem. But <u>like Jesus</u> on the way to Jerusalem for the last time, he refused to turn back. He'd burned his bridges behind him. His life was <u>expendable</u>. And he had <u>a job</u> to do: to bring the good news to Jews and Gentiles—a mission in fulfillment of which Paul considered chains and death a reasonable price to pay (Acts 20:24; 21:13).

<br>

**Agabus**
Acts 11:27–30

**style of Old**
1 Kings 11:29–31;
Isaiah 20:3–4;
Jeremiah 13:4;
27:2–3;
Ezekiel 4, 5:1–4

**like Jesus**
Matthew 16:21

**expendable**
Acts 20:24; 21:13

**a job**
Matthew 28:19–20;
Acts 9:15–16

**belt**
leather sash worn around outer robe to keep it close to the body while working

**go to**

commitment
Matthew 26:39;
Luke 11:2

James
Jesus's half brother,
leader of the
Jerusalem church
elders

The argument ended with a shrug of shoulders and a prayer of <u>commitment</u>, "The will of the Lord be done" (Acts 21:14 NKJV). Ultimately, our decisions must be guided by the Holy Spirit, not the emotions and opinions of other people.

**what others say**

### Dietrich Bonhoeffer

As we embark upon discipleship we surrender ourselves to Christ in union with his death—we give over our lives to death. Thus it begins; the cross is not the terrible end to an otherwise God-fearing and happy life, but it meets us at the beginning of our communion with Christ. When Christ calls a man, he bids him come and die.[3]

## The Good News: Paul Arrives in the Holy City

ACTS 21:15–20a *And after those days we packed and went up to Jerusalem. Also some of the disciples from Caesarea went with us and brought with them a certain Mnason of Cyprus, an early disciple, with whom we were to lodge. And when we had come to Jerusalem, the brethren received us gladly. On the following day Paul went in with us to James, and all the elders were present. When he had greeted them, he told in detail those things which God had done among the Gentiles through his ministry. And when they heard it, they glorified the Lord. (NKJV)*

Arrangements had been made for Paul and his team to stay at the home of a transplanted Cypriot Jew named Mnason. Mnason had been part of the Jerusalem church from its beginning. "An early disciple" (Acts 21:16 NKJV) indicates he may have been one of the original three thousand believers (see Acts 2:41). It was easier for a foreign-born Jew than for a Judean-born Jew to host Gentiles.

After unpacking at Mnason's pad, the travelers met **James** and the Jerusalem elders. They presented the gift from the Gentile churches (see Romans 15:25; Acts 24:17). Luke doesn't mention the gift. Evidently the gift seemed incidental compared with the exciting things Paul had to report about God's work among the pagans:

- Opening Europe (Macedonia, Greece) to the gospel (see Acts 16)

- Introducing Athenian philosophers to their "unknown God" (see Acts 17)

- Transforming lives in Corinth (see Acts 18; 1 Corinthians 6:10–11)
- The bonfire of magic books and occult paraphernalia in Ephesus (see Acts 19)

The Gentile brothers with Paul shared their spiritual experiences and verified his report. The Jewish brothers responded with worship.

## Jews for Jesus

**ACTS 21:20b** *And they said to him, "You see, brother, how many myriads of Jews there are who have believed, and they are all zealous for the law;* (NKJV)

The Jerusalem elders shared the good news that "many myriads" of Jews—literally, "tens of thousands"—had put their faith in Jesus. With the addition of the phrase "and they are all zealous for the law," the elders delicately introduced their greatest concern about Paul's arrival.

### The Bad News: Paul Arrives in the Holy City

Not everyone, even among the Christians, was happy to see Paul sauntering into town with that mixed crew of Jew and Gentile buddies of his. It was almost time for the Feast of Pentecost, and Jewish feasts always ignited nationalist fire and anti-Gentile sentiment. Anti-Gentile attitudes were magnified by hunger and deprivation. When crops failed across the empire, pervasive anti-Semitic prejudice assured that trade in essential foodstuff would go to other places before it came to "troublesome Israel." Jews hated Romans and other Gentiles for leaving them to starve. These anti-Gentile sentiments made it tricky for the Jerusalem Christians to accept help from the Gentile Christians.

## The Scuttlebutt About Paul

**ACTS 21:21** *but they have been informed about you that you teach all the Jews who are among the Gentiles to forsake Moses, saying that they ought not to circumcise their children nor to walk according to the customs.* (NKJV)

The elders knew these rumors were untrue. Paul never told Jewish Christians to stop being Jewish. He taught that Gentile Christians should "not deny their cultural heritage and assume that by becom-

**go to**

**church's decision**
Acts 15:19

**new creation**
John 3:3–8;
2 Corinthians 5:17

ing 'Jewish' they would be more pleasing to God."⁴ This teaching was consistent with the <u>church's decision</u> to free Gentiles from the Law (Acts 21:25). What Paul taught is clear from the things he did and wrote:

- A person's standing before God is not based on circumcision but faith and <u>new creation</u> (see Galatians 2:15–16; 5:6; 6:15).

- To circumcise or not to circumcise one's son is a matter of parental choice (see Acts 16:3; 1 Timothy 1:1).

- A Christian Jew is free to observe Jewish traditions and feast days (see Acts 18:18; 20:6, 16; Romans 14:2–8).

- Winning people to Christ is more important than observance of religious traditions (see 1 Corinthians 9:20–21). To communicate the gospel, Paul accommodated both Jewish and Gentile preferences, depending on which he was trying to reach.

In his autobiography, *Just As I Am*, Billy Graham tells of receiving the invitation to conduct a preaching mission in 1984 in the Soviet Union. He was not certain he should accept it, because a previous visit had been misused for propaganda purposes.

As he struggled with his decision, he thought of the apostle Paul and his desire to preach the gospel in Rome, the seat of infamous Nero's empire. Just before retiring one night he read Paul's statement in 1 Corinthians 9:20–21 from *The Living Bible*:

> *When I am with the Jews I seem as one of them so that they will listen to the Gospel and I can win them to Christ. When I am with Gentiles who follow Jewish customs and ceremonies I don't argue, even though I don't agree, because I want to help them. When with the heathen I agree with them as much as I can, except of course that I must always do what is right as a Christian. And so, by agreeing, I can win their confidence and help them too.*

Dr. Graham wrote: "During the night, I woke up with these words clearly in my mind. They seemed to be God's direct answer to my quandary. When morning came . . . I had a settled peace about going."⁵

The daring, go-anywhere spirit of the twentieth century's greatest evangelist is traceable, at least in part, to the same theology of "accommodation for the sake of communication" that helped make Paul the first century's greatest evangelist. To both, winning people to Christ was more important than observance of arbitrary and limiting traditions and protocols. Both were willing to reach people outside the envelope of their own culture, even if it meant being misunderstood and criticized.

## Jesus Fills Old Rites with New Meaning

**ACTS 21:22** *"What then? The assembly must certainly meet, for they will hear that you have come." (NKJV)*

Christian Jews in Jerusalem were in a precarious position. They knew Jesus fulfilled the Jewish rituals. They knew salvation was based on faith in him, his death and resurrection. Yet, they remained loyal to the traditions—Jesus filled the old rites with new meaning!

But Israel was divided about Jesus (one-third believed; two-thirds did not). Most Jewish leaders rejected Christ. Pressures on believers to renounce the new faith or get out of Judaism were intensifying. A decade after Paul's visit, Christian Jews would find themselves **excommunicated** from the Temple!

## Polishing Paul's Image

**ACTS 21:23–25** *Therefore do what we tell you: We have four men who have taken a vow. Take them and be purified with them, and pay their expenses so that they may shave their heads, and that all may know that those things of which they were informed concerning you are nothing, but that you yourself also walk orderly and keep the law. But concerning the Gentiles who believe, we have written and decided that they should observe no such thing, except that they should keep themselves from things offered to idols, from blood, from things strangled, and from sexual immorality." (NKJV)*

Jerusalem's Christian leaders hoped that if Paul could be seen in the Temple carrying out Jewish religious rituals, doubts about his **orthodoxy** could be diffused. Their plan called for him to participate in the purification rites of four Jewish Christians.

The Nazarite vow, which is apparently what the four were doing, was a ritual expressing gratitude for God's special blessing. It involved abstaining from eating meat and drinking wine for thirty days, during which the hair was allowed to grow. The last seven days were spent in the Temple. Offerings were made—a lamb for a sin

**Nazarite vow**
Numbers 6

**excommunicated**
censured, denied access, excluded from Jewish religious life

**orthodoxy**
devotion to an accepted set of beliefs and practices

**theology of accommodation**
1 Corinthians 9:19–23; 10:23–33; Romans 14:1–15:7

**purification rites**
required of pilgrims from pagan lands before participating in temple worship

offering, a ram for a peace offering, unleavened bread, cakes made of fine flour and oil, a meat offering, and a wine offering—not an inexpensive process. Finally, the hair of the vow-taker was cut and burned with the sacrifice as an offering to God. If you saw a guy leaving the Temple with his head shaved, chances are he wasn't just being "cool." He had just said "Thanks, God!" by taking the Nazarite vow.

Jewish law allowed a person who had not done the thirty days of self-denial to join in the Nazarite ceremonies of others by participating in their **purification rites**, paying their expenses, and going through the last seven days with them. Even though he didn't do the whole Nazarite thing, paying the Nazarites' expenses was considered an especially fine, godly thing to do.

That is what Paul was asked to do (Acts 21:24).

## Caught in the Act of Making Peace

**ACTS 21:26** *Then Paul took the men, and the next day, having been purified with them, entered the temple to announce the expiration of the days of purification, at which time an offering should be made for each one of them.* (NKJV)

Paul's show of solidarity with the four Nazarites was consistent with his "theology of accommodation." His reasons for following the elders' public relations scheme included these ideas:

- To express confidence in the wisdom of the Jerusalem elders
- To preserve peace in the church
- To ease tensions between Christian Jews and their culture
- To remove barriers to acceptance of the gospel by Jews
- To open the way for the elders to accept aid from the Gentiles
- To express unity between Gentile and Jewish wings of the church
- To demonstrate loyalty to his Jewish roots

Willingness to accommodate the likes and dislikes of others, where accommodation does not hinder spiritual growth or violate some clear instruction of the Lord, is part of a sound church growth strategy.

## Peace Process Boomerangs!

ACTS 21:27–30 *Now when the seven days were almost ended, the Jews from Asia, seeing him in the temple, stirred up the whole crowd and laid hands on him, crying out, "Men of Israel, help! This is the man who teaches all men everywhere against the people, the law, and this place; and furthermore he also brought Greeks into the temple and has defiled this holy place." (For they had previously seen Trophimus the Ephesian with him in the city, whom they supposed that Paul had brought into the temple.) And all the city was disturbed; and the people ran together, seized Paul, and dragged him out of the temple; and immediately the doors were shut. (NKJV)*

The Jerusalem Christian elders' scheme backfired. With the Nazarites in the Temple for seven days, Paul was highly visible. Old enemies—Jews from Asia Province who'd failed to silence him in Ephesus (see Acts 19:8–10)—recognized him. They grabbed him, shouting that he was guilty of teaching anti-Judaism and adding the inflammatory accusation that he'd brought Greeks into the Temple! Both charges were 100 percent baloney.

### Gentiles Not Allowed in the Temple

Gentiles were not allowed in the Temple. They could only come to the outer Court of the Gentiles (see illustration, page 42). Between the outer and inner courts was a fence. On the fence was a sign in Greek and Latin: "No foreigner may enter within the barricade which surrounds the temple and enclosure. Anyone who is caught trespassing will bear personal responsibility for his ensuing death."[7]

The Roman occupation government did not allow Jews to execute anyone without the governor's permission with this exception: a Gentile (even a Roman) who crossed the fence line was a dead man!

**shut their hearts**
Acts 28:25–27

**destruction**
Luke 21:6

**Away with him**
Luke 23:18

**tribune**
commander of one
thousand troops
with ten centurions

**Pax Romana**
Roman peace
enforced by a
powerful military

Earlier, the Asian Jews had seen Paul and Trophimus, a Greek, together in the city and assumed Paul had brought him into the Temple.

Hearing the accusations, people rushed Paul and dragged him out into the Court of Gentiles. Immediately the gates slammed shut.

Bible scholars see the shutting of the temple gates as a symbol of the deliberate choice of leaders and people of Israel to <u>shut their hearts</u>, minds, and religious life to God, his message, and his Messenger. The Temple was now ripe for <u>destruction</u>. In AD 70, less than a decade later, destruction came.

## Roman Justice to the Rescue!

*ACTS 21:31–36 Now as they were seeking to kill him, news came to the commander of the garrison that all Jerusalem was in an uproar. He immediately took soldiers and centurions, and ran down to them. And when they saw the commander and the soldiers, they stopped beating Paul. Then the commander came near and took him, and commanded him to be bound with two chains; and he asked who he was and what he had done. And some among the multitude cried one thing and some another. So when he could not ascertain the truth because of the tumult, he commanded him to be taken into the barracks. When he reached the stairs, he had to be carried by the soldiers because of the violence of the mob. For the multitude of the people followed after, crying out, "<u>Away with him!</u>" (NKJV)*

Just northwest of the temple area overlooking the Court of Gentiles was the Fortress Antonia, built by Herod and named in honor of Roman General Mark Antony. The fortress served as barracks for a thousand Roman soldiers deployed under the command of a **tribune**, to keep the peace at feast times. The fortress was connected to the Court of Gentiles by two flights of stairs, strategically close so the garrison could intervene quickly at the first sign of civil disturbance.

Rome demanded civil order in its provinces. A riot was a serious breach of the **Pax Romana** carrying serious repercussions.

When word of the uproar reached the tribune, at least two hundred soldiers stormed down the steps to where the mob was beating Paul. When the rioters saw the troops, swords drawn, they quickly backed away.

Since Paul was the focus of the ruckus, the tribune ordered him chained. When the tribune asked the crowd what crime Paul had committed, he got a confused cacophony of shouted accusations that made no sense. He ordered the prisoner inside the fortress for questioning. As Paul was being led away, the crowd again lunged at him, trying to tear him from the soldiers, screaming for his death! The mob became so violent, the soldiers had to pick Paul up bodily and carry him up the stairs.

**assassins**
"dagger men"; whose tactic was to mingle with festival crowds, stab pro-Roman Jews, then disappear into the crowd

what others say

**William Barclay**

There was never a time when Paul was nearer death than this and it was the impartial justice of Rome which saved his life.[8]

## The Tenacious Truth Teller

ACTS 21:37–22:2 *Then as Paul was about to be led into the barracks, he said to the commander, "May I speak to you?" He replied, "Can you speak Greek? Are you not the Egyptian who some time ago stirred up a rebellion and led the four thousand assassins out into the wilderness?" But Paul said, "I am a Jew from Tarsus, in Cilicia, a citizen of no mean city; and I implore you, permit me to speak to the people." So when he had given him permission, Paul stood on the stairs and motioned with his hand to the people. And when there was a great silence, he spoke to them in the Hebrew language, saying, "Brethren and fathers, hear my defense before you now." And when they heard that he spoke to them in the Hebrew language, they kept all the more silent. Then he said:* (NKJV)

This conversation reveals some interesting facts:

• Paul was multilingual. He spoke Greek, universal language of the Roman Empire, and Aramaic, everyday language of Palestinian Jews (Acts 21:37, 40; 22:2). As a trained rabbi, he was also fluent in Hebrew, the language of the Old Testament.

• When the trouble started, the tribune jumped to the conclusion that Paul was an Egyptian assassin who had led "four thousand **assassins**" in a failed revolt in AD 54. The Egyptian was on both the Jewish and Roman "Ten Most Wanted" lists.

• Paul came to Jerusalem with one consuming passion: to share the good news of Jesus Christ with his countrymen (see Acts

go to

**Christ-obsessed**
Galatians 2:20

**national identity**
2 Corinthians 11:22;
Philippians 3:4–5

**Gamaliel**
Acts 5:34

**glory**
radiance, reflection,
image

9:15). A less <u>Christ-obsessed</u> man would be yelling, "Please! Get me to the ER!" Paul was asking, "Please let me speak to the people."

The tribune, hoping to get information to report to his superiors on the reason for the riot, granted Paul's request. A wall of tough legionnaires kept the crowd from coming too close. The beat-up, upbeat little Jew from Tarsus stood at the top of the stairs. Surprisingly, the crowd fell silent at the wave of his hand and the sound of his voice speaking their language. "Brethren and fathers," he began. These were the same words Paul had heard the martyr Stephen speak to begin his defense (see Acts 7:2).

## The Saul/Paul of Tarsus Story

ACTS 22:3–5 *"I am indeed a Jew, born in Tarsus of Cilicia, but brought up in this city at the feet of Gamaliel, taught according to the strictness of our fathers' law, and was zealous toward God as you all are today. I persecuted this Way to the death, binding and delivering into prisons both men and women, as also the high priest bears me witness, and all the council of the elders, from whom I also received letters to the brethren, and went to Damascus to bring in chains even those who were there to Jerusalem to be punished." (NKJV)*

Paul called it "my defense" (Acts 22:1 NKJV). It was the story of his conversion. Acts contains two other accounts of this same story: Luke's third-person report in Acts 9:1–19 and another first-person account before Governor Festus and King Agrippa II in Acts 26:4–23. It's a model for Christians telling the stories of their personal spiritual journeys.

### Who I Was

When speaking about Jesus, speak in language listeners can understand.

Paul was a Jew. He never forgot his <u>national identity</u>. He identified with his listeners.

- A Roman citizen—"Born in Tarsus."

- A citizen of Jerusalem—"Brought up" in the Holy City, probably arrived at age thirteen for rabbinical education.

- A lawyer and rabbi—"Taught according to the strictness of our fathers' law" under the famed Pharisee teacher, <u>Gamaliel</u>, renowned as "the **glory** of the law."

key point

- Zealous for God—"As you!" he added. The zeal was real, but misguided.
- Persecutor of Christians—He hunted down, arrested, jailed, and even killed the followers of "**this Way**"—Jesus's followers.

## How I Met Jesus

go to

this Way
John 14:6;
Acts 9:2; 22:4

saw
Acts 26:16;
1 Corinthians 9:1; 15:8;
Galatians 1:16

chosen
Ephesians 1:4;
Romans 8:28–29

new life
2 Corinthians 5:17;
Ephesians 2:1

guarding
Acts 7:58; 8:1

**the big picture**

### Acts 22:6–16

Paul tells the story of how God got his attention, corrected his understanding, blinded him, sent Ananias to heal him, and transformed him into a messenger for God.

chosen
"handpicked"9

this Way
term for Christians
emphasizing their
unique way of living

Paul, known as Saul at the time of his conversion, told what happened on his way to Damascus to hunt Christians (Acts 9). It was high noon. A blazing light dazzled him and knocked him down. A voice called his name. The speaker was Jesus, who, until that moment, Saul believed was dead. Not only did Saul hear the voice, but he <u>saw</u> the resurrected Lord Jesus—person to person (Acts 22:14–15).

Ananias, a Christian believer highly respected by both Jews and Christians in Damascus, came to see the blinded, shaken Saul. He restored Saul's sight, assured him God had **chosen** him and that he wasn't dreaming—he'd really seen Messiah Jesus. He gave Saul God's assignment: Tell everyone you meet about Jesus.

Ananias instructed Saul how to begin his walk with Jesus: (1) Call on Jesus for salvation and cleansing from your sins; (2) be baptized as an outward sign of your <u>new life</u>; and (3) act now!

## How My Life Has Changed Since I Met Jesus

ACTS 22:17–21 *"Now it happened, when I returned to Jerusalem and was praying in the temple, that I was in a trance and saw Him saying to me, 'Make haste and get out of Jerusalem quickly, for they will not receive your testimony concerning Me.' So I said, 'Lord, they know that in every synagogue I imprisoned and beat those who believe on You. And when the blood of Your martyr Stephen was shed, I also was standing by consenting to his death, and <u>guarding</u> the clothes of those who were killing him.' Then He said to me, 'Depart, for I will send you far from here to the Gentiles.'" (NKJV)*

**go to**

**no longer concerned**
Hebrews 10:17;
1 John 1:9

From what Paul said before his voice was drowned out by renewed demands for his death, we detect these changes:

- Paul did not stop being Jewish. The difference was that now when he prayed Jesus met him.

- Paul could now hear the Lord's voice directing his life.

- Paul saw his sins clearly and was honest in admitting them.

- When he talked about sins committed before he met Christ, he discovered the Lord was <u>no longer concerned</u> about his past, only his present and future.

- Paul had been trained to teach Jews God's law. But now the Lord sent him to teach pagans God's grace.

what others say

**Johnny Cash**

A few years ago I was hooked on drugs. I dreaded to wake up in the morning. There was no joy, peace, or happiness in my life. Then one day in my helplessness I turned my life completely over to God. Now I can't wait to get up in the morning and study my Bible. Sometimes the words out of the Scriptures leap into my heart. This does not mean that all my problems have been solved, or that I have reached any state of perfection. However, my life has been turned around. I've been born again![10]

## First-Century Religious Hot Button

**ACTS 22:22–23** *And they listened to him until this word, and then they raised their voices and said, "Away with such a fellow from the earth, for he is not fit to live!" Then, as they cried out and tore off their clothes and threw dust into the air,* (NKJV)

At the mention of the Gentiles, Paul struck the raw nerve that triggered the riot in the first place. The crowd remembered why they wanted to kill him. The horror of his "crime" swept over them again: Taking a filthy heathen, a lawless, godless, ceremonially unclean, unblessed, despised, hell-bound Gentile into the house of God! In "righteous" rage they tore off their cloaks and shook the dust off them as a sign of condemnation. In horrified grief over the imagined desecration of the sacred place, they threw dust into the air till the Court of Gentiles was a choking cloud of suspended dirt.

go to

**citizen**
Luke 20:22–25;
Romans 13:1–8;
Ephesians 2:19;
Philippians 3:20

what others say

**William Barclay**

If Paul had preached the yoke of Judaism to the Gentiles all would have been well; it was because he preached the grace of Christianity to them that the Jews were enraged.[11]

# Citizen Paul

ACTS 22:24–29 *the commander ordered him to be brought into the barracks, and said that he should be examined under scourging, so that he might know why they shouted so against him. And as they bound him with thongs, Paul said to the centurion who stood by, "Is it lawful for you to scourge a man who is a Roman, and uncondemned?" When the centurion heard that, he went and told the commander, saying, "Take care what you do, for this man is a Roman." Then the commander came and said to him, "Tell me, are you a Roman?" He said, "Yes." The commander answered, "With a large sum I obtained this citizenship." And Paul said, "But I was born a citizen." Then immediately those who were about to examine him withdrew from him; and the commander was also afraid after he found out that he was a Roman, and because he had bound him. (NKJV)*

Standard interrogation procedure under Roman justice was not questioning with one's lawyer present. To get at the truth in the shortest time possible, Roman police simply stretched the accused spread-eagle on the ground and literally whipped the living stuffing out of him until he either died from it or was willing to say whatever it took to get the torture to stop! This is what Paul was facing when he played his trump card!

The attitude of the Romans changed quickly when they learned Paul was a freeborn Roman <u>citizen</u>. Everyone from the commander and centurion to the scourge-wielding dog-faced soldier suddenly backed off in shock at how close they'd come to mistreating a fellow Roman without due process. It was a serious crime to chain or flog a Roman citizen. The commander could lose his military commission or even his life.

## Roman Citizenship

A Roman citizen was treated as if he were a resident of the city of Rome.

*Advantages of Roman Citizenship*

- A Roman citizen was subject only to Roman courts and laws.

- A Roman citizen was protected from interrogation by torture or imprisonment before trial.

- A Roman citizen was free to travel anywhere in the empire he wished to travel.

- A Roman citizen was under the protection of the local Roman garrison in any city in the empire.

*Four Ways One Became a Roman Citizen*

1. By birth in a free Roman city, such as Tarsus or Philippi.

2. By birth to parents who were Roman citizens.

3. By having citizenship conferred in recognition of special service to the emperor or empire.

4. By bribing an official who could grant citizenship (this is how the tribune in Acts 22:28 obtained it).

what others say

**Stanley Hauerwas and William H. Willimon**

The church is a colony, an island of one culture in the middle of another. In baptism our citizenship is transferred from one dominion to another, and we become, in whatever culture we find ourselves, resident aliens.[12]

# Chapter Wrap-Up

- As Paul headed for Jerusalem, he knew he was headed for danger. Fellow Christians tried to convince him not to go. Agabus prophesied his arrest and that he would be turned over to the Romans. (Acts 21:1–14)

- In Jerusalem Paul met with church leaders. After exchanging reports of God's work among Gentiles and Jews, they proposed a plan for Paul to participate in purification rites to put down rumors that he was guilty of anti-Jewish teaching. (Acts 21:15–19)

- The plan backfired. Paul was recognized in the Temple by his enemies, who falsely accused him of anti-Jewish teaching and taking a Gentile into the Temple. A riot ensued. Roman soldiers rescued Paul from the murderous mob. (Acts 21:20–36)

- Paul asked the Roman commander to let him speak to the people from the top of the fortress stairs. He told the story of his conversion. When he mentioned being sent to the Gentiles, the crowd again erupted in cries for his death. (Acts 21:37–22:23)

- Just as the Romans were about to interrogate him by flogging, Paul told them he was a Roman citizen. The torture stopped. Paul was taken into protective custody and treated with greater respect. (Acts 22:24–29)

# Study Questions

1. How did Agabus pantomime his prophecy concerning Paul's arrest in Jerusalem? How did Agabus know what Paul would face? How did Paul's response to the prophecy differ from his Christian friends' response?

2. What did James and the Jerusalem church elders want Paul to do to prove he was not anti-Jewish? Why did Paul go along with their plan?

3. Identify the three main points in Paul's conversion story (Acts 22:1–21).

4. Identify three of the five changes that took place in Paul's life as a result of his encounter with Jesus (Acts 22:17–21).

# Acts 22:30–23:35 Paul Pleads "Not Guilty"

*Chapter Highlights:*
• Who's on Trial Here?
• The Truth Will Drive You Crazy
• Tribune Transfers Paul to Governor

## Let's Get Started

According to Acts, the presence of Jesus Christ in a person can change his or her life from a road to nowhere to high adventure. In the final chapters, Luke traces the journey of Paul from one dramatic event to another. With each paragraph risks increase, intrigue deepens, action intensifies. We observe the Jew from Tarsus ultimately rising—soaring like an eagle—above it all. One dangerous, painful, or horrific situation after another becomes an opportunity to tell the story the early Christians seemed ready to tell if it was the last thing they did!

As the drama unfolds, we see with increasing clarity one emerging reality: Jesus Christ is alive! He is present with his people in the midst of it all. And his presence turns calamity into a victory for believers and another chance for unbelievers to turn to God!

## Who's on Trial Here?

ACTS 22:30–23:1 *The next day, because he wanted to know for certain why he was accused by the Jews, he released him from his bonds, and commanded the chief priests and all their council to appear, and brought Paul down and set him before them. Then Paul, looking earnestly at the council, said, "Men and brethren, I have lived in all good conscience before God until this day."* (NKJV)

The day after Paul's arrest (see Acts 21:33), the tribune of the Roman garrison at Jerusalem summoned the Sanhedrin, Israel's supreme court, to a meeting to determine the exact nature of the charges against Paul. This seventy-member council was composed of high priests, city officials, and Pharisee, Sadducee, and Herodian party reps.

With Roman soldiers on alert nearby, the tribune escorted Paul, no longer in chains, into the council chamber.

**go to**

**fair-haired boy**
Acts 7:58; 8:1, 3;
9:1–2; 22:4–5

**strike**
John 18:22–23

The normal way to address the Sanhedrin was to say, "Rulers of the people and elders of Israel."[1] By saying "Men and brethren," Paul declared himself an equal with the council. Before becoming a Christian he'd been deeply involved in Sanhedrin affairs, either as a Pharisee delegate or a rabbinical student. He had once been the Sanhedrin's "fair-haired boy."

### Assertions of Innocence

The accusation of the Asian Jews who stirred up the previous day's riot was that Paul had brought Gentiles into the Temple and was teaching against Judaism (see Acts 21:28). In this meeting before the Sanhedrin those charges were never mentioned. Paul, taking control of his own trial, opened with a ringing plea of *Not guilty!*

## Ananias—Spiritual Leader or Flimflam Man?

ACTS 23:2–5 *And the high priest Ananias commanded those who stood by him to strike him on the mouth. Then Paul said to him, "God will strike you, you whitewashed wall! For you sit to judge me according to the law, and do you command me to be struck contrary to the law?" And those who stood by said, "Do you revile God's high priest?" Then Paul said, "I did not know, brethren, that he was the high priest; for it is written, 'You shall not speak evil of a ruler of your people.'"* (NKJV)

Ananias had been the high priest for ten years. He was corrupt and violent. Jewish historian Josephus reports that Ananias sent servants to Judean farmers' threshing floors during harvest and illegally confiscated tithes that were supposed to go to the common priests.[2] Another source tells how he misappropriated sacrifices dedicated to God.

Infuriated by Paul's disregard of Sanhedrin protocols, Ananias ordered the sergeant-at-arms to hit him in the mouth! We can't be sure the blow ever landed, because Paul instinctively responded with verbal blows to stagger his opponent.

Paul accused Ananias of breaking the law (Acts 23:3). Under Jewish law defendants were presumed innocent until proven guilty. To mistreat a person before trial was forbidden. Paul had not been properly charged, nor tried and convicted. The law also stated that to strike a fellow Israelite was to attack the glory of God![3]

Paul called Ananias a fake. The metaphor "whitewashed wall" (Acts 23:3 NKJV) pictured a cracked structure whose disintegration is thinly disguised by a coat of cheap paint. The high priest hid hypocrisy and wickedness behind a facade of religious piety.

Paul didn't recognize Ananias as the legitimate high priest. He agreed that insulting Israel's ruler violated the Law. When he said, "I did not know, brethren, that he was the high priest" (Acts 23:5 NKJV), did he mean he wasn't physically familiar with the man or "I apologize for my unthinking outburst"? Or was he being sarcastic?— "I did not know a man as disreputable as this could hold the office of high priest!"

Paul prophesied Ananias's judgment. He told the man who ordered him struck, "God will strike you" (Acts 23:3 NKJV). The prophesied judgment began a year later when he was removed from office. His ill-gotten wealth continued to give him influence. The final strike came in AD 66 at the point of assassins' daggers, as Jewish guerrillas dragged him from his hiding place in an aqueduct and killed him.

**go to**

**whitewashed wall**
Ezekiel 13:10–13;
Matthew 23:27

**hypocrisy**
Matthew 23:13

**insulting Israel's ruler**
Exodus 22:28

> what others say
>
> **F. F. Bruce**
>
> The warm impetuousness of a man [Paul] of like passions with ourselves is vividly portrayed in this trial scene, and there is no doubt who presents the more dignified bearing— Paul or the high priest.[4]

## The Truth Will Drive You Crazy

ACTS 23:6–9 *But when Paul perceived that one part were Sadducees and the other Pharisees, he cried out in the council, "Men and brethren, I am a Pharisee, the son of a Pharisee; concerning the hope and resurrection of the dead I am being judged!" And when he had said this, a dissension arose between the Pharisees and the Sadducees; and the assembly was divided. For Sadducees say that there is no resurrection—and no angel or spirit; but the Pharisees confess both. Then there arose a loud outcry. And the scribes of the Pharisees' party arose and protested, saying, "We find no evil in this man; but if a spirit or an angel has spoken to him, let us not fight against God." (NKJV)*

**Pentateuch**
first five books of
the Bible

**traditions**
interpretations of
rabbis, added reli-
gious rules

**predestination**
belief that events
are determined by
God ahead of time

Paul knew the makeup of the Sanhedrin like the back of his hand. Its seventy members were religious "experts." One thing you can count on is that religious scholars will argue at the drop of a Bible passage! Especially this bunch of experts.

## The Sanhedrin

| The Majority: Sadducee Party | The Minority: Pharisee Party |
| --- | --- |
| High priestly aristocracy | Experts in Jewish law |
| Roman sympathizers | Silent protesters against Rome |
| Accepted authority of only the **Pentateuch** | Accepted rabbinical **traditions** as authoritative |
| Believed in human free will | Believed in **predestination** |
| Denied existence of spirit world, angels, demons | Believed in spirit world, angels, demons |
| Denied life after death or resurrection | Believed in resurrection of the dead |
| A few became Christians (see Acts 6:7) | Many became Christians (see Acts 15:5) |

## The Guts of the Gospel

Paul's announcement that he was a second-generation Pharisee on trial over the issue of the Resurrection was like an apple thrown to a herd of pigs. It turned Israel's rulers into a scrapping aggregation of squealing creatures incapable of decision making!

Some think Paul's Resurrection statement was designed to bring out the worst in the Sanhedrin. But there was more to it than trickery to create a diversion. Paul turned the spotlight on the real reason some Sanhedrin members wanted to terminate him. They could not prove him guilty of bringing Gentiles into the Temple or anti-Jewish teaching. What many (especially the Sadducean rulers) despised about him and all Christians was their teaching of the *Resurrection*. If a person believed in the Resurrection, it was possible to believe the Christians' claim that Jesus rose from the dead. And from there it was only a short distance to faith in Jesus as the Messiah, sent from God to redeem people from their sins and bring Judaism to its fulfillment.

## The Resurrection—Good News or Grand Nuisance?

It's a pattern. As the early church's story is traced in Acts, the subject of resurrection repeatedly incites hostility and conflict:

- *Acts 3:12–4:3*—Peter and John teach the people about Jesus's resurrection. The Sadducees get all hot and bothered and throw them in jail.
- *Acts 5:30–33*—The Twelve mention the Resurrection. Council members want to kill them.
- *Acts 7:55–60*—Stephen says he sees Jesus alive and standing at God's right hand. The council goes wild and stones him to death.
- *Acts 17:32*—Paul mentions the Resurrection to the Athenian philosophers. They jeer him and walk out.

## Why Was the Resurrection Such a Turn-Off?

The problem with the resurrection as the early Christians taught it—the Easter story—is that Resurrection demonstrates Jesus is who he claimed to be. The fact that Jesus rose from the dead shows the following:

- *Acts 2:24–36*—He is <u>Lord</u> and Christ (Savior-King).
- *Acts 3:15–16*—His name can bring healing.
- *Acts 4:10–12*—<u>Salvation</u> (rescue from sin and separation from God) is found nowhere else. Jesus is the **capstone** of everything God is doing.
- *Acts 5:29–32*—He is Prince and Savior.
- *Acts 13:37–39*—Through him, sins are forgiven and people get right with God—something the law (human works) could never do.
- *Acts 17:31*—Jesus is God's appointed judge of the world.

It is not the Resurrection idea itself that drives people crazy. It is what the resurrection says about Jesus. A theoretical Jesus who exists on the level of ideas, religious traditions, institutional trappings, and history does not disturb most people. But a Jesus who died for the world's sins, rose from the dead, and presently lives in his followers, calling for real change in the way all people live—that Jesus cannot be ignored. That Jesus makes people mad.

**Lord**
Romans 1:4

**salvation**
1 Corinthians
15:14–22

**capstone**
keystone that holds the whole building together

**needed**
Acts 16:9; 18:9–10;
27:23–24

# The Resurrection—Up Close and Personal

*ACTS 23:10–11 Now when there arose a great dissension, the commander, fearing lest Paul might be pulled to pieces by them, commanded the soldiers to go down and take him by force from among them, and bring him into the barracks. But the following night the Lord stood by him and said, "Be of good cheer, Paul; for as you have testified for Me in Jerusalem, so you must also bear witness at Rome." (NKJV)*

That night, back in the safety of the fortress, Paul reflected on the events of the last two days. He'd boldly challenged the powerful men of Israel. He'd thrown the council into pandemonium with one volley of truth. He'd declared the resurrection of Jesus. But after being mauled by an angry crowd, he may have been experiencing a healthy dose of discouragement. No one had been converted. His presence and words in the Holy City only seemed to inspire rage and conflict. And what of his dreams of witnessing in Rome?

At that moment the reality of the Resurrection stood beside him in the cell! The Lord Jesus came to him and turned his questions into promises.

At decisive points in his walk of faith, Paul heard the Lord say what he most <u>needed</u> to hear. In this jailhouse vision Jesus gave at least four reassurances:

1. Jesus was with Paul.

2. Paul had accomplished what he'd come to Jerusalem to do—"bear [Jesus's] name before Gentiles, kings, and the children of Israel" (Acts 9:15 NKJV). His testimony at the top of the stairs (Acts 21:40–22:21) and declaration of faith in the Resurrection in the Sanhedrin (Acts 23:6) fulfilled the assignment. "You have testified for Me in Jerusalem," the Lord said.

3. Paul would get to Rome and fulfill his dream of telling the Jesus story there, as in Jerusalem (Acts 23:1). Prison would not keep him from being Christ's witness!

4. Paul would leave Jerusalem alive.

With Jesus's comforting appearance to Paul in his jail cell, we (and Paul) are assured that everything that is happening—the anger and error of religious men, the military force of pagan Rome, the events that have brought Paul to this point, and all that will follow—is being used by the Lord (Romans 8:28) to position Paul to do what he longs to do—witness for Christ to the most powerful man in the world, the Roman emperor.

**pact**
Numbers 30:2

**Zealots**
militant party committed to protecting Judaism by violence

## what others say

### John McRay

Paul may have spent as much as 25% of his time as a missionary in prison.[5]

### Billy Graham

God does not always deliver us out of catastrophe, but he promises to be with us throughout.[6]

### Henry Alford

So one crumb of divine grace and help [was] multiplied to feed five thousand wants and anxieties [for Paul].[7]

## Get Paul!

ACTS 23:12–15 *And when it was day, some of the Jews banded together and bound themselves under an oath, saying that they would neither eat nor drink till they had killed Paul. Now there were more than forty who had formed this conspiracy. They came to the chief priests and elders, and said, "We have bound ourselves under a great oath that we will eat nothing until we have killed Paul. Now you, therefore, together with the council, suggest to the commander that he be brought down to you tomorrow, as though you were going to make further inquiries concerning him; but we are ready to kill him before he comes near." (NKJV)*

Frustrated in their attempt to lynch Paul at the Temple and unable to press charges against him because of Sanhedrin infighting, his enemies concocted another assassination plot. More than forty men—probably **Zealots**—bound themselves together in a rash pact: They would not eat or drink until Paul was dead by their hand! Ruling members of the council—mostly Sadducees—joined the conspiracy.

The oath taken by these dagger men probably followed a familiar Jewish pattern: "So may God do to us, and more also, if we eat or drink anything until we have killed Paul."[8]

# Cat's Out of the Bag

ACTS 23:16–22 *So when Paul's sister's son heard of their ambush, he went and entered the barracks and told Paul. Then Paul called one of the centurions to him and said, "Take this young man to the commander, for he has something to tell him." So he took him and brought him to the commander and said, "Paul the prisoner called me to him and asked me to bring this young man to you. He has something to say to you." Then the commander took him by the hand, went aside, and asked privately, "What is it that you have to tell me?" And he said, "The Jews have agreed to ask that you bring Paul down to the council tomorrow, as though they were going to inquire more fully about him. But do not yield to them, for more than forty of them lie in wait for him, men who have bound themselves by an oath that they will neither eat nor drink till they have killed him; and now they are ready, waiting for the promise from you." So the commander let the young man depart, and commanded him, "Tell no one that you have revealed these things to me." (NKJV)*

Not much is known about Paul's family. His father was a Pharisee (see Acts 23:6) and a Roman citizen from Tarsus. Paul mentions relatives in greetings to Christians in Rome (see Romans 16:7, 11, 21), but we can't be sure he's speaking of spiritual or blood relatives. Since so little is said of his immediate family it is usually assumed that when he became a Christian his family disowned him, and are included in his statement that for Christ's sake "I have suffered the loss of all things" (Philippians 3:8 NKJV).

We know from Acts 23:16 that Paul had a sister, whose son, a young man—a boy or a teenager—was in Jerusalem. We don't know if he or his mother was a believer, but he obviously cared what happened to his uncle. Somehow the lad got wind of the conspiracy and went to the Fortress Antonia to blow the wannabe assassins' cover.

After telling what he knew to Paul, he was taken to the tribune, who responded with uncharacteristic gentleness and listened carefully as the boy revealed what he knew about the conspiracy.

Christianity often spreads with the help of nonbelievers whose hearts are open to individual Christians they admire (see Matthew 10:40).

**Talmud**
ancient commentary
on Old Testament
laws

### Howard Marshall

The fact that the tribune took the boy by the hand has also been the subject of scholarly sarcasm: "Never was a tribune so amiable," said [one commentator]. But the impression we get is rather that the lad was quite young, and the tribune's action is appropriate. The ancient world would not have seen any incompatibility between his ordering Paul to be scourged and his kindly treatment of the boy.[9]

## Tribune Transfers Paul to Governor

### Acts 23:23–33

Wasting no time the tribune assigned a force of 470 Roman legionaries to escort Paul in the middle of the night to Antipatris, then on the next day to Caesarea. They carried a letter from Tribune Claudius Lysias to Felix, Roman governor of Judea, transferring Paul's case to the governor's jurisdiction.

Quick action by the tribune changing the venue of Paul's trial from Jerusalem to Caesarea with a show of overwhelming force frustrated the assassins who must have felt silly for making their brash oath. Poor fools! They went without breakfast for nothing! Paul was long gone before they strapped on their cloaks and daggers the next morning. It's unlikely any starved because they were unable to keep their vow. The Jewish **Talmud** conveniently provided that such oaths could be annulled by getting a rabbi to cancel the obligation.

Paul's removal to Caesarea took the steam out of a problem that had created three days of high tension for the Jerusalem garrison. The commander's letter to the governor (Acts 23:26–30) followed the typical format of official first-century correspondence. Like any good politician, the noble tribune gave a spin to the facts making him look slightly more knowledgeable and in charge than he really was. Still, give Tribune Claudius Lysias a medal for effective crowd control and riot dousing.

Caesarea was about sixty miles (one hundred kilometers) northwest of Jerusalem. It was the governmental center of the province of Judea, and site of Herod's palace, which was occupied by Governor Marcus Antonius Felix.

The military escort with Paul left Jerusalem about 9:00 P.M. and traveled thirty-seven miles by forced march, arriving at Antipatris before dawn. Next day the four hundred infantry and spearmen returned to Jerusalem. The cavalry took the prisoner the last twenty-seven miles.

## First Stop on the Rugged Road to Rome

> ACTS 23:34–35 *And when the governor had read it, he asked what province he was from. And when he understood that he was from Cilicia, he said, "I will hear you when your accusers also have come." And he commanded him to be kept in Herod's Praetorium. (NKJV)*

The cellblock of Herod's magnificent Caesarean palace was no royal guest suite. It was as ugly as the rest of the place was elegant. Paul slept on the floor wrapped in his own cloak, his hands manacled with a chain (see Acts 26:29). It was a miserable place, but safer than Jerusalem.

The governor would hear his case when his accusers arrived with formal charges. Paul's journey to Rome had begun as promised (Acts 23:11). God was using everything from theological arrogance to family loyalty to religious hatred to military power to Roman justice to spiritual vision, as he moved his witness to where he could use him best. In his letter to the Christians at Rome, Paul says he learned to see everything that happened as something useful in God's process of carrying out his grand design:

"And we know that all things work together for good to those who love God, to those who are the called according to His purpose" (Romans 8:28 NKJV). God can use all the happenings of our lives to accomplish good things.

# Chapter Wrap-Up

- The Roman tribune called a meeting of the Sanhedrin to clarify charges against Paul. Paul claimed innocence. When the high priest ordered him struck, Paul struck back with charges and prophecies against the high priest. (Acts 22:30–23:5)

- Paul declared that the key issue that had gotten him into trouble was belief in the Resurrection. The Sanhedrin became a shouting match between Pharisees who believed in resurrection and Sadducees who did not. (Acts 23:6–9)

- Roman troops again rescued Paul from being mauled by the warring council members. In his cell that night, Jesus reassured Paul he was doing what he'd been called to do and would soon witness in Rome. (Acts 23:10–11)

- Forty terrorists took an oath to kill Paul before they ate again. Some rulers joined the conspiracy. Paul's nephew discovered the plot and told Paul. (Acts 23:12–22)

- A large force of soldiers and cavalry escorted Paul to Caesarea, where he was turned over to Governor Felix for trial. (Acts 23:23–35)

# Study Questions

1. In his response to the order that he be hit in the mouth, what four negative things did Paul say to or about Ananias, the high priest (Acts 23:3–5)?

2. Why did Paul's mention of the Resurrection in the Sanhedrin create such turmoil? What is it about the Resurrection that upsets people?

3. According to what is said about it in Acts, identify at least three things the Resurrection reveals about Jesus.

4. Identify three of the four reassurances Jesus gave Paul when he visited him in the barracks.

# Acts 24-26 Christ's Ambassador on Trial

*Chapter Highlights:*
- **Courtroom Strategy**
- **Politics of Compromise**
- **Paul Happy to Tell Good News**

## Let's Get Started

Five days after his delivery to Herod's palace prison at Caesarea, the iron gates leading to Paul's cell clanged open. Two pairs of military boots stomped toward his cell. Two tough legionnaires hustled the little prisoner to Governor Felix's audience hall.

He stood in the great hall to face his accusers and his judge, on trial for his life. Always the Lord's promise echoed in the back of his mind: "You must also bear witness at Rome" (see Acts 23:11 NKJV).

In Acts, Roman justice is presented in a fairly favorable light.

Even with its inconsistencies, the <u>system often worked</u> to the advantage of Paul and his team. As a Roman citizen he did not hesitate to demand the protections the system offered.

**go to**

**system often worked**
Acts 16:37–39;
18:16; 19:35–41;
22:25–29; 23:23–33

**procurator**
ruler of a minor
province

## Politics of Corruption

> ACTS 24:1 *Now after five days Ananias the high priest came down with the elders and a certain orator named Tertullus. These gave evidence to the governor against Paul. (NKJV)*

The governor was Marcus Antonius Felix. He was born a slave in the household of Antonia, mother of Claudius Caesar. Claudius freed him. In AD 38 he was appointed **procurator** of Judea. Felix married a succession of three wives, all princesses. The first was the granddaughter of Antony and Cleopatra, the name of the second is not known, and the third was Drusilla (Acts 24:24), youngest daughter of King Herod Agrippa I.

Roman historian Tacitus wrote that Felix "exercised kingly power with the mind of a slave."[1] His rule on Judea was marked by a series of insurrections, which he brutally crushed. The Jews hated him. His governance gave rise to the sicarii terrorists who assassinated Romans and Roman sympathizers. (The tribune at Jerusalem had assumed Paul was one of these terrorists when he had Paul arrested and jailed.)

# Courtroom Strategy

**go to**

worldwide trouble-
maker
Acts 17:6

**Nazarenes**
Hebrew and Arabic
name for Jewish
Christians

*ACTS 24:2–9 And when he was called upon, Tertullus began his accusation, saying: "Seeing that through you we enjoy great peace, and prosperity is being brought to this nation by your foresight, we accept it always and in all places, most noble Felix, with all thankfulness. Nevertheless, not to be tedious to you any further, I beg you to hear, by your courtesy, a few words from us. For we have found this man a plague, a creator of dissension among all the Jews throughout the world, and a ringleader of the sect of the Nazarenes. He even tried to profane the temple, and we seized him, and wanted to judge him according to our law. But the commander Lysias came by and with great violence took him out of our hands, commanding his accusers to come to you. By examining him yourself you may ascertain all these things of which we accuse him." And the Jews also assented, maintaining that these things were so. (NKJV)*

Paul's accusers had hired a professional orator (that is, expert baloney slicer!) named Tertullus as prosecution counsel. Tertullus had a way with words! But very little regard for the truth. Flattery is a manipulative substitute for truth, a warning of more lies to come.

## Quick! Bring a Shovel!

Tertullus waxed eloquent about the "great peace" the province had enjoyed under Felix. Actually, few periods in Judean history were marred by more unrest and terrorism. Tertullus told how grateful the people were for Felix's "foresight." The years AD 52–59 when Felix was procurator were years of unparalleled government corruption!

Did Tertullus actually believe that this unabashed attempt to manipulate the court through flattery would win the tough-minded Felix to his cause?

The delegation from Jerusalem charged Paul on three counts: First, he was a worldwide troublemaker (Greek: *loimos*—a pest, a plague). Second, he was ringleader of the sect of the **Nazarenes**. Third, he violated the sanctity of the Temple by bringing in Greeks. In the tradition of successful lawyers everywhere, Tertullus put his clients' unique spin on the facts. According to his made-for-the-courtroom yarn, the Jews narrowly averted disaster by taking Paul into custody (Acts 24:7). The lawyer-propagandist makes the lynch mob of Acts 21:30–31 sound like an orderly police action!

# Paul for the Defense

## Acts 24:10-21

**the big picture**

When Paul was allowed to speak, he boldly made his defense in a logical fashion. Paul told Tertullus what he did not do, what he did do, why he was in Jerusalem, and that there was no evidence to prove the charges against him.

The defendant spoke respectfully and truthfully, foregoing the verbal shallowness with which Tertullus filled the courtroom. The charges against him were without substance (Acts 24:13). The following chart outlines his argument:

## Paul's Defense Points

| Outline of Paul's Defense Points | That Support His Defense |
| --- | --- |
| What I'm not guilty of doing (Acts 24:12–13) | • I did not argue with anyone.<br>• I did not stir up trouble in the city. |
| What I admit (Acts 24:14–16) | • I worship the God of Israel—a freedom granted by Roman law.<br>• I follow "the Way"—lifestyle taught by Jesus of Nazareth.<br>• My faith agrees with the Old Testament—"the Law" and "the Prophets."<br>• I share hope of a future resurrection—as Old Testament patriarchs and prophets did.<br>• I try to live with a clear conscience before God and man. |
| Why I came to Jerusalem (Acts 24:17) | • I came with gifts to help the poor.<br>• I came to worship—"to bring alms and offerings." |
| What I was doing at the Temple (Acts 24:18) | • I was participating in a ceremony of cleansing in preparation for worship. |
| There is no evidence to prove the charges against me (Acts 24:19–20) | • The Asian Jews who started this (Acts 21:28) should be here to be cross-examined if they have any charges to bring. But they are not here. Their allegations are invalid.<br>• The Sanhedrin could not agree on the crime for which I should be charged (see Acts 23:7–9). |
| What I've done is no crime (Acts 24:21) | • I am guilty of believing in the resurrection of the dead. This is why I am on trial! (Paul knew if Felix became convinced the issue had nothing to do with Roman law, but was about a point of Jewish theology, he'd throw the case out of court.) |

## The Politics of Expediency

ACTS 24:22–23 *But when Felix heard these things, having more accurate knowledge of the Way, he adjourned the proceedings and said, "When Lysias the commander comes down, I will make a decision on your case." So he commanded the centurion to keep Paul and to let him have liberty, and told him not to forbid any of his friends to provide for or visit him.* (NKJV)

As Felix responded to Paul's defense, the rough-and-tumble slave-turned-politician revealed thorough knowledge of the Jesus movement. Did he know some Christians? Caesarea had some live ones, including the Roman centurion Cornelius (see Acts 10) and evangelist Philip and his preacher-girls (see Acts 21:8–9). Some scholars think he got his information from his Jewish wife, Drusilla.

He could have dismissed the charges and let Paul go. Instead, to keep from offending the Sanhedrin, Felix postponed the verdict and left Paul in jail under the pretext of needing to hear more testimony.

Meanwhile, Paul was kept under guard, but given limited freedom. Roman jailhouse procedure was that a prisoner's food and personal needs were not provided. Paul's friends (Luke, Philip, and others) could visit and care for his needs.

## Too Close for Comfort

ACTS 24:24–26 *And after some days, when Felix came with his wife Drusilla, who was Jewish, he sent for Paul and heard him concerning the faith in Christ. Now as he reasoned about righteousness, self-control, and the judgment to come, Felix was afraid and answered, "Go away for now; when I have a convenient time I will call for you." Meanwhile he also hoped that money would be given him by Paul, that he might release him. Therefore he sent for him more often and conversed with him.* (NKJV)

It would be two years before Paul's trial resumed (Acts 24:27; 25:1). During that time, Paul received visitors and strengthened the Caesarean Christians from his place of confinement. Scholars believe Luke, who was with Paul, used these two years to gather information needed for his two books about the life of Christ and the early church.

During those two years, Paul and Felix had many conversations. His talks with Paul betrayed a hungry heart with a genuine interest in Jesus. Corrupt politician that he was, he hoped Paul (whose family was wealthy) might grease his palms with a significant bribe to buy his freedom!

**God loves**
Romans 5:6–8

## Drusilla, Beautiful, Rich, Powerful . . . and Starving!

Acts 24:24 reports that Felix's third wife, Drusilla, joined her husband in some of the conversations with Paul. Drusilla was Jewish. She was the daughter of King Herod Agrippa I (see Acts 12). Drusilla was sixteen when Felix seduced her and convinced her to leave her Jewish husband for him. Now at nineteen she was a beautiful woman who had already experienced what wealth, power, social advantage, and self-indulgence could provide.

Even people who look like they have it "together" need Christ. Early Christians knew this and used every opportunity, including their own difficulties, to share the good news with others. Christian witnesses leave people free to make their own decisions about Christ—even if they make the wrong one!

## Don't Call Me—I'll Call You!

You can bet your last shekel Paul's chitchats with Felix and Drusilla were not little sermonettes, comedy routines, or heady discussions on how many angels can dance on the head of a pin! Paul zeroed in on themes of "the faith in Christ . . . righteousness, self-control, and the judgment to come" (Acts 24:24–25 NKJV). In other words, Paul talked about God's love demonstrated in Jesus, God's moral and spiritual demands, and the need for personal redemption—with a little hellfire and damnation thrown in for good measure. The hair stood up on the back of Felix's dirty neck! He ended one conversation with the famous line: "That's enough for now! You may leave. When I find it convenient, I will send for you." We know they talked many times. We don't know if Felix or Drusilla ever found it "convenient" to trust in Jesus. We do know God loves dirty politicians and self-indulgent beauty queens!

Paul and the early Christians turned courtroom appearances into fulfillment of Jesus's call to carry his name everywhere. Their accusers, who demanded the Christians answer for their faith, often found themselves on trial in the court of their own consciences.

## The Noble Roman Festus Replaces the Brutal Felix

ACTS 24:27 *But after two years Porcius Festus succeeded Felix; and Felix, wanting to do the Jews a favor, left Paul bound. (NKJV)*

Felix's talent for bad government went too far. Racially driven mob violence broke out between Jews and Greeks in Caesarea. Felix gave his approval as thousands of Jews were killed and the houses of the wealthy were sacked. (He may have taken a cut of the loot for himself.) Rome recalled him. His corruption in office never led to official charges because his brother, a close friend of Caesar, used his influence to hide discrepancies in provincial accounts.

Felix was out. Festus replaced him as governor. But Paul was still stuck in the palace prison.

Porcius Festus doesn't get many lines in the history books. He was appointed Procurator of Judea in AD 59 or 60. A kinder, gentler man to deal with a bitterly divided province, he was committed to Roman justice and an expert in the art of political compromise.

## Politics of Compromise

ACTS 25:1–8 *Now when Festus had come to the province, after three days he went up from Caesarea to Jerusalem. Then the high priest and the chief men of the Jews informed him against Paul; and they petitioned him, asking a favor against him, that he would summon him to Jerusalem—while they lay in ambush along the road to kill him. But Festus answered that Paul should be kept at Caesarea, and that he himself was going there shortly. "Therefore," he said, "let those who have authority among you go down with me and accuse this man, to see if there is any fault in him." And when he had remained among them more than ten days, he went down to Caesarea. And the next day, sitting on the judgment seat, he commanded Paul to be brought. When he had come, the Jews who had come down from Jerusalem stood about and laid many serious complaints against Paul, which they could not prove, while he answered for himself, "Neither against the law of the Jews, nor against the temple, nor against Caesar have I offended in anything at all." (NKJV)*

"Poor old hate-filled men!"[2] Eugenia Price calls Jewish leaders still harboring their bitterness and pressing their allegations against Paul.

When Festus arrived they tried to get him to return Paul to Jerusalem for trial. They had no intention of trying him. Although their brash fast had obviously been called off, the two-year-old plot by forty assassins to terminate Paul was still alive and breathing fire (Acts 25:3; 23:12–15).

After the two-year postponement, the trial resumed in Caesarea. Like turkey vultures flocking to road kill, Sanhedrin leaders clustered around the prisoner, flapping and pecking. From Paul's one-line defense (Acts 25:8) we can surmise the nature of their complaints— breaking Jewish law; desecrating the Temple; violating Caesar's decrees. The one about Caesar's decrees had been added since the trial before Felix. It's the charge to which Festus would pay most attention. Again, none of the accusations were provable and no evidence was offered.

## "To Caesar You Will Go!"

ACTS 25:9–12 *But Festus, wanting to do the Jews a favor, answered Paul and said, "Are you willing to go up to Jerusalem and there be judged before me concerning these things?" So Paul said, "I stand at Caesar's judgment seat, where I ought to be judged. To the Jews I have done no wrong, as you very well know. For if I am an offender, or have committed anything deserving of death, I do not object to dying; but if there is nothing in these things of which these men accuse me, no one can deliver me to them. I appeal to Caesar." Then Festus, when he had conferred with the council, answered, "You have appealed to Caesar? To Caesar you shall go!"* (NKJV)

Festus's proposal to move the trial to Jerusalem was the politics of compromise, pure and simple. He knew no Roman law had been violated (Acts 25:18–19). As new governor he simply wanted to avoid upsetting Jewish leaders his first month in office.

Paul knew he'd never get a fair trial in Jerusalem. He hadn't forgotten the murder pact. Roman law provided that if a case being tried—especially a capital case—was beyond the competence of a provincial governor, a Roman citizen had the right of *provocatio ad Caesarem*—appeal to the emperor. Only murderers, pirates, or bandits caught in the act were denied this right. The Jewish leaders' charge that Paul had violated Caesar's decrees opened the way for his bold and strategic legal move: "I appeal to Caesar!"

The current **caesar** was Nero. Paul's trial took place in the fifth year of Nero's reign, during the early years when he ruled well and under the wise influence of the Stoic philosopher Seneca. Nero's insane crusade against Christians did not begin until five years later.

## King Makes a State Visit to Welcome New Governor

the big picture

### Acts 25:13-22

King Herod Agrippa II from the neighboring province of Chalcis (part of modern Lebanon) and his sister Bernice paid a state visit to welcome Festus, the new governor. Agrippa was considered an expert in Jewish affairs. Festus was unfamiliar with Jewish customs and theology, and uncertain as how to proceed with Paul's appeal to Caesar, so he asked the king's advice. Agrippa revealed he would like to hear Paul for himself. So a hearing was arranged for the next day.

Legally, the hearing was unofficial, since Agrippa had no jurisdiction in the case. Unofficial or not, it became a grand spectacle (Acts 25:23). Agrippa and Bernice put on their purple robes and golden crowns. Festus dressed in the scarlet cape worn by Roman governors on high state occasions. Agrippa was attended by his royal entourage and surrounded by Caesarean Jewish leaders, all dressed to kill. With Festus came the captains of the five cohorts stationed at Caesarea, along with an escort of legionnaires at attention.[3]

Agrippa's full name was Marcus Julius Agrippa II. He was the great-grandson of Herod the Great, who slaughtered the babies of Bethlehem (see Matthew 2:16) and son of Herod Agrippa I who beheaded James (Acts 12:2). With his appointment by the Romans as "King of Chalcis" came the right to appoint Jewish high priests. He knew the Jews well and was deeply interested in Jewish theology.

Bernice's full name was Julia Bernice (Latin: Veronica). She was not Agrippa's wife, but his younger sister. Rumors persisted of an incestuous relationship between them. For her activities on behalf of the Jews before the **fall of Jerusalem**, she was later revered as "Julia Bernice, the great queen."

There is no record of Bernice or Drusilla putting their faith in Christ. We know they were hungry to know about him. Their interest and urging may have influenced the male leaders around them to call Paul to testify repeatedly.

**aggregation**
group

what others say

### Simon Kistemaker

The contrast between the dazzling garb of the high and mighty and the humble clothes of the chained prisoner suddenly becomes meaningless, for Paul displays the quiet dignity of a man with a message.[4]

## Paul Goes Before the King

ACTS 25:23–27 *So the next day, when Agrippa and Bernice had come with great pomp, and had entered the auditorium with the commanders and the prominent men of the city, at Festus' command Paul was brought in. And Festus said: "King Agrippa and all the men who are here present with us, you see this man about whom the whole assembly of the Jews petitioned me, both at Jerusalem and here, crying out that he was not fit to live any longer. But when I found that he had committed nothing deserving of death, and that he himself had appealed to Augustus, I decided to send him. I have nothing certain to write to my lord concerning him. Therefore I have brought him out before you, and especially before you, King Agrippa, so that after the examination has taken place I may have something to write. For it seems to me unreasonable to send a prisoner and not to specify the charges against him." (NKJV)*

When the beautiful, rich, and powerful had paraded in and assumed the places in the room demanded by the protocols of the day, Procurator Festus called for Paul to be brought in. The little tentmaker from Tarsus, hands in chains, stood before the king and the high muckety-mucks of Caesarea. It was high drama and great entertainment.

Festus explained the purpose of this fancy-but-informal hearing: Paul had appealed to Caesar. Before sending him to Rome, it was necessary to prepare an official report documenting the case. This imposing **aggregation**—especially King Agrippa—had been invited to help the governor prepare the wording of the report.

## Early Christians on Trial in Acts

| Scripture Record | Defendant(s) | Judge(s) | Sentence or Result |
|---|---|---|---|
| Acts 4:1–22 | Peter and John | Sanhedrin | Threatened and released |
| Acts 5:17–40 | The Twelve | Sanhedrin | Flogged and released |
| Acts 6:8–7:60 | Stephen | Sanhedrin | Death by stoning |
| Acts 12:1–2 | James (the apostle) | Herod Agrippa I | Beheaded |
| Acts 12:3–19 | Peter | Herod Agrippa I | Escaped, never tried |
| Acts 16:19–39 | Paul and Silas | Philippian magistrates | Caned, jailed overnight |
| Acts 17:6–9 | Jason and brothers | Thessalonian city officials | Posted bond |
| Acts 18:12–17 | Paul | Gallio | Case thrown out |
| Acts 19:23–41 | Paul, Gaius, Aristarchus | Ephesian mob (unofficial) | Dismissed |
| Acts 21:27–22:22 | Paul | Temple mob (unofficial) | Rescued by Roman troops |
| Acts 23:1–10 | Paul | Sanhedrin | Hung jury (no decision) |
| Acts 24:1–23 | Paul | Felix | Postponed, Paul in jail two years |
| Acts 25:1–12 | Paul | Festus | Appealed to Caesar |
| Acts 25:1–26:32 | Paul | Festus and Agrippa II | Sent to Rome |

# Paul Happy to Tell Good News

### the big picture

### Acts 26:1-18

As he began his defense before Agrippa, Paul acknowledged the king's familiarity with Jewish customs and theology, and then proceeded to tell his story. Initially he had opposed Jesus and mistreated Christians. But Jesus confronted him on his way to persecute Christians in Damascus, and his life was totally changed. Jesus called him to go to both Jews and Gentiles and tell them their lives could be changed and they could be forgiven too.

Paul felt "happy" to be able to tell his story (Acts 26:2 NKJV). Sharing the good news of Jesus with an audience of movers and shakers was better than a trip to Disneyland!

Once again Paul insisted he was on trial because he believed in the Resurrection. From childhood his personal hope of spiritual survival had always depended on Israel's survival as a nation. A member of Judaism's strictest sect, Pharisee, he was committed to the Law—"God's thunder from the mountain . . . carved in stone, written on parchment, etched on the heart of Israel"⁵—and Judaism's survival (Acts 26:4–6).

Resurrection <u>hope</u> is deeply embedded in the history of Israel. God has raised Israel repeatedly! (The modern world watched him do it again with the establishment of the present state of Israel in 1948.) In fact, it is incredible that any Jew should ever "thought incredible . . . that God raises the dead" (Acts 26:6–8 NKJV). Paul had believed Jesus was a threat to the survival of Judaism and should be opposed. So he threw himself lock, stock, and barrel into what he thought was <u>God's work</u>. He attacked Jesus's "**saints,**" jailed and voted to kill them, tried to force them to **blaspheme,** and tracked them down in foreign cities (Acts 26:9–11).

Paul was on his way to Damascus armed with arrest warrants. Jesus confronted Paul, knocked him flat on his face, exposed his inner struggle against the Holy Spirit, personally introduced himself, and sent Paul to share with Jews and non-Jews alike what he'd seen and heard (Acts 26:12–18).

Paul's orders from God included a summary of what Jesus does for people (Acts 26:18):

- Opens their eyes making them <u>able to see</u> things they never saw before

- Turns them from spiritual darkness (deceit, evil) <u>to light</u> (transparency, holiness)

- <u>Transfers</u> them from the power of Satan to the **power** of God, making them able to live obediently, victoriously

- Gives them forgiveness of sins and a share with the **sanctified,** re-creating and purifying their lives as they trust in Jesus

Early Christians refused to let another person's immoral lifestyle hinder them from sharing Jesus's love with that person.

**go to**

**hope**
Job 19:25–27;
Ezekiel 37:1–14

**God's work**
Philippians 3:4–6

**able to see**
John 3:3

**to light**
John 3:19–21;
1 John 1:5–7

**transfers**
Colossians 1:12–14

**saints**
ordinary believers in Jesus

**blaspheme**
renounce faith in Jesus

**power**
rule, kingdom

**sanctified**
set apart as special, holy

key point

**in Damascus**
Acts 9:19–25

**suffered**
Isaiah 53:5–6

**rose**
Psalm 16:9–10

**light**
Isaiah 60:1–3

# One Vision, One Master

ACTS 26:19–23 *"Therefore, King Agrippa, I was not disobedient to the heavenly vision, but declared first to those <u>in Damascus</u>, and in Jerusalem, and throughout all the region of Judea, and then to the Gentiles, that they should repent, turn to God, and do works befitting repentance. For these reasons the Jews seized me in the temple and tried to kill me. Therefore, having obtained help from God, to this day I stand, witnessing both to small and great, saying no other things than those which the prophets and Moses said would come—that the Christ would suffer, that He would be the first to rise from the dead, and would proclaim light to the Jewish people and to the Gentiles."* (NKJV)

"I was not disobedient to the heavenly vision!" Paul had seen the crucified Jesus alive. In fact, Jesus's Spirit had invaded the feisty Pharisee's heart and life (see Acts 9:17). As soon as he knew what the Lord wanted him to do, Paul began doing it with the same intensity with which he'd persecuted Christians (see Acts 9:19–22).

Paul's gung ho obedience and effectiveness in communicating God's law-free grace to Gentiles and Jews was, in fact, the reason behind the attack against him in the Temple. "For these reasons the Jews seized me in the temple and tried to kill me," Paul said (Acts 26:21 NKJV). Their hostility could be traced to envy over the life-changing results of his ministry in Ephesus (see Acts 19:8–20).

As proof he had violated neither Judaism's laws nor Caesar's decrees, Paul repeated the main points of the message he preached everywhere. He was not merely defending himself—he was offering Agrippa and the others the hope that goes with resurrection:

- All people must repent and prove their heart change by their life change (Acts 26:20).

- Jesus fulfilled the predictions of the Old Testament prophets (Acts 26:22).

- He <u>suffered</u> on the cross to pay the penalty for human sin (Acts 26:23).

- He <u>rose</u> from the dead, the first to do so (Acts 26:23).

- Christ alive is active in the lives of Jews and Gentiles, showing them <u>light</u>—revealing God (Acts 26:23).

**mentally sound**
2 Timothy 1:7

## In Touch with Reality

ACTS 26:24–25 *Now as he thus made his defense, Festus said with a loud voice, "Paul, you are beside yourself! Much learning is driving you mad!" But he said, "I am not mad, most noble Festus, but speak the words of truth and reason."* (NKJV)

Agrippa knew the Jews and had studied their theology. The Romans considered him an expert adviser on Judaism. He understood what Paul was saying. Festus, on the other hand was in over his head! When Paul pressed the issue of Jesus rising from the dead, it was too much for the pragmatic Roman mind to process. "You're crazy, Paul!" he shouted. "You think too much!" (Acts 26:24, paraphrased).

Paul was highly educated and intellectually brilliant. In Festus's opinion (or was it a derisive joke?) superior learning had driven the prisoner over the edge. No sensible man would turn his whole nation against him (see Acts 25:24) for such fantastical philosophical foolishness. Paul used two Greek words to defend what he'd been saying (Acts 26:25): *aletheias*—"true," in harmony with reality,[8] and *sophrosunes*—"reasonable," mentally sound.

When a person knows Jesus, nothing makes more sense than that Jesus is alive! His being alive is what makes life in this crazy world finally make sense. To genuinely link up with God is to be in touch with reality.

## Charles H. Spurgeon

To be laughed at is no great hardship to me. I can delight in scoffs and jeers. Slanders are my glory. But that you should turn from mercy, this is my sorrow. Spit on me, but, oh, repent! Laugh at me, but, oh, believe in my Master! Make my body as dirt of the streets, but damn not your own souls![9]

# The Wisecrack Heard Round the World

## Acts 26:26–32

Paul asked, "King Agrippa, do you believe the prophets?" Agrippa responded, "You almost persuade me to become a Christian." Paul said he prayed to God the people listening to him would all become Christians. The dignitaries left, convinced Paul did not deserve to be in prison.

It's a story repeated in the court appearances of early Christians—the judges find themselves on trial. Paul is right. Agrippa knew the Old Testament prophets. Not only that, the events that fulfilled the ancient prophecies were well known in Israel. The stories of Jesus's miracles, death, and resurrection were common knowledge, not a secret carefully kept from the public (Acts 2:22).

The community of Christian believers was not a secret society, but highly visible and active.

Paul knew the truth: Agrippa believed! That is, he was intellectually convinced Jesus fulfilled the prophets' predictions. What was the king to say? If he said he believed the prophets, Paul would say, "Surely, then, you accept Jesus as the Messiah!" If he said he did not believe the prophets, it would be politically disastrous for his relationship with the Jews he's trying to govern. To complicate matters, the Roman governor had just equated Christianity with insanity.

Agrippa comes up with a wisecrack that brings down the house! "Keep this up much longer and you'll make a Christian out of me!"[10] (Acts 26:28).

Paul was not laughing. "I would to God that not only you, but also all who hear me today, might become both almost and altogether such as I am [a follower of Jesus], except for these chains"

(Acts 26:29 NKJV). With that Paul smiled and raised his right hand, and with it the left arm of the silent soldier standing beside him, to whom he was manacled wrist to wrist with what Eugene Peterson calls "prison jewelry"![11]

The beautiful people paraded from the room as they'd entered—each with secret questions he or she would answer before God. They agreed: Paul's imprisonment was unjust. Nonetheless these "powerful" people were too politically and morally weak to free him. He was a step closer to preaching the gospel in Rome (Acts 26:30–32).

what others say

### Lawrence O. Richards

Strip away the palaces and the jewels, the pomp and fine clothes, and we realize that history's beautiful people are as frail and empty as the rest. They search among the world's treasures, but cannot find anything that will give their lives meaning, or give themselves a value divorced from material possessions. . . . How desperately every human being needs to look beyond what the world has to offer, to find true fulfillment in a personal relationship with God.[12]

### Crosspoint

Believing requires more than our minds. Believing requires our hearts and our wills. Believing requires that our passions line up with the words we have said and the testimonies we have made. Believing requires hard work as we submit all that we are to the one who can transform us into people of faith.[13]

# Chapter Wrap-Up

- Paul appeared before Governor Felix, in Caesarea. Paul pleaded not guilty, repeating his contention that he was on trial because he believed in the Resurrection. (Acts 24:1–21)

- Felix postponed his verdict and kept Paul in prison for two years. Felix had several conversations with Paul. He trembled with fear as Paul spoke. (Acts 24:22–26)

- Felix was recalled. Festus took his place. He asked Paul if he'd be willing to be tried in Jerusalem. Knowing of the assassination plot, Paul used his Roman citizen's right of appeal to Caesar. (Acts 25:1–12)

- King Agrippa visited Festus. A meeting was scheduled to hear Paul. Paul told an audience of government and military leaders about his conversion. (Acts 25:13–26:23)

- When Paul spoke of Jesus's resurrection, Festus called him "mad." Paul asked Agrippa if he believed the prophets, and the king responded with the joke-line: "You almost persuade me to become a Christian." (Acts 26:24–32)

# Study Questions

1. On what three counts did Tertullus and the Jerusalem leaders charge Paul before Felix? What charge was added in the trial before Festus?

2. In answering the charges before Felix, what two reasons did Paul give for coming to Jerusalem? What was he doing at the Temple when the crowd tried to kill him?

3. Identify four things Jesus does for people according to Acts 26:18.

4. What issue did Paul press that made Festus say Paul was insane? What did Paul insist King Agrippa already believed?

5. What wisecrack did Agrippa use to avoid answering Paul's question about believing the prophets?

# Acts 27 Dangerous Passage

*Chapter Highlights:*
- **Anchors Aweigh!**
- **Rough Sailing**
- **Euroquilo!**
- **Admiral Paul**
- **Shipwreck!**

## Let's Get Started

King Agrippa agreed with Governor Festus that Paul had done nothing worthy of capital punishment or imprisonment. He could have been released but for one thing: He had appealed his case to the Roman emperor (see Acts 26:30–31). The appeal took the decision out of the governor's hands. Roman law required that an appeal to Caesar had to be carried to completion. Paul would stand trial in Rome. Unmentioned at this point by the author of Acts were the facts (already in evidence to the reader of Acts) that (1) a radical assassination squad still waited outside to "welcome" Paul with daggers (Acts 23:12; 25:2–3); and (2) the Lord had told him in a vision (Acts 23:11) that he was on his way to Rome to witness for Christ. He'd be traveling courtesy of Roman justice, under whose protection he sat in jail.

The trip to Rome would be made by sailing ship, by far the fastest form of long-distance travel from the eastern to western Mediterranean. If you like a good sea story, you'll be captivated by Luke's masterpiece of descriptive writing in Acts 27. It's a salty yarn in the tradition of sections of Melville's *Moby Dick*. The language of this tale shows the author knew the sea well. Because of this and other clues in Acts some scholars theorize Luke had spent at least part of his medical career as a ship's surgeon. We know he took several sea voyages with Paul, including this in Acts 27. (Luke tells us he was there by his use of "we" and "us.")

### what others say

**F. F. Bruce**

Luke's narrative of the voyage and shipwreck of Paul on his way to Italy is a small classic in its own right.[1]

**James Smith**

No sailor would have written in a style so little like that of a sailor; no man not a sailor could have written a narrative of a sea voyage so consistent in all its parts, unless from actual observation.[2]

# Anchors Aweigh!

**coaster**
ship that sailed
close to land and
called at ports along
the coast

> ACTS 27:1–2 *And when it was decided that we should sail to Italy, they delivered Paul and some other prisoners to one named Julius, a centurion of the Augustan Regiment. So, entering a ship of Adramyttium, we put to sea, meaning to sail along the coasts of Asia. Aristarchus, a Macedonian of Thessalonica, was with us.* (NKJV)

Agrippa advised Festus on wording for official documents sent to Rome with Paul (see Acts 25:26–27). Legal documents prepared, the prisoners at Caesarea were turned over to a centurion named Julius of the honored Augustan Regiment. Troops of the Augustan Regiment were all Romans recruited in Italy and were trusted with special assignments for the emperor.

The Roman fleet had no passenger ships. Passengers sailed aboard cargo ships as space was available. This voyage (see Illustration #18) would take place on three ships: a **coaster** from Caesarea to Myra (Acts 27:2–5) and two Egyptian grain ships on regular runs from Alexandria to Rome (Acts 27:6–28:1; Acts 28:11–13).

### what others say

**Edwin M. Yamauchi**

The ships left when the winds and omens were favorable. The expense for passage was not high; it cost a family but two drachma (about two days' wages) to sail from Alexandria to Athens. The fare included the provision of water and cabins but not food.[3]

## Paul's Loyal "Slaves"

Luke, as noted, was with Paul on this voyage. Another apostolic coworker, Aristarchus the Macedonian, was also there. It is possible Luke signed on as ship's doctor. Another intriguing possibility mentioned by some scholars is that both Luke and Aristarchus went as Paul's slaves. Roman law permitted prominent Roman citizens under arrest to take with them one or two slaves to care for their personal needs.

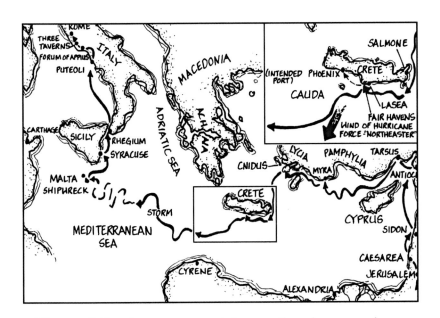

**Illustration #18**
Paul's Voyage to Rome—This map shows the route of Paul's last journey beginning in Caesarea and Sidon. He boarded a ship at Caesarea, sailed close to land and then toward Crete, was shipwrecked at Malta, and traveled to Rome. The inset shows the way the ship was blown off course at Crete.

The possibility that two men might actually volunteer to become slaves in order to stay with Paul on one of his most dangerous trips reveals the surprising depth of their love for the apostle and the Lord they all served! Continuous church growth depends on the willingness of Christians to make personal sacrifices and to go to the ends of the earth to tell the Jesus story.

### what others say

**W. M. Ramsay**

[Luke and Aristarchus would have gone] not merely performing the duties of slaves . . . but actually passing as slaves. In this way not merely had Paul faithful friends always beside him; his importance in the eyes of the centurion was much enhanced, and that was of great importance.[4]

## Society of Friends

ACTS 27:3 *And the next day we landed at Sidon. And Julius treated Paul kindly and gave him liberty to go to his friends and receive care.* (NKJV)

In just one day at sea, Paul won the friendship of Centurion Julius. Luke says Julius treated Paul "kindly." When the ship called at the port of Sidon, Julius allowed Paul to leave the ship and visit "his friends," the Sidonian Christians. The original Greek reads "the friends," another way early Christians referred to one another—like "the Way" (see Acts 24:22), "the brethren" (see Acts 28:15), or "the disciples" (see Acts 21:16). Nothing convinces people that Christianity is real like the lengths to which Christians will go to express their love.

# Rough Sailing

> ACTS 27:4–9a *When we had put to sea from there, we sailed under the shelter of Cyprus, because the winds were contrary. And when we had sailed over the sea which is off Cilicia and Pamphylia, we came to Myra, a city of Lycia. There the centurion found an Alexandrian ship sailing to Italy, and he put us on board. When we had sailed slowly many days, and arrived with difficulty off Cnidus, the wind not permitting us to proceed, we sailed under the shelter of Crete off Salmone. Passing it with difficulty, we came to a place called Fair Havens, near the city of Lasea. Now when much time had been spent, and sailing was now dangerous because the Fast was already over,* (NKJV)

The safe Mediterranean sailing season was summer—May to September. Sailing from east to west after mid-September was considered "iffy," impossible by November, and suicidal from November to February. For weeks between November and March cloudy skies hid the sun and stars on which first-century sailors depended for their bearings. Without sextant or compass, staying on course was impossible. Most of Paul's voyage took place when "the Fast was already over" (Acts 27:9 NKJV), Yom Kippur, the Jewish Day of Atonement, which in that year, AD 59, was late—October 5, well into the scary season!

When they put to sea after the Sidonian stopover, late summer winds from west and northwest made going north and west difficult. To take advantage of the steady westward current along the south coast of Asia Minor (modern Turkey) and night breezes from the shore, the ship hugged the coast of Cilicia and Pamphylia. When westerly winds made progress impossible, the ship lay at anchor in the shelter of the coastline. Finally, they arrived at Myra, a chief port of the imperial grain service.

There the centurion found an Alexandrian ship headed for Rome with a load of Egyptian corn or wheat and put his soldiers and prisoners aboard.

Egypt was Rome's "granary." Hundreds of thousands of tons of grain were shipped to the Imperial City on what, for that day, were huge ships (see Illustration #19). **Fore** and **aft** these vessels were basically the same shape. Rudderless, they were steered with two huge paddles on each side of the stern. Power depended on a single gigantic square sail made of heavy Egyptian linen or animal hides stitched together. They were not designed for sailing against the wind—which is exactly what sailors faced on this ill-fated voyage in early October AD 59.

**Illustration #19**
Egyptian Grain Ship—Paul was a prisoner put aboard an Egyptian grain ship such as this one. The biggest ships were 140–180 feet long, 36–45 feet wide, and 33–45 feet deep with a cargo capacity of up to 1,200 tons of grain. Some ships had more than one figurehead, usually a carving of a god. Castor and Pollux, twins of the constellation Gemini, were the favorite gods and good luck sign of mariners.

With difficulty the ship made the port of Cnidus, a peninsula on the southwest coast of Asia Minor. From there they intended to sail directly to Crete and along the north side of the island, then to Italy. But a persistent **nor'wester** off Cnidus forced them to give up the direct course. They sailed south to the leeward side of Crete and struggled along the south coast, arriving at Fair Havens well into the danger season.

## By the Time I Get to Phoenix

**ACTS 27:9b–12** *Paul advised them, saying, "Men, I perceive that this voyage will end with disaster and much loss, not only of the cargo and ship, but also our lives." Nevertheless the centurion was more persuaded by the **helmsman** and the owner of the ship than by the things spoken by Paul. And because the harbor was not suitable to winter in, the majority advised to set sail*

**three shipwrecks**
2 Corinthians 11:25

*from there also, if by any means they could reach Phoenix, a harbor of Crete opening toward the southwest and northwest, and winter there. (NKJV)*

Paul was a tentmaker not a seaman, but he was an experienced sea traveler who had already been through <u>three shipwrecks</u>! He urged officers of the ship to winter at Fair Havens. Adequate accommodations could be found in the nearby city of Lasea (Acts 27:8). From personal experience he warned of loss of ship and lives. Later, an angel revealed to him that the ship would wreck, but with no loss of life (see Acts 27:24).

The centurion, senior military officer on board, would make the final decision. He chose to rely on the wisdom and experience of the ship's owner (who was probably also ship's captain) and the pilot who knew these waters like the back of his hand. The fact that Phoenix (modern Phenika) would be safer and more comfortable for spending the winter tipped the scales. The decision was made to sail the fifty miles along the coast to Phoenix and winter there.

## Euroquilo!

**ACTS 27:13–15** *When the south wind blew softly, supposing that they had obtained their desire, putting out to sea, they sailed close by Crete. But not long after, a tempestuous head wind arose, called Euroclydon. So when the ship was caught, and could not head into the wind, we let her drive. (NKJV)*

Phoenix was west from Fair Havens, around the southwestern tip of Crete, then a short distance north across the Gulf of Messara. A gentle southern breeze was the answer to the sailors' prayers. Hugging the shore for a few hours would put them safely into their winter haven. But not even the saltiest salt pulling ropes and hoisting sail on that ship could have predicted what happened next, even though it was "a common occurrence in those seas," according to nautical expert James Smith.[5]

At the center of the island of Crete rose Mount Ida. Without warning the south wind changed as a violent northwest wind roared down the slopes of the mountain—"a tempestuous head wind." The New King James Version calls it "Euroclydon," which is from *Euroquilo*, a hybrid Greek word combining Euros (east wind) with Aquilo (north wind). It described well the wild, unpredictable, twisting motion of sea and clouds caused by contrary currents of air moving opposite directions at high speed.[6]

The unexpected arrival of Euroclydon meant that when the ship tried to turn north around Cape Matala to reach Phoenix, she would be turning directly into the fierce gale—something the big grain ships simply were unequipped to do in heavy seas. All they could do was to run with the wind. They suddenly found themselves being driven hard away from land. She would never see Phoenix!

## Lay To on the Starboard Tack!

ACTS 27:16–17 *And running under the shelter of an island called Clauda, we secured the skiff with difficulty. When they had taken it on board, they used cables to undergird the ship; and fearing lest they should run aground on the Syrtis Sands, they struck sail and so were driven. (NKJV)*

Twenty-five miles (forty kilometers) south of Crete lay the tiny isle of Clauda. The leeward side of the island gave slight and temporary relief from the fiercest blast of the Euroclydon. This gave the crew an opportunity to perform some precautions. Above the roar of the storm commands something like these were given:

"Hoist the lifeboat!" The "lifeboat" was a single wooden dinghy towed astern of the main vessel. By now it was full of water, making securing it more difficult.

"Winch the hawsers!" This was known as "frapping" the ship. It involved passing ropes or cables (called "hawsers") under the ship, and drawing them tight with winches to keep the ship from breaking its back ("hogging") and to prevent the wood-plank hull from coming apart.[7]

"Drop the sea anchor!" A "drift anchor" dragged astern slowed the ship's descent as she plunged down from the crest of wave after wave. The reason for deploying this anchor was the fear that the winds, if they continued for several days, might drive the ship across the Mediterranean into an area of sandbars called "the Greater Syrtis" off the African Coast west of Cyrene, a legendary ships' graveyard!

"Lay to on the **starboard tack**!" To slow her further the ship was turned so her right side was to the wind.[8] This done, the best they could do was "let [the ship] drive" (Acts 27:15 NKJV).

**starboard**
right side of a ship looking forward
(port: left side)

**tack**
ship's direction

# All Hope Lost for Storm-Tossed Ship

ACTS 27:18–20 *And because we were exceedingly tempest-tossed, the next day they lightened the ship. On the third day we threw the ship's tackle overboard with our own hands. Now when neither sun nor stars appeared for many days, and no small tempest beat on us, all hope that we would be saved was finally given up. (NKJV)*

During the next three days two last-gasp actions were taken in hope of saving the lives of the 276 passengers and crew (that's how many Acts 27:37 says were on board). First, some of the cargo was thrown overboard. Two days later the relentless storm raged on, and the ship showed more signs of breaking up. So together, crew and passengers (note the use of "we") **jettisoned** some of the ship's tackle—probably the heavy **mainsail** and **yard**. Frantic last rites for a dying ship!

Night and day, storm clouds hid the sun and stars so the pilot could not tell where they were. The ship was taking on water and riding low in the water.

Luke's terse statement expresses the terrified resignation that gripped everyone on board: "All hope that we would be saved was finally given up" (Acts 27:20 NKJV).

# Admiral Paul

ACTS 27:21–26 *But after long abstinence from food, then Paul stood in the midst of them and said, "Men, you should have listened to me, and not have sailed from Crete and incurred this disaster and loss. And now I urge you to take heart, for there will be no loss of life among you, but only of the ship. For there stood by me this night an angel of the God to whom I belong and whom I serve, saying, 'Do not be afraid, Paul; you must be brought before Caesar; and indeed God has granted you all those who sail with you.' Therefore take heart, men, for I believe God that it will be just as it was told me. However, we must run aground on a certain island." (NKJV)*

Seasick and demoralized, the crew and passengers hung on to whatever they could to keep from being washed overboard, and waited for the ship to be swamped. In the midst of this milieu of hopelessness Paul talked with God. It was two-way communication:

**go to**

**instinctively**
1 Thessalonians 5:17

**terrified shout**
Matthew 14:30

**silent wish**
Psalm 37:4;
John 15:7

**request**
Philippians 4:6

**resignation**
Matthew 26:42;
Luke 22:42;
Acts 21:14

**promise**
Acts 22:11

1. The phrase "God has granted you all those who sail with you" indicates Paul had prayed not just for himself but for the other 275 who shared his situation. (Believers <u>instinctively</u> pray in the predicaments of life.) It may have been a <u>terrified shout</u> as he struggled with the others to save the ship, a <u>silent wish</u>, a specific <u>request</u>, or a sigh of <u>resignation</u> to God's will.

2. God's response was communicated by an angel:

   - Remember God's <u>promise</u>: You will stand before Caesar in Rome. (It's only reasonable: How can you do that if you go down with this ship?)

   - The ship will be destroyed.

   - No one will die in the shipwreck.

Armed with this revelation and promise, Paul became the doomed ship's unofficial "admiral." As the storm raged, he stood up, hanging on to some rigging to keep from being thrown off his feet by the pitching ship. After an irresistible "I told you so!" the "admiral" issued an incredible order: "Cheer up, fellas! We're going to make it!" He passed on the angel's message and ended with a shout of confidence, "I have faith in God!"

**what others say**

**Billy Graham**

When the "evil day" comes, we do not have to be dependent upon the circumstances around us, but rather on the resources of God![9]

The situation appeared so hopeless it was understandable for even Christian men to think they were beyond help. But in the midst of the blackest, stormiest night, the Lord sent a messenger to reveal he was in control—even a shipwreck could not sink his program for reaching the world with his message of love.

## The Sound of Land

ACTS 27:27–29 *Now when the fourteenth night had come, as we were driven up and down in the Adriatic Sea, about midnight the sailors sensed that they were drawing near some land. And they took soundings and found it to be twenty fathoms; and when they had gone a little farther, they took soundings again and found it to be fifteen fathoms. Then, fearing lest we should run aground on the rocks, they dropped four anchors from the stern, and prayed for day to come.* (NKJV)

The tempest had driven the drifting ship for two weeks! The Adriatic Sea mentioned is the first-century name for the central Mediterranean, distinguished from the "Gulf of Adria" to the north, known today as the Adriatic Sea.[10] In the middle of the pitchdark fourteenth night, the sailors, whose ears were tuned to the sounds of the sea, "sensed that they were drawing near some land." One ancient manuscript of this story says, "The land was resounding" (Acts 27:27). In other words, they heard breakers!

Approaching the bay the breakers were especially violent and noisy. Standard practice as the ship approached land was to check the depth of the water at half-hour intervals.[11] Depth soundings confirmed the ship was being driven toward an unknown shore. Four anchors were dropped from the stern to keep the ship from crashing against shoreline rocks. The anchors pointed her toward the shore in preparation for beaching at dawn.

## Rats Try to Leave the Sinking Ship

ACTS 27:30–32 *And as the sailors were seeking to escape from the ship, when they had let down the skiff into the sea, under pretense of putting out anchors from the prow, Paul said to the centurion and the soldiers, "Unless these men stay in the ship, you cannot be saved." Then the soldiers cut away the ropes of the skiff and let it fall off.* (NKJV)

Pretending to deploy more anchors, the crew decided they'd have a better chance of survival if they took the only lifeboat and skedaddled. There were no other lifeboats. This one was only large enough for the crew. In the sailors' ratty scheme the soldiers and passengers would be left behind to go down with the ship!

Paul realized what was happening and warned the centurion that the safety of everyone on board depended on the sailors staying with the ship and doing what they alone were trained to do—sail! A couple of whacks by legionnaires' swords and the mariners' malevolent escape scheme washed away with the deserted dinghy.

what others say

### F. F. Bruce

By this time the centurion had learned that it was unwise to disregard Paul's advice, although his advice was probably misinterpreted when the soldiers cut the hawsers and let the dinghy go adrift. The dinghy could have been very useful in getting the ship's company ashore had it proved impossible to beach the ship. . . . However, the centurion may have decided that the soldiers' action was the most effective way of keeping the sailors on board.[12]

## Breakfast with the Admiral

ACTS 27:33–38 *And as day was about to dawn, Paul implored them all to take food, saying, "Today is the fourteenth day you have waited and continued without food, and eaten nothing. Therefore I urge you to take nourishment, for this is for your survival, since not a hair will fall from the head of any of you." And when he had said these things, he took bread and gave thanks to God in the presence of them all; and when he had broken it he began to eat. Then they were all encouraged, and also took food themselves. And in all we were two hundred and seventy-six persons on the ship. So when they had eaten enough, they lightened the ship and threw out the wheat into the sea. (NKJV)*

What was just ahead would require all the strength they could muster. So Paul urged the passengers and crew to do something they hadn't done for two weeks—eat. Again he assured them all would survive. Like a Jewish father beginning a family meal, he took bread, thanked God, broke the bread, and began to eat. As they ate they caught some of Paul's confident spirit. After their predawn breakfast, they threw the last of the cargo into the sea to raise the ship in the water so she'd run closer to shore before being beached.

what others say

### William Barclay

Into the tempest there seems to come a strange calm. The man of God has somehow made others sure that God is in charge of things. The most useful people in the world are

go to

**presence**
Genesis 18:26–32

**bay**
now called "St.
Paul's Bay"

**foresail**
small sail used to
aid steering

those who, being themselves calm, bring to others the secret of confidence.[13]

### F. F. Bruce

Human society has no idea how much it owes, in the mercy of God, to the <u>presence</u> in it of righteous men and women.[14]

## Shipwreck!

*ACTS 27:39–41 When it was day, they did not recognize the land; but they observed a <u>bay</u> with a beach, onto which they planned to run the ship if possible. And they let go the anchors and left them in the sea, meanwhile loosing the rudder ropes; and they hoisted the mainsail to the wind and made for shore. But striking a place where two seas met, they ran the ship aground; and the prow stuck fast and remained immovable, but the stern was being broken up by the violence of the waves. (NKJV)*

By dawn's early light the pilot saw a sandy beach. "They"—the pilot and owner-captain—decided to try to run the ship aground on the beach. The cables on the aft anchors were cut, the **foresail** (which hadn't been jettisoned in Acts 27:19) was hoisted to the wind. The battered ship picked up speed as she headed for land. It never made the beach. Her bow stuck fast in an offshore sandbar. The storm-churned surf immediately tore the stern to splinters.

## Centurion Calls Halt to Mass Execution

*ACTS 27:42–44 And the soldiers' plan was to kill the prisoners, lest any of them should swim away and escape. But the centurion, wanting to save Paul, kept them from their purpose, and commanded that those who could swim should jump overboard first and get to land, and the rest, some on boards and some on parts of the ship. And so it was that they all escaped safely to land. (NKJV)*

Roman military discipline made soldiers responsible for their prisoners. If they escaped, the guards were given the penalty intended for the fugitive. An escaped prisoner could mean death for the guard on whose watch he got free. Killing prisoners was one way to assure that none escaped! To save Paul's life, the centurion called a halt to this mass execution before it could happen. And he ordered everyone to abandon ship.

As the ship disintegrated, 276 passengers and crew swam or floated on parts of the wreckage. All crawled out of the surf, soaking wet, bone weary, and greatly relieved to be alive!

what others say

**W. M. Ramsay**

Thus the foreship was held together, until every passenger got safe to dry land. Only the rarest conjunction of favorable circumstances could have brought about such a fortunate ending to their apparently hopeless situation.[15]

## Chapter Wrap-Up

- Paul and other prisoners sailed the first leg of their journey to Rome aboard a "coasting vessel." Luke and Aristarchus were with Paul. At Sidon, the centurion allowed Paul to visit Christian friends. (Acts 27:1–3)

- At Myra they boarded an Egyptian grain ship. Contrary winds made staying on course impossible. At Fair Havens, Crete, Paul urged them to stop for the winter. The ship's owner and pilot overruled him. (Acts 27:4–12)

- When a southern breeze began to blow, they set sail for Phoenix but never got there. A sudden hurricane-force wind (Euroclydon) swept down from the northeast, and the ship was caught in a terrible storm. (Acts 27:13–20)

- All on board gave up hope of survival. But an angel gave Paul God's promise that, though the ship would be lost, everyone on board would survive. (Acts 27:21–26)

- On the fourteenth stormy night sailors sensed land was near. They tried to escape in the only lifeboat, leaving passengers to go down with the ship. Paul told the centurion, who cut the lifeboat adrift to keep the crew aboard. (Acts 27:27–34)

- Before beaching the boat Paul urged them all to eat. At dawn the ship was headed to the beach. It struck a sandbar, stuck fast, and broke up in the waves. The centurion ordered everyone to abandon ship and to swim or grab a plank and float to shore. All 276 aboard survived! (Acts 27:35–44)

## Study Questions

1. Name two Christians who accompanied Paul on his voyage to Rome. What were they likely willing to do in order to go with him?

2. What made sailing so difficult? When did Paul's ship reach Fair Havens, Crete? Why did the ship's owner and pilot decide to sail on to Phoenix?

3. Identify three parts of the message the "angel of God" brought Paul in the midst of the storm.

4. What happened when sailors tried to escape in the lifeboat? What did the centurion do when soldiers wanted to kill prisoners to keep them from escaping? Why?

# Acts 28 The Unchained Truth

## Let's Get Started

Sailors, soldiers, prisoners, and other passengers from the Alexandrian corn ship lay drenched and exhausted amid the splintered wreckage of their ship, on a strange beach even their pilot did not recognize (see Acts 27:39). The realization that they had actually survived two weeks of endless struggle to survive, at the mercy of tempestuous seas, must have, in itself, seemed incredible. Were they dreaming, or was this solid ground beneath them? And when the count was taken and it was discovered that all on board had made it to shore alive, incredulity must have given way to sheer astonishment and joy.

## Hope Island

ACTS 28:1–2 *Now when they had escaped, they then found out that the island was called Malta. And the natives showed us unusual kindness; for they kindled a fire and made us all welcome, because of the rain that was falling and because of the cold.* (NKJV)

The survivors discovered they had washed up on the small island of Malta. Luke's original word to describe "the natives" is *barbaroi*, literally translated "barbarians." In the first century that did not mean they were uncivilized. Greek-speaking people used the word to refer to non-Greek-speaking people. These natives turned out to be quite civil. Survivors found a blazing fire, built by the natives, waiting to warm them.

## Shaking Snake

ACTS 28:3–6 *But when Paul had gathered a bundle of sticks and laid them on the fire, a viper came out because of the heat, and fastened on his hand. So when the natives saw the creature hanging from his hand, they said to one another, "No doubt this man is a murderer, whom, though he has escaped the sea, yet jus-*

**go to**

**not drop dead**
Mark 16:18

**a god**
Acts 14:8–13

**Justice**
goddess of
retribution

*tice does not allow to live." But he shook off the creature into the fire and suffered no harm. However, they were expecting that he would swell up or suddenly fall down dead. But after they had looked for a long time and saw no harm come to him, they changed their minds and said that he was a god. (NKJV)*

As Paul gathered a bunch of brushwood to add to the fire he inadvertently picked up a poisonous snake, a viper, stiffened by the cold. (It's interesting that today there are no poisonous snakes on the island.) As he laid wood on the fire, the snake, revived by the warmth, grabbed Paul's hand with its fangs. Paul shook it off into the fire.

Superstitious islanders watched for the worst to follow. They'd no doubt heard the story of the murderer who escaped a shipwreck on the Libyan coast but **Justice** caught up with him when he died of a viper's bite.¹ As they watched Paul shake the snake into the fire, they concluded he, too, was a murderer getting what he deserved. To their surprise, Paul did <u>not drop dead</u> from the venom. The Maltese then decided he must be <u>a god</u>!

## Winter of Hope and Healing

ACTS 28:7–10 *In that region there was an estate of the leading citizen of the island, whose name was Publius, who received us and entertained us courteously for three days. And it happened that the father of Publius lay sick of a fever and dysentery. Paul went in to him and prayed, and he laid his hands on him and healed him. So when this was done, the rest of those on the island who had diseases also came and were healed. They also honored us in many ways; and when we departed, they provided such things as were necessary. (NKJV)*

The islanders took the survivors into their homes. Paul and Luke were entertained for three days at the home of Publius, Malta's top government official. While there, Paul prayed for Publius's father, who was sick with dysentery. He got well. Word of this spread, and Paul and Luke (notice "us," Acts 28:10) spent the winter healing the island's sick. Knowing Paul's compulsion for sharing Christ, we can be sure medical treatment and healing were dispensed with rich doses of the good news.

Shipwrecked, still a prisoner, and stuck for three months on a strange island, Paul and Luke found themselves with opportunities for ministry arranged, not by their careful planning, but by the secret sovereign arranging of God.

**serendipity**
unexpected, delightful happening

## On the "Road" Again

ACTS 28:11–13 *After three months we sailed in an Alexandrian ship whose figurehead was the Twin Brothers, which had wintered at the island. And landing at Syracuse, we stayed three days. From there we circled round and reached Rhegium. And after one day the south wind blew; and the next day we came to Puteoli,* (NKJV)

Another Egyptian grain ship had wintered on Malta. The ship was decorated with figures (see Illustration #19) for good luck. When the ship sailed in early February, Centurion Julius put his prisoners and soldiers aboard. Early February was usually considered too early to resume Mediterranean sailing. But according to the Roman writer Pliny,[2] ships sailing near shore could put to sea after February 8 when westerly and southerly winds began to blow.

It was forty miles—a one-day trip—to Syracuse, main port of the island of Sicily. From Syracuse the ship sailed to the toe of the Italian peninsula, putting in at Rhegium. Another day's sailing brought it to Puteoli, which, in the first century, was the busiest port in southern Italy, located in the most sheltered part of the Bay of Naples. There passengers disembarked and traveled the rest of the way to Rome on the famous Appian Way.

## The Roman Welcoming Committee

ACTS 28:14–15 *where we found brethren, and were invited to stay with them seven days. And so we went toward Rome. And from there, when the brethren heard about us, they came to meet us as far as Appii Forum and Three Inns. When Paul saw them, he thanked God and took courage.* (NKJV)

Evidently Centurion Julius had a week's worth of official red tape to attend to before continuing to Rome. In a welcome **serendipity** it was discovered there were some Christian brothers in Puteoli. Paul and his companions were permitted, under guard, to spend the week with them.

Evidently the Puteoli Christians sent word to Rome that Paul had arrived. Two delegations of Christians hiked down the Appian Way

**meet**
Greek: official dele-
gation welcoming a
dignitary

**omnipresent**
present everywhere

to **meet** and escort him to Rome. The Forum (marketplace) of Appii was forty-three miles from the capital. Tres Tabernae ("the Three Inns") was a familiar Appian Way stopping place thirty-three miles from Rome.

### Who Started the Church at Rome?

The best guess is that the church at Rome got its start when Roman Jews heard Peter preach in Jerusalem on the Day of Pentecost, AD 30 (see Acts 2:10). No doubt some were among the three thousand who believed in Jesus as Messiah and were baptized that day (see Acts 2:41). They had returned home to share the good news and began meeting as believers.

Paul's friends Aquila and Priscilla were from Rome and would have told him about the Christians there (see Acts 18:2).

Three years before his arrival, Paul wrote his letter to the Roman Christians in which he expressed his longing to come to Rome and share with them for mutual encouragement (see Romans 1:8–13). At last he was looking into the faces of Roman Christians. The dream was becoming a living reality.

what others say

**William Barclay**

The Christian is never alone. (1) He has the consciousness of the unseen cloud of witnesses around him and about him. (2) He has the consciousness of belonging to a worldwide fel-lowship. (3) He has the consciousness that wherever he goes there is God. (4) He has the certainty that his Risen Lord is with him.[3]

Through his **omnipresent** Spirit, the Lord leads and empowers people in many places at once to be witnesses and to function as the church. Because he is not limited to time and space, God may direct Christians to a traveler in all sorts of strange and faraway places.

## Paul Under House Arrest in Rome

the big picture

**Acts 28:16–22**

Upon arrival in Rome Paul was placed under house arrest. Three days after arrival in Rome, Paul introduced himself to the leaders of the Jewish community. He told them about his arrest and appeal to Caesar. He declared he was a prisoner "for the **hope of Israel**." They responded that they'd heard nothing bad about him and they'd like to hear what he had to say.

go to

hope of Israel
Acts 23:8; 24:15;
26:6–8

hope of Israel
national survival,
renewal, eternal life
through the risen
Jesus

While awaiting trial in Rome, Paul was allowed to rent his own house (perhaps working with leather or making tents to provide funds). He was still a prisoner, chained twenty-four hours a day, wrist-to-wrist, to a soldier of the Praetorian Guard (Acts 28:20).

"A prominent individual, or one expected to be released, might be kept under house arrest if he or she could afford the rent. In Rome, where housing prisoners was excessively expensive, Paul was given the privilege of house arrest, and he paid the rent himself. . . . He probably lived in a third-floor apartment; first floors were used for shops, and the second floor was expensive."[4]

Many people came to see him. As each guard stood his watch, he overheard Paul's conversations and watched him. In one of his letters Paul reports that the whole Praetorian Guard had come to know that his "chains [were] in Christ" (Philippians 1:12–14 NKJV). Some of these soldiers may have become Christians (see Philippians 4:22). Through many years, in city after city, Paul offered the gospel to Jews before anyone else. He never gave up hope that his countrymen would believe in Jesus as Messiah. The story almost always had the same ending—some Jews believed and joined the Jesus movement, others refused to believe and dug in their heels in bitter opposition to Christ. It happened again in Rome.

Roman Jews had heard nothing bad about Paul (Acts 28:21)—amazing, considering the bitterness against him in Jerusalem. Here are possible reasons for this happy lack of negative communication: (1) A letter or representative may have been delayed by the complexities of winter travel; (2) Jerusalem leaders realized they didn't have a chance of success after failing to convict Paul in Judea; or (3) Roman law could make life difficult for unsuccessful prosecutors, and they didn't want to take the risk.[5]

They'd heard nothing bad about Paul, but the Roman Jews did have some unfavorable hearsay information about the Christian movement (Acts 28:22).

# Hot Debates and Demands for Proof

the big picture

### Acts 28:23–27

The Jewish leaders arranged a meeting and large groups of people came to where Paul was staying. From dawn to dusk Paul told them about Jesus Christ, trying to convince them that Jesus was Messiah by quoting from the Law of Moses and from the Prophets.

The leaders arranged an extended meeting with Paul at his rented place. From morning till evening he told the story of Jesus, explaining how Jesus's life, death, and resurrection fulfilled Old Testament promises concerning the Messiah. It wasn't a monologue. That wasn't the Jewish way or Paul's style. There were tough questions. Hot debates. Demands for proof. Appeals to believe and welcome Jesus as Savior and Lord.

Some became convinced and believed in Jesus (Acts 28:24). Others refused. In Acts 28:26–27 Paul quoted and applied to them the dire words God gave the prophet Isaiah for his unbelieving generation in Isaiah 6:9–10.

Many people, Jews and Gentiles, do not believe because they choose not to believe, they deliberately close their eyes, ears, and hearts, and harden themselves against the truth about themselves and God's plan for their spiritual **healing**.

what others say

### William Barclay

There is something wonderful in the fact that to the end of the day, wherever he went, Paul began with the Jews. For rather more than thirty years now they had been doing everything they could to hinder him, to undo his work, and even to kill him: and even yet it is to them first he offers his message. Is there any example of undefeatable hope and unconquerable love like this act of Paul when, in Rome too, he preached first to the Jews?[6]

For the probable contents of Paul's daylong session with the Jews at Rome, check these passages:

- Acts 13:17–41; 17:2–3; 26:4–23.

For the Old Testament messianic prophecies that early Christians quoted when talking with Jews, check these passages:

**will hear it**
Acts 13:48

## Messianic Prophecies Quoted by Christians

| Old Testament Source | Christian Quote in Acts |
| --- | --- |
| Acts 2:16–21 | Joel 2:28–32 |
| Acts 2:25–28 | Psalm 16:8–11 |
| Acts 2:34–35 | Psalm 110:1 |
| Acts 3:22–23 | Deuteronomy 18:15, 18–19 |
| Acts 3:25 | Genesis 22:18 |
| Acts 4:11 | Psalm 118:22 |
| Acts 4:25–26 | Psalm 2:1–2 |
| Acts 8:32–33 | Isaiah 53:7–8 |
| Acts 13:33–35 | Psalm 2:7; Isaiah 55:3; Psalm 16:10 |

# No Chain Can Hold the Truth!

ACTS 28:28–31 *"Therefore let it be known to you that the salvation of God has been sent to the Gentiles, and they <u>will hear it</u>!" And when he had said these words, the Jews departed and had a great dispute among themselves. Then Paul dwelt two whole years in his own rented house, and received all who came to him, preaching the kingdom of God and teaching the things which concern the Lord Jesus Christ with all confidence, no one forbidding him. (NKJV)*

Rejecting Jews left the meeting in disarray. The door they chose to slam shut became a swinging door, wide open to the Gentiles. For two years Paul waited in Rome for his appeal to be heard before Emperor Nero. He welcomed all comers, all the while coupled to Roman soldiers day and night by a chain. He told everyone who visited about the good news of Jesus and the difference in people's lives the kingship and practical reign of God could make.

None of this was any secret to the Roman authorities, yet no official attempt was ever made to stop it. In the Greek manuscript of Acts, the last word is *axolutos*—"no one forbidding him." A wonderful note, considering Paul's physical situation. The Ambassador of Christ was chained, but the good news was unchained!

**go to**

**quietly invaded**
Matthew 13:33;
Luke 17:20–21

what others say

**William Barclay**

This rejection of Jesus by the Jews is the very thing which has opened the door to the Gentiles. There is a purpose in everything; on the helm of things is the hand of the unseen steersman—God.[7]

### The End?

This is where the book stops. With Paul under house arrest in Rome.

"Print it!"

But . . . we wish Luke had told us more.

What happened at the trial? Did Paul witness for Jesus to Nero? What happened to the early Christians? We are left to get our information from other sources. But for Luke it was like Income Tax Day: "Gotta get it postmarked before midnight!" The deadline for publication had arrived.

Luke ends with a note of triumph: "Preaching the kingdom of God and teaching the things which concern the Lord Jesus Christ with all confidence, no one forbidding him" (Acts 28:31 NKJV).

But the rest of the story is left untold in the Bible narrative. In reality, Luke cannot write the end because the story is still being told in the twenty-first century, in the lives of the Christians today.

## Paul in Rome: The Rest of the Story

Acts gives only a glimpse of what happened in Rome. Beginning in the chained ambassador's unchained heart, from his rented house, the gospel quietly invaded the city and the empire. From prison Paul accomplished four things vitally important to the spread of the gospel:

1. *He wrote.* While under house arrest in Rome, Paul wrote letters to (1) Philippians, (2) Ephesians, (3) Colossians, and (4) Philemon.

## 2. He directed a team of ambassadors for Christ:

- Luke and Aristarchus were with him (see Acts 27:1–2). Luke stayed to the end (see 2 Timothy 4:11).

- Timothy came and went with apostolic instructions for churches (Philippians 1:1; Colossians 1:1; Philemon 1).

- Tychicus served Paul's needs; he delivered Paul's letter to the Ephesians (Ephesians 6:21).

- Epaphroditus spent time with Paul and brought money to supply his needs (Philippians 4:18).

- John Mark became Paul's valued aide and ministered with him in Rome (Colossians 4:10; 2 Timothy 4:11).

## 3. He personally introduced people to Jesus.
(1) The soldiers of the Praetorian Guard all knew Paul was in chains because of Christ (Philippians 1:13); some became believers. (2) Paul's fearless preaching while in chains inspired his fellow Christians to witness more boldly (Philippians 1:14). (3) Members of Caesar's personal staff (relatives and others) became believers (Philippians 4:22).

## 4. He witnessed to Caesar.
There is no New Testament record of an appearance before the emperor, unless it was the trial Paul refers to in 2 Timothy 4:16–17. In God's message to Paul during the storm, he promised Paul would stand trial before Caesar (Acts 27:23–24). We may assume the Lord kept that promise as he did the promise that no lives would be lost in the shipwreck (Acts 27:44).

You'd think being under arrest would stifle a man's witness and keep him from effective ministry. But Jesus knows what he's allowing. Powerfully, God worked through Paul in prison. Had he not been confined, the busyness of ministry may have delayed the writing of the New Testament letters so vital to our Christian faith. Members of his team may have remained overly dependent on Paul and failed to find their own ministries. Paul's experience reveals: No confinement can stop the Lord's work!

## To the Ends of the Earth

When you stop to think about it, Acts 28 was a pretty good place to stop. With Christ on the offensive in Rome, the table of contents for Luke's early church history, outlined by Jesus in Acts 1:8, reached its climax:

1. "You shall receive power when the Holy Spirit has come upon you"—story in Acts 1:12–2:4.

2. "You shall be witnesses to Me in Jerusalem"—story in Acts 2:5–7:60; Acts 22:1–23:10.

3. "You shall be witnesses to Me . . . in all Judea and Samaria"—story in Acts 8:1–11:18.

4. "You shall be witnesses to Me . . . to the end of the earth"—story in Acts 11:19–21:14; 23:11–28:31.

Acts is the story of people responding to God's invitation to be rescued from alienation from him by believing and acknowledging Jesus as Lord of their lives (see Acts 9:3–5; 26:19).

The truth by which they find their way to God is found in the Bible, which they consider to be the Word of God (see Acts 2:16–36). Their lives are shaped by its teachings (see Acts 15:13–21;

19:18–20). Their sole aim in life is to glorify God and tell the story of Jesus to everyone, depending on the Spirit to lead and enable them (see Acts 4:29; 20:24; Ephesians 1:12).

As they catch that vision—the vision Jesus himself gives them—they do not live as "rugged individuals," but live and work in the context of the family of faith (see Acts 2:41–47; 20:1–11). The fellowship of the living church becomes the "matrix for mission"—the place where spiritual maturity is encouraged and Christ's vision is born in his followers, and from which Christ's witnesses emerge to tell the world!

## what others say

**Richard C. Halverson**

At Pentecost . . . by the supernatural power of the Holy Spirit, those 120 individual disciples were galvanized into one, inseparable, indivisible, indestructible living organism—the body of which Christ is the head. They literally became members of one another, needing one another, responsible to one another as the members of a physical body are responsible and necessary to each other. . . .

What that first century world saw was a phenomenon of people of all walks of life loving one another, praying for one another. Slaves and free men were in that community. Rich and poor were in that fellowship. Roman citizens and non-Roman citizens were in that community. Members of the establishment and those violently opposed to the establishment were part of that community. The intelligentsia and the illiterate were members of that community. To the utter amazement of the world outside, they were bound together in an unexplainable love and unity.[9]

Emperors would come and go. Anti-Christian forces would be fierce. Fiery persecutions, including ten ordered by Roman emperors, would try to silence the truth. Courage would always be demanded of witnesses. It is today.

The gospel impacted not only Rome but the world. The Christian movement expanded quietly—one person at a time confessing faith in Jesus as Savior and Lord.

Two and a half centuries after Acts 28, in AD 313, Emperor Constantine officially called an end to persecution of Christians.

**feet of Christ**
Ephesians 1:9–10, 22;
Philippians 2:9–11;
Colossians 1:17–20;
Revelation 4:1–11

Eleven years later, in AD 324, the emperor himself confessed his faith in Christ and declared his intention to make Christianity the religion of the Roman Empire.

Within a few years of Luke's writing Acts 28, Paul was martyred for his faith. Acts 28:31 could serve as his epitaph. What do you need to be building into your life right now, so that your faith in Christ will be what people remember about you when you die?

Luke's story of the early church is designed to give Christian witnesses in the twenty-first century insights into their resources in the Holy Spirit, hope in the storms into which following Jesus inevitably led, and peace in the relentless working of God to fulfill his divine plan to bring people of all nations to their knees at the <u>feet of Christ</u>.

> **what others say**
>
> **Billy Graham**
>
> As we have seen in this book, Pentecost was the day of power of the Holy Spirit. It was the day the Christian church was born. We do not expect that Pentecost will be repeated any more than that Jesus will die on the cross again. But we do expect pentecostal blessings when the conditions for God's moving are met, and especially as we approach "the latter days." We as Christians are to prepare the way. We are to be ready for the Spirit to fill and use us.[10]

## Chapter Wrap-Up

- Survivors of Paul's wrecked ship washed up on the island of Malta. Islanders were kind. Paul and Luke ministered to the sick. (Acts 28:1–10)

- Centurion Julius took prisoners and soldiers aboard an Egyptian ship from Malta to Puteoli. Two groups of Romans came to escort Paul to Rome. (Acts 28:11–15)

- In Rome Paul lived under house arrest. Leaders and members of the Jewish community came and listened to his message. Sharp division developed among them about Jesus. (Acts 28:16–27)

- Having given Jews first chance Paul then took the gospel to Gentiles. He remained under arrest and preached Christ without government hindrance. (Acts 28:28–31)

- Paul's ministry in Rome was effective. He wrote letters, directed apostolic teams, and won many to Christ. Luke ends his telling of the story of the early Christians as the "ends of the earth" phase of Christian witness was just getting under way. (Acts 1:8)

## Study Questions

1. When a poisonous snake bit Paul's hand what did the Maltese islanders think? What did they expect to happen to him? When it didn't, what did they conclude?

2. What did Paul mean when he quoted the verses from Isaiah 6:9–10 to the people who rejected Christ (Acts 28:25–27)?

3. With what note of triumph does Luke end his story of the early church's witness to the world in Acts 28:31?

4. Identify three or four things his New Testament letters reveal Paul accomplished in Rome in addition to what is reported in Acts 28.

# Appendix A – Time Line of Paul's Life

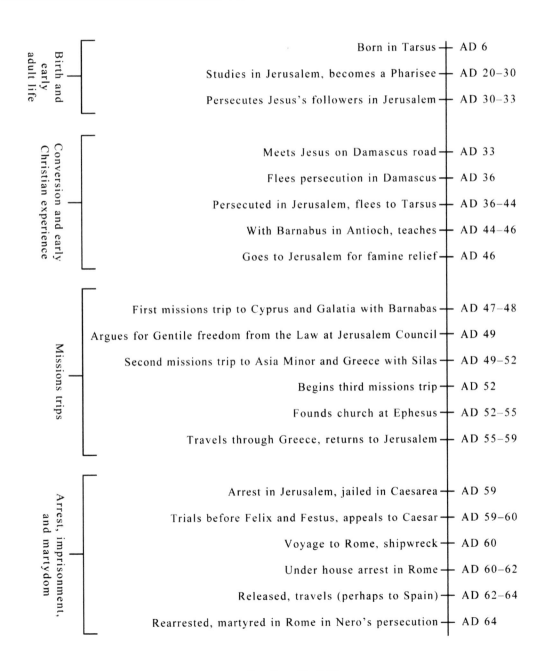

**Birth and early adult life**

| | |
|---|---|
| Born in Tarsus | AD 6 |
| Studies in Jerusalem, becomes a Pharisee | AD 20–30 |
| Persecutes Jesus's followers in Jerusalem | AD 30–33 |

**Conversion and early Christian experience**

| | |
|---|---|
| Meets Jesus on Damascus road | AD 33 |
| Flees persecution in Damascus | AD 36 |
| Persecuted in Jerusalem, flees to Tarsus | AD 36–44 |
| With Barnabus in Antioch, teaches | AD 44–46 |
| Goes to Jerusalem for famine relief | AD 46 |

**Missions trips**

| | |
|---|---|
| First missions trip to Cyprus and Galatia with Barnabas | AD 47–48 |
| Argues for Gentile freedom from the Law at Jerusalem Council | AD 49 |
| Second missions trip to Asia Minor and Greece with Silas | AD 49–52 |
| Begins third missions trip | AD 52 |
| Founds church at Ephesus | AD 52–55 |
| Travels through Greece, returns to Jerusalem | AD 55–59 |

**Arrest, imprisonment, and martydom**

| | |
|---|---|
| Arrest in Jerusalem, jailed in Caesarea | AD 59 |
| Trials before Felix and Festus, appeals to Caesar | AD 59–60 |
| Voyage to Rome, shipwreck | AD 60 |
| Under house arrest in Rome | AD 60–62 |
| Released, travels (perhaps to Spain) | AD 62–64 |
| Rearrested, martyred in Rome in Nero's persecution | AD 64 |

# Appendix B - The Answers

## CHAPTER 1: ACTS 1
## LIGHTING THE FUSE

1. Jesus got his power to teach and work from the Holy Spirit. (Acts 1:2)

2. Baptism with the Spirit changes a person into Christ's likeness (2 Corinthians 3:18); cleanses from sin (Acts 15:8); and fills with the Spirit's presence and character (Acts 2:4) by placing the person into the stream of Christ's resurrection life (Romans 8:2) and making him or her a member of Christ's body (1 Corinthians 12:13).

3. Major offensives in Jesus's strategy for world conquest call for Christians to be witnesses (1) in Jerusalem, (2) in Judea and Samaria, and (3) to the ends of the earth. (Acts 1:8)

4. The people in the upper room were constantly in prayer. (Acts 1:14)

5. Judas's replacement must be someone who (1) met the risen Jesus, (2) knew Jesus well by being with him during his earthly ministry, and (3) knew and could work with the other apostles (Acts 1:21–22). Joseph and Matthias met the qualifications (Acts 1:23).

6. After listening to the job description and qualifications, they prayed for the Lord to reveal his choice (Acts 1:24) and cast lots to see whom he had chosen (Acts 1:26).

## CHAPTER 2: ACTS 2
## FIREWORKS AT THE FIESTA

1. When the Spirit came, the disciples heard wind (Acts 2:2) and saw fire (Acts 2:3). They were filled with the Spirit and enabled to speak new languages (Acts 2:4).

2. The gift of tongues is the ability, given by the Holy Spirit, to speak a language one was unable to speak before (Acts 2:6, 11). It allowed communication with people who otherwise could not have understood their message (Acts 2:5–11). In new languages they communicated God's wonders (Acts 2:11). Reactions included bewilder-

ment (Acts 2:6), amazement (Acts 2:7, 12), questions (Acts 2:7–8, 12), perplexity (Acts 2:12), discussion (Acts 2:12), ridicule (Acts 2:13), and slander (Acts 2:13). More information on speaking in tongues is found in 1 Corinthians 12–14.

3. The Resurrection proves Jesus is Lord and Christ. (Acts 2:36)

4. The gift of the Holy Spirit is given to all who respond to the invitation to repent, declare faith in Jesus (baptism is a sign of faith), and receive forgiveness of sins.

5. Early believers devoted themselves to (1) apostles' teaching, (2) fellowship, (3) bread breaking (sharing meals and the Lord's Supper), and (4) prayer. (Acts 2:42)

6. Early believers expressed oneness and love by making available everything they had to meet each other's needs (Acts 2:44). If they had nothing to give, they sold something and gave the proceeds (Acts 2:45).

7. Luke reports, "The Lord added to the church daily" (Acts 2:47 NKJV).

## CHAPTER 3: ACTS 3–4
## SETTING THE WOODS ON FIRE

1. The man at the Beautiful Gate asked for money (Acts 3:3). Peter and John gave him healing (verses 6–8). The power to heal came through faith in Jesus's name (verse 16).

2. To act "in Jesus's name" means to act under authority from Jesus; consistent with his person, character, goals, values, and instructions; with motives and desires in harmony with his motives, desires, and will. (John 14:12–14, 26; 16:23–24; 1 John 5:14–15)

3. Two reasons given in Acts 4:2 for the arrest of Peter and John are (1) they taught the people, and (2) they proclaimed Jesus's resurrection. Sadducees wanted to stop the Resurrection teaching because they didn't believe in the Resurrection (Luke 20:27).

4. When Peter and John were ordered not to teach in Jesus's name, they insisted (1) they had to do what was right in God's sight, and (2) they could not help telling what they had seen. (Acts 4:19–20)

5. Jerusalem Christians demonstrated love and solidarity by (1) considering their material possessions as belonging to the community of believers, (2) sharing what they had, (3) selling property and houses to get money for distribution to the needy (Acts 4:32, 34–37). In this way (4) all known needs were met (verse 34).

## CHAPTER 4: ACTS 5
## THE PERFECT CHURCH—NOT!

1. Satan was behind Ananias and Sapphira's hypocrisy (Acts 5:3). They lied to the Holy Spirit, God (Acts 5:3–4). Giving was not demanded; Peter told Ananias the land belonged to him and the proceeds were his to do with as he pleased (Acts 5:4).

2. An "obvious" miracle is one in which natural laws seem to be suspended. Example: Opening the eyes of the blind (John 9:32), healing a lame man (Acts 3:6–8). A "hidden" miracle is one in which God shapes and uses natural events and processes to accomplish his purposes (Romans 8:28; Acts 2:5, 44–47; 4:32, 34).

3. Facts about Christian healing ministry observed in Acts 5:12–16 include these: (1) Like Jesus, they gave healing high priority. (2) Ministry to the sick was evidence of God's power at work (Acts 5:12). (3) Healings were done through the apostles (Acts 5:12) and others (Acts 5:16). (4) Healing ministry makes the church attractive (Acts 5:16).

4. The priests were jealous because of crowds coming to the apostles (Acts 5:16–17). An angel of the Lord let them out of jail (Acts 5:19). They went directly to the Temple and started preaching Jesus again, as the angel had instructed them to do (Acts 5:21).

5. A Pharisee named Gamaliel spoke in favor of letting the apostles go (Acts 5:34–39). His fellow teachers called him "The Beauty of the Law."

6. The apostles rejoiced because they'd been "counted worthy to suffer shame" for Jesus (Acts 5:41 NKJV).

## CHAPTER 5: ACTS 6–7
## A TEMPLE TO DIE FOR

1. Qualifications for people caring for the poor were being well known, being full of the Holy Spirit, and being wise. (Acts 6:3)

2. Christian beliefs were twisted to form charges against Stephen: (1) The Temple isn't the only place people can meet God (John 4:23–24; Matthew 18:20). (2) The Law and Temple are fulfilled (fully understood) in Christ (Matthew 5:17). (3) The Holy Spirit writes God's laws on people's minds and hearts (Hebrews 8:10; 10:16). (4) God's grace is not exclusively for Jews, but also for Gentiles (Matthew 28:19; Acts 2:39).

3. Stephen said his accusers were guilty of persistent resistance against the Holy Spirit (Acts 7:51); persecution and martyrdom of the prophets (Acts 7:52); betrayal and murder of the Messiah (Acts 7:52); and disobedience of the Law they claimed to defend (Acts 7:53).

4. As he died Stephen prayed, "Lord Jesus, receive my spirit" (Acts 7:59 NKJV) and "Lord, do not charge them with this sin" (Acts 7:60 NKJV). As he died Jesus prayed, "Father, into Your hands I commit My spirit" (Luke 23:46 NKJV) and "Father, forgive them" (Luke 23:34 NKJV).

## CHAPTER 6: ACTS 8  SCATTERGUN!

1. God used Saul's persecution to get Christians to take Christ to Judea and Samaria. (Acts 8:1, 4)

2. Crowds heard Philip preach and saw his miracles. Many believed in Jesus and were baptized. His most notable "convert" was Simon the magician. (Acts 8:5–13)

3. Three things that were different were (1) the apostles prayed for them (Acts 8:15); (2) the delay between believing in Jesus and receiving the Spirit (Acts 8:16); and (3) the need for the apostles to lay hands on them when the Spirit was given (Acts 8:17). It was important for the apostles to be there (1) to assure the Samaritans they were accepted; (2) to demonstrate the apostles' authority; (3) to assure Jewish Christians that Samaritans were true followers of Christ.

4. Simon was confused about (1) God's grace—he thought he could buy it (Acts 8:18–20); (2) power— the difference between magic and the Holy Spirit's power; (3) ministry—he saw it as showmanship (Acts 8:21); and (4) the purpose of the Spirit's work—he saw it as a means of personal gain.

## CHAPTER 7: ACTS 9
## U-TURN ON STRAIGHT STREET

1. Jesus confronted Saul with the question: "Why are you persecuting Me?" (Acts 9:4 NKJV). The spiritual principle revealed by the question is that Jesus and his followers are one—to persecute Jesus's followers is to persecute Jesus.

2. The five spiritual processes involved in Saul's spiritual reconstruction/conversion were these: (1) personal encounter with Jesus; (2) forgiveness by Jesus and others for the harm he'd done to Christians (Acts 9:17); (3) filling with the Spirit (Acts 9:17); (4) baptism (Acts 9:18); and (5) commissioning as Christ's ambassador (Acts 9:15).

3. At first Saul was rejected because the Jerusalem believers thought Saul's conversion was a new attempt to infiltrate their group. Barnabas listened to Saul's story, believed him, and introduced him to the others. (Acts 9:26–27)

4. As a result of Peter's healing of Aeneas and raising of Tabitha, many people in and around Lydda and Joppa heard the gospel and believed in Jesus. (Acts 9:35, 42)

## CHAPTER 8: ACTS 10–11
## PETER GOES WALL CRASHING

1. In his vision Peter saw a sheet containing animals he believed were unclean. The voice told him to "kill and eat" the so-called unclean animals. When he protested the voice said: "Do not call anything impure that God has made clean." (Acts 10:11–15)

2. To show his change of mind, Peter (1) welcomed the Gentiles (Acts 10:23); (2) returned to Caesarea with them, no questions asked (Acts 10:23, 29); (3) entered the house of the Gentile Cornelius (Acts 10:25, 27); (4) confessed his change of mind (Acts 10:28–29); and (5) declared the gospel's inclusiveness (Acts 10:34–35).

3. Witnesses who went to Antioch shared the good news about Jesus with Gentiles. (Acts 11:20)

4. Barnabas's ministry accomplished four things: (1) affirmed God's work (Acts 11:23); (2) introduced people to Jesus (Acts 11:24); (3) linked him up with Saul (Acts 11:25–26); and (4) discipled (trained and taught) new converts (Acts 11:26).

5. Visible proofs of grace that may have caused Antiochenes to call disciples "Christians" include (1) willingness to cross racial, cultural, and social barriers to share Christ (Acts 11:20); (2) unity based on accommodation to each other's differences; (3) eagerness to grow (Acts 11:26); and (4) generosity (Acts 11:18–30).

## CHAPTER 9: ACTS 12  KING OF HOT AIR
## AND MAGGOTS

1. James was put to death "with the sword" (beheaded) (Acts 12:2). This persecution was different because it was the first attack on the church by a secular government.

2. To get Peter out of jail, the church got together and prayed (Acts 12:5). Groups met at members' homes; one prayer group met at Mary's house (Acts 12:12).

3. In response to their prayers, an angel was sent to Peter to wake him up and lead him to freedom (Acts 12:6–10). The real power is in the hands of God, the Lord of the church, who can overrule the plans and orders of kings and governments.

4. When Rhoda said Peter was at the door she got two responses: (1) You're crazy! (2) It's his angel (Acts 12:15). What their responses reveal about their prayers is that they prayed and God answered even though their prayers and faith were not perfect or doubt-free.

5. Herod Agrippa's fraudulence was revealed when he let the Phoenicians call him a god. (Acts 12:22–23)

## CHAPTER 10: ACTS 13–14
## WORLD AMBASSADORS

1. Two types of ministry used by the shepherds (pastors) of Antioch were prophecy and teaching: prophecy is communicating God's message; teaching is explaining the meaning and application of God's message. (Acts 13:1)

2. When they got together, the prophets and teachers worshiped the Lord and fasted. While they were together the Holy Spirit told them to set Barnabas and Saul apart for a wider mission. (Acts 13:2)

3. Paul told the sorcerer (1) he was a child of the devil; (2) he was an enemy of all that is right; (3) he was full of deceit; (4) he always made right seem wrong and wrong seem right; and (5) the Lord was against him. (Acts 13:10–11)

4. After the lame man's healing, the people of Lystra thought Barnabas and Paul were the pagan gods Zeus and Hermes (Acts 14:11–12). To show they were human the apostles tore their clothes and went into the crowd so they could be seen up close (Acts 14:14–15).

5. A testimony to God's reality and kindness that all humans can see is the natural world—rain, sunshine, seasons, crops, supply of food, and things that give joy. (Acts 14:17)

## CHAPTER 11: ACTS 15  OUTSIDERS CRASH
## THE CHRISTIAN PARTY

1. When the legalistic teachers came to Antioch, Paul and Barnabas debated them (Acts 15:2). The controversy was about whether people are saved by faith or by keeping religious laws (Galatians 2:15–16).

2. The six points Peter stressed were these: (1) God initiated the outreach to the Gentiles (Acts 15:7). (2) God verified his acceptance by giving them the Holy Spirit (Acts 15:8). (3) God makes no distinction between Jews and Gentiles, purifying the hearts of both by faith (Acts 15:9). (4) Laying law on people God has accepted amounts to questioning God (Acts 15:10). (5) If the Law is an impossible burden to Jews, it makes no sense to expect Gentiles to live by it (Acts 15:10). (6) The law never saved anyone—both Jews and Gentiles are saved through grace (Acts 15:11).

3. James was convinced the Gentiles should be accepted because of (1) God's actions (Acts 15:14), and (2) God's Word (Acts 15:15–18).

4. Two accommodations Gentiles were asked to make in order to make fellowship with their Jewish brothers easier were these: (1) Don't serve food that has been offered to idols before being sold in the market. (2) Don't serve meat that has not been properly bled. (Acts 15:20)

5. The issue that led to the breakup of Paul and Barnabas was whether or not John Mark should accompany them on their next missionary journey.

### CHAPTER 12: ACTS 16 JAILHOUSE ROCK

1. Four "higher principles" that guided Paul are (1) personal obedience to Christ (2 Corinthians 10:5); (2) living by the spirit, not the letter of the Law (2 Corinthians 3:6); (3) accommodation on nonessentials (1 Corinthians 9:19–23); and (4) love (1 Corinthians 13:4–8).

2. Two reasons Tim submitted to "the surgery" were (1) to assure Jews that following Christ didn't mean to stop being Jewish, and (2) to assure credibility with Jews.

3. Paul and the team were convinced by a vision that going to Macedonia was God's will (Acts 16:9–10). Luke joined the team. We know because he, as author, uses first person pronouns "we" and "us" when describing team movements (Acts 16:10–12).

4. Three whose stories are in Acts 16 are (1) Lydia, a wealthy businesswoman trading in purple cloth (Acts 16:14–15); (2) the demon-possessed girl who was a fortune-teller and slave (Acts 16:16); and (3) the jailer who was a middle-class Roman soldier (Acts 16:23–34).

5. Paul and Silas answered, "Believe on the Lord Jesus Christ, and you will be saved, you and your household" (Acts 16:31 NKJV). As proof of his conversion (Acts 16:33–34), the jailer (1) made amends, washing their wounds; (2) was baptized

with his family; (3) shared table fellowship with Paul and Silas; and (4) experienced joy.

### CHAPTER 13: ACTS 17 JUNKYARD OF THE GODS

1. Thessalonian enemies accused Christians of (1) causing trouble, (2) defying Caesar's decrees, and (3) promoting a king to replace Caesar. (Acts 17:6–7)

2. In contrast to others, the Bereans eagerly received the message and studied the Scriptures to see if the message was true. (Acts 17:11)

3. Paul's starting place in his Mars Hill speech was the altar "To an Unknown God" (Acts 17:23).

4. The statements from Paul's Mars Hill speech are as follows:

    a. People are dependent on God for "life, breath, and all things" (Acts 17:25).

    b. God is "not far from each one of us" (Acts 17:27).

    c. "In Him we live and move and have our being" (Acts 17:28).

    d. "We are also His offspring" (Acts 17:28).

5. Areopagus members sneered when Paul mentioned the Resurrection. (Acts 17:32)

### CHAPTER 14: ACTS 18 SIN CITY SAINTS

1. In Corinth Paul linked up with Aquila and Priscilla (Acts 18:2). They were tentmakers, Jews, and Christians (Acts 18:2–3).

2. Paul went to the home of Titius Justus, next door to the synagogue, to continue preaching. Crispus, synagogue president, believed and followed Christ, along with his entire family. Many Corinthians believed and were baptized. (Acts 18:7–8)

3. The three reasons the Lord gave Paul for staying in Corinth and continuing to preach were (1) the Lord was with him, (2) the Lord would protect him, and (3) the Lord had people in Corinth who would respond to the message. (Acts 18:9–10)

4. Apollos was influenced and helped by Aquila and Priscilla. He was a good orator, comfortable in public debates. (Acts 18:25, 28)

### CHAPTER 15: ACTS 19 FREEDOM AND FURY IN THE CITY OF THE NO-GODS

1. Missing elements in the faith and spiritual experience of the "Ephesian twelve": They had not heard of the Holy Spirit, so they had not received him. (Acts 19:2)

2. Paul stopped teaching at the synagogue when people became obstinate, refused to believe his message, and slammed the Christian way of life (Acts 19:9). During the two years he taught at Tyranus's hall, "all who dwelt in Asia heard the word of the Lord" (Acts 19:10 NKJV).

3. The new Christians at Ephesus broke free from their superstitious ways and demonstrated commitment to Christ by burning their occult and magic books (Acts 19:17–19). Result: The "word of the Lord grew mightily and prevailed" (Acts 19:20 NKJV).

4. Demetrius and the silversmiths were angry because the number of people turning to Christ was depleting the profits of their Diane trinket business (Acts 19:23–27). They represent people today who oppose spirituality, morality, and justice when profit margins are threatened—the "idolatry of the bottom line."

## CHAPTER 16: ACTS 20 THE VULNERABLE AMBASSADOR

1. Five characteristics of the church meeting at Troas were (1) they met on Sunday, (2) they ate together, (3) they met at night, (4) they met in a third-floor room, and (5) the length of the meeting was not regulated by the clock. (Acts 20:7–11)

2. A young man named Eutychus fell asleep and fell out the window. (Acts 20:9)

3. The three "titles" for local church leaders mentioned in Acts 20 are (1) elders (Acts 20:17)—emphasizes the need for leaders to be spiritually mature; (2) overseers (Acts 20:28)—emphasizes their role as guides and protectors; and (3) shepherds (Acts 20:28)—emphasizes leaders' role as caregivers.

4. The "final answer" to the $1,000 question: d. The Holy Spirit (Acts 20:28). The "final answer" to the $10,000 question: c. God, because he shed his blood (Acts 20:28). The "final answer" to the $100,000 question: a. Be on guard, and d. Warn people of the danger (Acts 20:31).

## CHAPTER 17: ACTS 21:1–22:29 STARING DOWN DANGER

1. Agabus bound his own hands and feet with Paul's belt and said, "So shall the Jews at Jerusalem bind the man who owns this belt" (Acts 21:11 NKJV). The Holy Spirit revealed this to him. Paul's friends begged him not to go to Jerusalem, but the prophecy only strengthened Paul's determination to go (Acts 21:12–14).

2. The elders asked Paul to join the purification rites of four men (Acts 21:21–25). The main reason

he agreed was his "theology of accommodation"—his personal commitment to adapt to the preferences and desires of both Jews and Gentiles to remove barriers to the gospel so he could win them to Christ (1 Corinthians 9:19–23).

3. Paul's three main points were these: (1) Who I was; (2) how I met Jesus; and (3) how my life has changed since I met Jesus.

4. Changes in Paul's life after his encounter with Christ were these: (1) Jesus met him when he prayed (Acts 22:17–18). (2) The Lord was leading him (Acts 22:18, 21). (3) He could be honest about his sins (Acts 22:19–20). (4) He discovered the Lord was not concerned about his past but about his present and future (Acts 22:21). (5) He was able to tell people about God's grace (Acts 22:21).

## CHAPTER 18: ACTS 22:30–23:35 PAUL'S TICKET TO RIDE

1. In his response to Ananias's order to hit him in the mouth, Paul (1) accused Ananias of breaking the law (Acts 23:3); (2) called him a fake—a "whitewashed wall" (Acts 23:3); (3) refused to recognize him as legitimate high priest (Acts 23:5); and (4) prophesied that God would strike him (Acts 23:3).

2. Paul's mention of the Resurrection threw the Sanhedrin into turmoil because Pharisees believed in it and Sadducees did not. What upsets people about the Resurrection is that it reveals things about Jesus that make him difficult to ignore. (Romans 1:4)

3. According to Acts, the Resurrection reveals (1) Jesus is Lord and Christ (Acts 2:24–36); (2) his name heals (Acts 3:15–16); (3) salvation is in him (Acts 4:10–12); (4) he is Prince and Savior (Acts 5:29–32); (5) he forgives sins and puts people right with God (Acts 13:37–39); and (6) he is God's appointed judge (Acts 17:31).

4. Jesus's visit (Acts 23:11) reassured Paul that (1) the Lord was with him; (2) Paul had accomplished what he came to Jerusalem to do—testify about Jesus to the people of Israel; (3) Paul would witness in Rome; and (4) Paul would leave Jerusalem alive.

## CHAPTER 19: ACTS 24–26 CHRIST'S AMBASSADOR ON TRIAL

1. In the trial before Felix (Acts 24:5–7), Tertullus accused Paul of (1) being a troublemaker; (2) being ringleader of the Nazarene sect; and (3) violating the Temple (Acts 21:28). Before Festus they also said Paul violated Caesar's decrees (Acts 25:8).

2. On trial before Felix, two reasons Paul gave for coming to Jerusalem were (1) to bring gifts to the poor, and (2) to present "offerings" (Acts 24:17). When the crowd attacked him, he was participating in a cleansing ceremony (Acts 24:18).

3. Four things Jesus does for people (Acts 26:18) are (1) opens their eyes, (2) turns them from darkness to light, (3) transfers them from the power of Satan to God, and (4) gives them forgiveness of sins and a share with the sanctified (holy, special to God).

4. Festus said Paul was insane when he insisted that Jesus rose from the dead (Acts 26:23). Paul said King Agrippa believed the prophets (Acts 26:27).

5. The wisecrack Agrippa used to avoid answering Paul's question about believing in the prophets was, "You almost persuade me to become a Christian?" (Acts 26:28 NKJV).

## CHAPTER 20: ACTS 27
## DANGEROUS PASSAGE

1. Two Christians who accompanied Paul to Rome were Luke (note "we" in Acts 27:1–2), and Aristarchus (Acts 27:2). Luke and Aristarchus may have gone as Paul's slaves.

2. Sailing was difficult because "the winds were contrary" (Acts 27:4 NKJV). They reached Fair Havens after the Fast (Acts 27:9)—after Yom Kippur, the Day of Atonement, October 5, AD 59. The owner and pilot decided to sail on to Phoenix because accommodations were better there for spending the winter (Acts 27:11–12).

3. The angel (1) reminded Paul of God's promise that he would testify for Jesus in Rome, (2) revealed that the ship would be lost, but (3) no one traveling with Paul would die in the shipwreck. (Acts 27:21–26)

4. When sailors tried to escape, Paul told the centurion they had to stay on board if everyone was going to be saved (Acts 27:30–32). When soldiers decided to kill the prisoners, the centurion stopped them. He wanted to spare Paul (Acts 27:42–43).

## CHAPTER 21: ACTS 28—
## THE UNCHAINED TRUTH

1. When the snake bit Paul, the Maltese thought he was a murderer getting justice (Acts 28:4). They expected him to die (Acts 28:5–6). When he didn't, they concluded he was a god (Acts 28:6).

2. By quoting from Isaiah (Acts 28:25–27) Paul said that people do not believe in Jesus Christ because they choose not to believe, deliberately close their eyes, ears, and hearts, and harden themselves

against the truth about themselves and God's plan for their spiritual healing.

3. Luke's final note of triumph is to tell of Paul's bold, unhindered preaching of the kingdom of God and teaching about the Lord Jesus Christ. (Acts 28:31)

4. Paul's letters reveal that, in Rome, in addition to what is reported in Acts 28, Paul (1) wrote New Testament letters (Philippians, Ephesians, Colossians, and Philemon); (2) directed a team of Christian workers (Acts 27:1–2; Philippians 1:1; 4:18; Colossians 1:1; 4:10; 2 Timothy 4:11; Philemon 1; Ephesians 6:21); (3) personally introduced people to Jesus (Philippians 1:13–14; 4:22); and (4) witnessed to Caesar (Acts 27:23–24; 2 Timothy 4:16–17).

# ENDNOTES

## Chapter 1: Acts 1—Lighting the Fuse

1. Flavius Josephus, *The Wars of the Jews*, 7 vols. of *The Works of Flavius Josephus*, translated by William Whiston (Grand Rapids, MI: Associated Publishers & Authors, n.d.).

2. Maude De Joseph West, *Saints in Sandals* (Grand Rapids, MI: Baker, 1975), 9.

3. William Barclay, *The Gospel of Luke* (Philadelphia: Westminster, 1956), 2.

4. Ben Wirthington III, "Primary Sources," *Christian History* 17, no. 3 (issue 59): 18.

5. Howard A. Snyder, *Community of the King* (Downers Grove, IL: InterVarsity, 1977), 12.

6. Billy Graham, *The Holy Spirit: Activating God's Power in Your Life* (Nashville: W Publishing Group, 1976), 32.

7. F. F. Bruce, *The New International Commentary on the New Testament: The Book of Acts* (Grand Rapids, MI: Eerdmans, 1988), 36.

8. Graham, *The Holy Spirit*, 14.

9. William Barclay, *The Acts of the Apostles* (Philadelphia: Westminster, 1975), 11.

10. Snyder, *Community of the King*, 16–17.

11. I. Howard Marshall, *The Acts of the Apostles* (Grand Rapids, MI: Eerdmans, 1980), 62.

12. Sue Monk Kidd, "Learning to Wait on God: Prayer," *Daily Guideposts*, 1989 (Carmel, NY: Guideposts, 1988), 131.

13. Eugene Peterson, *The Message* (Colorado Springs, CO: NavPress, 1993), 210.

14. Lawrence O. Richards, *Victor Bible Background Commentary: New Testament* (Wheaton, IL: Victor, 1994), 280.

## Chapter 2: Acts 2—God's Promise to the Jewish Believers

1. Michael Card, *Immanuel: Reflections on the Life of Christ* (Nashville, TN: Thomas Nelson, 1990), 24.

2. Graham, *The Holy Spirit*, 45.

3. Richards, *Victor Background Commentary*, 280.

4. Dallas Willard, *The Divine Conspiracy* (San Francisco: Harper, 1998), 279.

5. Paul Tournier, *The Person Reborn* (New York: Harper & Row, 1966), 4.

6. Cyril of Jerusalem, quoted in *Crosspoint* 12, no. 3 (fall 1999): 16.

7. Kilian McDonnell, "The Spirit and the Believer," *Crosspoint* 12, no. 13 (fall 1999): 17.

8. Graham, *The Holy Spirit*, 140–141.

9. Krister Stendahl, "Come Holy Spirit—Renew the Whole Creation," *Crosspoint* 12, no. 3 (fall 1999), 13–14.

10. Watchman Nee, *A Table in the Wilderness* (Wheaton, IL: Tyndale, 1965), reading for January 16.

11. Barclay, *Acts*, 26–27.

12. George MacDonald, quoted in *NRSV Classics Bible* (Grand Rapids, MI: Zondervan, 1996), 1273.

13. J. Gresham Machen, *The Christian Faith in the Modern World* (Grand Rapids, MI: Eerdmans, 1947), 63.

14. Bruce, *Acts*, 69.

15. Liddell & Scott, *Greek-English Lexicon* (London: Oxford/ Clarendon, 1944), 607.

16. Tertullian, *Apologeticus*, quoted in Philip Schaff, *The History of the Christian Church*, vol. 2: *Anti-Nicene Christianity* (Grand Rapids, MI: AP & A, n.d.), 167.

17. Lawrence O. Richards, *A Theology of Christian Education* (Grand Rapids, MI: Zondervan, 1975), 30.

18. Sherwood Wirt, *Afterglow* (Grand Rapids, MI: Zondervan, 1975), 82.

19. Tertullian, *Apology*, chapter 39, quoted in *Crosspoint* 13, no. 2 (fall 2000): 27.

20. Jim Wallis, *Agenda for Biblical People* (San Francisco: Harper & Row, 1984), 65.

21. Snyder, *Community of the King*, 124–125.

**Chapter 3: Acts 3–4—Fresh Enthusiasm for the Ancient Faith**

1. *The Revell Bible Dictionary* (Old Tappan, NJ: Revell, 1990), 142.

.2. Richard C. Halverson, *Relevance: The Role of Christianity in the Twentieth Century* (Waco, TX: Word, 1968), 87–88.

3. Bruce, *Acts*, 82.

4. Walter Wangerin, *The Book of God* (Grand Rapids, MI: Zondervan, 1996), 847.

5. Peterson, *The Message*, 214.

6. Nee, *Table*, October 14.

7. John R. W. Stott, *The Cross of Christ* (Downer's Grove, IL: InterVarsity, 1986), 59–60.

8. C. J. Klausner, *From Jesus to Paul* (London: Allen & Unwin, 1944), 282–283.

9. Peterson, *The Message*, 215.

10. Barclay, *Acts*, 42.

11. West, *Saints in Sandals*, 34.

12. Ronald J. Sider, *Rich Christians in an Age of Hunger* (Downer's Grove, IL: InterVarsity, 1977), 103.

13. Wallis, *Agenda for Biblical People*, 71.

14. Graham, *The Holy Spirit*, 282.

**Chapter 4: Acts 5—The Perfect Church—Not!**

1. Charles Colson, *The Body: Being Light in Darkness* (Dallas: Word, 1992), 130.

2. Barclay, *Acts*, 44–45.

3. Graham, *The Holy Spirit*, 298.

4. Peterson, *The Message*, 216.

5. Colson, *The Body*, 382–384.

6. Richards, *Bible Background Commentary*, 288.

7. Ibid., 289.

8. Peterson, *The Message*, 217.

9. J. A. Findlay, quoted in Bruce, *Acts*, 115.

10. Bruce, *Acts*, 117–118.

11. West, *Saints in Sandals*, 44.

**Chapter 5: Acts 6–7—Opposition Adds Fuel to Faith's Fire**

1. Gene Edwards, *The Early Church* (Goleta, CA: Christian Books, 1974), 69.

2. Richards, *Background Commentary*, 291.

3. Keith Miller, *A Second Touch* (Waco, TX: Word, 1967), 154.

4. Sherwood Eliot Wirt, *Jesus, Man of Joy* (Nashville, TN: Nelson, 1991), 71.

5. Peterson, *The Message*, 218.

6. Ibid.

7. Billy Graham, *Peace with God* (Nashville: W Publishing Group, 2000), 204.

8. Barclay, *Acts*, 52.

9. Colson, *The Body*, 114, 116.

10. Bruce, *Acts*, 135.

11. Festo Kivengere, "Love Triumphs in Suffering," *Crosspoint* 13, no. 2 (fall 2000): 17.

**Chapter 6: Acts 8—Scattergun!**

1. Bruce, *Acts*, 161.

2. Barclay, *Acts*, 63.

3. Everett Ferguson, "Did You Know," *Christian History* 9, no. 3 (issue 27): inside front cover.

4. Halley, *Bible Handbook*, 465.

5. Robert E. Coleman, *The Master Plan of Evangelism* (Old Tappan, NJ: Revell, 1964), 102–103.

6. Graham, *The Holy Spirit*, 318.

7. Barclay, *Acts*, 141.

8. Audrey I. Girard, from her unpublished journals.

9. Bruce, *Acts*, 170.

10. Acts 8:20, J. B. Phillips, *The New Testament in Modern English* (New York: Macmillan, 1972), 250.

11. Bruce, *Acts*, 166, citing Justin Martyr and Tertullian.

12. Nee, *Table*, June 26.

13. Barclay, *Acts*, 69.

**Chapter 7: Acts 9—Saul's Astonishment at Christians' Joy**

1. Kivengere, "Love Triumphs in Suffering," 17.

2. *Acts of Paul*, quoted in Stephen M. Miller, "Bald, Blind, and Single?" *Christian History* 14, no. 3 (issue 47): 33.

3. Price, *Learning to Live*, 65.

4. Barclay, *Acts*, 71.

5. John R. W. Stott, *Basic Christianity* (Grand Rapids, MI: Eerdmans, 1998), 125–126.

6. Barclay, *Acts*, 71.

7. Ibid., 72.

8. Billy Graham, *How to Be Born Again* (Waco, TX: Word, 1977), 162–163, 165–166.

9. Basilea Schlink, *Ruled by the Spirit* (London: Oliphants, 1969), 50–51.

10. Ajith Fernando, *NIV Application Commentary:*

*Acts* (Grand Rapids, MI: Zondervan, 1998), 311.

## Chapter 8: Acts 10–11—Challenging Phase of the New Revolution

1. Barclay, *Acts*, 79.
2. West, *Saints in Sandals*, 80.
3. John Kennedy, *The Torch of the Testimony* (Bombay: Gospel Literature Service, 1965), 3–4.
4. *The Analytical Greek Lexicon* (Grand Rapids, MI: Zondervan, 1970), 147.
5. Richards, *Background Commentary*, 290.
6. *Revell Bible Dictionary*, 228.
7. Schlink, *Ruled by the Spirit*, 115.
8. Bruce, *Acts*, 217.
9. *Good News Bible: The Bible in Today's English Version* (New York: American Bible Society, 1976), Acts 11:2.
10. Edwards, *The Early Church*, 162.
11. Ibid., 167–168.
12. *Revell Bible Dictionary*, 450.
13. West, Saints in Sandals, 92.

## Chapter 9: Acts 12—King of Hot Air and Maggots

1. Mrs. Howard Taylor, *The Triumph of John and Betty Stam* (Chicago: Moody, 1935), 136.
2. James Reapsome, *Evangelical Mission Information Service*, "Persecuted Christians Today," 37.
3. Samuel Rutherford, quoted in Billy Graham, *Till Armageddon: A Perspective on Suffering* (Waco, TX: Word, 1981), 115.
4. Graham, *Till Armageddon* 108, 110.
5. Vegetius, *On Military Affairs*, quoted in Bruce, Acts, 234.
6. Barclay, *Acts*, 94.
7. Paul Billheimer, *Destined for the Throne* (Ft. Washington, PA: Christian Literature Crusade, 1975), 52.
8. Charles Wesley, from the hymn, "And Can It Be?"
9. Peterson, *The Message*, 231.
10. Nee, *Table*, February 25.
11. Bruce, *Acts*, 237.
12. Flavius Josephus, *Antiquities of the Jews*, Book 19, 8:2.
13. West, *Saints in Sandals*, 102–103.

## Chapter 10: Acts 13–14—World Ambassadors

1. Oswald Chambers, *My Utmost for His Highest* (Grand Rapids, MI: Discovery House, 1963), 290.
2. Edwin M. Yamauchi, "How Far Did Paul Travel?" *Christian History* 14, no. 3 (issue 47): 18.
3. Peterson, *The Message*, Acts 13:8.
4. Bede, *Commentary on Acts*, quoted in Bruce, Acts, 249.
5. Graham, *The Holy Spirit*, 294.
6. Wangerin, *Book of God*, 848.
7. Barclay, *Acts*, 100–101.
8. J. R. Dumelow, *Commentary on the Holy Bible* (New York: Macmillan, 1923), 836.
9. Oswald Chambers, *So Send I You* (Ft. Washington, PA: Christian Literature Crusade, 1930), 163.
10. Barclay, *Acts*, 110.
11. Billheimer, Destined, 133.

## Chapter 11: Acts 15—Outsiders Crash the Christian Party

1. Marshall, *Acts*, 249.
2. Peterson, *The Message*, 237.
3. Barclay, *Acts*, 114–115.
4. Ibid., 115.
5. Bruce, *Acts*, 296 (footnote).
6. West, *Saints in Sandals*, 133.
7. Richards, *Background Commentary*, 302.
8. Marshall, *Acts*, 249.
9. Larry Richards, *Bible Difficulties Solved* (Grand Rapids, MI: Revell, 1993), 323.

## Chapter 12: Acts 16—Penetration into the Roman World

1. R. W. Emerson, "Essay on Self-Reliance," *Essays, Lectures and Orations* (London: n. p., 1848), quoted in Bruce, *Acts*, 304.
2. Barclay, *Acts*, 114–115.
3. Fernando, *Acts*, 433 n. 11.
4. Bruce, *Acts*, 308.
5. Fernando, *Acts*, 433.
6. Pollock, *Apostle*, 124.
7. Barclay, *Acts*, 124.
8. *Christian History* 7, no. 3 (issue 19): 37.
9. Barclay, *Acts*, 127.

10. Richards, *Background Commentary*, 307.

11. Howard Marshall, "Acts," in *Eerdmans Handbook to the Bible*, ed. David and Pat Alexander (Grand Rapids, MI: Eerdmans, 1973), 561.

### Chapter 13: Acts 17—Junkyard of the Gods

1. J. B. Phillips, *The New Testament in Modern English* (New York: Macmillan, 1972).

2. Marshall, "Acts," 562.

3. Barclay, *Acts*, 127.

4. Bruce, *Acts*, 323.

5. Billy Graham, *The Jesus Generation* (Grand Rapids, MI: Zondervan, 1971), 117–118.

6. Calvin Miller, *The Singer* (Downer's Grove, IL: InterVarsity, 1975), 106.

7. *Revell Bible Dictionary*, 510.

8. Marshall, "Acts," 562.

9. Digenes Laertius, *The Lives of Eminent Philosophers* vol. 1, 110; Plato, *Laws*; Aristotle, *The Art of Rhetoric* (Book 3, 17:10); quoted in Richardson, *Eternity in Their Hearts*, 14–21.

10. Don Richardson, *Eternity in Their Hearts* (Ventura, CA: Regal, 1981), 24.

11. Bruce, *Acts*, 337.

12. Peterson, *Message*, 243.

13. Epimenides, quoted in Richards, *Background Commentary*, 308.

14. Michael Green, "Early Christian Preaching," *Eerdmans Handbook*, 555.

15. Bruce, Acts, 343.

16. West, *Saints in Sandals*, 163.

17. John Pollock, *Apostle*, 155.

### Chapter 14: Acts 18—Sin City Saints

1. Pollock, *Apostle*, 161–162.

2. Bruce, *Acts*, 346.

3. Ibid.

4. Bernard of Clairvaux, quoted in Richard Foster, *Celebration of Discipline* (San Francisco: Harper, 1978), 110.

5. Maria, in Rogers and Hammerstein's *The Sound of Music*.

6. Seneca, quoted in Barclay, *Acts*, 137.

7. Bruce, *Acts*, 354.

8. Barclay, *Acts*, 139.

9. Vickie Baker, Denver, Colorado, quoted in "The Quiet Heart," *Decision*, October 2000, 41.

### Chapter 15: Acts 19—Freedom and Fury in the City of the No-Gods

1. John Kennedy, *The Torch of the Testimony* (Bombay: Gospel Literature Service, 1965), 238.

2. Peterson, *The Message*, 245.

3. Graham, *The Holy Spirit*, 178–179.

4. Ibid., 143.

5. Bruce, *Acts*, 366.

6. Peterson, *The Message*, 245.

7. Richards, *Background Commentary*, 309.

8. Mark Galli, "Did You Know?" *Christian History* (issue 57): inside front cover.

9. Barclay, *Acts*, 147.

### Chapter 16: Acts 20—The Vulnerable Ambassador

1. Girard, from her unpublished journals.

2. Barclay, *Acts*, 148.

3. William G. Bixler, "How the Early Church Viewed Martyrs," *Christian History* 9, no. 3 (issue 27): 30.

4. Everett Ferguson, "Did You Know?" *Christian History* 9, no. 3 (issue 27): inside front cover.

5. John O. Gooch, *Christian History* 12, no. 1 (issue 37): 2.

6. Philip Yancey, *Christianity Today*, May 20, 1996, 80.

7. Audrey Girard, from the song "Reflection of Grace," *Adult Teaching Guide* (Wheaton, IL: Scripture Press, March-May 1997). Property of the composer: Audrey Girard, P.O. Box 5148, Lake Montezuma AZ 86342. All rights reserved.

8. Marshall, *Acts*, 333.

9. Lawrence O. Richards, *Expository Dictionary of Bible Words* (Grand Rapids, MI: Zondervan, 1985), 181.

10. Ruth Bell Graham, *Decision*, October 2000, 39.

### Chapter 17: Acts 21:1–22:29—Staring Down Danger

1. Fernando, *Acts*, 554–555.

2. Richards, *Background Commentary*, 312–313.

3. Dietrich Bonhoeffer, *The Cost of Discipleship*, quoted in Christian History (issue 32): 29.

4. Richards, *Background Commentary*, 213.

5. Graham, *Just as I Am*, 613–614.

6. Barclay, *Acts*, 156.

7. Bruce, *Acts*, 409.

8. Barclay, *Acts*, 157.

9. Peterson, *The Message*, 252.

10. Johnny Cash, quoted in Billy Graham, *How to Be Born Again*, 153.

11. Barclay, *Acts*, 162.

12. Stanley Hauerwas and William H. Willimon, *Resident Aliens: Life in the Christian Colony* (Nashville, TN: Abingdon, 1989), 12.

### Chapter 18: Acts 22:30–23:35—Paul Pleads "Not Guilty"

1. Barclay, *Acts*, 164.

2. Josephus, *Antiquities of the Jews* 20:206, quoted in Bruce, *Acts*, 425.

3. Barclay, *Acts*, 164.

4. Bruce, *Acts*, 426.

5. John McRay, "Stench, Pain, and Misery—Life in a Roman Prison," *Christian History* 14, no. 3 (issue 47): 14.

6. Billy Graham, "What Will You Do When Disaster Comes?" *Decision*, November 2000, 3.

7. Alford, *The New Testament for English Readers*, 806.

8. Bruce, *Acts*, 431.

9. Marshall, *Acts*, 368.

### Chapter 19: Acts 24–26—Christ's Ambassador on Trial

1. Tacitus, quoted in Bruce, *Acts*, 437.

2. Eugenia Price, *Learning to Live from the Acts*, 131.

3. Barclay, *Acts*, 175.

4. Simon Kistemaker, *New Testament Commentary: Exposition of the Acts of the Apostles* (Grand Rapids, MI: Baker, 1990), 884.

5. West, *Saints in Sandals*, 228.

6. Bruce, *Acts*, 467–468.

7. Billy Graham, *Till Armageddon: A Perspective on Suffering* (Waco, TX: Word, 1981), 200.

8. Richards, *Background Commentary*, 315.

9. Charles H. Spurgeon, "New Park Street Pulpit," vol. 4 (Pasadena, TX: Pilgrim Publications, 1970), quoted in "Life Lived on the Edge," *Decision*, October 2000, 40.

10. Peterson, *The Message*, 260.

11. Ibid.

12. Richards, *Background Commentary*, 317.

13. "Concerning the Word of Life," *Crosspoint* 13, no. 2 (summer 2000): 75.

### Chapter 20: Acts 27—Dangerous Passage

1. Bruce, *Acts*, 474.

2. James Smith, *The Voyage and Shipwreck of St. Paul* (London: Longmans, Green, 1848, 1880), quoted in E. F. Harrison, *The Acts of the Apostles: A Commentary* (Philadelphia: Westminster, 1971), 412.

3. Ewin M. Yamauchi, "On the Road with Paul," *Christian History* 14, no. 3 (issue 47): 18.

4. W. M. Ramsay, *St. Paul the Traveler*, quoted in Bruce, Acts, 477–478.

5. Smith, *Voyage and Shipwreck*, 102.

6. Bruce, *Acts*, 485.

7. Marshall, *Acts*, 408–409.

8. Bruce, *Acts*, 486.

9. Billy Graham, *Hope for the Troubled Heart* (Minneapolis: Grason, 1991), 177.

10. Bruce, *Acts*, 489–490.

11. Smith, *Voyage and Shipwreck*, 121.

12. Bruce, *Acts*, 491.

13. Barclay, *Acts*, 186.

14. Bruce, *Acts*, 488.

15. W. M. Ramsay, *St. Paul the Traveller and the Roman Citizen* (London: Hodder & Stoughton, 1895, 1920), 341.

### Chapter 21: Acts 28—The Unchained Truth

1. Bruce, *Acts*, 498.

2. Pliny, *Natural History*, quoted in ibid., 500.

3. Barclay, *Acts*, 190.

4. McRay, "Stench, Pain, and Misery," 14.

5. Fernando, *Acts*, 625.

6. Barclay, *Acts*, 191–192.

7. Ibid., 192.

8. Richards, *Handbook*, 599.

9. Richard C. Halverson, *How I Changed My Thinking about the Church* (Grand Rapids, MI: Zondervan, 1972), 41–42.

10. Graham, *The Holy Spirit*, 328.

# Index

## A

Abraham, 81, 82
acropolis, 222
Acts (*see* book of Acts, characteristics)
Acts of the Apostles (*see* book of Acts, characteristics)
Agabus
    prophesies famine, 140
    prophesies Paul's bondage, 267
Age of the Holy Spirit, 28
Agrippa, Herod, II, 308–10, 313, 314
    *See also* Herod
Akel Dama, 16
Alexander (of Ephesus), 246
Alexander (priest), 47, 48
Alexander the Great, 195
Alford, Henry
    on divine reassurance, 289
aliens, in Bible, 16
all things in common, 36, 54
Amin, Idi, 153
Amos, 182–83
Ananias (disciple), 63, 111–14, 277
Ananias (high priest), 284–85, 295–96
Ananias (struck dead), 57–60
Andrew (apostle), 14
angels
    angel of the Lord, 64
    as giving law to Israel, 85
    guardian angel, 149
    Stephen's face like angel, 81
    *See also* angels in Acts
angels in Acts
    angel assures Paul none will drown, 320
    angel rescues apostles from prison, 64–65
    angel rescues Peter from prison, 147–48
    angel speaks to Cornelius, 125–26, 128, 130
    angel speaks to Philip, 101
    angel strikes Herod Agrippa, 152–53
    at Jesus's ascension, 11
    at Jesus's resurrection, 5

Annas, 47, 48, 51
Antioch (Orontes), 135, 174–75
    church at Antioch, 137–38, 159
Antioch (Pisidia), 166
Antonia, 146, 274
Aphrodite, 221–23
apocalyptic, 10
Apollo (god), 222, 231, 235
Apollos (evangelist), 230–31
apologist, 63
apostles
    choose Judas's replacement, 13–14
    imprisoned, beaten by Sadducees, 64–69
    at Jerusalem Council, 179
    at Jesus's ascension, 11–12
    miracles post-Pentecost, 36
    and Saul's persecution, 93–96
    *See also* apostles, characteristics;
        Barnabas; Paul; Peter
apostles, characteristics
    approach to Jewish people, 168–69
    as chosen by Jesus, 13
    defined, 10
    listed, 13–14
    as martyrs, iv
    qualifications for apostleship, 16–17
    as sinners, 13–14
    where they took gospel message, 10–11
Aquila, 223–25, 330
    and Ephesus church, 229–231, 236, 240
    teamwork with wife, 231–32
    travels, 224
Aramaic, 74
Aratus, 216
Areopagus, 212–17
Aristarchus, 240, 246, 314
    awaits Paul at Troas, 250, 251
    stays with Paul till end, 335
Artemis of Ephesus, 235
    *See also* Diana of the Ephesians
ascension
    its significance, 11–12
    as prophesied in Old Testament, 12
    *See also* Jesus

Asia, meaning in Acts, 235
assassins, 275
Athens
    its idols, 211
    its philosophers, 211–12
Augustan Regiment, 314
authority, and Jesus's name, 43

## B

Babel, 26
Baker, Vickie
    on holy boldness, 232
baptism
    at Corinth, 226
    with fire, 6–7
    of Gentiles, 130–32
    with the Holy Spirit, 6–7, 8, 13, 98–99
    in Jesus's name, 98–99
    John's baptism, 6–7
    Lydia's household baptized, 196
    meaning in New Testament, 7, 103
    at Pentecost, 32–34
    with water, 6–7
Bar-Jesus Elymas, 163–64
Barabbas, 44
Barclay, William
    on appropriate compromise, 272
    on astrologers, 97–98
    on baptism in early church, 103
    on Barnabas's humility, 165
    on Christian as never alone, 330
    on Christianity as The Way, 231
    on deacons as chosen for service, 78
    on futility of rebellion against good, 53
    on God's gift of confidence, 323–24
    on grace of Christianity as offensive, 279
    on importance of waiting, 10
    on Jews' rejection as Gentiles'
        opportunity, 334
    on kindness essential for Christianity, 201
    on law vs. grace, 181–82
    on leadership of James, brother of
        Jesus, 182

**Index**

# W

Wallis, Jim
  on disciples and money, 37
  on sharing of resources, 55
Wangerin, Walter
  on Saul's name change to Paul, 165
  on threatened religious leaders, 47
water baptism, 6
Way, the, (Christians) 107–8, 138, 243, 276, 277, 298
Wesley, Charles
  on salvation as escape from prison, 148
West, Maude De Joseph
  on Agrippa's death, 152
  on avoiding immorality, 184
  on calling believers "Christians," 139–40
  on God bringing good from evil, 53
  on heroism of early Christians, 3
  on intelligentsia and faith, 217
  on Jews avoiding Gentiles, 125
  on persecutors, 69
whipping, apostles whipped, 68–69
whitewashed wall, 284–85
widows in Acts, 73–77
Willard, Dallas
  on engulfment by Holy Spirit, 24
Willimon, William H.
  on church as resident aliens, 280
wind, symbolizing Holy Spirit, 23
Wirt, Sherwood
  on getting out of God's way, 76
  on loving vs. unloving churches, 35
witnesses, Christians as witnesses, 9–10
wizards, in Scripture, 164
wolves, image of false pastors, 258
women, in early church
  outnumbering men, 196
  Philip's four daughters, 266
  Priscilla's role, 231–32
  at resurrection, 5
  in upper room, 14–15

*See also* Lydia; Mary; Priscilla
wonders and signs, 28, 79
Word, Word of God, v
worship, 207

# Y

Yamauchi, Edwin M.
  on ancient sea travel, 314
Yancey, Philip
  on church as meeting of equals, 254–55

# Z

Zealots, 289
Zeno, 212
Zeus, 171

CPSIA information can be obtained at www.ICGtesting.com
Printed in the USA
LVOW09s0102180214

374116LV00001B/1/P

9 781418 509972